The Family-School Connection

Issues in Children's and Families' Lives
AN ANNUAL BOOK SERIES

Senior Series Editor

Thomas P. Gullotta, *Child and Family Agency of Southeastern Connecticut*

Editors

Gerald R. Adams, *University of Guelph, Ontario, Canada*

Bruce A. Ryan, *University of Guelph, Ontario, Canada*

Robert L. Hampton, *University of Maryland, College Park*

Roger P. Weissberg, *University of Illinois at Chicago, Illinois*

Drawing upon the resources of Child and Family Agency of Southeastern Connecticut, one of this nation's leading family service agencies, **Issues in Children's and Families' Lives** is designed to focus attention on the pressing social problems facing children and their families today. Each volume in this series will analyze, integrate, and critique the clinical and research literature on children and their families as it relates to a particular theme. Believing that integrated multidisciplinary approaches offer greater opportunities for program success, volume contributors will reflect the research and clinical knowledge base of the many different disciplines that are committed to enhancing the physical, social, and emotional health of children and their families. Intended for graduate and professional audiences, chapters will be written by scholars and practitioners who will encourage the reader to apply their practice skills and intellect to reducing the suffering of children and their families in the society in which those families live and work.

Volume 1: **Family Violence: Prevention and Treatment**
LEAD EDITOR: Robert L. Hampton
CONSULTANTS: Vincent Senatore, *Child and Family Agency, Connecticut*; Ann Quinn, *Connecticut Department of Children, Youth, and Family Services, Connecticut*

Volume 2: **The Family-School Connection**
EDITORS: Bruce A. Ryan and Gerald R. Adams

Volume 3: **Adolescent Dysfunctional Behavior**
EDITORS: Gary M. Blau and Thomas P. Gullotta

Volume 4: **Preventing Violence in America**
EDITORS: Robert L. Hampton, Pamela Jenkins, and Thomas P. Gullotta

Volume 5: **Primary Prevention Practices**
AUTHOR: Martin Bloom

Volume 6: **Primary Prevention Works**
EDITORS: George W. Albee and Thomas P. Gullotta

The Family-School Connection

Theory, Research, and Practice

Editors

**Bruce A. Ryan
Gerald R. Adams
Thomas P. Gullotta
Roger P. Weissberg
Robert L. Hampton**

Vol.
2

*Issues in Children's
and Families' Lives*

SAGE Publications
International Educational and Professional Publisher
Thousand Oaks   London   New Delhi

Copyright © 1995 by Sage Publications, Inc.

For information address:

 SAGE Publications, Inc.
2455 Teller Road
Thousand Oaks, California 91320
E-mail: order@sagepub.com

SAGE Publications Ltd.
6 Bonhill Street
London EC2A 4PU
United Kingdom

SAGE Publications India Pvt. Ltd.
M-32 Market
Greater Kailash I
New Delhi 110 048 India

Printed in the United States of America

Library of Congress Cataloging-in-Publication Data

Main entry under title:

The family-school connection: Theory, research, and practice / edited
by Bruce A. Ryan . . . [et al.].
    p.   cm.—(Issues in children's and families' lives; v. 2)
Includes bibliographical references and index.
ISBN 0-8039-7306-3 (cloth: alk. paper).—ISBN 0-8039-7307-1
(paper: alk. paper)
    1. Home and school—United States.   2. Education—Parent
participation—United States.   3. Parent and child—United States.
4. Family—United States—Social conditions.   I. Ryan, Bruce A.
II. Series.
LC225.3.F38   1995
649'.68—dc20   95-11383

This book is printed on acid-free paper.

96 97 98 99 00 01 10 9 8 7 6 5 4 3 2

Sage Production Editor: Tricia K. Bennett
Sage Typesetter: Andrea D. Swanson

Contents

Series Editor's Introduction:
It Is in Our Best Interest

The theme for the 1995 Hartman Biennial National Conference is Schools and Families: Reciprocal Influences and Implications for Research and Practice. This latest volume in the Child and Family Agency book series **Issues in Children's and Families' Lives** reflects the meaning of that theme well. The editors on this project, Bruce A. Ryan and Gerald R. Adams, have recruited and worked with a talented group of scholars to share the present state of theoretical and research knowledge in this area of vital importance.

As in so many other areas of social science research, the education and psychology graduate students and the scholars in those disciplines for whom this volume is intended have been frustrated with the paucity of evaluative research. Here the reader will be introduced, by Ryan and Adams in Chapter 1, to a theoretical model for evaluative research that will prove useful in future years for scholars determining the nature of relationships among family variables and children's success in school. In Chapter 2, Ellen S. Amatea and Peter A. D. Sherrard build on the first chapter with their insightful exploration of understanding. They eloquently demonstrate that reality and the perception of reality are both different and relative constructs at best. In the third chapter, Diane Scott-Jones relates how school achievement is influenced by parent-child interactions. Joyce L. Epstein and Seyong Lee in Chapter 4, using the theoretical perspective of overlapping spheres of influence, examine school,

family, community, and peer group connections among early adolescents. This part of the volume concludes with a critical analysis
of how family environment influences educational attainment by
Jay D. Teachman, Randal D. Day, and Karen Price Carver.

In the second half of this volume, the reader explores with
Robert-Jay Green the family's influence on learning for youth with
learning disabilities. In Chapter 7, Rex Forehand, Lisa Armistead,
and Karla Klein examine the influence parental discord and divorce
have on learning. Approaches to reducing the frequency of truancy
are discussed in Chapter 8 by Jane Corville-Smith. In Chapter 9,
Robert W. Plant and Patricia A. King discuss one promising approach to strengthening parent, child, and school ties—the Family
Resource Center. In the final chapter, Annette U. Rickel and Evvie
Becker-Lausen focus on the influences of families on children.

This volume and the 1995 Hartman Conference devoted to this
topic are timely additions to the growing literature and public
dialogue on families, children, and schools in the United States. As
we pass the midway point of the last decade of the 20th century
with so many pressing challenges facing this nation, it is appropriate
to examine our current knowledge and chart a course for expanding
and refining that knowledge base.

It is appropriate because families matter.

It is appropriate because schools matter.

It is appropriate because children matter.

And yet although many acknowledge the importance of families,
schools, and children, it seems to me that as a people we are either
unable or unwilling to take the steps necessary to forge a successful
linkage between them. It is in our best interest to do so, not because
it is the right thing to do—though it is—but because our survival
as a nation demands that we develop methods to accomplish this
goal. It is not philanthropy, charity, or a liberal social conscious that
leads me to this conclusion, but self-interest driven by certain
demographic realities.

What does demography have to do with children, schools, and
families? It has been said that demography is destiny. If that is the
case then this nation has charted a course in the treatment of its
schools, its young families, and its children that will inevitably lead
it onto the rocks of social conflict if change does not occur soon.

Presently, 50.8% of the youth in this country live in traditional
families, that is, families with a mother and father in a first marriage

(U.S. Bureau of the Census, 1994b). Many (24%) live with only one parent, the majority of whom have either never married or have not yet reached the age of majority. Many (22%) live in families reshaped by divorce or remarriage, and others (2.7%) live with adults other than their biological parents. Common to many of these families is the absence of adequate economic resources.

Presently, 20.1% of the youth living in this country find themselves living in poverty (Annie E. Casey Foundation, 1991). Disturbingly, the probability that the child lives in an impoverished setting is larger, the younger the child. The chances that these youth will escape poverty in childhood is slim.

Presently, 24% of black and 41% of Hispanic youth leave school prematurely (Adams, Gullotta, & Markstrom-Adams, 1994). This decision has profound economic consequences for these youth. It is estimated that over a lifetime high school graduates earn $211,100 more than dropouts ($821,000 vs. $609,900). Greater career opportunities and lifetime earnings accompany each increase in educational attainment, so that a person with some college education is estimated to have lifetime earnings of $993,000; with a college degree, $1,421,000; and with a professional degree, $3,013,000 (U.S. Bureau of the Census, 1994a).

Against this bleak backdrop, consider just these two realities. First, assuming the United States does not alter its immigration policies to accept, let alone recruit large numbers of well-educated Europeans to its shores, in the coming decades the labor force of this nation will be unlike ever before in this nation's history. The people will not have lived in "traditional" families. Many will have experienced profound economic hardship. The majority of this labor force will not be white and male, but female, black, Asian, or Hispanic.

The second reality is that the Social Security system on which this nation's retired citizenry has come to depend will be severely stressed by the early part of the next century. The Social Security system is designed as a pay-as-you-go system; that is, current payroll deductions are drawn on to support eligible enrollees who during their working years supported those before them. From a historical perspective, it is useful to note that at the time of its development during the Great Depression roughly six employed individuals supported every Social Security recipient. At the present time, this employee-to-recipient base has declined to slightly less than three workers to one recipient. By the early part of the next century, at just about the time this baby boomer editor will be retiring, that labor pool, now predominately female and minority, will have declined in size to less than two workers for every Social Security recipient. The pyramid on which the system was developed, with the many supporting the eligible few, will be reversed in the next three decades. Assuming benefits in future years are not severely curtailed for most Americans, it will be this new and proportionately much smaller labor force supporting a very large elderly, retired, and benefit-seeking population.

Why dwell on this last point? I dwell on this last point because it is in my self-interest and the self-interest of others to invest in today's young families who are raising tomorrow's labor force. We must engage these young families now and nurture their abilities to educate their children now because we will not have the opportunity to revisit them and their children in the future. It will be too late. It is in my self-interest and the self-interest of others to invest in today's children, who in the matter of a few years will replace us as workers and policymakers. Unless we care for the child today while that child still seeks our care, our love, and our attention, and nurture in that child charity and fairness, we surely will confront the angry and embittered faces of adults whose hatred will spill forth over those who did not care for them in their time of need. It is in my self-interest and the self-interest of others to invest in today's schools and demand that they well educate this future labor force. Self-interest demands that schools reach out in new ways to involve parents because quite literally we cannot afford to waste a single young person to ignorance.

—Thomas P. Gullotta
Child and Family Agency

References

Adams, G. R., Gullotta, T. P., & Markstrom-Adams, C. (1994). *Adolescent life experiences.* Pacific Grove, CA: Brooks/Cole.

Annie E. Casey Foundation. (1991). *Kids count data book.* Greenwich, CT: Author.

U.S. Bureau of the Census. (1994a). College degree can make you a $ million. *Census and You, 29*(8), 12.

U.S. Bureau of the Census. (1994b). Families "traditional" and otherwise. *Census and You, 29*(10), 1-2.

Acknowledgments

As with all edited books, this one could not have been created without the contributions of many people. We are especially indebted to the authors of the chapters, who willingly responded to very tight deadlines. Without their important contributions, there would be no book.

Thomas P. Gullotta, CEO of the Child and Family Agency of Southeastern Connecticut and senior series editor, deserves special appreciation for his constant support, encouragement, and wise counsel. His faith in the book's theme sustained us at the numerous points when the deadlines seemed impossible. We also want to thank William Malone, David Bernon, and Tom Dalicandro of the Wellington County Roman Catholic Separate School Board for standing behind us as we began to explore the intersection between families and schools. The technical support of Marie McGlone, Barbara Merritt, and Cathy Walsh in the Department of Family Studies of the University of Guelph is most appreciated. We further want to acknowledge the financial support from the John and Kelly Hartman Foundation and the Hospital for Sick Children Foundation in Toronto.

—Bruce A. Ryan
—Gerald R. Adams

Dedication

The Child and Family Agency traces its history to the Female Benevolent Society founded in 1809 in Hartford, Connecticut. In 1944, the Eastern District Committee of that organization, then known as the Connecticut Children's Aid Society, was formed. From that Eastern District Committee emerged the Child and Family Agency in 1972. Across those many decades and in spite of the numerous waves of change that periodically sweep across the waters, the Child and Family Agency remains to this day true to a governing model that emphasizes the volunteer efforts of the layperson. This volume is dedicated to the 34 Board Chairmen who, by their efforts, have enabled this Agency to serve children in the context of their families in the context of their communities.

1944-1945 Mrs. O. Pomeroy Robinson
1946-1947 Mrs. Alfred M. Bingham
1948-1950 Mrs. Robert O. Anderson
1951 Mrs. Thomas B. Klakring
1952 Mrs. Robert S. Chappall
1953-1954 Mrs. Pyam Williams
1955 Mrs. Rand Jones
1956 Mrs. Jacques Wimpfheimer
1957-1958 Mrs. Thomas Ahern
1959 Mrs. R. Austin Battles
1960-1961 Mrs. Charles LaCour
1962-1963 Mrs. Edward Williams
1964 Mrs. Allan Dunning
1965 Mrs. William Brewster
1966 Mrs. Frederick Hartman
1967 Mrs. Henry D. Towers
1968 Mrs. Donald J. Charbonnier
1969 Mrs. Angus Park
1970 Mrs. Charles La Cour and Mrs. Pyam Williams
1971 Mrs. William Anderson and Mrs. Thomas Cramer
1972-1974 Merrill Dreyfus
1974-1976 Mrs. Angus Park
1976-1978 Mr. Fred Larson
1978-1980 Mr. Grover Lassen
1980-1983 Mrs. Carol Ryland
1983-1984 Dr. Ira Schwartz
1984-1985 Dr. Ross Johnson
1986-1987 Mrs. Patricia Rogerson
1988-1989 Dr. Robert Hampton
1990-1991 Mrs. Alva G. Gahagan
1992-1994 Mr. Ward "Hap" Johnson
1994- Mr. Thomas Mitchell

PART I

Processes

• CHAPTER 1 •

The Family-School
Relationships Model

BRUCE A. RYAN

GERALD R. ADAMS

In her thoughtful book, *Worlds Apart: Relationships Between Families and Schools,* Sara Lawrence Lightfoot (1978) observed with a tone of regret that the culture had set the home and the school, the two main developmental contexts of childhood, into separate spheres and erected powerful barriers between them. She found parents and teachers hewing to their separate roles with only a minimum of contact with each other across the family-school boundary. She further noted that this schism even extended to researchers in education and child development, who tended to keep their scholarly efforts focused on either the child in the school or the child in the home. A major exception to this generally divided world was, of course, the study of the preschool child (Levenstein, 1977); but the day the child went off to school, it seems, was the day the world for Lightfoot's child came apart.

An inspection of the research literature on the relationship between families and schools prior to 1978 appears to confirm Lightfoot's view.[1] Ryan (1994; see Appendix, this volume) has assembled an extensive

AUTHORS' NOTE: Preparation of this chapter was supported in part by a research grant from the Hospital for Sick Children Foundation (Toronto). The authors are particularly grateful to William Malone, Maureen Busby-O'Connor, and Jane Smith for their support and assistance.

3

bibliography of about 300 research reports, clinical studies, book chapters, and books focused on the school-family link. Of these, 188, or nearly two thirds, are empirical studies (the remainder being a mixture of issue-raising articles, clinical reports, or theory development papers). Only 26 of these empirical studies were published prior to 1978.

An early study by Milner (1951) appeared in *Child Development* and signaled a trend for the initial research on the family-school link to appear mainly in child development, social psychology, or family research journals. It was another 20 years before Peck (1971) published his study on family processes and reading in the *Journal of School Psychology* that education-oriented journals began to carry studies of family factors and children's school outcomes. Even then, it was another 5 years before the *Journal of Experimental Education* published Swanson and Henderson's (1976) study of how achievement motives developed at home could be seen to generalize to the school. After the late 1970s, research articles on family-school linkages appeared with increasing regularity in a broad spectrum of social science as well as research/professional journals in education.

A study of this rapidly growing body of research and scholarship since Lightfoot's book appeared reveals a literature that is highly dispersed in themes with much of it atheoretical in character. On the whole, the work on the family-school link does not appear to represent consistent or coherent research programs. Instead, the majority of publications in this area arise from single-episode studies, once-only clinical reports, and the apparently short-lived interests of isolated scholars. Still, amid what might be described as scholarly chaos, there are islands of order and coherence. Particularly over the last decade, a number of research-focused individuals and groups have indeed developed significant and meaningful research programs that in their individual ways are accumulating a considerable body of knowledge about the effects of family relationships on children's school outcomes. One can point to the work of Amato (1989) on family resources from a sociological viewpoint; Cowen's (Cowen, Lotyczewski, & Weissberg, 1984; Pedro-Carroll, Cowen, & Hightower, 1986) interest in risk and personal resource factors from a community psychology perspective; Emery's (Emery, 1982; Emery & O'Leary, 1982, 1984) and Forehand's (Forehand, McCombs, & Brody, 1987) specific concerns with interparental conflict; Epstein's (Epstein, 1987, 1992) attention to parent involvement in schooling; Hetherington's (Hetherington, Cox, & Cox, 1982) and Guidubaldi's (Guidubaldi, Cleminshaw, Perry, Nastasi, & Lightel, 1986) focus on divorce; Hess's (McDevitt et al., 1987) exploration of maternal-child interactions; Marjoribanks's (1979, 1981) psychometric approaches to a wide range of parental and home variables; and Steinberg's (Steinberg, Lamborn, Dornbusch, & Darling, 1992; Steinberg, Mounts, Lamborn, & Dornbusch, 1991) exploration of parenting styles and practices.

Regardless of the integrity of these productive individual lines of research, the fact remains that the accumulated evidence resists integration. In the mid-1980s two general literature reviews (Hess & Holloway, 1984; Scott-Jones, 1984) appeared. Although very different from each other, these reviews both became highly cited and were regarded as authoritative accounts of the state of the field to that time. Interestingly, both reviews had to draw primarily on research concerned with preschool children to adequately cover the topics the respective authors judged important. Seemingly, even in the early 1980s the available research on school-aged children was very limited; studies of school-aged children and adolescents simply were not available with respect to many important conceptual themes. More recently, Christenson, Rounds, and Gorney (1992), having the advantage of a much richer literature base, revisited the field in developing the basis for advising school psychologists on how they might deal with the reality of family effects on school achievement. In contrast to the two earlier reviews, Christenson et al. (1992) eschewed a consideration of family background variables such as socioeconomic status (SES) in favor of a family process focus. Over the course of the 1980s the balance of research shifted away from status variables to process studies as scholars began to favor the study of risk mechanisms over risk indicators (Rutter, 1994).

In spite of the strong scholarship demonstrated in these reviews, the fact remains that the research in the field is still largely unintegrated and underutilized. The large variety of constructs that have been investigated, let alone the even more various strategies that researchers have used to measure these constructs, leaves the would-be reviewer of literature gasping. As the reviews noted above reveal, the scholar who seeks to examine this literature has been left largely to the mercy of the content of the research studies themselves along with his or her own purposes as guides to where the internal structures of the literature might lay. To date, there has been a paucity of large-enough theoretical models or conceptual schemes for organizing the myriad of pieces involved in accounting for the family's role in its children's learning and success in school. Some recent steps toward the development of more encompassing models have appeared (Grolnick & Slowiaczek, 1994; Steinberg et al., 1992), but these have not dealt with the full range of potential variables that previous research has shown are relevant to the family-school link.

The purpose of this chapter is to propose a more encompassing model of the link between family processes and school outcomes than has heretofore been available. The remainder of the chapter is organized around four themes. First, a number of foundational principles governing the development of the model will be considered. Second, the model will be described and its component parts defined. Third, its usefulness as a tool for integrating the existing literature on the family-school link will be illustrated. Finally, a number of studies using path-analytic techniques will be examined to provide an initial assessment of the model's validity.

Essential Features of a Model of Family-School Relationships

Ideally, any model that seeks to account for the ways families affect the success of their children in school should satisfy four criteria.

1. The model should be *inclusive*—that is, it should encompass, at some level of abstraction, all of the characteristics of individual family members, the patterns of family relationships, and the contextual circumstances of the family that might be seen to affect or be affected by the child's academic and social school-outcomes.

2. The model should *organize the relevant variables along a dimension of proximity to the child's school outcomes.* This criterion is consistent with the recent report by Wang, Haertel, and Walberg (1993), who found that variables (e.g., psychological, instructional, home environment) that were proximal and more intimately related to school learning were stronger determinants of learning than were distal variables (e.g., demographics, policy, institutional/organizational). Recent path analytic studies (e.g., Grolnick & Slowiaczek, 1994; Steinberg

et al., 1992) of family process effects on school learning also point to the importance of a proximal-distal dimension in the model's structure.

3. The model should *recognize that influence effects will be strongest between adjacent classes of variables*—that is, the more widely separated the variables are along the proximal-distal dimension, the weaker are the interactions between those variables. In general, those variables distal from the child's school outcome affect the outcome variable through the mediating actions of variables and processes more intimately connected to the outcome. In the language of path analysis, direct effects between variables are possible at all levels of the model, but indirect effects should be expected to predominate.

4. The model should *acknowledge the bidirectionality of influence along the proximal-distal dimension*. It is to be expected that all variable classes represented in the model have the capacity to exert some influence over all other variable classes. Within the context of the single dimension of the model, for example, the levels of general family conflict can be seen as affecting parent-child relations that in turn affect school outcomes. Similarly, it is also likely that school outcomes sometimes affect parent-child relations that in turn could lead to changes in the overall level of conflict in the family.

The Family-School Relationships Model

Figure 1.1 describes a model intended to encompass all of the relevant family characteristics and processes that might be implicated in children's school achievements and adjustments. It is structured along a proximal-distal dimension where Child Outcomes is placed at Level 0 and Child's Personal Characteristics at Level 1, with successive levels extending out to Exogenous Social/Cultural and Biological Variables at Level 6. The order of effects along the proximal-distal dimension are assumed to be bidirectional, with the intensity of interaction normally greatest between adjacent levels. The levels themselves are not to be seen as particular variables, constructs, or processes. Rather, they are styled as classes of constructs within which literally hundreds of specific variables could be defined depending on the objectives of a given research project or interests of a researcher.

It is important to note that the model essentially pertains to *within-the-family processes* and is not intended to account for all the ways family members or other social agents, such as peers or teachers, could influence children's school outcomes. It does not,

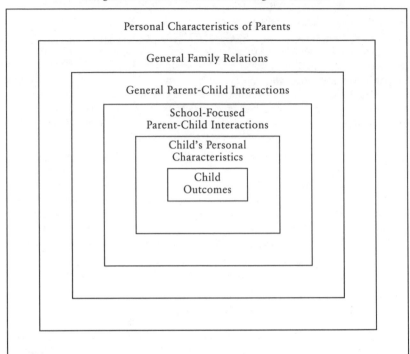

Figure 1.1. The Family-School Relationships Model

for example, address the various ways parents become involved in their children's schooling within the school context by volunteering, membership on advisory committees, or even running for office on a local school board. Epstein's (1987, 1992) explication of the different types of parental school involvement deals with these issues much more directly.

Level 0: Child Outcomes. It is possible to envision a very large range of different school outcomes that could be investigated, but in general, these fall into two classes: academic achievement and social behaviors in the classroom and/or about the school. Academic achievement can be measured through the use of grades, teacher ratings of achievement, or standardized achievement tests. Social behaviors can be determined from an inspection of school records to assess major behavioral disruptions such as truancy, suspensions, or even detention. More commonly seen in the literature, however, are studies involving the use of teacher ratings, usually on standardized checklists or rating scales where the focus is on the child's capacity to work within the rules of the school, the child's relationships with teachers, or peer relationships. Less frequently, child-teacher interactions are observed, coded, and analyzed.

In general, any construct that could be considered a legitimate schooling outcome could be placed at Level 0 in the model. It might be argued that the list of possible outcomes could include characteristics such as self-esteem, assertiveness, maturity, and confidence. In fact, these same characteristics are often explicit objectives of early childhood education programs, and if they are also among the important goals of a particular program for school-aged children, the model is open to their inclusion at Level 0. As will be seen, however, the model's presumption, for children who attend regular school, is that schooling outcomes will be limited to academic achievement and social behaviors within the school. Constructs such as self-esteem and maturity are classified with the Child's Personal Characteristics at Level 1 and are understood to be among the qualities the child brings to the learning situation, which contribute to the schooling outcomes and may be affected in turn by the outcomes.

Level 1: Child's Personal Characteristics. Level 1 includes all those personal qualities that are intimately connected with the outcomes however they are defined. It is assumed that when some condition or process in the family affects a child's success in school, the effect of that condition or process is always mediated in some way through the psychological processes within the child. Conflict in the home, for example, might undermine achievement because it might first reduce the child's motivation to succeed or reduce the amount of energy the child has available for homework and study. The potential list of constructs or variables located at this level is very long and includes various forms of intellectual ability and academic skills along with a wide range of psychosocial characteristics such as self-esteem, sociability, assertiveness, confidence, and enthusiasm.

Level 2: School-Focused Parent-Child Interactions. The constructs and processes found at Level 2 reflect a specific focus on the ways parents (and sometimes older siblings) take particular action with respect to school issues. The particular variables of interest at this level include help with homework; support and general encouragement in learning and schoolwork; monitoring of homework and school attendance; exerting pressure or using aversive strategies to motivate the child; taking steps to ensure the general development of literacy, numeracy, and cultural interests; and even simply being a parent who is easy to talk to about relationship problems at school.

These Level 2 variables can be distinguished from the more general varieties of parent-child interaction identified at Level 3 on the basis of the special focus on the school. If the outcomes of interest were child development outcomes of a more general nature, there would be little reason to divide Level 2 processes from those in Level 3. But with school outcomes being the focus, it makes practical sense to locate these two classes of variables in different levels of the model. Certainly, within a path analysis framework, the partitioning of these different varieties of parent-child interaction makes it easier to see how general parenting behaviors come to affect school-related parenting, thus revealing something of the mechanisms, for example, that link parenting style with school achievement (Dornbusch, Ritter, Leiderman, Roberts, & Fraleigh, 1987).

Level 3: General Parent-Child Interactions. As has already been alluded to, the variables placed at Level 3 are those that characterize, in a general way, the interactions or relationships between parents and their children. There is no particular focus on schooling or school problems in these interactions; at this distance from Level 0 on the proximal-distal dimension, the school is already becoming a more remote issue. The constructs or variables located at this level are those traditionally associated with parenting research and include authoritative, authoritarian, and permissive parenting styles as well as measures of coercive parenting strategies, parental control, parental rejection, and expressions of warmth. Once again, the list is potentially long and the model remains open to the particular research interests of scholars.

Level 4: General Family Relations. At the next step away from Level 0, attention shifts from a consideration of interactions between parents and children to a concern for the overall nature of the family. Constructs at this level attempt to communicate how families present themselves as a group or unit. Constructs such as cohesiveness, conflict, organization, family sociability, enmeshment, disengagement, and democratic family style illustrate the kinds of variables this level accommodates.

Also placed at this level are constructs that define the nature of the marital relationship between the parents. Although an argument can be made to assign marital or interparental relationship constructs to a level of their own beyond Level 4, they are placed within Level 4 because such relationships likely appear to most children as an integral part of the overall nature of the family. In fact, the exact placement of the marital relationship variables in this model is most probably an empirical question best answered with reference to path analytic data. Certainly, no data are currently available that clearly indicate where to place these processes in relation to the proximal-distal dimension.

Level 5: Personal Characteristics of Parents. Parents' personal characteristics are placed at Level 5 because they are not strictly a part of the relationship processes that characterize the family system. Thus, they are rather distant from school outcomes, but clearly highly relevant to how the family operates in general and how the parents interact with their children around school issues in particular. The constructs at this level include parental personality characteristics such as introversion, expressiveness, dominance, and flexibility as well as psychiatric disorders such as depression, excessive anxiety, and psychoses. Parental beliefs about education and parents' expectations about educational achievement would also be located at Level 5.

Level 6: Exogenous Social/Cultural and Biological Variables. The variables at Level 6 consist of two general types. First, there are the social/cultural variables: SES, type of neighborhood, marital status, family structure, and ethnicity, for example. Second, this level includes the biological "givens" such as the sex of the parent, sex of the child, and the child's congenital characteristics whether or not they are due to inheritance. Among the latter could be physical disabilities such as missing limbs, degrees of paralysis, or general disabilities such as Down's syndrome.

Compared to the variables included within each of the other levels of the model, Level 6 variables seem more like an arbitrary assemblage. The characteristics and processes located at the other levels all bear a natural and logical linkage with each other and with the characteristics and processes in the neighboring levels. Each identifies a feature of a person or a family process that is substantially formed by other events or processes in the system of family relationships. In a sense, there is a strong organic linking among the variables in the levels from 0 through 5.

Level 6, on the other hand, is intended to include all those characteristics and conditions of the family that can have a significant impact on the family system and family members but are not themselves in significant degree the consequence of those same family processes, especially those that are particularly germane to children's school success. The direction of effects with respect to Level 6 variables is assumed to be rather more strongly unidirectional.

The inclusion of variables such as SES, ethnicity, and type of neighborhood are most easily seen as part of the Level 6 grouping. Marital status or family type are a little more troublesome. Each of these could be seen, for example, to be an outcome of family conflict coupled with low cohesion and disengagement. In a sense, it might be argued that marital status is a "family outcome" and could be placed in Level 0 of the model. If this were a model of family processes and marital outcomes, this would indeed be a reasonable placement. But because the model is focused on children's schooling outcomes, variables such as this seem more logically placed at Level 6.

Perhaps most difficult to justify for Level 6 inclusion are the sex of the parents and the biological characteristics of the children themselves. Sex of parent could be included in Level 5, but the model would then imply that parental sex is determined, in part, by, for example, SES-type variables. Such a placement would be illogical. A similar objection could be made to placing sex of child at Level 1 with the other personal characteristics of the child. Where to locate a variable such as Down's syndrome seems more difficult. If intelligence is to be placed at Level 1, it makes some sense to place variables such as Down's there as well, especially if Down's serves as a surrogate for an intelligence measure.

In fact, although logic and knowledge of the field can be used to determine the best placement of some of these Level 6 variables, the placement of other variables (such as type or degree of retardation) probably have to be decided empirically. As data on the relationships between these various classes of variables are examined in future research, the best location for these variables in the model will become clearer. In fact, the literature to date has generally placed them in an exogenous position in relation to ongoing family relationship processes.

Assessing the Model's Validity

The adequacy with which the model represents the varieties and constructs in the field cannot be fully assessed simply by examining the logic of its internal structure. Beyond this minimal internal consistency requirement, it is possible to identify at least three additional adequacy criteria. First, it is necessary to show that the model is helpful in finding meaningful organization in the existing family-school literature. Second, it is important to show that the model's own structure is consistent with the recently emerging studies using structural equation strategies to map the linkages among family characteristics, family processes, and school outcomes. Third and finally, the model must also be seen to be useful in identifying important future research questions and suggesting effective intervention procedures. A consideration of the third of these three criteria is beyond the scope of this chapter, but there is potential benefit in examining the first two. It is to these that attention is now turned.

The Model as a Tool
for Organizing the Existing Literature

As has already been observed, the complexity of the family-school literature with its wide range of constructs, variables, and measures has made it extremely difficult to draw strong conclusions from the published research. In the brief review of the literature that follows, no attempt has been made to be exhaustive or fully authoritative. Rather, the objective is to illustrate the way the model might be used to locate order in the literature, and perhaps even more important, to identify important conceptual gaps in the research literature.

Level 0: Child Outcomes. Of the approximately 300 scholarly papers or books concerned with the family-school link that are in Ryan's (1994) bibliography, 211 are reports of empirical or clinical research. Almost 100% of these studies employed correlational methods in exploring the relationship between child outcome measures and relevant associated processes or conditions. More than 60% of these empirical studies report data on academic measures; more than 40% report on measures of behavior problems or social relationships (some examined both kinds of outcomes). The large majority of studies used measures of math and reading skills although some (e.g., Anderson & Evans, 1976; Campbell & Mandel, 1990; Dornbusch et al., 1987) employed standardized achievement tests or GPA to obtain more general assessments of academic success.

Measures of behavior problems or social relationships have mainly involved the use of interviews with parents or teachers, or checklists and rating scales such as the Behavior Problem Checklist, the Walker Problem Behavior Checklist, and the Classroom Adjustment Rating Scale.

Level 1: Child's Personal Characteristics. It is clear that the child's own characteristics make an important contribution to his or her own school adjustment and achievement. Not only are intellectual capacity and specific conditions such as learning disabilities related to all forms of school success, but a host of personality variables such as maturity, self-esteem, self-confidence, self-control, anxiety, depression, shyness, and emotionality have been found to be significantly correlated with school functioning (Amato, 1989; Anderson & Evans, 1976; Beer, 1989; Bornstein, Bornstein, & Walters, 1988; Forehand, McCombs, Long, Brody, & Fauber, 1988; Grolnick & Ryan, 1989; Kurdek & Sinclair, 1988).

Level 2: School-Focused Parent-Child Interactions. Some particular parent behaviors have been found to be positively related to school success. Among these are parental help with school subjects (Amato & Ochiltree, 1986; Chen & Uttal, 1988; Hewison, 1988; Hewison & Tizard, 1980; Hoover-Dempsey, Bassler, & Brissie, 1987; Keith, Reimers, Fehrmann, Pottebaum, & Aubey, 1986; Laosa, 1982; Milne, Ginsburg, Myers, & Rosenthal, 1986; Milner, 1951; Seginer, 1986; Swanson & Henderson, 1976), achievement training (Anderson

& Evans, 1976), monitoring of school behaviors by parents (Campbell & Mandel, 1990; Loeber & Dishion, 1984; Milne et al., 1986; Natriello & McDill, 1986; Ramsey, Walker, Shinn, O'Neill, & Stieber, 1989), parental teaching strategies (Barber, 1988; Hess, Holloway, Dickson, & Price, 1984; Hess & McDevitt, 1984; Hoover-Dempsey et al., 1987; Laosa, 1982), and a general interest by parents in their children's school affairs (Hoover-Dempsey et al., 1987; Milne et al., 1986; Parkinson, Wallis, Prince, & Harvey, 1982; Seginer, 1986; Stevenson & Baker, 1987; Watson, Brown, & Swick, 1983). Although these studies do begin to specify the parent-child interactions that might be said to have special relevance for children's school adjustment and achievement, it is far from clear how these interactions are associated with the characteristics of the children, parent characteristics, or with wider sociocultural context variables, all of which have been shown to be correlated with children's school difficulties in other studies.

Level 3: General Parent-Child Interactions. In recent years, a number of studies have shown that authoritative parenting styles have more positive effects on children's school success and achievement than either permissive or authoritarian parenting (Brown, Mounts, Lamborn, & Steinberg, 1993; Dornbusch et al., 1987; Lamborn, Mounts, Steinberg, & Dornbusch, 1991; Steinberg, Elmen, & Mounts, 1989; Steinberg et al., 1991; Steinberg et al., 1992). Moreover, this relationship between school success and parenting style appears to hold across a variety of family context conditions, including SES, family structure, and ethnic groups (Steinberg et al., 1992).

Level 4: General Family Relations. The assessment of global family interactions has involved interview schedules and questionnaires developed for particular studies (Amato, 1989; Loeber & Dishion, 1984), direct observations (Cohn, 1990; McDevitt et al., 1987), and standardized self-reports and rating scales (Emery & O'Leary, 1982; Kurdek & Sinclair, 1988; Shybunko, 1989). Unfortunately, the variety of measures used, differing levels of measurement, lack of consistency in the operational definitions of concepts of the same name, and widely varying circumstances in which the measures have been employed make it extremely difficult to offer uncluttered accounts of the research outcomes in this area.

In general, however, it seems evident that a number of family interaction patterns are related to poor school achievement and adjustment. These include families that are in conflict, are not very cohesive, are overprotective and intrusive, have poor internal organization, do not reflect an orientation toward achievement and intellectual or cultural activities, have poor parenting quality, are enmeshed, and are not nurturant. At the same time, however, it is not obvious from the available data how these various conditions and circumstances impact school success; the specific mechanisms by which general family processes come to affect particular school or achievement behaviors of children have not typically been studied.

Level 5: Personal Characteristics of Parents. There is an extensive literature that shows that school achievement and adjustment are positively associated with raised parental educational expectations (Amato & Ochiltree, 1986; Bacon & Ichikawa, 1988; Hess et al., 1984; Milne et al., 1986; Milner, 1951; Parkinson et al., 1982; Seginer, 1986; Wagner & Spratt, 1988), parents' educational aspirations for their children (Amato & Ochiltree, 1986; Laosa, 1982; Marjoribanks, 1981; Natriello & McDill, 1986; St. John, 1972), knowledge of the child's schooling (Baker & Stevenson, 1986), and parental satisfaction with parenting (Crandall, Dewey, Katkovsky, & Preston, 1964; Guidubaldi et al., 1986). Negative associations with school success have been found with maternal rejection of homemaking (Davids & Hainsworth, 1967), parental depression (Forehand, Long, Brody, & Fauber, 1986), controlling, nonnurturant mothers (Heilbrun & Waters, 1968), authoritarian parental attitudes (Humphries & Bauman, 1980), and parental psychotic disturbance (Janes, Weeks, & Worland, 1983). Once again, how these characteristics affect or are affected by the wider context of the family and internal family processes remains largely unexamined.

Level 6: Exogenous Social/Cultural and Biological Variables. The literature concerned with family form offers a relatively clear and simple picture. Divorce tends to have a damaging effect on children's school adjustment (Beer, 1989; Dornbusch et al., 1987; Guidubaldi, Cleminshaw, Perry, & Mcloughlin, 1983; Hetherington et al., 1982; Kurdek & Sinclair, 1988). Nearly all researchers, however, agree that the effects of divorce are sometimes temporary, that some children are not necessarily adversely affected, and that the absence of parental conflict significantly alters the impact of divorce (Emery, 1982; Long & Forehand, 1987). Further research needs to be directed at how divorce and conflict affect those parenting behaviors specially relevant to school success and adjustment.

It is now almost a truism that other ecological variables such as SES, parental education, parental income, social class, ethnicity, race, and the language spoken in the home all have an impact on children's school adjustment. What has not been explored adequately in the literature is the relationship between these kinds of variables, including family form variables, and those parent-child interactions that are critical in determining school adjustment.

Is the Model Consistent With Existing Structural Equation Studies?

Although it is useful to demonstrate how the general literature on family-school relationships can be interpreted through the use of the model, a more detailed consideration of studies especially focused on the structure of those relationships is also valuable. Indeed, a considerable body of such evidence exists in numerous structural equation studies of family-school link. It is to this body of research evidence that attention is now turned.

Table 1.1 offers a summary of 17 structural equation studies of the link between family relationship processes and children's social and academic success in school. These studies represent a nearly exhaustive sampling of such studies extant in the literature since 1976. No studies of this type were found prior to 1976. The left side of the table identifies each study and shows whether or not it included variables that can be mapped onto the Family-School Relationships Model. Each X indicates the presence of at least one variable from a specified level in the model. In the right side of the table, three columns contain assessments of the degree to which the study can be said to support the validity of the model. These two parts of the table are discussed separately.

An inspection of the left side of Table 1.1 shows that all studies, as might be expected, employed some form of school outcome measure (Level 0). Two thirds of the studies assessed academic outcomes whereas the remainder focused on various forms of social adjustment. The next two most frequently studied levels were Level 6 (Exogenous Social/Cultural and Biological Variables) and Level 1

Table 1.1 Path Analysis Studies, 1976-1994: Their Relevance to the Family-School Relationships Model

Study	Levels in the Model							Variables Not Included in Model	Dimension of Proximity to Outcome?	Adjacent Level Effects?
	L6	L5	L4	L3	L2	L1	L0			
Anderson & Evans (1976)	X				X		X	None	Yes	Yes
Keith (1982)	X						X	None	Yes	Yes
Parsons et al. (1982)	X					X	X	None	Yes	Yes
Stolberg & Bush (1985)	X	X	X	X			X	a	Yes	Largely
Keith et al. (1986)	X				X	X	X	None	Largely	Partially
Seginer (1986)	X	X			X		X	None	Yes	Largely
Widlak & Perrucci (1988)	X				X		X	None	Yes	Yes
Scott & Scott (1989)				X		X	X	None	Yes	Yes
Steinberg et al. (1989)				X	X	X	X	None	Yes	Largely
Forehand et al. (1990)	X		X		X		X	None	Yes	Partially
Campbell & Mandel (1990)	X				X		X	b	Yes	Yes
Simons et al. (1991)	X			X		X	X	None	Largely	Yes
Conger et al. (1992)	X	X	X	X			X	None	Yes	Yes
Steinberg et al. (1992)					X	X	X	None	Partially	Yes
de Jong (1993)	X					X	X	None	Largely	Yes
DeBaryshe et al. (1993)		X		X		X	X	None	Yes	Yes
Grolnick & Slowiaczek (1994)			X	X	X	X	X	c	Yes	Yes

NOTES: a = Child's recent life events; b = Membership in gifted class or program; c = Parents' participation in activities at school.

(Child's Personal Characteristics). The most common Level 6 variables were SES, sex of child, ethnicity/race, and parents' marital status. Typical Level 1 variables included ability, self-concept/self-esteem, and some measure of academic effort.

Table 1.1 also shows that when researchers elected to focus on family relationships, they tended to select variables that represent Level 3 (General Parent-Child Interactions) on the model. More than 50% of the studies employed measures of general parent-child interactions whereas fewer took measures from Level 2 (School-Focused Parent-Child Interactions) or from Level 4 (General Family Relations). Interest in Level 5 (Personal Characteristics of Parents) variables has been sporadic and infrequent with highly divergent measures ranging from parental expectations through parent depression and parent perceptions of child's ability to parents' social adjustment.

There appears to have been a weak but apparent change over the years toward family variables that are closer on the proximity dimension to the child outcomes. Possibly, there is a declining interest among researchers for data involving SES, parents' personal characteristics, and general family relations and growing attention to family interactions involving children. This trend, to the extent that it exists, is in keeping with the growing sense that variables proximal to school outcomes are more important in determining those outcomes (Wang et al., 1993). Regardless of these possible shifts in the variables of interest, it is clear that these path analytic studies have employed variables that represent a wide range of family and family-member characteristics relevant to understanding the link between family relationship processes and children's school outcomes.

The right side of Table 1.1 consists of three columns that together describe how closely the data from the 17 path analytic studies conform to the model. As stated earlier, the model must satisfy four criteria before it can be regarded as adequately representative of social reality. To recap, these are inclusiveness, organization of variables along a dimension of proximity to outcome, demonstration that effects among variables are strongest between variables in adjacent levels, and bidirectionality of effects. This last property of the data cannot be adequately tested from an inspection of the data in these studies and is therefore not addressed in Table 1.1. Nevertheless, the notion of bidirectionality of influence along the proximity dimension remains an important assumption in the model. Table 1.1 is limited to a consideration of the first three of these criteria. The column headed "Variables Not Included in Model" indicates that a large majority of the variables included in these studies are fully accounted for by the model. Only three studies used constructs outside the domains making up the model. Because the model is solely concerned with the characteristics of, and processes within, families, variables such as "child's recent life events" (Stolberg & Bush, 1985), "membership in a gifted program or class" (Campbell & Mandel, 1990), and "parent participation in activities at school" (Grolnick & Slowiaczek, 1994) cannot be accommodated. They represent events and processes outside the family. It would appear, then, that none of these studies investigated within-family constructs or variables that could not be mapped onto the model. The support for the model's inclusiveness is strong.

The validity of the proximity-to-outcome dimension is assessed in the column, "Dimension of Proximity to Outcome?" Of the 17 studies, 13 appear to conform completely to the dimensionality of the model. Of the remaining four, three are largely consistent with the model, with the fourth showing a significant number of variable relationships that suggest another construct structure. An inspection of the data from the conforming studies shows that in each case nearly all of the relationships explored are presented with outcomes positioned on the extreme right in the path diagrams and the predictor variables arrayed in steps toward the left. In virtually all cases, the ordering of variables as determined by path coefficients in these studies conforms to the levels of the model. Conger et al. (1992), for example, found that mother and father depression (Level 5) led to marital conflict (Level 4), which affected how involved the parents were in parenting (Level 3), which was linked to the level of positive adjustment in the children (Level 0). Although not all levels of the model are represented in Conger et al. (1992), those that are present reflect the model's structure.

An example of a study that does not conform completely to the model is Steinberg et al. (1992). These authors found authoritative parenting (Level 3) linked to both parental involvement in schooling and parental encouragement to succeed (Level 2). The latter two Level 2 variables were themselves shown as being bidirectionally linked with each other. Parental involvement, but not parental encouragement, then linked further and significantly with achievement (Level 0). So far, this pattern is generally consistent with the model. Steinberg et al. (1992), however, also found that achievement linked to school engagement (child reports of own effort, concentration, attention, and frequency of mind wandering), which is a Level 1 variable in the model. No direct links were found between school engagement and any of the parent-child interaction measures.

Findings at variance to the basic structure of the model, like those in Steinberg et al. (1992), remain exceptional. The bulk of the evidence supports the proximity-to-outcome dimensional structure of the model.

Having established that the model appears to encompass virtually all family relationship processes relevant to school success and that these processes seem to be distributed along a proximal-distal dimension in relation to school outcomes, it remains to consider the third of the three criteria for assessing the adequacy of the model. The final column in Table 1.1, "Adjacent Level Effects?" indicates which studies show the associations between variables to be strongest between adjacent levels. Fifteen of the 17 studies are completely or largely consistent with the model's assumption of adjacent level effects. None of the studies contain findings contradicting the model's assumption of such effects. Regarding the least supportive evidence, the studies by Keith et al. (1986) and Forehand, Thomas, Wierson, and Brody (1990), in particular, found a larger number of direct effects between widely separated levels than the model suggests might be expected. In Keith et al. (1986), for example, family background (Level 6) links directly with parent involvement (Level 2), child's ability (Level 1), and achievement (Level 0). No measures from Levels 5, 4, or 3 were used in the study. Similarly, in Forehand et al. (1990), marital status (Level 6) links directly with parent functioning (Level 4), parenting (Level 3), and adolescent functioning (Level 0). No Level 5, 3, or 1 measures were investigated. Still, the bulk of the evidence supports the model's general assumption that variables at different levels would have their strongest effects on variables in adjacent levels.

At the same time, it must be acknowledged that the model does not rule out direct effects between distant levels. It is highly likely, for example, that marital conflict (Level 4) could be intense enough to have a negative impact on achievement (Level 0) regardless of what happens to parent-child interactions (Level 3) or the child's personal characteristics (Level 1).

Conclusions and Implications

It seems fair to conclude that the model adequately captures the nature of the relationship among family relationship variables and children's success in school. The general literature examining the family-school link is clearly amenable to the organizational structure the model offers. Data arising from structural equation studies of the family-school relationship are also highly consistent with the model's structure. The use of the model as a guide for the design of future research or interventions appears to be warranted.

Even the brief exploration of the literature presented in this chapter identified numerous lines of future research. It is clear that much more research needs to be done to adequately explore the linkages among the variables at different levels of the model. Most obvious among these is to explain how family context variables (Level 6) come to have their impact on children at the personal level (Level 1) and on their school success (Level 0). Are the effects of Level 6 variables mainly mediated through general family functioning (Level 4), or are parent-child interactions (Levels 3 and 2) more important? In other words, is it possible for a child in depressed economic circumstances, whose family is generally well functioning, to still be disadvantaged at school because his or her parents are simply not able, in terms of time, to be as supportive, encouraging, and helpful with school responsibilities? Would the intellectual ability of the child in this situation make a difference to how disadvantaging it would be to have parents too busy to be focused on school activities? The potential number of relationships to be explored is enormous.

Another very important task, which remains largely undone, is the investigation of developmental shifts in the relative importance of different levels and variables. Is it possible that in the junior grades the effects of SES and other Level 6 variables might be more easily ameliorated by school-based accommodations, whereas at higher grade levels the long-term effects of these conditions might be too strong for the schools to overcome? Do the effects of different patterns of parent-child relations (Level 3) change as the child develops a more defined sense of self (Level 1)? Do particular family processes begin to affect the social and academic domains of school adjustment as the child grows older and the school shifts its focus from a balanced concern of social and academic development to a much stronger emphasis on achievement?

The Family-School Relationships Model offers a promising tool to assist researchers and practitioners in the design of their research and interventions. It is sufficiently open in definition and broad in scope to permit application to a wide variety of problem areas. It is hoped that its use will enable scholars to overcome problems with the integration and utilization of research findings. Perhaps, in due course, children will not be treated as if they lived in "worlds apart."

Note

1. Excluded from this discussion are the numerous investigations, appearing frequently in the 1970s, that employed behavioral strategies in the home to achieve behavior change in the classroom (Atkeson & Forehand, 1979). Normally, such approaches sought to make the home an extension of the classroom by enlisting the parent as an agent of the school. The ongoing nature of family relationship processes or parent-child interactions and how they might bear on school success were rarely of interest in such studies.

References

Amato, P. R. (1989). Family processes and the competence of adolescents and primary school children. *Journal of Youth and Adolescence, 18,* 39-53.

Amato, P. R., & Ochiltree, G. (1986). Family resources and the development of child competence. *Journal of Marriage and the Family, 48,* 47-56.

Anderson, J. G., & Evans, F. B. (1976). Family socialization and educational achievement in two cultures: Mexican-American and Anglo-American. *Sociometry, 39,* 209-222.

Atkeson, B. M., & Forehand, R. (1979). Home-based reinforcement programs designed to modify classroom behaviors: A review and methodological evaluation. *Psychological Bulletin, 86,* 1298-1308.

Bacon, W. F., & Ichikawa, V. (1988). Maternal expectations, classroom experiences, and achievement among kindergartners in the United States and Japan. *Human Development, 31,* 378-383.

Baker, D. P., & Stevenson, D. L. (1986). Mothers' strategies for children's school achievement: Managing the transition to high school. *Sociology of Education, 59,* 155-156.

Barber, B. L. (1988). The influence of family demographics and parental teaching practices on Peruvian children's academic achievement. *Human Development, 31,* 370-377.

Beer, J. (1989). Relationship of divorce to self-concept, self-esteem and grade point average of fifth and sixth grade school children. *Psychological Reports, 65,* 1379-1383.

Bornstein, M. T., Bornstein, P. H., & Walters, H. A. (1988). Children of divorce: Empirical evaluation of a group-treatment program. *Journal of Clinical Child Psychology, 17,* 248-254.

Brown, B., Mounts, N., Lamborn, S., & Steinberg, L. (1993). Parenting practices and peer group affiliation in adolescence. *Child Development, 64,* 467-482.

Campbell, J. R., & Mandel, F. (1990). Connecting math achievement to parental influences. *Contemporary Educational Psychology, 15,* 64-74.

Chen, C., & Uttal, D. H. (1988). Cultural values, parents' beliefs, and children's achievement in the United States and China. *Human Development, 31,* 351-358.

Christenson, S. L., Rounds, T., & Gorney, D. (1992). Family factors and student achievement: An avenue to increase students' success. *School Psychology Quarterly, 7,* 178-206.

Cohn, D. A. (1990). Child-mother attachment of six-year-olds and social competence at school. *Child Development, 61,* 152-162.

Conger, R. D., Conger, K. J., Elder, G. H., Lorenz, F. O., Simons, R. L., & Whitbeck, L. B. (1992). A family process model for economic hardship and adjustment of early adolescent boys. *Child Development, 63,* 526-541.

Cowen, E. L., Lotyczewski, B. S., & Weissberg, R. P. (1984). Risk and resource indicators and their relationship to young children's school adjustment. *American Journal of Community Psychology, 12,* 353-367.

Crandall, V., Dewey, R., Katkovsky, W., & Preston, A. (1964). Parents' attitudes and behaviors and grade school children's academic achievement. *Journal of Genetic Psychology, 104,* 53-66.

Davids, A., & Hainsworth, P. K. (1967). Maternal attitudes about family life and childrearing as avowed by mothers and perceived by their underachieving and high-achieving sons. *Journal of Consulting Psychology, 31,* 29-37.

DeBaryshe, B. D., Patterson, G. R., & Capaldi, D. M. (1993). A performance model for academic achievement in early adolescent boys. *Developmental Psychology, 29,* 795-804.

de Jong, P. F. (1993). The relationship between students' behaviour at home and attention and achievement in elementary school. *British Journal of Educational Psychology, 63,* 201-213.

Dornbusch, S. M., Ritter, P. L., Leiderman, P. H., Roberts, D. F., & Fraleigh, M. J. (1987). The relation of parenting style to adolescent school performance. *Child Development, 58,* 1244-1257.

Emery, R. E. (1982). Interparental conflict and the children of discord and divorce. *Psychological Bulletin. 92,* 310-330.

Emery, R. E., & O'Leary, K. D. (1982). Children's perceptions of marital discord and behavior problems of boys and girls. *Journal of Abnormal Child Psychology, 10,* 11-24.

Emery, R. E., & O'Leary, K. D. (1984). Marital discord and child behavior problems in a nonclinic sample. *Journal of Abnormal Child Psychology, 10,* 11-24.

Epstein, J. (1987). Toward a theory of family-school connections: Teacher practices and parent involvement. In K. Kurrelmann, F. Kaufmann, & F. Losel (Eds.), *Social intervention: Potential and constraints* (pp. 121-136). New York: Aldine de Gruyter.

Epstein, J. (1992). School and family partnerships. In M. Alkin (Ed.), *Encyclopedia of educational research* (pp. 1139-1151). New York: Macmillan.

Forehand, R., Long, N., Brody, G. H., & Fauber, R. (1986). Home predictors of young adolescents' school behavior and academic performance. *Child Development, 57*, 1528-1533.

Forehand, R., McCombs, A., & Brody, G. H. (1987). The relationship between parental depressive mood states and child functioning. *Advances in Behavior Research and Therapy, 9*, 1-20.

Forehand, R., McCombs, A., Long, N., Brody, G., & Fauber, R. (1988). Early adolescent adjustment to recent parental divorce: The role of interparental conflict and adolescent sex as mediating variables. *Journal of Consulting and Clinical Psychology, 56*, 624-627.

Forehand, R., Thomas, A. M., Wierson, M., & Brody, G. (1990). Role of maternal functioning and parenting skills on adolescent functioning following parental divorce. *Journal of Abnormal Psychology, 99*, 278-283.

Grolnick, W. S., & Ryan, R. M. (1989). Parent styles associated with children's self-regulation and competence in school. *Journal of Educational Psychology, 81*, 143-154.

Grolnick, W. S., & Slowiaczek, M. L. (1994). Parents' involvement in children's schooling: A multidimensional conceptualization and motivational model. *Child Development, 65*, 237-252.

Guidubaldi, J., Cleminshaw, H. K., Perry, J. D., & Mcloughlin, C. S. (1983). The impact of parental divorce on children: Report of the nationwide NASP study. *School Psychology Review, 12*, 300-323.

Guidubaldi, J., Cleminshaw, H. K., Perry, J. D., Nastasi, B. K., & Lightel, J. (1986). The role of selected family environment factors in children's post-divorce adjustment. *Family Relations, 35*, 141-151.

Heilbrun, A. B., & Waters, D. B. (1968). Underachievement as related to perceived maternal child rearing and academic conditions of reinforcement. *Child Development, 39*, 913-921.

Hess, R. D., & Holloway, S. D. (1984). Family and school as educational institutions. In R. D. Parke (Ed.), *Review of child development research, Vol. 7: The family* (pp. 179-122). Chicago: University of Chicago Press.

Hess, R. D., Holloway, S. D., Dickson, W. P., & Price, G. G. (1984). Maternal variables as predictors of children's school readiness and later achievement in vocabulary and mathematics in sixth grade. *Child Development, 55*, 1902-1912.

Hess, R. D., & McDevitt, T. M. (1984). Some cognitive consequences of maternal intervention techniques: A longitudinal study. *Child Development, 55*, 2017-2030.

Hetherington, E. M., Cox, M., & Cox, R. (1982). Effects of divorce on parents and children. In M. E. Lamb (Ed.), *Nontraditional families: Parents and child development* (pp. 233-288). Hillsdale, NJ: Lawrence Erlbaum.

Hewison, J. (1988). The long term effectiveness of parental involvement in reading: A follow-up to the Haringey Reading Project. *British Journal of Educational Psychology, 58*, 184-190.

Hewison, J., & Tizard, J. (1980). Parental involvement and reading attainment. *British Journal of Educational Psychology, 50*, 209-215.

Hoover-Dempsey, K. V., Bassler, O. C., & Brissie, J. S. (1987). Parent involvement: Contributions of teacher efficacy, school socioeconomic status, and other school characteristics. *American Educational Research Journal, 24*, 417-435.

Humphries, T. W., & Bauman, E. (1980). Maternal child rearing attitudes associated with learning disabilities. *Journal of Learning Disabilities, 13*, 54-57.

Janes, C. L., Weeks, D. G., & Worland, J. (1983). School behavior in adolescent children of parents with mental disorder. *Journal of Nervous and Mental Disease, 171,* 234-240.

Keith, T. Z. (1982). Time spent on homework and high school grades: A large sample path analysis. *Journal of Educational Psychology, 74,* 248-253.

Keith, T. Z., Reimers, T. M., Fehrmann, P. G., Pottebaum, S. M., & Aubey, L. W. (1986). Parental involvement, homework, and TV time: Direct and indirect effects on high school achievement. *Journal of Educational Psychology, 78,* 373-380.

Kurdek, L. A., & Sinclair, R. J. (1988). Relationship of eighth graders' family structure, gender, and family environment with academic performance and school behavior. *Journal of Educational Psychology, 80,* 90-94.

Lamborn, S., Mounts, N., Steinberg, L., & Dornbusch, S. (1991). Patterns of competence and adjustment among adolescents from authoritative, authoritarian, indulgent, and neglectful families. *Child Development, 62,* 1049-1065.

Laosa, L. M. (1982). School, occupation, culture, and family: The impact of parental schooling on the parent-child relationship. *Journal of Educational Psychology, 74,* 791-827.

Levenstein, P. (1977). The mother-child home program. In M. C. Day & R. K. Parker (Eds.), *Preschool in action: Exploring early childhood programs* (pp. 28-49). Boston: Allyn & Bacon.

Lightfoot, S. L. (1978). *Worlds apart: Relationships between families and schools.* New York: Basic Books.

Loeber, R., & Dishion, T. J. (1984). Boys who fight at home and school: Family conditions influencing cross-setting consistency. *Journal of Consulting and Clinical Psychology, 52,* 759-768.

Long, N., & Forehand, R. (1987). The effects of parental divorce and parental conflict on children: An overview. *Developmental and Behavioral Pediatrics, 8,* 292-296.

Marjoribanks, K. (1979). *Families and their learning environments.* London: Routledge & Kegan Paul.

Marjoribanks, K. (1981). Family environments and children's academic achievement: Sex and social group differences. *Journal of Psychology, 109,* 155-164.

McDevitt, T. M., Hess, R. D., Kashiwagi, K., Dickson, W. P., Miyake, N., & Azuma, H. (1987). Referential communication accuracy of mother-child pairs and children's later scholastic achievement: A follow-up study. *Merrill-Palmer Quarterly, 33,* 171-185.

Milne, A. M., Ginsburg, A., Myers, D. E., & Rosenthal, A. S. (1986). Single parents, working mothers, and the educational achievement of school children. *Sociology of Education, 59,* 125-139.

Milner, E. (1951). A study of the relationship between reading readiness in grade one school children and patterns of parent-child interaction. *Child Development, 22,* 95-112.

Natriello, G., & McDill, E. L. (1986). Performance standards, student effort on homework, and academic achievement. *Sociology of Education, 59,* 18-31.

Parkinson, C. E., Wallis, S. M., Prince, J., & Harvey, D. (1982). Research note: Rating the home environment of school-age children: A comparison with General Cognitive Index and school achievement. *Journal of Child Psychology and Psychiatry, 23,* 329-333.

Parsons, J. E., Adler, T. F., & Kaczala, C. M. (1982). Socialization of achievement attitudes and beliefs: Parental influences. *Child Development, 53,* 310-321.

Peck, B. (1971). Reading disorders: Have we overlooked something? *Journal of School Psychology, 9,* 182-190.

Pedro-Carroll, J. L., Cowen, E. L., & Hightower, A. D. (1986). Preventive intervention with latency-aged children of divorce: A replication study. *American Journal of Community Psychology, 14,* 277-290.

Ramsey, E., Walker, H. M., Shinn, M., O'Neill, R. E., & Stieber, S. (1989). Parent management practices and school adjustment. *School Psychology Review, 18,* 513-525.

Rutter, M. (1994). Family discord and conduct disorder: Cause, consequence, or correlate? *Journal of Family Psychology, 8,* 170-186.

Ryan, B. A. (1994). *Family relationship processes and children's school achievement and adjustment: A bibliography of research and comment.* Unpublished manuscript, Department of Family Studies, University of Guelph, Guelph, Ontario.

St. John, N. (1972). Mothers and children: Congruence and optimism of school-related attitudes. *Journal of Marriage and the Family, 34,* 422-430.

Scott, W. A., & Scott, R. (1989). Family correlates of high-school student adjustment: A cross-cultural study. *Australian Journal of Psychology, 41,* 269-284.

Scott-Jones, D. (1984). Family influences on cognitive development and school achievement. *Review of Research in Education, 11,* 259-304.

Seginer, R. (1986). Mothers' behavior and sons' performance: An initial test of an academic achievement path model. *Merrill-Palmer Quarterly, 32,* 153-166.

Shybunko, D. E. (1989). Effects of post-divorce relationships on child adjustment. *Journal of Divorce, 12,* 299-313.

Simons, R. L., Conger, R. D., Whitbeck, L. B., & Conger, K. J. (1991). Parenting factors, social skills, and value commitments as precursors to school failure, involvement with deviant peers and delinquent behavior. *Journal of Youth and Adolescence, 20,* 645-664.

Steinberg, L., Elmen, J., & Mounts, N. (1989). Authoritative parenting, psychosocial maturity, and academic success among adolescents. *Child Development, 60,* 1424-1436.

Steinberg, L., Lamborn, S., Dornbusch, S., & Darling, N. (1992). Impact of parenting practices on adolescent achievement: Authoritative parenting, school involvement, and encouragement to succeed. *Child Development, 63,* 1266-1281.

Steinberg, L., Mounts, N., Lamborn, S., & Dornbusch, S. (1991). Authoritative parenting and adolescent adjustment across various ecological niches. *Journal of Research on Adolescence, 1,* 19-36.

Stevenson, D. L., & Baker, D. P. (1987). The family-school relation and the child's school performance. *Child Development, 58,* 1348-1357.

Stolberg, A. L., & Bush, J. P. (1985). A path analysis of factors predicting children's divorce adjustment. *Journal of Clinical Psychology, 14,* 49-54.

Swanson, R., & Henderson, R. W. (1976). Achieving home-school continuity in the socialization of an academic motive. *Journal of Experimental Education, 44,* 38-44.

Wagner, D. A., & Spratt, J. E. (1988). Intergenerational literacy: Effects of parental literacy and attitudes on children's reading achievement in Morocco. *Human Development, 31,* 359-369.

Wang, M. C., Haertel, G. D., & Walberg, H. J. (1993). Toward a knowledge base for school learning. *Review of Educational Research, 63,* 249-294.

Watson, T., Brown, M., & Swick, K. J. (1983). The relationship of parents' support to children's school achievement. *Child Welfare, 62,* 175-180.

Widlak, P. A., & Perrucci, C. C. (1988). Family configuration, family interaction, and intellectual attainment. *Journal of Marriage and the Family, 50,* 33-44.

CHAPTER 2

Inquiring Into Children's Social Worlds: A Choice of Lenses

ELLEN S. AMATEA

PETER A. D. SHERRARD

The woman who was forcing herself up the steps of the school looked very tired and old. She was 68. They had called her yesterday, angry about what Andrew had done, and insisted she come for a "conference." She felt tired, so tired. Her heart was heavy and filled with shame and despair. She muttered to herself: "What is wrong with that boy? He seems so angry. . . . Nothing seems to make him mind."

It was the fall, and Ida Maude's grandson Andrew was in trouble. The oldest of three, he and his younger brother and sister had come to live with their grandmother the year before when their mother was hospitalized in a drug treatment unit. The older two boys, ages 11 and 8, seemed to constantly be in trouble. They were always fighting with each other, cursing and hitting and pushing, till she took a switch to them. They ran away when they saw the switch, so she hadn't really had to use it. But they seemed so stubborn and mean at times. What had gone wrong? Her daughter, Glenda, had been such a sweet young girl—just like her little granddaughter, Katy. How had Glenda gotten so mixed up with drugs and booze? And why were Glenda and her children so miserable and unhappy? Who and what were to blame?

She thought about her talks with Glenda. Glenda had blamed her husband, Tim. Tim "got mean" when he drank too much and knocked the kids and Glenda around. Ida Maude and Glenda had talked about this each time that Glenda had left him and moved back in with her mother. But why did Tim get so drunk? He had blamed Glenda, saying she was always nagging him. "And sure enough those two did have some terrible fights," Ida Maude thought. "But why did it lead to the boozing and the drugs? Why did Glenda and Tim leave their young-un's for me to raise? Didn't I teach Glenda to be a good mom? Someone had done somethin' bad wrong to have these children turn out like this. But who? Who is really to blame?" As she hurried down the hall into the school office, Ida Maude's stomach churned and she turned these troubling questions over and over in her mind: "What do they think of me having a grandson who does such shameful things as peeing on all the toilet paper rolls? He tells me they don't like him; they think he is stupid. What do they think I can do to make him act right? These children don't listen to me. I don't know what to do so he won't do these awful things!"

The problem troubling the heartsick Ida Maude, that of figuring out how to help Andrew "act right" in school and at home, is faced by many parents and school professionals. Examining the questions Ida Maude asks herself about her grandchild's situation reveals a perspective on Andrew's problem that is shared by the majority of U.S. educators and mental health professionals. This perspective, variously called a technical-rational, mechanistic, or positivistic worldview (Auerswald, 1987), assumes that the world in which we live, the world that contains the problems we try to solve, operates similarly to a machine—that is, everything has a predictable structure with fixed and movable parts, and a problem is an event that occurs as a result of a "part" malfunctioning. Thus, if Ida Maude's grandson or his family is experiencing problems, it is a result of some faulty part; someone or a group is not "acting" properly. Or someone has put too much pressure on certain parts of the system that cannot bear the load, and thus the system "breaks down." Solving problems within this epistemological perspective assumes that one must search for the part or parts that are damaged, weak, or missing, and fix them.

Although most of us are familiar with this mechanistic view of the nature of the world and the way it "works," we may not be aware of how this worldview not only shapes what we know about children and their social worlds, but how we know it and how we decide to use the knowledge we gain from such an inquiry. It is only with our own discovery of alternative worldviews that we have begun to appreciate how each one serves as a lens that stimulates the creation of certain kinds of knowledge about children and their social worlds and at the same time eliminates the possibility of other types of knowledge ever being formed. In this chapter we describe some of the perceptual and conceptual shifts we have experienced in our "ways of knowing" and inquiring into the social worlds of children as we differentiated distinctively different epistemological lenses through which to view their world. We then consider the application of these lenses in the design of existing research and theory on children's family life and school adjustment, and discuss the political and ethical implications of choosing such different lenses.

Discovering a Choice of Lenses

Like many clinicians and educators who work with children, we have experienced a series of transforming moments in our understanding of and inquiry into the social worlds of children—moments that have generated significant political and ethical implications for our clinical and research practice. In the 1970s our attention moved from viewing the individual child alone to attempting to understand the child's behavior within the various systems in which he or she lived. This first shift, what Neill and Kniskern (1982) referred to as the move from "psyche to system," challenged us as clinicians and educators to contextualize the child—noting the child's situation-in-life and the impact of the child's network of relationships on his or her behavior. In the 1980s our thinking shifted further from viewing the designated system from the outside as an "objective" observer to acknowledging our position inside a designated system as a "participant-observer." This second shift, what Keeney (1983) documents as the move from "simple" cybernetics to "second-order" cybernetics (or the cybernetics of cybernetics) has challenged us to contextualize ourselves and to account for the impact our observations and stories have on ourselves and on the human systems with which we are involved. In the 1990s, our thinking is shifting again—from an either/or perspective to both/and, from universe to multiverse—in an effort to gain the benefits of double description (Bateson, 1979). The cumulative perspective emerging from these shifts of consciousness promotes a shift in our ideas as to whom we should work with, a shift in *how we think* about the construction and reconstruction of reality, and a shift in position vis-à-vis that reality—a shift in epistemology.[1]

So what is "epistemology" and what is its relevance to educational practice with and clinical research into children and their social worlds? Held and Pols (1985) suggest that two different meanings have been attributed to the concept of epistemology in the behavioral sciences literature: The first meaning addresses "the nature of knowledge—both with *what* knowledge is as distinct, say, from mere belief or prejudice; and with *how* we know" (p. 510). By contrast, the second meaning "is more concerned with what we know (or think we know)," that is, "with what philosophers call metaphysics or ontology: the inquiry into the nature of the world as it is" (p. 510).

G. Bateson (1977) believed that each of us—whether educator, clinician or researcher—formulates our own answer to what knowledge is and how we know it. He asserted that one cannot *not* have an epistemology: "You cannot claim to have no epistemology. Those who so claim have nothing but a bad epistemology. Every description you make is based on, and contains implicitly, a theory of how to describe" (p. 147). Epistemology is, according to Bateson (1979), "always and inevitably personal. The point of the probe is always in the heart of the explorer; what is *my* answer to the question of knowing?" (p. 98).

We join Bateson (1979) and Keeney (1982) in giving attention to the nature of knowledge, particularly, "the process of knowing, constructing and maintaining a world of experience" (Keeney, 1982, p. 165). By consciously reflecting on "how we know," we as educational researchers and clinicians are attending to how we "edit" the universe and how we participate in the "social construction of reality" (Berger & Luckman, 1966). "The fundamental act of epistemology is to draw a distinction—distinguishing an 'it' from the 'background' that is 'not it' " (Keeney, 1982, p. 156). Bateson referred to this activity as "punctuation." A particular punctuation organizes or patterns events in a certain way:

> Punctuating or mapping a world follows from how an observer *chooses* to see. . . . What we see is always a map, never the territory or thing in itself. . . . In cybernetics, seeing a world follows from how we draw it. It is as if one's hand draws outlines on one's own retina. The process is recursive—what one draws, one sees, and what one sees, one draws. (Keeney, 1982, p. 157)

Thus, the act of punctuating, or drawing distinctions, involves everyone—grandmother and grandson, teacher and student, counselor and client, researcher and subject—in the construction and reconstruction of "reality."

Each of the shifts of consciousness we have experienced since the 1970s has evolved into choice points regarding punctuation. The first involves *focus and boundary,* the "self/other/context" distinction advanced by Satir (1972), where context includes both system and ecosystem (i.e., the cultural and geopolitical environment): Are we focusing on an individual, others in communication with that individual, or the systems within which the event is taking place?

The second shift highlights *position and relationship,* the first-order and second-order distinction advanced by Keeney (1982): Are we taking the position of observer or participant-observer? Are we inside or outside of the system(s) we are observing? Wiener (1948) believed that looking at the whole picture meant including the observer: "Essentially your ecosystem, your organism-plus-environment, is to be considered as a single circuit . . . and you're not really concerned with an input-output, but with the events within the bigger circuit, and you are part of the bigger circuit" (quoted in Brand, 1976, p. 37). M. C. Bateson (1977) argued that the views from both positions (as inside or outside observer) were significant and valuable, as evident in his observation regarding a projected study of dolphins that "there are at least *two levels* to be studied all the time, dolphin events, relationships, and meanings, and events, relationships, and meanings involving *scientist and dolphin*" (p. 72). The first level marks the scientist as observer; the second level references his or her participation, its impact on the event observed, and the event's impact on him or her.

The third shift of consciousness we have experienced involves *inquiry and description,* the explanatory distinctions drawn by Dewey and Bentley (1949/1973). To what do we attribute action and cause? To what (or whom) do we assign responsibility (or blame) for how (or why) something (or someone) moves (or changes) while something (or someone) else does not? Dewey and Bentley (1949/1973) identified "three levels of organization and presentation of inquiry in the order of historical importance" (p. 107):

> *self-action:* where things are viewed as acting under their own powers, . . . *interaction:* where thing is balanced against thing in causal

interconnection, . . . and *transaction:* where systems of description
and naming are employed to deal with aspects and phases of action
. . . such that no one [part] can be adequately specified apart from
the specification of [the whole]. (p. 108)

Each of the action modes of inquiry direct our attention to the
construction of a particular "social reality" that generates very
different causal explanations—all of which can be "true." Consider,
for example, propositions advanced in quantum physics that all
being at the subatomic level can be described equally well either as
solid particles (like so many minute billiard balls) or as waves (like
the undulations of the surface of the sea). Neither description is
really accurate on its own:

> Both waves and particles are equally fundamental. Each is a way
> matter can manifest itself, and both together are what matter *is.* And
> while neither "state" is complete in itself, and both are necessary to
> give us a complete picture of reality, it turns out that we can never
> focus on both at once. . . . Either we can measure the exact position
> of something like an electron when it manifests itself as a particle, or
> we can measure its momentum (its speed) when it expresses itself as
> a wave, but we can never measure both, exactly, at the same time.
> (Zohar, 1990, p. 26)

This is the nub of the uncertainty principle; although the wave and
particle descriptions of being reveal its essential duality, they preclude each other because we can never focus on both at once.
Nonetheless, we do without either description at great peril.

When reflecting on these shifts of consciousness, we have discovered that significant benefits have been gained when we oscillate
through the choice points described in "what if" fashion, benefits
analogous to binocular vision and the "bonus" of depth perception.
Just as one can choose among lenses of varying power on a micro-
scope, so can an educational and clinical researcher choose among
a variety of modes of description (i.e., epistemologies) when viewing the realities of a research inquiry into children and their social
worlds. And as we have stated elsewhere:

> Just as each microscopic lens can introduce the observer to realities
> not observed before, so can each epistemology introduce the clinician
> (or social scientist) to social realities not recognized before, social

realities that often contradict each other. Furthermore, just as each microscopic lens can elicit an awareness that what one thought looked irrevocably one way, can, in fact, be seen another way, so can each epistemology elicit an awareness that the view of reality one has held as "true" may be alternated with another view, often contradictory with the first, which is equally convincing. This awareness arises as a benefit of "double description" (Bateson, 1979) and constitutes the essence of the ecosystemic revolution that has generated an epistemological framework synthesizing cybernetics, ecology, and systems theory. (Amatea & Sherrard, 1994, p. 7)

This discovery of a set of opposing "truths" reminds us that we participate in "choosing" from a larger range of options the "thought rules" by which we construct the particular reality of our research inquiry; furthermore, knowledge of these alternative lenses (or positions) can aid us in clarifying the particular epistemological assumptions that undergird our research practice. We invite you to join us in "seeing and choosing" more clearly the epistemological lenses by which each of us think and organize our research inquiry. To this end, we illustrate through the case of Andrew how our choice of lenses—that is, our choice of focus, position, and mode of inquiry and explanation—allows us to see different realities. We will then highlight the use of the lens of position in the current research literature on children's family life and school performance to demonstrate the implications for the educational and clinical researcher of exercising a particular "choice of lenses."

Seeing Different Realities

From Psyche to System: Choosing One's Focus

One of the first cases referred to the new school counselor in the fall of the year was Andrew. A fifth grader who lived with his 68-year-old grandmother and a younger brother and sister (ages 8 and 5), Andrew was a teacher's worse nightmare—he stole, he lied, and when provoked by his peers, he did the most outlandish things he could think of—like urinating on all the rolls of toilet paper in the boy's bathrooms at the school. He and his siblings had been placed with their maternal grandmother a year earlier due to the fact that their father, who struggled with chronic alcoholism, and their mother, who was addicted to cocaine, had physically and emotionally abused all three children. The family was considered "no good" by members of the small community in which they lived, with the father often returning to town between jail terms, becoming drunk, and beating up his wife in public. Andrew and his younger brother had already developed a negative reputation among the teaching staff, who had little hope that the children would turn out any different from their parents. In considering who was involved with Andrew and how they were defining and responding to his problem, the counselor learned from Andrew's teachers that despite his placement in a class for emotionally handicapped children, Andrew constantly created problems in this as well as the larger school facility, had many confrontations with teachers and the other children, and exhibited considerable difficulty with learning. The teachers perceived that Andrew was "severely disturbed" and that he had not mastered even the most basic interpersonal skills. They attempted to manage Andrew's outbursts by sending him to the principal's office (where he often spent the majority of the school day), calling his grandmother and insisting that she make him behave, or temporarily suspending him from school. It was quite evident that many of the teaching staff felt that Andrew was a "hopeless case" and that the family was at fault for his behavior.

The description above clearly targets Andrew as the guilty party in a series of disturbances and it leads us to believe there is something wrong with him. All eyes (and blame) are focused on the "no-good" son of a "no-good" family. There appears to be a massive consensus that locates the disturbance in Andrew himself and produces a major effort to discharge the "bad apple" before it spoils the brew. Andrew, however, has a different story, as the counselor discovered:

Meeting with Andrew individually, the counselor observed that Andrew was quite guarded and had few skills for expressing how he felt. It took a great deal of gentle nudging for him to talk about himself. Over a few weeks, however, using play media, Andrew began to reveal how upset he was that his family, and his father, in particular, were made fun of by the other students. He described a number of situations in which he had initiated serious fights after being teased by a group of boys about "his Daddy being a no-good drunk." He now seemed to go out of his way to keep his classmates and teachers in an uproar, and had managed to get himself completely ostracized by his peers because of his behavior.

Should the counselor believe Andrew's story? To do so would certainly place the counselor in opposition to prevailing opinion, unless there was more to the story.

> Dropping by to chat with Andrew's grandmother (as she had no phone) to see how she was aligned with the others involved with Andrew, the counselor said, "I'm worried about your grandson, and I'll bet you are too. I am new to the school and I know you know your grandson better than I do. Would you help me understand what has happened and how we might be able to get him on track at school?" The counselor learned that the grandmother seemed overwhelmed as to where to start to deal with him. She complained angrily about Andrew's problems at schools, which she described as "his being bad," yet acknowledged that she felt completely helpless as to how to manage him. The school had called her numerous times and was now threatening to expel Andrew permanently, her health was fragile, and she was completely exhausted from trying to manage him and the other two children. Although outside therapy had been recommended by the school several earlier times, the grandmother felt that it would be useless.

By seeking out Andrew's grandmother, the counselor is shifting attention from psyche (i.e., the problem is only in the individual) to system (i.e., the problem is contextual). As the counselor gathers information and compares the various descriptions of "the problem," a fuller picture emerges, revealing both complexity and possibility.

From Outside to Inside: Choosing One's Position

The counselor has already taken initiative to participate in the system observed. And that participation, as Andrew's case reveals, is the key to change.

> It was obvious that the school and home were caught in an escalating complementary pattern. The more desperate the school became that something be done with Andrew and the more school officials indicated to his grandmother that he was seriously disturbed, the more powerless the grandmother felt at having any impact on his behavior, and the less she did to control him, triggering the school to grow even more concerned, and press her harder. To alter this vicious cycle the

counselor decided to frame Andrew's behavior differently so that the grandmother might be more hopeful that she could have some impact on him and the counselor could build an alliance with her in which the grandmother felt she had some power. In addition, it would be important to interdict the negative feedback cycle so that the grandmother would not constantly be told how hopeless things were. Volunteering to serve as a conduit for information about Andrew from the school to the grandmother could serve this purpose. Thus, the counselor asked the grandmother if she knew exactly what the fights that Andrew had gotten into at school seemed to involve. The grandmother admitted that she did not. The counselor then indicated that she had learned from Andrew that most of his fighting seemed to involve protecting the family's, and particularly his father's, honor. The counselor stated, "It was as if Andrew feels he has to be the 'family's champion.' " As the counselor described a number of the situations in which Andrew had initiated serious fights after being teased about his family, the grandmother visibly softened. She admitted that although she often scolded him when he got into trouble she did not question him about the circumstances of the fights. The counselor acknowledged how difficult it was for her too to get Andrew to describe how he felt. She then proposed that she would like to drop by and chat with the grandmother every so often, because maybe between the two of them they could get some idea where Andrew was coming from.

The counselor has created an alliance with the grandmother standing *with* her (and *with* Andrew) rather than against her (as if from the outside as an observer). Clearly the counselor has a personal stake in the outcome of this drama.

Interaction to Transaction: Choosing
One's Mode of Inquiry/Explanation

One always has a choice as to one's "readiness to see" certain events and not others. Such readiness shows up in the choice of meaning one gives to people's actions. One can highlight meanings that underscore how things are always moving and changing and what is important in this movement (a wave lens), or one can emphasize the essential, unchanging nature of people's actions and intentions (a particle lens). Explanations that concern the essential nature of a person (self-action modes of inquiry) or of a relationship or set of relationships (interactional modes of inquiry) might be thought of as modes of inquiry and explanation that highlight stability. In contrast, transactional modes of inquiry/explanation that acknowledge how the observer's participation ripples through the system, and that emphasize explanations of overlooked possibilities, can enable people to recognize different aspects of what is already there. In the following excerpt the counselor's use of a transactional mode of explanation is illustrated:

Over the next several weeks, the counselor met with Andrew on an individual basis several times. Andrew slowly began to develop some language for describing his feeling experience and shared more and more about his anger and disappointment with school. He began to see the counselor as someone who did not treat him like a "bad kid," but was nurturing and playful with him. At the same time, the counselor consulted with Andrew's teachers at school and indicated that she agreed with them that Andrew did not know how to behave in school and said she would be willing to work with him if and when he behaved disruptively. During this same time the counselor dropped by the grandmother's house on a regular basis, and rather than sharing Andrew's school mishaps with the grandmother, she shared things that Andrew had said that showed his soft, nurturing side and asked for the grandmother's help in trying to understand what he meant.

As the grandmother began to be treated like a coequal by the counselor, she became less defensive and discouraged and began to ask how to handle certain situations with the children. She disclosed in response to the counselor's inquiry as to what she would like to be different that when her husband had died recently, each of the three children "went nuts, tearing up the house, and everything in it" rather than acting sad. She was confused and upset by their response and unsure what to do. The counselor suggested that the grandmother was probably the first person in these children's lives who cared about how they felt and would take time to talk to them about their feelings. She encouraged the grandmother to talk with the children about how they felt about the situation with their father and their mother. As the grandmother became more confident about nurturing, she admitted that she probably needed to be firmer with the children. The counselor stated that she knew that these children had been through a lot, and that both she and the grandmother might need some help figuring out what to do. The counselor then suggested that one of the family counselors in the local mental health clinic might be able to help them.

With the grandmother agreeing, the counselor then arranged a meeting with an agency counselor she knew. In this initial meeting, which both the family and school counselor attended, they all decided that the grandmother and the children would meet with the agency counselor and deal with family matters, and the school counselor would continue to drop by for a chat with the grandmother every so often and fill her in on school matters. In addition, the school counselor would continue to meet with Andrew on a regular basis. The grandmother and her family followed this arrangement conscientiously, meeting with the agency counselor regularly for the next several months and experiencing a lot of success in developing a clearer routine and structure for the children at home, and in building more opportunities to talk to the children about emotional issues. The counselor worked with Andrew and his teachers to reinforce his behavior in the classroom and with other students. By the spring, Andrew had developed a much more cooperative attitude with his teachers, was working up to grade level in all his subjects, and had begun to develop more positive relationships with some of his peers.

The counselor recognized that her participation could have an influence in the system. However, the only person that the counselor could directly influence was herself and how she participated in the system. This was illustrated in her decision to visit with each of the key members of the system and in her selection of what she would emphasize with each during the visit. Her deliberate selection of certain meanings for Andrew's behavior enabled the persons involved to recognize different aspects of what was already there— Andrew's nurturing side, the grandmother's nurturing side, and the school's nurturing side—and to collaborate in developing a version of themselves as a nurturing rather than a hostile community.

As this case vignette illustrates, the perspective emerging from the choice of focus (Andrew, grandmother, or the "problem-determined system"), the choice of position (observer or participant-observer), and the choice of mode of inquiry/explanation (self-action, interaction, or transaction), generates very different constructions and reconstructions of reality (what is meant by a child's social world; how it might be conceptualized; and how it functions, adapts, and changes). Furthermore, each choice defines the nature of children's problems differently (i.e., how problems in children's social worlds develop and how they are to be defined and investigated). Finally, each choice depicts a different set of beliefs about the ethical and political consequences of the child's action(s) and the school's response.

Inquiring Into Children's Family Life and School Adjustment

Like many other social scientists and educators, we have found ourselves shifting between use of a first-order and a second-order lens to guide our inquiry into children's family life and school adjustment. Are we viewing our research participants from the *outside* (a first-order view) as an "observer" or from *inside* of the system of interest (a second-order view) as a "participant-observer"? Let us look at the nature of these two lenses, considering the political and ethical implications of their use, and examining how each has been applied by social scientists, clinicians, and professional educators engaged in research and practice with children and key members of their social worlds.

Using a First-Order Lens: Choosing to Be an Observer

Many social scientists and educators prefer to operate from the *outside* of a child's social world in order to more effectively observe and analyze inputs to and outputs from those worlds. Such first-order thinkers often embrace the traditional scientific method that not only ties problem solving to explicit problem definition, hypotheses formation, and a systematic search for disconfirming evidence (Harrison & Bramson, 1982), but also assumes that knowledge is "about" something external to the knower and can present itself objectively to the knower. Thus, the basic question is causal: What caused this event that I'm observing? Or as Ida Maude stated: "Who and what are to blame?" It is presumed that the discovery of the cause will lead one to a workable solution to the dilemma at hand. For example, historically, psychiatry has focused on the individual, attributing the cause of a child's difficulties to a chemical imbalance, organic predisposition, personality disorder, "poor" self-concept, or social learning deficit as though the child's distress is a consequence of the laws of mechanics.

This way of thinking has also influenced social scientists who focus on the family system and transfer their search for causal factors from the individual child's psyche to the ecology of the child. Rather than looking atomistically at Andrew by dissecting his insides (i.e., psyche) to find the cause of his difficulties, first-order system observers look at both the intimate social network of the family in which Andrew is embedded and the superordinate social network of the school and community in their search for clues as to the relevant causal system supporting the problem. Stachowiak and Briggs (1984) advocate this point of view in their description of human ecology:

> In human ecology, the person-environment context constitutes the totality of relationships among individuals and their environments. . . . Theoretically, system levels can be identified from the smallest subatomic particles to the interaction of galaxies. In human services, the focus extends from the level of physiological functioning to that of social and cultural influences. Given this range, selection of the system levels relevant to a specific problem is a crucial first step in the process of diagnosis and treatment. (pp. 8-9)

It is assumed, from a first-order systems perspective, that the source of Andrew's problems can be found in the way system levels relate to each other. According to Anderson and Goolishian (1988), this view of human systems constitutes the "onion theory":

> Each system is like a layer of the onion that is encircled by another layer. . . . Each layer subsumes and controls subordinate layers in the service of its own requirement—the homeostatic maintenance of social order, stability and equilibrium. The individual is encircled by the family, the family by the larger system (e.g., school, neighborhood, social services agency), the larger system by the community, and so on. This imposed restriction of social role and structure acts as a social harness that exists independently of people and provides the order that society calls culture and civilization. (p. 376)

Given this complex cybernetic hierarchy of layered human systems, problematic behavior or deviance within particular components or levels of the system is interpreted as representing inadequacies in social role and structure. Thus, when components (i.e., people, families, peer groups, neighborhoods, specific subcultural groups) demonstrate problems, it is because they are functioning erroneously because of not having been sufficiently socialized as to their proper role and structure by the hierarchical layer immediately above the layer demonstrating deviance. (Note the reference to Andrew's "no-good" family as explanation for his deviance.) The focus of research inquiry is defined in the language of social structure and role, and the task of the researcher is defined as "identifying the social defect in the structure of the appropriate social system layer" (Anderson & Goolishian, 1988, p. 377). The methods used by the researcher in ferreting out this flaw may be characterized as very much like those of an impartial investigator or detective "trying to unravel a complex mystery" (Tomm, 1988) by using basic questions such as: Who did what? To whom? Where? When? and Why? in order to discern who and what to blame (e.g., a family, a peer group, a community neighborhood). And the presumption is that having found out what in the system caused the problem, the investigator can set in motion a process for correcting the malfunction.

At the heart of this first-order view is a positivist, or logical empiricist, orientation that assumes that truth is (and can be) completely represented by observable phenomena and scientifically verifiable facts, that is, that truth occurs in only one valid version: "Science, seen from this perspective, is the process of using an empirical method to pare down alternatives descriptions and explanations of phenomena until there is a single version remaining. This surviving version is seen as possessing intrinsic truth, in that it possesses as much truth in one context as it does in another" (Griffith & Griffith, 1990, p. 16).

Furthermore, human systems are assumed to exist as an objective reality independent of the observer. It is assumed that the social scientist or educator can abstract him- or herself from his or her object of study in order to "discover" and accumulate objective knowledge. Being a distant, impartial observer, the social scientist, clinician, or educator can discover how the system should function without participating in it, determine the degree of defect of the system (via assessment) without changing anything in the system's functioning by means of his or her observation, and identify what should be done to fix the system (i.e., what proper corrective actions should be taken) without ever consulting his or her study participants (Hoffman, 1990). Within this perspective, the social scientist operates from a free-standing pursuit of truth independent of his or her values and worldview, and privately formulates hypotheses (which are never disclosed to the participant/client) as to the structure of the system. Implicit in this set of assumptions is the belief that research subjects themselves are nonexperts; that the personal, familial, political, and economic domains are inherently different and operate autonomously; and that only the social scientist can select the appropriate field or level of experience to be assessed, decide what is right or wrong (i.e., functional or dysfunctional), and through the results of this inquiry, suggest the appropriate consequences in terms of who or what should be changed in order to remedy the child's difficulties.

Because we have been well anchored in this first-order tradition, we have looked with intrigue at what researchers are discovering about the connections between children's family life and school performance. Believing that children's capacities and competence develop in response to their social world, we wondered what causal connections existed between children's family experience and their school learning and how such findings could influence educational practice. Paralleling our own frequent choice of a first-order way of knowing, many of these social scientists sought to establish a link between children's school competence and aspects of their family world by using a group comparison design in which a group of families of children experiencing some learning difficulty/pathology were contrasted with a group of families with children demonstrating no known difficulties.

We found three lines of pertinent research linking family life and children's learning particularly intriguing: (a) research investigating parent-child communication deviance, (b) research on family organizational structures, and (c) research on family beliefs and worldviews. Inherent in the design of each of these research efforts were assumptions that there were inherently stable or static features that characterized family life as it really was, that these static features of family life could be studied without consideration of the context in which they were being called forth (i.e., the nature of the demand situation in which family features were being demonstrated), that the investigator could serve as a value-free reporter of the events under investigation (i.e., that his or her narrowing down of the focus of investigation in no way influenced what was observed), and that a causal connection could be established between family characteristics and children's school performance.

Parent-Child Communication Deviance

Building on a long tradition of research on parental communication deviance and adult thought disorders (Doane, 1978, 1985;

Singer, Wynne, & Toohey, 1978), a number of researchers have sought in recent years to understand children's learning and achievement difficulties within a family communication deviance model. Green (1989), for example, proposed that the family is the child's primary classroom experience—that is, children's experience in the family shapes their ability to function cognitively at school in terms of learning to orient themselves to tasks, to stay focused on tasks, and to ask clarifying questions. In a study comparing the performance of learning-disabled and normally achieving middle school students, Ditton, Green, and Singer (1987) reported a significant relationship between parental communication deviances and children's placement in a learning disability program, with parental communication deviance being defined "as oddities in spoken language that impair the establishment and maintenance of a shared focus of attention in communication" (Green, 1989, p. 191). Proposing that just as confusing and disorienting styles of parental communication are reflected in the confused and disoriented thought processes of schizophrenic offspring, so children's cognitive performance reflects the confusing style of parental communication with them. Recently, Rasku-Puttonen, Lyytinen, Poikkeus, Laakso, and Ahonen (1994) extended the investigation of this relationship between the child's learning disabilities and the conversational competence of the child and the parent through observation of a parent-child learning task. Working with 60 mother-child pairs in which half of the children were learning disabled and the other half were normally achieving children, the researchers reported that the mothers of learning-disabled (LD) children were found to give less exact instructions and more ambiguous messages than the mothers of non-LD children, whereas the LD and non-LD children did not differ in the degree of clarification they requested from their mothers.

Although these studies are viewed as yielding evidence that deviant styles of parental communication *contribute* to the etiology of learning disabilities in children, there are a number of studies presenting competing research evidence. For example, observations of parent-child interactions have indicated that mothers' behavior toward their learning-disabled children is different from that toward their nondisabled children (Bryan, Donahue, Pearl, & Herzog, 1984). According to Kistner and Torgesen's (1987) review, interactions between LD children and their parents contain more negative feedback, directives, and control of the children's behavior than do interactions between normally achieving children and their parents.

An alternative perspective might be that the behavior of mothers toward their LD children reflects adaptive efforts to deal with their children's learning problems. Mothers of learning-disabled children, for example, have been reported to take more initiative than do mothers of nondisabled children in play situations (Bryan et al., 1984). A similar trend has been found between mothers and their dysphasic children (Rasku-Puttonen, Lyytinen, & Vilkman, 1991) and between parents and communicationally handicapped children (Pellegrini, Brody, & Sigel, 1985). These findings seem to indicate that parents of handicapped children make an extra effort to involve their children in the discourse by asking them questions and thereby providing them with the possibility to respond appropriately.

One of the challenges to this line of research is that this explanation ignores the existence of underlying neuropsychological causes of learning disabilities and dismisses the increasing evidence of the contribution of genetic factors to verbal or other learning disabilities. Another challenge is that this research ignores the larger social context in which the child and family are operating. Given the narrow focus of these research efforts on parent-child communication, it is hard to see whether there are other factors in the environment that may contribute to a child's learning and school adjustment difficulties. A child may be more susceptible, for example, to school failure because of being treated in a distant, put-down manner by the school staff. A final challenge lies with the bidirectionality of these parent-child communication patterns. More often than not, correlational patterns such as those reported above are interpreted as unidirectional by an unsophisticated audience—that it, that the influence is from parent to child. Such correlational patterns could, however, suggest a causal pattern in the opposite direction—the chronically demanding child who thinks and learns differently might solicit a response from parents that is different from the response they would make to children without this disorder.

Pathological Family Role Structures

There has been a fascination for many years in studying the link between how families organize themselves and the type of psychological symptom found in a family, suggesting a typology of family role structure by symptom. This conceptual focus has been applied in examining the link between the interactional role structure of the family and a child's learning performance as well. One of the most prominent efforts to develop a family organization typology came from the work of Salvadore Minuchin, Braulio Montalvo, and their associates (Minuchin, Montalvo, Guerney, Rosman, & Schumer, 1967), who studied the socialization processes of families with severely delinquent, lower socioeconomic class boys. These boys' families seem to fall into two categories: one characterized as "enmeshed," the other as "disengaged." Although both were composed of poverty-level families, they differed in substantial ways and were described by Minuchin and his associates (1967) as representing opposite ends of a bipolar continuum. In the disengaged family (also called the underorganized or underinvolved family), there seemed to be a relative absence of strong connections, and relationship ties between family members were weak or nonexistent. The enmeshed family, by contrast, was characterized by a "tight interlocking" (Hoffman, 1981) of its members, with each highly attuned to the emotional reactions of the other. In the latter group of families, conflict was continually deflected through the use of third parties. Whenever two persons disagreed and attempted to work out some problem, a third would intervene. For example, if a parent criticized one of the children, the other parent or a sibling would join in to protect the child, and then another family member would join the critic or the criticized. Thus, attention to the original issue would be deflected, only to emerge again later in a similar sequence and then to be similarly deflected and left unresolved. According to Minuchin, the enmeshed, or as Aponte (1976b) terms it the "overinvolved or overorganized," family is characterized by parental intrusiveness, overinvolvement, and overprotectiveness or restrictiveness.[2] In these families, parents tend to be too involved and too controlling of their children's lives, including their school performance. This shows up as both parents (or one parent very involved and the other peripheral) taking over, pressuring, nagging, and dominating. The child symptoms produced in these family organizations are "obsessional worry, performance anxiety, procrastination, passive-negativism, or oppositional behavior in reference to academic tasks" (Green, 1989, p. 194).

Various researchers have described parent-child interactional patterns that differ in degree of rigidity, overinvolvement, and lack of conflict resolution in the families of underachieving children (Dornbush & Ritter, 1992; Humphries & Bauman, 1980; Kohn & Rosman, 1974). Although in some families the quality of parental intrusiveness is benevolently protective, in others it is reported to be harshly punitive, attacking, and authoritarian. In either case, researchers characterize the parents in these families as taking on too much responsibility for the child's school performance, and the child, on the other hand, as taking on too little responsibility for his or her achievement in school.

In contrast to the overorganized, rigid involvement of the enmeshed families, the polar opposite family structure (the chaotically disorganized, disengaged family), has been linked by Green (1989) to a different set of school performance problems: "Whereas the overorganized structure seems to be associated with internalizing symptoms such as obsessional worry, performance anxiety or passive-negativism, the underorganized structure has been linked to child attentional deficits and conduct disorders" (p. 193). The organizational structure of these types of families has been characterized by Minuchin and his associates (1967) as having (a) highly conflictual interaction with resolution of conflict escalating by threats and counterthreats rather than discussion; (b) an overall deficit of communication through words and logic, which are replaced by an intensity of physical action and sound in which members resort to yelling because they do not expect to be listened to; (c) parental styles of control that are global, erratic, and based primarily on parental mood with the result that clear and consistent behavioral contingencies (rules) for rewards and punishments are lacking; and (d) an extreme focus on hierarchical relatedness and immediate compliance by the use of force rather than cognitively mediated long-term solutions.

A number of researchers have hypothesized that children coming from this type of family organization demonstrate difficulties in focusing attention (i.e., attentional deficits), a disruptive communication style that precludes taking in new information, and behavior focused on eliciting authoritarian/proximal control by the teacher rather than as a result of the classroom task per se. Owen, Adams, Forrest, Stolz, and Fisher (1971), for example, rated the families of LD children as more disorganized and unstable than the families of normal controls. Kohn and Rosman (1974) studied the academic achievement of elementary school students longitudinally and reported a relationship between disorganized family structure and children's poor task orientation and academic achievement. In a study of three groups of predominantly white, middle-class families having emotionally disturbed, learning-disabled, or normal children, Amerikaner and Omizo (1984) reported that the parents of emotionally disturbed and learning-disabled children reported more chaotic family environments characterized by less cohesive relations than did the parents of normals. Finally, in examining the impact of different family processes on high school students' school performance across various ethnic groups, socioeconomic classes, and family structures (e.g., single parent vs. two parent), Dornbush and Ritter (1992) conducted a series of studies involving several thousand high school students differing in school achievement. They found several distinctive styles of family decision making and parental involvement in children's school life that were strongly associated with different student achievement patterns.

Each of these studies attempts to establish the predictive validity of a typology of interactional/organizational family structures to explain certain types of school achievement and adjustment problems. Such typologies of interactional/organizational structure have also been used to describe school life and family-school interaction. Schwartzman and Kneifel (1985), for example, reviewed the literature on how school systems often replicate dysfunctional family patterns in responding to children. They contend that school staffs could be classified along the same bipolar continuum (as underinvolved or overinvolved) in their degree of involvement and organization. Aponte (1976a), for example, reports a case of such structural context replication wherein a child acting out in school is described as belonging to a family characterized by a rigid, overinvolved structure and a school staff organized along similar lines. Other clinicians (Lusterman, 1989) have utilized the dimensions of family cohesion (e.g., interpersonal warmth and connectedness) and family adaptability (e.g., rule setting and changing) to characterize not only the nature of the family's interaction but also the school's interaction around a child experiencing academic performance problems.

This role structure typology, like many other family typologies, tends to imply an either/or continuum, as if one is simply talking about families having too much or too little cohesion or role structures. Many family theorists have become dissatisfied with this continuum concept. Hoffman (1981), for one, states:

There are some serious drawbacks in this typology. It [Minuchin's typology] does not cover enough variables, nor is it rich or interesting enough. . . . In addition, these studies that try to establish an etiology different from the traditional individually-oriented one have assumed a causal link between family role structure and deviant behavior. But to say that a particular condition is contingent on a given type of family organization or role structure, or to think that there is a direct connection, is to make the mistake of linear thinking. (pp. 85-86)

A major dilemma faced by these theorists is their focus on pathology. Are there positive and adaptive aspects of family life that are not seen by the researcher? Furthermore, are these organizational traits unchanging?

Family Beliefs and Worldviews

Uncomfortable with the too-simple dichotomy of pathology/non-pathology epitomized by much of the family role structure research, several family theorists and researchers began in the early 1980s to formulate more complex views of the family and its relationship to children's school performance. They talked of family worlds, calling on a new and important concept: the "family paradigm." This was illustrated in the work of David Reiss (1981) and Larry Constantine (1986), who were committed to broadening their focus to consider a set of key variables that would not just describe families with symptomatic members but the whole rich variety of families. Reiss (1981) proposed that family members operate with each other as if guided by a family paradigm, which he defined as

An overarching image of their family and of families in general, which influences the nature of the ways they relate together as a family. These images function as points of reference against which family members check their experience with each other; define their priorities among competing ends; develop the ground rules which guide their everyday actions and the values by which their behavior is judged. Thus, a paradigm is not only a model of what a family is, can be and should be, but is also a world view through which experiences in relationships are interpreted. It is a particular image, a way in which the members of a family view how they should operate internally and in relation to the rest of the world. (p. 53)

In an initial series of research studies linking family interaction styles with individual thinking processes, Reiss (1981) described a series of problem-solving experiments that drew on three populations: eight families with offspring diagnosed "schizophrenic," eight families whose members had "character disorders" (i.e., severe delinquencies), and eight with offspring who had no known disorder. The entire families, consisting of parents, the symptomatic child, and all other siblings, were included in the experiment. The families were required to sort a group of 15 cards, each containing a patterned sequence of letters or nonsense syllables. Their task was broken down into three steps: First, each family member—sitting in a separate booth—was asked to sort the group of cards; next the family as a whole was given the task of putting the same series of cards in order; and finally, each individual again was given the task of sorting the cards. During the family task each member was given 2 cards, and when these were sorted was instructed to press a "finished" button to get another card, until all 15 were sorted. Family members could communicate with each other by earphone and share ideas and information. The families could use whatever strategy they wished to solve the task—they could trade ideas or go it alone, they could wait for enough cards to see an overall pattern or decide on a sequence based on the first few cards they got. (The experiment was set up so that it was easier to arrive at a correct hypothesis for sorting the cards after they were almost all in, but the rule for sorting still had to be guessed at.)

According to Reiss (1981), these initial experiments revealed some fascinating differences among the participating families. It was almost as if each group of families operated from very different "family miniuniverses," which were very different from each other yet correlated closely to the clinical groupings. Reiss identified three categories of miniuniverse—*consensus-sensitive, interpersonal-distance sensitive,* and *environment-sensitive*—corresponding to the schizophrenic families, the delinquent families, and the normal families, respectively. According to Reiss, "The characteristics which seemed to mark off these groups of families were: (a) family members' ability to use cues or suggestions from each other; (b) their ability to use cues from the laboratory; and (c) their ability to reach closure" (p. 34). Reiss found that families with schizophrenic members were very clued in to each other but very walled off from everything else. Their internal sensitivity did not help them with the test, but hindered them. In Reiss's words, "In this kind of family, there is a joint perception that the analysis and solution of the problem are simply a means to maintain a close and uninterrupted agreement at all times" (p. 56). He explained that this group of families seemed to need to be close and in agreement, and that they seemed to experience the environment as threatening and dangerous. Thus, the testing situation was viewed as a threat to be warded off. Consequently, people in these families would reach a solution very quickly, before much information had become available, and hang onto their position even when later facts or a better solution arrived at by another family member contradicted it. They often failed because of premature closure. "They would rather be wrong than fight" (Hoffman, 1981, p. 89). Reiss (1981) believed that this view of family life was not characteristic just of problem families. He cited, for example, the cultural variant of certain southern Italian clans, with their code of family solidarity and their perception of the outside world as menacing and unpredictable.

In contrast to these consensus-sensitive families were the interpersonal-distance-sensitive families. These families tended to attend very well to clues from the outside environment, but did not attend to cues from each other. During the test, for example, family members behaved as though it would be a mistake to accept the opinions of other members of their family. They seemed to need to show they could be independent and could master the outside world on their own. Reiss (1981) stated: "These individuals seem to share a perception that the environment was split into as many pieces as there were family members; each member had access to his own piece and therefore attended to environmental cues from his piece only" (p. 72). These families seemed to experience the laboratory as a way to demonstrate individual mastery rather than family mastery. Although these families seemed to Reiss to have a better appreciation of the "out-there reality" than the consensus-sensitive group, their stance as independent thinkers seemed to constrain their ability to work together as a family to solve the problem-solving tasks. Reiss drew the parallel of this style to highly individualistic middle-class families who tolerate a high degree of conflict to enable members to do their own thing. The third category, the environment-sensitive group, was composed of families whose members seemed to have an optimal balance between using cues from other family members and at the same time accepting and incorporating clues from their environment. "Flexibility about both the degree of internal connectedness and connection with the outside worlds seemed to distinguish this group on the problem solving tasks" (Reiss, 1981, p. 82).

Over time, Reiss broke away from this static family qualities model of internal and external connectedness and closure and began to emphasize how families *change* their paradigm or worldview rather than stay the same. Instead of characterizing families in fixed categories and comparing families with known pathologies, Reiss and his associates became fascinated with how "normal" families view their world and with how such families change their paradigm over time. He states: "I propose that family crisis fills a positive function in the life of every family. Though filled with risk it ultimately opens the family to new experience, altering their sense of themselves and the outside world and thereby transforming a paradigm which may have guided them for years or even generations" (Reiss, 1981, p. 134). In subsequent years, Reiss and his associates examined how normal families evolve and change their paradigms as they manage various developmental transitions such as that of adolescence (Reiss, Oliveri, & Curd, 1983).

One of the researchers to adapt Reiss's interest in how normal families view their world through a particular family paradigm and its impact on child rearing was Larry Constantine. Constantine (1986) proposed that although all families are organized by certain basic themes through which they construct their worlds and organize their actions and beliefs, they can differ dramatically in how they set their priorities and structure family life. These variations in family style and structure have been organized by Constantine according to two fundamental themes of family life: (a) the commitment to continuity versus variety in family life and (b) the extent to which the interests of individual family members are valued versus the interests of the family group as a whole. Four distinctive paradigms of family life emerge from the variations on these themes: (a) the *closed/traditional,* (b) the *random/individualistic,* (c) the *synchronous/harmonious,* and (d) the *open/collaborative.*

According to Constantine (1986) each of the four paradigms can form the basis for successful family life; there need not be only one best formula, right answer, or functional family. Instead, families can draw from a variety of different approaches to problem solving that are useful in different circumstances. Through a series of clinical case studies linking type of family paradigm to adolescent development, Constantine (1987) demonstrated how support for adolescent differentiation from the family and separation or autonomous functioning varies with the family's paradigm, and how adolescents raised under different paradigms may face quite different developmental challenges. For example, issues that were salient for adolescents from closed/traditional families with strong parental authority may not be as important developmentally for those raised in the more permissive style of a random/individualistic paradigm.

Intrigued by the fundamental distinctions about family life suggested by Reiss and Constantine, by Constantine's (1991) recent focus on work organizations, and by the observation that many of the cases in which children were reported to be experiencing difficulties at school seemed to involve differences between the home and school in basic assumptions and values, Amatea, Brown, and Cluxton (1992) devised a framework for (a) identifying how children's school problems might be amplified by school and family paradigm diversity and (b) fitting interventions to the basic nature and operating assumptions of the school and the family. Assuming that schools as well as families can be seen as human systems guided by overarching paradigms that reflect inherent assumptions as to how interaction within and between systems will be coordinated, these researchers identified the types of strengths and vulnerabilities (see Table 2.1) inherent in the school's and family's paradigms so that approaches to resolving differences between the home and school could be identified.

As we consider these various research efforts in the first-order tradition, we see illustrated not only a particular choice of position, but of focus and mode of inquiry/explanation as well. For example, the focus of each of these research endeavors has broadened to include not just the problem child and his or her family, but the school and normal families. In contrast, the mode of inquiry/explanation illustrated in these research efforts highlights interaction (rather than self-action or transaction). We have readied ourselves to see stabilities—things about children and their families and schools that stay the same—and when we notice a relationship we tend to think in linear terms, assigning a cause (and often assigning blame). We have not been as ready to see the instabilities, the aspects of children and their social worlds that are constantly changing and evolving. Finally, we have chosen a position outside

Table 2.1 Defining Features, Strengths, and Limitations of School and Family Paradigms

	Closed/Traditional	Random/Individualistic	Open/Collaborative	Synchronous/Serene
Individual and Family/Classroom Group	Promotes dependence, loyalty, subordination to group	Promotes counterdependence, independence from group	Promotes flexible interdependence; admixture of dependent, independent	Promotes "nondependence," parallel independent functioning
Autonomous Action	Relatively low; limited support except when regulated by rules	Relatively high; actively promotes "separate solutions"	Relatively low; favors collaborative action	Relatively high; favors compatible independent action
Parenting/Teaching	Authority-based; explicit expectations of obedience and conformity; expresses established views	Laissez-faire, free individual expression; natural emergence of unique potential	Collaboration; children as respected partners; rules and expectations "worked out" through open communication	High but unstated expectations based on "understood" needs; identification with parents/teachers
Stability and Change	Builds stability	Creates change	Generates flexibility; combines stability and change	Timelessness
Decision Making	Based in authority, tradition; commands, directions passed	Based in originality; spontaneity; autonomous actions	Based in consensus; open communication; negotiation	Based in tacit agreement, mutual identification; automatic
Power and Control	Hierarchy, fixed roles	Anarchic, egalitarian, independent solutions	Mutual collaboration, joint solutions	Indirect or covert; implied understandings
Provides	Security, belonging	Freedom, variety	Emotional support, adaptiveness	Tranquillity
Promotes	Conformity, loyalty	Individuality, independence	Mutuality, cooperation	Harmonious identification
May Sacrifice	Individuality, variety	Security, stability	Tranquillity	Emotional support and involvement
Probable Direction	Rigidity, overinvolvement	Chaos, underinvolvement	Chaos, overinvolvement	Rigidity, underinvolvement

SOURCE: Amatea, Brown, and Cluxton (1992); adapted from Constantine (1986).

55

the system we are observing. Rather than considering how we as the researchers are the ones taking the parts and pieces apart and deciding that one part "controls" another or that one part "causes" another, we see the properties we study as standing outside ourselves. Thus, our possible role as participant-observers in the research has remained hidden.

Using a Second-Order Lens:
Choosing to Be a Participant-Observer

It has been only gradually and with much reluctance, as we have discovered life outside the first-order perspective, that we have become aware of an alternative to use of the first-order lens. Social construction theory has been crucial in our developing awareness of an alternative—the second-order perspective. Basically, social construction theory holds that our beliefs about the world are social inventions. As we move through the world we build up our ideas about what the world is like by means of our conversation with other people. Thus, rather than viewing knowledge as a representation of facts and events in a real world as do the positivists, social constructionists view knowledge as a social phenomenon in which my perception of reality can only evolve within a cradle of communication with other people. Epitomizing this theoretical perspective, Gergen (1985) states: "The terms in which the world is understood are social artifacts, products of historically situated interchanges among people. From the constructionist position the process of understanding is not automatically driven by the forces of nature, but is the result of an active, cooperative enterprise of persons, in relationship" (p. 267).

An increasing number of clinicians and social scientists (Andersen, 1987, 1991; Anderson & Goolishian, 1988; Anderson, Goolishian, & Winderman, 1986; Avis, 1994; Gergen, 1988; Hoffman, 1990) are challenging the assumptions of objectivity and neutrality that have characterized the positivist view. They contend that it is not possible to "obtain an objective account of the world . . . not mediated by our language, by our interpretations, by our location in the field of social structures" (White, 1992, p. 35). They point out that knowledge is power, that power allows some persons to define what constitutes true knowledge, and that the dominant constructions of reality we often operate by in education and the social sciences oppress other alternative or subjugated knowledges

(Foucault, 1980) and limit their emergence. These social scientists contend that the critical questions are not what is the true nature of reality, but instead "which values and social institutions are favored by each of the multiple versions of reality [and] whose interests are served by these competing ways of giving meaning to the world" (Riger, 1992, p. 735).

These social scientists describe the process of social inquiry and intervention from the "inside" position: They consider themselves part of the "problem-determined system" (Daniels & White, 1994) that constructs the "story" of reality in which we each live. They believe that reality is socially constructed, that is, "how we describe reality is more about what can be said and thought [by participants of a social group] and about who can speak and with what authority" (Kaye, 1990, p. 28). Thus, a research inquiry is a linguistic event that takes place in a conversation wherein the participants together move from a position of "not knowing" to knowing.

Furthermore, these social scientists believe that they cannot influence others without being influenced; therefore, they include themselves as part of what must be examined. This belief has been nurtured by what has been called *second-order cybernetics* by cybernetics researchers like Keeney (1983), Maturana and Varela (1980), and Von Foerster (1981). Unlike the "first-order" cybernetics of the "hard" scientists, Von Foerster proposed that living systems were to be seen not as objects that could be programmed from the outside, but as self-creating, independent entities. Rather than view the purpose of scientific inquiry as the verification of reality through reducing events and processes to observable, quantifiable elements, and verifying the existence of these elements through replication, social scientists operating from a second-order perspective consider scientific inquiry to be a formative, constructive process in which both the researcher and those persons who are studied are involved together in creating, generating, and producing ideas in a process of "interpretive inquiry" (Kaye, 1990).

Obviously this view requires that one think about and participate in human systems differently as indicated by the term, *second order.* The second-order concept originated in mathematics and merely means taking a position that includes both the system and the observer so that you can perceive the operation reflexively. Thus, as Hoffman (1990) states, second-order views are really "views about views," which can often make one more aware of the way one's own relationship to an operation can influence it. In addition, taking such a view can assist the observer in seeing that a particular interpretation is only one among many possible versions. For example, the "new" math confronts those schooled in the "old" math with a new way to *think about* doing mathematics, beginning with the recognition that the decimal system of numbering based on groups of 10 is just one of any number of groupings that could be used for a numbering system. It could be five, it could be two. Similarly, when one can take a second-order view of children's social worlds, one thinks about how one thinks about such worlds. According to Hoffman (1990), in distinguishing between first- and second-order cybernetics, the single most important thought to keep in mind is that of the *observing system*. Von Foerster (1981) states that the observer enters into that which is observed in such a way that objectivity is not possible. Everything that is going on is entirely self-referential (Becvar & Becvar, 1993). Finally, because the way any observer perceives the world is through the lenses of culture, family, and language, the resulting product represents not something private and self-contained, but instead the product of an observer community. Bateson (1972), following Wiener (Brand, 1976), captured this view when he eliminated the line between observer and observed, subject and object, and proposed that these units and their contexts represented a larger circularity know as *mind*. In sum, these various ideas argue against the unilateral control of one part by another, affirm the perspective of cooperation rather than resistance (de Shazer, 1984), promote a human system as a self-referential system made up of the observer (i.e., the educator or social scientist) as well as the observed (the various participants in the child's social world), and reinforces the idea that one cannot observe something without in some way affecting it.

Thinking in these ways about reality, causality, and our position as researchers has radical implications for the conduct of research on children's family life and school performance. First, in contrast to those using the first-order perspective, researchers using the second-order lens acknowledge the nonreductionistic nature of the child's and family's experience. Rather than seeing a child's family or school world as static and *unchanging,* able to be broken down into essential elements that exist only in one version, this view emphasizes multiple perspectives and the changing nature of the child's social world. As Anderson and Goolishian (1988) put it,

The conceptualization of reality as a multiverse of meanings created in dynamic social exchange and conversational interaction moves us away from concerns about issues of unique truths and into a multiverse that includes a diversity of conflicting versions of the world. Within this framework, there are no "real" external entities, only communication and languaging human individuals. There is only the process of the constantly evolving reality of language use. Thus, there are no "facts" to be known, no systems to be "understood" and no regularities to be "discovered." (p. 378)

Second, rather than seeing the locus of the problem as residing in the character of the child or family system, researchers utilizing this second-order systems perspective view the larger social context in which children, their family, and their school are embedded in and *response-able* for jointly constructing the stories people live by. Third, rather than viewing the actions of the child, the family, and the school staff in a linear or sequential causal sequence, the actions and reactions of a child and persons at home and at school are seen as *simultaneously* influencing each other. For example, which stories about a child and his or her family held by the school constrain or support the child, the family, and/or school staff? Which stories held by the family constrain or support the child's school performance and his or her family's or school's *response-ability?* What stories in the larger culture support or constrain the school and family? How does the family affect beliefs in the school, and how in turn does the school affect the beliefs of the family? A child may be more susceptible, for example, to demonstrating school failure because of being treated in a distant, put-down manner by the school staff. In addition, a family may be less able to deal flexibly and imaginatively with a child's learning situation if its family expertise is denied.

Several recent lines of research and theory building on children's family and school worlds illustrate the use of this second-order lens: (a) research on solution-focused family-school consultation, (b) research on family-school climate building, and (c) ecosystemic family-school consultation. As might be expected given the legitimization of time in the second-order view, each of these lines of research and theory building is a form of action research tied to the design of novel educational and clinical intervention practices with children and their family and school worlds. Let us look at each of these research and theory-building efforts more closely.

Solution-Focused Family-School Consultation

An intriguing form of consultation known as brief, solution-focused family-school consultation (Carlson, Hickman, & Horton, 1992; Kral, 1992) epitomizes the changing, multiperspectival nature of reality characterizing the ecosystemic view. Rooted in the genre of therapy known as *solution-focused brief therapy* and the theory-building work of Kral (1986), Molnar and de Shazer (1987), and Molnar (1988), this model of consultation is characterized by a unique theory of change. Practitioners working within this approach assume that (a) change is constant (i.e., is always going on) and in fact inevitable; (b) individuals have within themselves the resources to resolve their difficulties; and (c) the change agent's role is to co-construct with the parties involved solutions that fit with the constraints of their situation. In this approach, the essential responsibility of the consultant is to change the context from a problem-saturated one to a resource-focused one—that is, one focused on the resources that clients already have for resolving their difficulties. Emphasis is placed on deconstructing the problem context (the old story of the problem) and co-constructing a resourceful mindset among the participants (i.e., dealing with what they already are changing rather than further concretizing their view of the problem as uncontrollable and unchanging by gathering only a detailed, sequential account of the problem and its causes and consequences). This requires that the consultant, the child, and involved others (the members of the child's family and school worlds) explore how they are already attempting to solve the problem rather than how they view the problem as staying the same. Asking questions such as "What is now going on in the family/classroom that they would like to continue to see happen?" is one way to focus on the positives that may be occurring but that may go unnoticed with the overfocus on the problems. This line of questioning not only allows participants to focus on what they are already doing to solve the problem, but also leads to participants viewing and understanding their experience of the problem differently (i.e., that it is changeable rather than unchangeable).

According to Carlson and her colleagues (1992), research on the effects of this approach with children, parents, and school staff in a public school setting revealed changes in how children, their parents and teachers, and the consultant viewed a child's problem and responded to it. Children reported feeling less blame and more problem improvement across the course of the intervention, and parents indicated feelings of greater involvement and optimism resulting from this mode of consultation. These results indicate that an emphasis on the strengths and resources of the child/family/ school ecosystem, and on the equal status of home and school— each as part of the solution rather than the problem—resulted in the construction of problem-solving versus problem-maintaining capacities in persons in the child's home.

Family-School Climate Building

Under the able leadership of Howard Weiss, a team of educators and clinicians were engaged over a 10-year period in a program of intervention to "initiate and sustain positive working partnerships between families and schools" (Weiss & Edwards, 1992, p. 215). Collaborating with staff in one of the most challenging public school systems in the country—the New York City public schools— they had as their goal: "establishing ongoing, routine vehicles for sharing information in a two-way dialogue between home and school, and developing educational plans and solving problems involving their children" (p. 215). Working with staff in schools varying in economic resources and status, this team of clinicians and educators was committed to re-visioning the roles of parents in the life of the school from that of peripheral players to active partners and co-decision makers in the education of the students. In addition to expanding the role of parents in schools, the goals of Weiss's series of projects were to assist schools in "establishing a general climate of family-school collaboration and designing a series of activities to reflect this climate . . . and to have each school assume ownership for their efforts to establish a collaborative climate for family-school relations" (pp. 218-219). Thus, the family-school system was viewed as the unit of intervention, and although strategies for solving children's school or mental health problems were one focus of activity, a wide range of other strategies designed to bring about organizational change in family-school relations was the focus of attention.

The specific family-school collaboration practices that Weiss and his team (Weiss & Edwards, 1992) sought to introduce included classroom family orientations, parent-teacher-child conferences held during the year, and family-school problem-solving meetings over concerns about a particular child. A major change implemented in these activities was the inclusion of the child as an active participant in the conversations involving the home and school. Recently, Weiss and his associates collected data regarding school staff, parent, and student perceptions of the extent to which these practices have occurred and the impact of these changes. In a recent study (Weiss, 1994) in which teachers in three Chapter I schools involved in an initial year of implementing these changes ("novice teachers") were compared with those teachers who had been involved for more than one year ("experienced teachers"), Weiss and his colleagues reported a shift from 0% to 85% in the percentage of teachers using family-classroom orientations. In a study comparing the family-teacher conferencing practices of 210 novice and experienced teachers in 12 schools, a significantly greater number of experienced teachers than novice teachers reported using family-teacher conferencing methods in which the child was included (95% vs. 55%) in their fall conferences. However, by the end of the school year, the novice teachers had significantly increased their frequency of using family-oriented conferencing methods (from 55% to 72%).

In addition, favorable changes appeared in parents' reported attitudes about the program. Not only were there significant increases in the number of parents participating in school orientations, parent participation in parent-school conferences also rose dramatically (from 32% to 68%) at midyear, and by the end of the year 90% of the children's parents had attended conferences. Parents rated the conferences as extremely useful in helping them understand school concerns, having school staff understand their concerns, and improving parent-teacher and parent-administration relationships. These shifts in teacher and parent attitudes and practices reveal that a concentrated focus on deliberately changing the relationships between schools and families could be successful.

Ecosystemic Family-School Consultation

An exciting revolution has been growing in the fields of education and mental health during the last decade—the application of ecosystemic thinking and practices in school contexts by educators as well as mental health professionals (Fine, 1992; Lincoln, 1992; White, Summerlin, Loos, & Epstein, 1992). Like most revolutions, this one has gone through a number of transformations. In the early 1980s, as a result of the growing popularization of family therapy, many educators began to view family therapy as an appropriate mode of treating children who demonstrated emotional or behavioral problems at school. Often, these educators would refer children and their families to family therapists for treatment. Undergirding this practice was the mechanistic belief that there was some causal relation between the child's problems at school and the transactions of his or her family members (i.e., that some structural flaw in the family was causing the child's school difficulty). Most mental health professionals during this era followed this same line of mechanistic thinking. More often than not the therapist would attempt to resolve the child's school problem by modifying the interaction of the student and his or her family members, giving only a modicum of attention to the dynamics between the family, the child, and the school staff. If members of the school staff were involved at all in the treatment effort, it was either to gather preliminary information about how the problem occurred at school in order to develop a particular treatment regimen that family members were to carry out, or to direct school staff to carry out a particular intervention decided on by the therapists and family during the family's therapy sessions.

In the late 1980s, this *flawed family* model came under increasing attack by several family therapists. Criticized as both oversimplifying the causes of many children's school behavior and learning problems, and as reinforcing the all-too-common symmetrical *struggle* between the school and family to determine who was to be judged to blame for a child's school difficulties, this model was also said to be less effective because it ignored the *resources for change* that both the school and family had to offer. Meanwhile, interest in applying ecosystemic thinking/practices to schools was growing among educators, fueled by both the increasing awareness of the impact of school climate on the performance of students and teachers and the burgeoning expectations brought about by federal legislation (such as Public Law 99-457) that mandated that children with special needs and their families be given adequate intervention resources during their preschool and school years.

A countertrend to the flawed family model began emerging in the late 1980s with the growing recognition by many family therapists that the school and family often shared in the communication about a child's school problem, thus together forming the membership of a *problem-determined ecosystem* (Amatea, 1989; Amatea & Brown, 1993; Amatea & Sherrard, 1989, 1994; Anderson et al., 1986). In taking this nonpathologizing view, a handful of family therapists, school counselors, and school psychologists working with cases involving children with some sort of school problem began to draw the boundaries of the system differently. They talked in terms of viewing not only family members, but a child's teachers, counselors, and peers as all having a part to play in defining a youngster's problem and attempting to resolve that problem. Consequently, these practitioners contended that although a child's problem could originate in any number of communication exchanges in a particular life arena (e.g., at school or at home), it was assumed that (a) the student's problem behavior was often maintained by the meanings and actions growing out of those meanings that were held by members of the problem-determined ecosystem, (b) these actions were often persisted in because the people involved believed that their efforts were the only right and logical ways to respond to the problem given the meanings they attributed to it, and (c) the student's problem behavior could be diminished if alternative meanings and the responses that evolved out of them could be constructed.

This way of thinking opened the door for a very different model of collaboration between school professionals and family members. Because it was assumed that a student's problem was often maintained by the meanings given the student's behavior and the actions emanating from those meanings—among school staff as well as the student's family—interventions were aimed at changing the beliefs and behaviors of school staff (e.g., a student's teachers or school counselor) to trigger a resolution of the student's problem instead of (or in addition to) those targeted at the student's family. In addition, it was assumed that changing or eliminating such beliefs and behaviors could often be done most effectively by examining both the beliefs/meanings and behaviors that trapped school staff, family members, and/or the children themselves into engaging in "more of the same" actions to resolve the child's difficulties.

As we consider the case of Andrew, his grandmother, and the school, we can see how practitioners of this approach explore and develop alternative meanings for the child's problem behavior within the broader ecosystem of the family, the school, and the practitioner. (Andrew's case was handled by a school counselor with whom one of us worked; she contacted us to assist her in deciding how she might respond differently to Andrew and the problem-determined ecosystem to which he and she belonged.) Rather than continuing to promote a meaning for Andrew's fighting and unruly school behavior that prevented his grandmother and teachers from changing their ways of responding to him in any real sense, the counselor explored the alternative meanings and beliefs around Andrew's fighting and constructed a context in which Andrew could move from being the victimizer of others to being victimized by his family's reputation. This allowed the grandmother and the counselor to begin to construct a less adversarial context with Andrew and with each other, which then elicited different behaviors from Andrew, his grandmother, and members of the school staff.

One empirical approach that could be adapted to assess the impact of this model of family-school change is depicted in the work of Rigazio-DiGilio (1994). Drawing on an adaptation of Piagetian theory developed by Ivey (1986, 1991) and his associates, Rigazio-DiGilio (1994) describes how the thinking and actions of individuals, families, and larger social networks (such as schools) evolve in a process of *dialectical interaction*. She states: "Throughout our development, the dialectical interaction that occurs between person and environment continually promotes the co-construction of worldviews that in turn influence how we approach our world, our life tasks, and or relationships" (p. 45). First, these theorists propose that individuals, families, and social agencies such as schools develop their thinking within four main orientations: the worlds of images and perceptions; of visible things, concrete actions, and thoughts; of abstractions and reflective thinking; and of dialectical awareness of complexity and interaction. As each of us face new experiences, we repeat all of these orientations. Each orientation involves a different perspective from which one understands and operates in the world; that is, a different pattern of thoughts, feelings, and behaviors characterizes each orientation. By listening to one's (or a family's or school staff's) languaging about an issue, a particular orientation can be identified.

Second, these theorists assume that through a process of dialogue, persons at home and at school jointly shape and reshape their patterns of thought, feelings, and behavior; that is, they change their basic cognitive orientation through dialogue with others. Research, for example, conducted by Rigazio-DiGilio and her associates (Rigazio-DiGilio, 1989, 1994; Rigazio-DiGilio & Ivey, 1990) has shown that using questioning strategies designed to promote personal exploration within each orientation (i.e., questions designed to identify the constraints and possibilities in a family's current cognitive-developmental orientation) actually facilitates the co-construction of different views and cognitive-developmental orientations with families of children experiencing school perform-ance difficulties. This illustrates a basic thought-rule of the ecosys-temic view that, as a researcher/clinician asks questions that affect the context the study participants operate in, the study participants' ways of viewing their world changes. Thus, describing how the thinking of those persons at home and at school involved in resolv-ing a child's problem changes in response to changes in the mean-ings introduced by the experimenter focuses our eye on how family-school systems change rather than on how they stay the same.

In summary, as we review the research efforts of practitioners choosing a second-order perspective we see illustrated a series of choices as to the focus, position, and mode of inquiry preferred. The choice of focus for the research inquiry is conceptualized as consisting both of themselves (i.e., the researchers) and the ob-served ecosystem (of the child and participants of his or her social worlds) bound together as an *observing system*. There is no refer-ence to an outside environment; the boundary around the observing system is unbroken and the system is closed (Becvar & Becvar, 1993). Thus, the choice of position of the researcher is that of participant-observer who is a part of an observing system (compris-ing researcher, child, and members of the problem-determined system), which constructs a common language and world of mean-ing and invites the telling of those private stories that explain the origin and continuing saga of a child's school performance, and contains resources for assessing possibilities and constructing ex-planations. In addition, the mode of inquiry/explanation illustrated by these research efforts is a transactional one; what the researcher does is to initiate reflexive activity among those participants who share a belief system about the child and his or her world, which in turn triggers reflexive action in the researcher. Thus, second-order researchers endeavor "to interact in a manner that opens space for the members of the ecosystem to see new possibilities" (Tomm, 1988, p. 9). This second-order perspective on research is epito-mized in Mary Gergen's (1988, p. 47) recommendations for new methodology standards for social science research. She suggests that social scientists (a) recognize the interdependence of experimenter and subject, (b) avoid the decontextualizing of subjects or experimenters from their social and historical surroundings, (c) recognize and reveal the nature of the scientist's values within the research context, (d) accept that facts do not exist independent of their producers' linguistic codes, (e) demystify the role of scientist and establish an egalitarian learning relationship with subjects, and (f) acknowledge the interdependent relationship between science makers and science consumers.

Conclusion

In conclusion, we assume that our selection of the lenses (or thought rules) by which we construct the particular reality of our research inquiry not only signals our beliefs as to who makes up the world we focus on, but also whom we hold accountable for it in its present state and how we function in relationship to them. If, for example, we report that Andrew's family role structure or family worldview is shaping Andrew's behavior, we will focus on only that particular aspect of the family's experience and hold Andrew's family accountable for changing Andrew by changing that aspect of themselves. In contrast, if we see the meanings given to Andrew's behavior by his family and school and the larger social context in which he and they are embedded as influential in shaping his behavior in a reciprocal way, we will favor explanations that include a description of the larger meaning context in which key persons in and outside the family (such as the school staff and mental health professionals) participate, and will inquire as to the meanings these persons at school and at home give to Andrew's situation. Developing an awareness of the alternative sets of lenses, or thought rules (i.e., of focus, position, and mode of inquiry/description), by which we can construct our research inquiry can help us to clarify the relative benefits and constraints of use of each set of lenses.

We assume that there are trade-offs involved in choosing to use any particular set of thought rules. The interactional/mechanistic mode of inquiry/description—which assumes that the actions and reactions of family and school staff are arranged in a counterbalanced way and can be objectively described—creates a sense of certainty that one can really know how things work. Such modes of inquiry are quite useful in overcoming demoralization and anxiety.

However, there are risks of oversimplification and overgeneralization involved with use of these particular thought rules. The discovery, for example, of a strong correlation between the presence of a learning disorder and parent's style of communication in a parent-child communication task may be seen as a description of reality and used to explain a whole range of other types of situations. According to Newmark and Beels (1994),

> This kind of simplification is possible when you believe you have got hold of a piece of scientific truth that permits you to ignore complexity and exceptions because it refers to something fundamentally "real." . . . This danger occurs because in doing research on a question, researchers usually break it down into simpler components, such that only a few features of a situation—isolated from the other components—are the focus of investigation. (p. 7)

An additional constraint to using these interactional thought rules becomes apparent when we look at how the findings from such inquiries into child-family relationships have commonly been used to finger the family as villain. We have often observed that findings of associations between a family's role structure, communication style, or worldview and children's school adjustment are interpreted to mean that the family is solely to blame for the child's difficulties. Such use of research findings that focus only on the child's family rather than the recursive contribution of the larger social context in which the family is embedded, and that look only at pathological aspects of the family's experience associated with a child's difficulty, give families the implicit negative message that they are the cause of a child's difficulties. One dangerous consequence of hearing the explanation—"You made/*caused* this situation, and now you must take responsibility for it"—as an accusation of guilt is that families react as though they are described as having some psychological or moral defect, and are driven away from the helping effort.

The choice of thought rules concerning the position of the researcher as an outside observer, distant from the research participants, may also affect what a child's family or school shows us in ways in which we are unaware. For example, is there an impact on the study participants of having secret knowledge about a family or school that our participants do not know about? What might be the impact on the family, the school, and the researcher of perceiving and thinking consensually with other members of the system of interest? Would the family's view of itself change? Would the researcher's view change? What would that show us about the nature of family-school processes and children's school adjustment?

Rather than consider the relative strengths and constraints of each lens with an eye to deciding that one set of lenses is inherently superior to another (e.g., that the second-order lens with which one positions oneself in the system as a participant-observer is inherently superior to the first-order lens with which one positions oneself outside the system one is observing), we believe that each set can be used in a complementary fashion shifting back and forth between them. For example, in choosing the lens of position, Andersen (1991) observed:

> It is easier to take a second order view when we have some distance on the issue in question (e.g., when we are "calm" in relation to it). On the other hand, it seems more natural to operate from a first order perspective when we are very eager in dealing with an issue (e.g., committed to an idea for how it should be resolved) or emotionally disturbed by it, (e.g., angry or sad or fearful). (p. 65)

Thus, rather than assert that one or the other set of lenses is a more useful way of thinking and conducting research, we consider each lens as essential to bifocal vision and that this quality of depth perception is necessary for efficacious school-family research. Rather than promoting either set of thought rules as the most appropriate way of inquiring into children's social worlds, we consider each lens a way of seeing differently.

Notes

1. After Auerswald (1985, 1987), we use the term *epistemology* to denote the set of rules used by a specific group of people (e.g., family mental health counselors and therapists) to define social "reality" (i.e., "what we cannot wish away"—Berger & Luckmann, 1966); *paradigm* to denote a set of rules that define a subunit of reality; *theory* to denote an idea or a set of ideas that actually or potentially contribute to a paradigm; and *map* or *model* to denote a concrete, metaphorical specification of an epistemology, a paradigm, or a theory.

2. In contrast, the disengaged family was called the "underorganized" by Aponte (1976b).

References

Amatea, E. (1989). *Brief strategic intervention for school behavior problems.* San Francisco: Jossey-Bass.

Amatea, E., & Brown, B. (1993). The counselor and the family: An ecosystemic approach. In J. Wittmer (Ed.), *Managing your school counseling program: K-12 developmental strategies* (pp. 142-150). Minneapolis, MN: Educational Media Corporation.

Amatea, E., Brown, B., & Cluxton, C. (1992). *Family-school paradigms: A framework for family-school intervention.* Unpublished manuscript, University of Florida, Gainesville.

Amatea, E., & Sherrard, P. (1989). Reversing the school's response: A new approach to resolving persistent school problems. *American Journal of Family Therapy, 17,* 15-26.

Amatea, E., & Sherrard, P. (1994) The ecosystemic view: A choice of lenses. *Journal of Mental Health Counseling, 16,* 6-21.

Amerikaner, M. J., & Omizo, M. M. (1984). Family interaction and learning disabilities. *Journal of Learning Disabilities, 17,* 540-543.

Andersen, T. (1987). The reflecting team: Dialogue and meta-dialogue in clinical work. *Family Process, 26,* 415-428.

Andersen, T. (1991). *The reflecting team: Dialogues and dialogues about dialogues.* New York: Norton.

Anderson, H., & Goolishian, H. (1988). Human systems as linguistic systems: Preliminary and evolving ideas about the implications for clinical theory. *Family Process, 27,* 371-393.

Anderson, H., Goolishian, H., & Winderman, D. (1986). Problem determined systems: Towards transformation in family therapy. *Journal of Strategic and Systemic Therapies, 5,* 1-14.

Aponte, H. J. (1976a). The family-school interview: An eco-structural approach. *Family Process, 15,* 303-311.

Aponte, H. J. (1976b). Under-organization in the poor family. In P. Guerin (Ed.), *Family therapy: Theory and practice* (pp. 432-448). New York: Gardner.

Auerswald, E. H. (1985). Thinking about thinking in family therapy. *Family Process, 24,* 1-12.

Auerswald, E. H. (1987). Epistemological confusion in family therapy and research. *Family Process, 26,* 317-330.

Avis, J. M. (1994). Advocates versus researchers: A false dichotomy? A feminist, social constructionist response to Jacobson. *Family Process, 33,* 87-92.

Bateson, G. (1972). *Steps to an ecology of mind.* New York: Ballantine.

Bateson, G. (1977). The thing of it is. In M. Katz, W. Marsh, & G. Thompson (Eds.), *Explorations of planetary culture at the Lindisfarne conferences: Earth's answer* (pp. 142-155). New York: Harper & Row.

Bateson, G. (1979). *Mind and nature: A necessary unity.* New York: E. P. Dutton.

Bateson, M. C. (1977). Daddy, can a scientist be wise? In J. Brockman (Ed.), *About Bateson* (pp. 57-74). New York: E. P. Dutton.

Becvar, D. S., & Becvar, R. J. (1993). *Family therapy: A systemic integration.* Boston: Allyn & Bacon.

Berger, P., & Luckman, T. (1966). *The social construction of reality*. Garden City, NY: Doubleday.

Brand, S. (1976). For god's sake, Margaret: Conversation with Gregory Bateson and Margaret Mead. *Co-Evolution Quarterly, 10*, 32-44.

Bryan, T., Donahue, M., Pearl, R., & Herzog, K. (1984). Conversational interactions between mothers and learning-disabled and nondisabled children during a problem-solving task. *Journal of Speech and Hearing Disorders, 49*, 64-71.

Carlson, C. I., Hickman, J., & Horton, C. B. (1992). From blame to solutions: Solution-oriented family-school consultation. In S. Christenson & J. C. Conoley (Eds.), *Home-school collaboration: Enhancing children's academic and social competence* (pp. 193-213). Silver Spring, MD: National Association of School Psychologists.

Constantine, L. (1986). *Family paradigms: The practice of theory in family therapy*. New York: Guilford.

Constantine, L. (1987) Adolescent process and family organization: A model of development as a function of family paradigm. *Journal of Adolescent Research, 2*, 349-366.

Constantine, L. (1991). Fitting intervention to organizational paradigm. *Organization Development Journal, 9*, 41-50.

Daniels, H., & White, L. J. (1994). Human systems as problem-determined linguistic systems: Relevance for training. *Journal of Mental Health Counseling, 16*, 104-118.

de Shazer, S. (1984). The death of resistance. *Family Process, 23*, 79-93.

Dewey, J., & Bentley, A. (1973). The knowing and the known. In R. Handy & E. C. Harwood (Eds.), *Useful procedures of inquiry* (pp. 192-231). Great Barrington, MA: Behavior Research Council. (Original work published 1949)

Ditton, P., Green, R.-J., & Singer, M. T. (1987). Communication deviances: A comparison between parents of learning disabled and normally achieving students. *Family Process, 26*, 75-87.

Doane, J. A. (1978). Family interaction and communication deviance in disturbed and normal families: A review of research. *Family Process, 17*, 357-376.

Doane, J. A. (1985). Parental communication deviance and offspring psychopathology. In L. L'Abate (Ed.), *Handbook of family psychology and therapy* (Vol. 2, pp. 71-96). Homewood, IL: Dorsey.

Dornbush, S. M., & Ritter, P. L. (1992). Home-school processes in diverse ethnic groups, social classes, and family structures. In S. Christenson & J. C. Conoley (Eds.), *Home-school collaboration: Enhancing children's academic and social competence* (pp. 111-125). Silver Spring, MD: National Association of School Psychologists.

Fine, M. (1992). A systems-ecological perspective on home-school intervention. In M. Fine & C. Carlson (Eds.), *The handbook of family-school intervention* (pp. 1-17). Boston: Allyn & Bacon.

Foucault, M. (1980). *Power/knowledge: Selected interviews and other writings, 1972-1977* (C. Gordon, Ed. and Trans.). New York: Pantheon.

Gergen, K. (1985). The social constructionist movement in modern psychology. *American Psychologist, 40*, 266-275.

Gergen, M. (1988). Building a feminist methodology. *Contemporary Social Psychology, 13*, 47-53.

Green, R.-J. (1989). "Learning to learn" and the family system: New perspectives on underachievement and learning disorders. *Journal of Marital and Family Therapy, 15,* 187-203.

Griffith, M., & Griffith, J. (1990). Can family therapy research have a human face? *Dulwich Centre Newsletter, 2,* 11-20.

Harrison, A. F., & Bramson, R. M. (1982). *The art of thinking.* New York: Berkley.

Held, B., & Pols, B. (1985). The confusion about epistemology and "epistemology" and what to do about it. *Family Process, 24,* 509-516.

Hoffman, L. (1981). *Foundations of family therapy.* New York: Basic Books.

Hoffman, L. (1990). Constructing realities: An art of lenses. *Family Process, 29,* 1-12.

Humphries, T. W., & Bauman, E. (1980). Maternal childrearing attitudes associated with learning disabilities. *Journal of Learning Disabilities, 13,* 54-57.

Ivey, A. (1986). *Developmental therapy: Theory into practice.* San Francisco: Jossey-Bass.

Ivey, A. (1991). *Developmental strategies for helpers.* Pacific Grove, CA: Brooks/ Cole.

Kaye, J. (1990). Toward meaningful research in psychotherapy. *Dulwich Centre Newsletter, 2,* 27-38.

Keeney, B. (1982). What is an epistemology of family therapy? *Family Process, 21,* 153-168.

Keeney, B. (1983). *Aesthetics of change.* New York: Guilford.

Kistner, J., & Torgesen, J. (1987). Motivational and cognitive aspects of learning disabilities. In A. Kazdin & B. Lahey (Eds.), *Advances in clinical child psychology* (pp. 289-333). New York: Plenum.

Kohn, M., & Rosman, B. L. (1974). Social-emotional, cognitive and demographic determinants of poor school achievement: Implications for a strategy of interventions. *Journal of Educational Psychology, 66,* 267-276.

Kral, R. (1986). Indirect therapy in schools. In S. de Shazer & R. Kral (Eds.), *Indirect approaches to therapy* (pp. 37-52). Rockville, MD: Aspen.

Kral, R. (1992). Solution-focused brief therapy: Applications in the schools. In M. Fine & C. Carlson (Eds.), *The handbook of family-school intervention* (pp. 330-346). Boston: Allyn & Bacon.

Lincoln, Y. (1992). The delivery of special services in the schools: Implications of systems theory. In M. Fine & C. Carlson (Eds.), *The handbook of family-school intervention* (pp. 428-439). Boston: Allyn & Bacon.

Lusterman, D. D. (1989). School-family intervention and the circumplex model. *Journal of Psychotherapy and the Family, 4,* 267-283.

Maturana, H., & Varela, F. J. (1980). *Autopoiesis and cognition: The realization of living.* Boston: D. Reidel.

Minuchin, S., Montalvo, B., Guerney, B., Rosman, B., & Schumer, F. (1967). *Families of the slums.* New York: Basic Books.

Molnar, A. (1988). *Changing children's behavior.* San Francisco: Jossey-Bass.

Molnar, A., & de Shazer, S. (1987). Solution-focused therapy: Toward the identification of therapeutic tasks. *Journal of Marital and Family Therapy, 13,* 349-358.

Neill, J. R., & Kniskern, D. P. (Eds.). (1982). *From psyche to system: The evolving therapy of Carl Whitaker.* New York: Guilford.

Newmark, M., & Beels, C. (1994). The misuse and use of science in family therapy. *Family Process, 33,* 3-17.

Owen, F. W., Adams, P. S., Forrest, T., Stolz, L. M., & Fisher, S. (1971). Learning disorders in children: Sibling studies. *Monographs of the Society for Research in Child Development, 36*,(4, Serial No. 144).

Pellegrini, A., Brody, G., & Sigel, I. (1985). Parents's teaching strategies with their children: The effects of parental and child status variables. *Journal of Psycholinguistics Research, 14*, 509-521.

Rasku-Puttonen, H., Lyytinen, P., Poikkeus, A. M., Laakso, M. L., & Ahonen, T. (1994). Communication deviances and clarity among the mothers of normally achieving and learning-disabled boys. *Family Process, 33*, 71-80.

Rasku-Puttonen, H., Lyytinen, P., & Vilkman, E. (1991). Communication between mothers and their normal or developmentally dysphasic children in experimental sessions. *Scandinavian Journal of Logopedics and Phoniatrics, 16*, 17-24.

Reiss, D. (1981). *The family's construction of reality*. Cambridge, MA: Harvard University Press.

Reiss, D., Oliveri, M. E., & Curd, K. (1983). Family paradigm and adolescent social behavior. In H. Grotevant & C. Cooper (Eds.), *New directions for child development* (pp. 29-50). San Francisco: Jossey-Bass.

Rigazio-DiGilio, S. (1989). *Developmental theory and therapy: A preliminary investigation of reliability and predictive validity using an inpatient depressive population sample*. Unpublished doctoral dissertation, University of Massachusetts, Amherst.

Rigazio-DiGilio, S. (1994). A co-constructive-developmental approach to ecosystemic treatment. *Journal of Mental Health Counseling, 16*, 43-74.

Rigazio-DiGilio, S., & Ivey, A. (1990). Developmental therapy and depressive disorders: Measuring cognitive levels through patient natural language. *Professional Psychology, 21*, 470-475.

Riger, S. (1992). Epistemological debates, feminist voices: Science, social values and the study of women. *American Psychologist, 47*, 730-740.

Satir, V. (1972). *Peoplemaking*. Palo Alto, CA: Science and Behavior Books.

Schwartzman, H. B., & Kneifel, A. W. (1985). Familiar institutions: How the child care system replicates family patterns. In J. Schwartzman (Ed.), *Families and other systems* (pp. 87-107). New York: Guilford.

Singer, M. T., Wynne, L. C., & Toohey, M. L. (1978). Communication disorders and the families of schizophrenics. In L. C. Wynne, R. L. Cromwell, & S. Matthyssee (Eds.), *The nature of schizophrenia* (pp. 260-288). New York: John Wiley.

Stachowiak, J., & Briggs, S. L. (1984). Ecosystemic therapy: A treatment perspective. In W. A. O'Connor & B. Lubin (Eds.), *Ecological approaches to clinical and community psychology* (pp. 7-23) New York: John Wiley.

Tomm, K. (1988). Interventive interviewing: Part 2. Intervening to ask lineal, circular, strategic, or reflexive questions? *Family Process, 27*, 1-15.

Von Foerster, H. (1981). *Observing systems*. Seaside, CA: Intersystems.

Weiss, H. M. (1994). *Family-school collaboration project: Evaluation summary*. Unpublished manuscript, Ackerman Institute, New York.

Weiss, H. M., & Edwards, M. E. (1992). The family-school collaboration project: Systemic interventions for school improvement. In S. Christenson & J. C. Conoley (Eds.), *Home-school collaboration: Enhancing children's academic and social competence* (pp. 215-243). Silver Spring, MD: National Association of School Psychologists.

White, L., Summerlin, M. L., Loos, V., & Epstein, E. (1992). School and family consultation: A language-systems approach. In M. Fine & C. Carlson (Eds.), *The handbook of family-school intervention* (pp. 347-362). Boston: Allyn & Bacon.

White, M. (1992). Men's culture, the men's movement, and the constitution of men's lives. *Dulwich Centre Newsletter, 3/4,* 33-52.

Wiener, N. (1948). *Cybernetics.* Cambridge, MA: Technology Press.

Zohar, D. (1990). *The quantum self.* New York: Quill/William Morrow.

CHAPTER 3

Parent-Child Interactions
and School Achievement

DIANE SCOTT-JONES

Ｈow do parents socialize their children toward high achievement in school? Families vary greatly in structure and functioning in U.S. society; variation exists also in schools and in children themselves. Given this diversity in families, schools, and children, what common themes can help us understand how children's experiences within the family contribute to their educational outcomes? The issue is important theoretically and also is of great practical importance. In spite of the educational reform movements of the recent past, schools are not successful in educating all U.S. children. Many educators look to the home for an understanding of children's achievement, although families cannot compensate for poor schools and family experiences alone will not provide a complete explanation for children's academic successes and failures.

Both families and schools are major contexts for children's development. The impact of these two institutions becomes linked

AUTHOR'S NOTE: The author acknowledges the research assistance of Carol Foltz. This chapter was completed while the author was supported by a grant from the national Center on Families, Communities, Schools, and Children's Learning, funded under the Educational Research and Development Center Program (Agreement No. R117Q00031) as administered by the Office of Educational Research and Improvement, U.S. Department of Education. The findings and opinions expressed in this report do not necessarily reflect the position or policies of the Office of Educational Research and Improvement or the U.S. Department of Education.

and interconnected as children grow and develop in their families, and then enter and advance through the formal educational system. Both institutions exist in and are influenced by the broad economic and sociohistorical context of U.S. society. The importance of the multiple, interconnected contexts of children's lives is widely acknowledged (e.g., Bronfenbrenner, 1979, 1986; Epstein, 1987).

The family context often has been conceptualized as status variables such as socioeconomic status (SES). Broad static measures of SES typically are used, without a detailed examination of the behaviors and experiences that may differ or remain constant across socioeconomic levels. A consensus is building, however, that status variables are not as important as are family process variables in predicting academic success (Dornbusch & Wood, 1989; Epstein, 1990; Scott-Jones, 1984; Slaughter, 1987; Walberg, 1984). Our knowledge of the relationships of SES, family structure, ethnicity, and other status variables to children's achievement in school needs to be bolstered by fine-grained knowledge of children's experiences in their homes.

Parental interaction with children in the home is one of six types of parental involvement in education and schooling outlined by Epstein and Connors (1992). Other types of parental involvement described by Epstein and Connors (1992), such as involvement in activities at school and involvement in school governance and decision making, are not examined in detail in this chapter, but discussed only in relation to interactions within families.

Of the parental interactions that may contribute to children's school performance, we hypothesize four levels: valuing, monitoring, helping, and doing. At the first level, parents convey to children the value of education in general and the value of specific aspects of education. In addition, parents monitor children's behavior and performance. Valuing and monitoring are assumed to affect students' motivation and engagement in the processes of learning and schooling. Helping interactions are focused on the acquisition of basic academic skills in mathematics, reading, or other subjects. These helping interactions can be thought of as part of *cognitive socialization*, which Ginsburg, Bempechat, and Chung (1992) define as the interactions in families that affect basic intellectual development in children. Valuing and monitoring fit Ginsburg et al.'s (1992) definition of *academic socialization*, a complementary process to cognitive socialization. Academic socialization includes

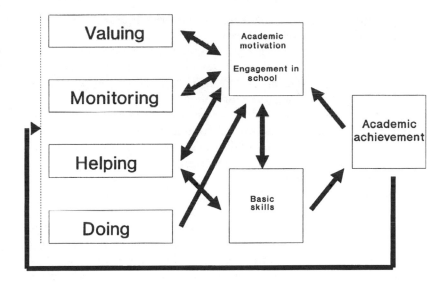

Figure 3.1. Family Interactions and Children's Academic Achievement

the interactions in families that affect how children respond to instruction in academic settings.

In communicating values, monitoring children's performance and behavior, and helping with academic tasks, parents must take into account the developing child's simultaneous and sometimes conflicting needs for autonomy and self-direction and for guidance and assistance. We hypothesize a fourth level—doing—in which parents are overly involved in their children's schoolwork. In these interactions, parents are actually doing the work for the children and diminishing students' autonomy or initiative.

This four-level framework—valuing, monitoring, helping, and doing—is a useful device for organizing existing research on parental interactions and children's school achievement. This framework, displayed graphically in Figure 3.1, acknowledges that parents contribute in different ways to their children's school achievement. Thus, support of achievement is possible in a range of families. High socioeconomic status or advanced formal education is not assumed to be a prerequisite for parental contributions to children's school achievement. Bidirectional influences between children and their parents are acknowledged. The framework is practical and can be communicated easily to teachers and parents.

As would be true of any model of social interactions or psychological processes, this framework assumes a number of complex processes and phenomena that are not included in the graphic in Figure 3.1. First, the affective component of parent-child relations is important. Parental warmth and responsiveness are not set aside as independent dimensions, but are important at each of the four levels of parental behavior. Children's peer relations also affect variables in the framework. The impact of peers increases as children get older. Generally, normal age-related changes in children and their parents affect the variables in the model, as do nonnormative life events such as divorce. School policies and practices, such as homework and grading policies, and changes in school structure from elementary to the upper grades are important; these may complement or conflict with parental behavior. Finally, broad sociohistorical conditions, such as employment opportunities or residential segregation, affect both parents and children.

In this chapter, I extend a previous description of the four-level framework for the family interactions of adolescents in the middle school years (Scott-Jones, in press). Each of the four levels is described in turn in the following sections. The chapter ends with a brief discussion of needed directions in research.

Valuing

The direct and indirect communication of the value of education is an important component of the academic socialization of children. Students from families who place a high value on education and achievement tend to perform well in school. Wood, Chapin, and Hannah (1988) found that high-achieving high school students rated their families significantly higher on scales of achievement orientation and intellectual/cultural orientation than did low achievers. Parents may state quite directly that education is important. In addition, parents convey educational values indirectly in a number of ways. Educational values are broader than good grades and good behavior in school. In addition to communicating the importance of doing well in school, parents, according to Nickerson (1992), can foster in their children a sense of inquisitiveness, a love of learning, a commitment to fair-mindedness, and an awareness of the child's own intellectual potential.

Aspirations and Expectations

In encouraging children to be aware of their own intellectual potential, parents may convey their aspirations and expectations for educational attainment and achievement. High-achieving children tend to have families who hold high educational expectations (Seginer, 1983). Parents' expectations for postsecondary education were positively related to 9th graders' achievement, intentions to remain in school past 10th grade, and educational plans in an Australian sample (Ainley, Foreman, & Sheret, 1991). Parental aspirations for their children's educational attainment were positively related to adolescents' grades in a sample of urban and rural black Xhosa-speaking monogamous and polygynous families in Transkei, South Africa (Cherian, 1992).

Parental expectations are related to performance in specific subject areas. Hess, Holloway, Dickson, and Price (1984) found that parents' press for achievement is related to children's reading performance. Parental educational expectations correlated more highly with students' science achievement than did SES (Reynolds & Walberg, 1992) and the relationship of math and science achievement to prior achievement appears to be mediated by parental expectations (Reynolds & Walberg, 1991). Seventh and ninth graders' perceptions of parents' encouragement and expectations for mathematics were positively related to achievement in mathematics (Visser, 1987). Parental expectations for mathematics grades were positively related to African American and white first graders' scores in mathematics reasoning and computation (Entwisle & Alexander, 1990). Additional analyses of these data indicate that parental expectations for grades in reading, mathematics, and conduct are not related to the first graders' conduct grades, absences, or tardiness (Thompson, Entwisle, Alexander, & Sundius, 1992).

Family structure is related to parents' educational expectations. Parents' educational expectations for their children are higher in two-parent than in single-parent or stepparent families (Astone & McLanahan, 1991; Seaborn-Thompson, Alexander, & Entwisle, 1988). Any difference in favor of stepparent families over single-parent families disappears once SES is controlled.

Cross-cultural differences in mothers' aspirations and expectations have been reported. Chen and Uttal (1988) compared Chinese and U.S. mothers of first, third, and fifth graders. Both Chinese and U.S. mothers expected their children to earn similar scores on a mathematics test—about 80 to 85 of 100 points. U.S. mothers, however, indicated they would be satisfied with scores 7 points lower than their expected scores. The score that would satisfy Chinese mothers was 10 points higher than their expectations. Thus, Chinese mothers appeared to have higher standards for their children than did U.S. mothers and the Chinese children scored higher on mathematics achievement tests. Similarly, Chung and Walkey (1989) found that Chinese third through fifth graders in New Zealand reported higher parental academic expectations, a greater sense of obligation to parents, and a greater fear of parents' response to failure than did students of European descent; Chinese students have significantly higher achievement than do students of other ethnic groups in New Zealand. Whang and Hancock (1994) reported that Asian American fourth-, fifth-, and sixth-grade students performed significantly higher than white students on mathematics achievement tests, but the Asian American students were less likely to believe they were meeting their parents' expectations, which presumably were higher than those of white parents.

In contrast to their seemingly lower expectations for elementary school children, U.S. mothers, compared to Japanese mothers, appear to have greater expectations for academic involvement of kindergartners. Bacon and Ichikawa (1988) reported that U.S. mothers were more likely to believe that kindergartners should have academic experiences and should be rewarded for school performance; U.S. mothers were less likely than Japanese to object to homework assignments and less likely to believe kindergarten should assist with children's socioemotional development. In this study, U.S. mothers' higher academic expectations are construed to be unrealistic and their early emphasis on academic experiences to be inappropriate.

Generally, talented ethnic minority youth in the United States have parents with high educational aspirations and expectations; these parents encourage their children to pursue high levels of education and challenging careers (Lee, 1985, 1989; Prom-Jackson, 1987). Parents of high-achieving third graders, in a predominantly Hispanic and African American sample, believed their children would go farther in school than did parents of low achievers (Clark, 1993). Ethnic minority parents also have high educational expectations for their children in samples that are not selected for high achievement. For eighth graders in the National Education Longitudinal Survey of 1988 (NELS:88), parents' expectations for college graduation were higher for ethnic minorities than for whites at each level of parental education from less than high school to graduate degrees (Muller & Kerbow, 1993). In the High School and Beyond (HSB) data, Mexican American high school seniors who were first-, second-, or third-generation Americans, and their mothers, had high expectations for educational attainment. For first- and second-generation students, the students' own expectations were significant predictors of mathematics and reading achievement; maternal expectations were not significant predictors, perhaps because of their similarity to students' expectations. For third-generation students, use of Spanish in the home was negatively associated with achievement; this relationship occurred even though the use of Spanish in the home declined from the first to the third generation (Buriel & Cordoza, 1988).

Parents' expectations for good performance and behavior in school and for children's conformity to rules are likely to increase as children get older. Dix and colleagues (Dix, Ruble, Grusec, & Nixon, 1986; Dix, Ruble, & Zambarano, 1989) have demonstrated that from preschool to Grade 6, mothers expected more conformity to rules and assumed their children were more responsible for negative behavior. Mothers also became increasingly upset and conveyed greater sternness and disapproval for negative behaviors. Dix et al (1986, 1989) focused on parents' attributions for children's misbehavior, but one can speculate that attributions for school behavior and performance would be similar. If so, as children increase in age, parents would increasingly respond negatively to poor performance in school and attribute responsibility for poor performance to the child.

Expectations for high achievement may be assumed in the family throughout a child's upbringing, even when these expectations are not stated directly. A consistent "yes" response over 3 years to the question "Is it taken for granted in your home that you will attend postsecondary education?" was positively associated with college attendance (Conklin & Dailey, 1981). School experiences, however, also affect children's expectations. Students who moved from a classroom with a high-efficacy teacher to a classroom with a low-efficacy teacher lowered their expectations for their own mathematics performance. Low achievers were most negatively affected (Eccles et al., 1993). The grades students earn in school may affect parental expectations. In an ethnically diverse sample in lower-middle-income neighborhoods, 9th and 10th graders' prior social studies grades were positively correlated with parental expectations for social studies grades. In turn, parental expectations, along with students' perceptions of self-efficacy, were positively correlated with the students' own grade expectations. The students' expectations were positively correlated with their actual social studies grades (Zimmerman, Bandura, & Martinez-Pons, 1992).

Effort and Ability

In communicating to children an awareness of their own intellectual potential, parents convey to children the value of effort and the role of ability in academic achievement. In general, parents' emphasizing the importance of effort and downplaying the role of ability appears to promote children's achievement.

Comparisons of Asian and U.S. parents, and comparisons of Asian American and other U.S. ethnic groups, indicate that Asian and Asian American parents emphasize the role of effort in children's achievement (Chen & Uttal, 1988; Siu, 1992). The high achievement of Asian and Asian American children may be due in part to parents' admonishing children to try hard and conveying to children the belief that outstanding performance will result from hard work.

Value of Specific Subjects

Parents convey to children the value of specific subjects such as reading and mathematics. Hess et al. (1984) found that the value placed on literacy in the home is related to reading performance in children. Marshall (1992) asserts that parents and students need the belief that mathematical knowledge gives them personal power in their lives.

A caution is that school experiences also influence the value students place on mathematics and other subjects. For example, the value placed on mathematics decreased for students moving from a classroom with a supportive teacher to one with an unsupportive teacher; the effect was greatest for low-ability students (Eccles et al., 1993). Talton and Simpson (1986) found that classroom environment variables were the strongest predictors of 6th through 10th graders' attitudes toward science. A set of variables called "family science," which considered whether family members like science, watch science programs on television, and help with science homework, were also predictive of students' science attitudes; a more general measure of the family, including disagreement and happiness, was not related to students' science attitudes. Similarly, the high school curriculum in mathematics and science was the strongest predictor of achievement in a postcollege follow-up of students identified as mathematically precocious in seventh and eighth grade. In addition, high achievers received more parental encouragement to study mathematics and science, to attend college, and to pursue their educational and career goals (Benbow & Arjmand, 1990); unfortunately, parental encouragement was assessed retrospectively in the follow-up.

Parents as Models

Parents are models that children observe in their everyday lives, and children may draw conclusions about the value of education from observing their parents (Nickerson, 1992). Parents may read and use other academic skills in their everyday lives; they may themselves be students on occasion; and children may hear stories about their parents' education and schooling.

Ethnicity and Educational Values

For parents who are not highly educated, education may be valued for social mobility, to the extent that parents see a clear connection between education and success. Families who are in unfavorable economic or social positions in society may embrace education as a means of social mobility. Historically, education has been pursued as an avenue of economic advancement in ethnic minority families (Billingsley, 1992). Marjoribanks (1987) found that students from families with "getting-ahead" ideologies have higher achievement test scores than students from families with similar SES but "getting-by" ideologies. Ginsburg et al. (1992)

suggest that adverse social and economic conditions may diminish the value parents place on education; the weakening of parental valuing of education may be especially likely to occur in low-income and minority families. Ogbu (1978, 1981, 1986) has been a leading proponent of the view that parents socialize their children toward the roles available to them in their society; castelike ethnic minority families and their children, according to Ogbu, perceive a discriminatory job ceiling that limits the value of education. Therefore, ethnic minority families and their children will not be oriented toward striving for success in school.

Some support for Ogbu's position can be found, but counterevidence can be found as well. For example, Abatso (1985), consistent with Ogbu, found that high-achieving African American college students exhibited a more positive perception of the career opportunity structure than did lower-achieving students. Similarly, Mickelson (1990) concludes that although African American and white students report the same abstract attitudes about education (e.g., education leads to economic prosperity), African American students' concrete experiences result in the belief that education leads to more economic opportunities for white students than for African American students. This belief may be translated into lower educational attainment, according to Mickelson (1990). Taylor, Casten, Flickinger, Roberts, and Fulmore (1994), however, did not find a relationship between awareness of discrimination and self-perceptions of academic ability in African American or white high school students.

Some researchers have suggested that ethnic minority students, in order to perform well in school, must place little emphasis on their ethnic identity (Matute-Bianchi, 1986) and must adopt "mainstream" values, even when doing so runs counter to their families' values. Thus, researchers have argued that acculturation of the family is positively related to ethnic minority students' performance in school (Manaster, Chan, & Safady, 1992). Manaster et al. (1992) found that Mexican American migrant high school students who were in an Upward Bound program and labeled successful differed on a measure of acculturation from students who had been retained in grade at least once and had failed a minimum skills test. Gonzales and Roll (1985) found that acculturation was positively related to students' verbal, but not analytic, IQ test scores. Velez

(1989) found that Cuban American students had a lower dropout rate than Puerto Rican or Chicano students and concluded that Cuban students' advantage stems from their higher SES and the greater similarity of their educational and political ideologies to mainstream U.S. values.

Evidence on the role of family acculturation, students' ethnic identity, and students' achievement is not clear, however. Taylor et al. (1994) found that African American high school students' ethnic identity was positively related to their achievement and engagement in school. Bowman and Howard (1985) found that for adolescent and young adult African American students, only one parental socialization practice—training children in awareness of racial barriers—was positively associated with grade point average. Youth taught to be aware of racism appeared to be at an advantage in possessing a sense of personal efficacy, compared to youth not taught anything about racism.

Asian American parents generally convey to their children a strong value of education, but the view of Asian Americans as the "model minority" is exaggerated. Siu (1992) points out that before World War II, Chinese Americans lived in hostile environments and had low levels of educational achievement. After World War II, Chinese Americans were treated more fairly and access to education improved. In addition, Chinese American students from middle- and upper-income families perform better in school than do Chinese Americans from low-income families. Siu (1992) concluded that parents' educational values must be supported by social and economic opportunity structures.

Provision of Educational Resources

Parents also may communicate the value of education indirectly through the provision of educational resources. Parents may provide books, computers, and other educational materials in the home and may provide a quiet place to study. Hess et al. (1984) found that availability of reading material in the home was related to children's reading performance. Low-income parents, however, may be unable to provide the resources they desire for their children and would need support from libraries, schools, and other community institutions.

Parents' Construction of Educational Values

Ginsburg et al. (1992) question whether programs can train parents to convey educational values to their children. These researchers suggest that programs instead may provide experiences that influence parents' construction of values. Eccles and Harold (1993) suggest that parental involvement in school governance may lead to stronger parental valuing of education. If parents are involved in setting school goals and priorities, they may be more invested in helping their children reach those goals. Few parents, however, are asked to become involved in school governance; a school committee typically would include only one or a few parents. Perhaps other means could be devised to involve parents in establishing joint goals with the school.

Parents may emphasize the prestige and authority of the teacher (Ginsburg et al., 1992) and parents may emphasize the importance of school as a respected institution. Cross-cultural research suggests that U.S. mothers may emphasize the role of the teacher less than do Chinese mothers (Chen & Uttal, 1988). When asked about the relative importance of parents and teachers in children's achievement, 66% of Chinese but only 19% of U.S. mothers believed that teachers were more influential than parents. The Chinese children in this study scored higher on their mathematics achievement tests than did the U.S. children.

Values promoted in settings other than the family may complement or be in opposition to parental values. Baumrind (1991) asserts that the diminishing importance of parental approval and the increasing importance of peer approval may create difficulties for adolescents. High achievement in school may not be valued by peers as much as conformity to group standards. Bacon and Ichikawa (1988) found that Japanese and U.S. kindergartens were organized in a manner consistent with mothers' expectations for children's kindergarten experiences. Japanese kindergartens were more oriented toward play and less structured than U.S. kindergartens; these differences were reflected in mothers' beliefs and expectations.

Values as Cognitive Mediators of Parent-Child Interactions

Parents' valuing of education is part of parents' belief system, which is a cognitive mediator of their interactions with children.

Broad values are translated into everyday interactions that support achievement. In the next sections, I describe these interactions.

Monitoring

Parents contribute to their children's academic achievement by monitoring school performance and activities that enhance or diminish school performance. Monitoring may include explicit or implicit rules regarding homework and other school-related activities, establishment of a routine for students' studying, checking that homework is completed, checking on the child's performance and behavior in school, and setting limits on activities such as watching television or spending time with friends. Parents' monitoring is most effective when it is accompanied by responsiveness and warmth toward the child and does not curtail the child's initiative and autonomy. Ideally, parents' monitoring leads to self-monitoring and self-management strategies in the child. The demands of parental monitoring of children may differ according to family structure and neighborhood conditions.

Parental Rules

Parents may establish rules regarding homework, including a routine and schedule for students' studying and completing homework. Parents also may establish rules for activities such as watching television or spending time with friends. Restriction of these activities may be necessary to ensure that the student has ample time for schoolwork.

For eighth graders in the NELS:88, parental restriction of television viewing time was significantly associated with less television viewing and higher achievement test scores, but not significantly associated with higher grades (Muller, 1993; Muller & Kerbow, 1993). For 7th and 10th graders, parents' rules about television viewing and parents' mediation or enforcement of television viewing standards were positively associated with students' grades (Lin & Atkin, 1989).

Parental Monitoring of Homework and Other Activities

Parents may check that homework is completed and monitor the amount of time children spend on homework. To monitor effectively, parents need to know the courses students are taking and students' performance levels. Parents also may monitor or supervise their children's other out-of-school activities that enhance or diminish academic achievement.

In the NELS:88, 45% of eighth graders reported that their parents often check their homework. Parental checking of homework was positively related to amount of time students spent on homework but was not related to students' grades (Muller & Kerbow, 1993).

In the NELS:88, eighth graders who spent more time at home alone after school had significantly lower achievement test scores and slightly but not significantly lower grades than those who spent less time alone (Muller, 1993; Muller & Kerbow, 1993). The majority (60%) of the eighth graders in this study were home alone less than 2 hours per day. An analysis of the NELS:88 data by Weishew and Peng (1993) indicated that eighth graders' time at home alone was also a significant predictor of self-reported preparedness for class.

In a study of parents of high- and low-achieving third graders, most of whom were Hispanic or African American, parents of high achievers were less likely to be at home to supervise their children from 3 p.m. to 5 p.m. In the homes of high achievers, mothers were more likely to work outside the home (Clark, 1993).

Parents' knowledge of their children's friends and of the friends' families may be an important aspect of parental monitoring. Muller and Kerbow (1993) report that among eighth graders in the NELS:88, white parents were more likely than parents in other ethnic groups to know the parents of their children's friends. Knowing the parents of their children's friends was significantly related to achievement test scores (Muller, 1993).

To monitor children effectively, parents need to talk with children about their school experiences. Muller (1993) found in the NELS:88 data that parents' talking with their eighth graders about current school experiences was positively associated with achievement test scores and with grades. In addition, parents' talking with eighth graders about high school plans was positively associated with grades. In a separate analysis of the same NELS:88 data, a composite parental involvement variable—including parents' talking about school experiences, high school plans, and post high school plans, along with parents' educational aspirations—was significantly related to achievement, with the strongest effects on mathematics and social studies (Keith et al., 1993).

Parental Control and Children's Self-Control

Parental monitoring should be geared toward helping children develop self-monitoring and self-management skills. A goal of parents' monitoring is to help the child develop skills such as planning the amount of time to be spent on homework and planning the timing and sequence of work from beginning to deadline for long-term projects. Especially as children move toward adolescence, they need to develop a sense of autonomy, at the same time that they enjoy the protection and guidance of their parents. Ultimately, students need self-control rather than strict control by parents.

Strict, direct, or harsh control by parents is negatively related to children's school performance. In a study of sixth graders, grade point average was negatively related to mothers' and fathers' harsh and inconsistent discipline and was positively related to students' self-restraint (Wentzel, Feldman, & Weinberger, 1991). The authors suggest that parents contribute to the child's self-restraint. In turn, self-regulation aids student achievement directly and indirectly through the positive reception of such behaviors by teachers (Feldman & Wentzel, 1990; Wentzel, Weinberger, Ford, & Feldman, 1990). Similarly, parental disciplinary style, defined as not harsh, was positively related to academic achievement in 12- and 13-year-olds (Portes, Dunham, & Williams, 1986). Patterson and colleagues (DeBaryshe, Patterson, & Capaldi, 1993), in their longitudinal study of white working- and lower-class boys in middle school, found that parents' use of coercive disciplinary practices was related to the boys' academic engagement in seventh grade. In turn, boys' seventh-grade academic engagement was positively related to eighth-grade achievement.

In a similar vein, Litovsky and Dusek (1985) found that seventh through ninth graders' perceptions of mothers' need for psychological control were negatively related to students' scores for self-esteem in school. Students' perceptions of both mother and father acceptance were positively related to self-esteem in school. Abraham and Christopherson (1984) found that mothers' controlling behaviors and mothers' and fathers' punishing behaviors were negatively related to perceived cognitive competence in rural predominantly white, middle- to lower-middle-income middle school students. Fathers' supporting behaviors, and for female students only, mothers' supporting behaviors, were positively related to students' perceived cognitive competence.

The negative relationship between direct parental control and cognitive performance can be found in early childhood and appears to persist in the transition to adolescence. Hess and McDevitt (1984) found that white mothers' (median education 14 years) appeals to their own authority and use of direct commands were negatively related to children's standardized test scores at ages 4, 5, 6, and 12. Effects of maternal direct control strategies persisted at age 12, even when controlling for children's intermediate ability. The negative effects of high degrees of control remained even after controlling for maternal variables such as intelligence, marital status, and SES. Interestingly, the negative effects of direct control appear to be tempered by the concurrent use of indirect control techniques (appeals to rules rather than to maternal authority; requests for generative verbalizations rather than direct commands). Mothers who used a combination of direct and indirect control techniques had children who performed as well as children whose mothers used few direct control techniques.

An exception to the finding of negative outcomes for parental direct control is the work of Amato (1989). For 3rd and 4th graders, parental control, along with parental support and allocation of household responsibilities, was positively related to general competence; parental punishment was negatively related to children's general competence. This study, however, does provide support for the need for decreased control in adolescence. In contrast to the data for 3rd and 4th graders, parental control was negatively related to general competence for 10th and 11th graders. Parental punishment also was negatively related to 10th and 11th graders' competence; parental support, allocation of household responsibilities, and family cohesion were positively related to competence.

Davey (1993) found that for adolescent boys, perceptions of their own control of decision making, along with family closeness and parents' knowing their whereabouts, were positively related to grade point average and negatively related to deviant behavior. Too much control relinquished to the adolescent, however, may be detrimental. For adolescents, early autonomy, defined as adolescents making decisions alone, was associated with lower grade point average and school effort, whereas joint parent-youth decision making was associated with higher grades and school effort. Although statistically significant for all ethnic groups, this relationship was strongest for white and Hispanic males, weaker among Asian Americans, and lowest among African Americans (Dornbusch, Ritter, Mont-Reynaud, & Chen, 1990). In a study of dropouts in one of the high schools in the Dornbusch et al. (1990) data, adolescents' making decisions alone distinguished dropouts from adolescents who had not dropped out of school (Rumberger, Ghatak, Poulos, Ritter, & Dornbusch, 1990).

Authoritative Parenting

Parents' exerting firm control over their children and establishing clear standards for their behavior is most effective when combined with warmth and responsiveness to the child. The combination of appropriately high levels of both control and responsiveness is labeled *authoritative parenting* in a long-standing typology developed by Baumrind (1966, 1975, 1978, 1983). This typology is useful, but ethnic and SES differences may exist.

Baumrind's conceptualization is based on research started in 1959 with middle-income white parents and their preschool children in Berkeley and Oakland, California. Her longitudinal sample, also middle-income whites in the same location, was assessed in 1968-1969 when the children were 4 to 5 years of age and again when children were 9 and 14.5 years of age. Baumrind employed a variety of data sources, including direct observations in natural and laboratory settings, structured interviews, standardized psychological tests, and psychological tests designed for the study. In the third assessment, teachers also were interviewed regarding the adolescents' behavior in school. Through cluster and factor analysis, scores for parents were reduced to two dimensions called "demandingness" (or control) and "responsiveness" (Baumrind, 1991).

From these two dimensions, Baumrind created the now widely known typology of parenting styles. The authoritative parenting style, in which parents exerted firm control, but also responded to children's needs and desires, was positively related to children's school performance and other measures of competence. Parents who exerted high levels of control but low levels of responsiveness were labeled authoritarian; parents low on control but high on responsiveness were labeled permissive. To the three major prototypes, Baumrind (1991) has added two additional types: rejecting-neglecting parents, who were high on neither control nor responsiveness, and traditional parents, who exhibited sex-stereotyped roles, with mothers more responsive than they were demanding and fathers more demanding than they were responsive.

During adolescence, the level of adult supervision required, especially in a period of social instability, may be perceived as constraining by the adolescent, unless the parent is also responsive and nonintrusive (Baumrind, 1991). Fostering the appropriate balance between parental control and children's self-control and autonomy may be especially difficult as children reach adolescence. Following puberty, a renegotiation of family members' roles and responsibilities is necessary to enable the adolescent to accept reasonable parental control (Baumrind, 1991). In times of social instability or great historical change such as the recent past, however, parents need to exercise increased authority in children's lives, especially in assisting adolescents in the transition to adulthood (Baumrind, 1991).

Baumrind asserts that authoritative control should be well accepted by adolescents whereas authoritarian control will be rejected. Furthermore, authoritarian methods should have greater negative effects on adolescents' than on young children's competence. Parents who were permissive with their young children, however, will experience difficulties when the children reach adolescence, according to Baumrind (1991). If parents continue to be permissive, adolescents may behave irresponsibly. Conversely, if formerly permissive parents exert more control, even if they do so authoritatively, adolescents are likely to reject the change.

Although based on longitudinal assessments and a variety of data sources, Baumrind's typology may not apply equally to families of different ethnic groups. Baumrind (1972) found that a small sample of black parents with preschool children appeared authoritarian when compared to white parents. The most intriguing finding of this study was that the authoritarian parenting style in black families, in contrast to white families, was associated with high levels of independence and self-assertiveness in children. The perception of parental authority or parental strictness may not be negative in ethnic minority families. In a sample of successful ethnic minority adolescents, parents were perceived as strict or between strict and lenient. The families were characterized by positive shared activities and a moderate-to-high degree of openness (Lee, 1985).

Baumrind's influential work has been expanded and revised by other researchers, most notably in the large multiethnic study of adolescents conducted by Dornbusch and colleagues and reported in many sources (e.g., Dornbusch, Ritter, Leiderman, Roberts, & Fraleigh, 1987). Consistent with Baumrind, Dornbusch et al. found that adolescents' school performance was positively associated with parents' exerting firm control, through clear standards for behavior, but also responding to adolescents' needs and desires, allowing them input into decisions, and maintaining open communication. Asian, African American, and Hispanic adolescents, however, reported higher levels of authoritarian parenting than did whites. Similarly, lower-socioeconomic-status adolescents rated their parents higher on authoritarian parenting than did middle-socioeconomic-status adolescents. Furthermore, the positive relationship between authoritative parenting and school performance was greatest for white students. Nevertheless, authoritative parenting style is considered important, as in Dornbusch and Wood's (1989) and Steinberg's (1989) literature summaries, which concluded that authoritative parenting style is one of three or four family factors (along with parental encouragement, parental involvement in school, and joint parent-student decision making) contributing to school success. Steinberg, Dornbusch, and colleagues (Steinberg, Dornbusch, & Brown, 1992) have concluded that peer influence—negative in the case of Hispanics and African Americans and positive for Asian Americans—diminishes the impact of parenting style on ethnic minority students' achievement. Additional conceptual and methodological work is needed, however, to accommodate findings on ethnic minority family interactions and academic performance.

Given that authoritative parenting is widely accepted as the optimal style, an important issue is its incidence. Baumrind's (1991) data from families with 9-year-olds suggests that the authoritative style occurs infrequently. In addition, Steinberg, Mounts, Lamborn, and Dornbusch (1991) classified as authoritative 11 of 82 (13%) working-class African American two-parent families in their sample. Similarly, Taylor, Casten, and Flickinger (1993) found that 9 of 44 (20%) two-parent African American families were authoritative; however, 40 of 81 (50%) single-parent African American families were authoritative.

An additional issue is whether parents tend to maintain a style consistently, as is assumed in a typology. An alternative view is that parenting is affected by the behavior of the child, the situation, and the overall social context. Although the "authoritative parent" serves an important function as an ideal type in our society, a more productive strategy may be to pursue the two dimensions Baumrind identified. Parents' control or monitoring, on the one hand, and parents' responsiveness or warmth, on the other, are important. In addition, specific school-related parenting practices are important.

As parents monitor school performance, the affective relationship between parents and children is important. Negative affect tends to narrow parents' attention, reduce their use of relevant information, activate rigid social responses, and interfere with problem solving (Dix, 1991). Dix and colleagues (Dix & Reinhold, 1991; Dix, Reinhold, & Zambarano, 1990) have found that authoritarian mothers were more likely to become upset or angry after a child displayed disobedience. Angry mothers, compared to neutral and happy mothers, expected that subsequent interactions would be more unpleasant and require greater sternness. Angry mothers also blamed the child more, were more upset with the child, and chose more derogatory traits to describe the child. The influence between angry mothers and misbehaving children may be bidirectional. Mothers of aggressive boys appear to be primed to perceive behavior more negatively than other mothers; however, the direction of this relationship is not clear (Dix & Lochman, 1990).

Family cohesiveness and adaptability are positively related to adolescents' grade point average and negatively related to their misconduct in school. For boys, the relationship between family adaptability and misconduct was curvilinear; misconduct was high for boys from both rigid and chaotic families, and was low for boys from structured and flexible families (Farrell & Barnes, 1993).

For young adolescent boys in two-parent well-educated families, parent-adolescent disagreement and maternal depression were predictive of conduct problems or externalizing behaviors in school and father-adolescent disagreement was predictive of grade point average. Surprisingly, none of the home variables were predictive of internalizing behaviors or anxiety-withdrawal in this small sample (Forehand, Long, Brody, & Fauber, 1986).

Family Structure and Parental Monitoring

Monitoring of children may be more difficult in some family structural arrangements, but the effect of single-parent family structure or of dual-parent employment may be exaggerated.

Although the time constraints on working mothers may be assumed to have a negative impact, Muller (1993) found that part-time employed mothers of eighth graders, compared to full-time employed and unemployed mothers, restricted television viewing more often and knew more of the parents of their children's friends. Both variables were positively related to the eighth graders' achievement test scores. It should be pointed out that the part-time employed mothers had higher incomes and educational levels, were older, and were more likely to live in suburbs than full-time employed or unemployed mothers.

The Role of Neighborhoods

Parents' monitoring of children may be affected by the neighborhood. For some parents, monitoring takes the form of protecting children from very real dangers in the surrounding neighborhood. Preliminary data reported by Eccles and Harold (1993) suggest that parents living in high-risk low-resource neighborhoods rely more on in-home management strategies that emphasize protection from dangers rather than developing skills. Parents from less risky neighborhoods spend more time developing talents and taking advantage of available resources. Families from all types of neighborhoods, however, can be highly involved in their children's education and psychological well-being, and there are also disengaged parents from all types of neighborhoods (Eccles & Harold, 1993). Nonetheless, demands placed on families by the need to monitor children's activities in the interest of safety may take time away from other family activities that might contribute more directly to the acquisition of academic skills. In a study of parents of high- and low-achieving third graders, parents of high achievers were more likely than parents of low achievers to believe their neighborhood was a safe place for their children (Clark, 1993).

Helping

Expert-Novice

Parents may help with school skills in an expert-novice relationship. Here, parents are knowledgeable about the topic students are learning, can establish the appropriate emotional tone in the teaching interaction, and can gauge when they have provided an appropriate amount of help—not too much and not too little. Highly skilled parents can act as tutors; individual tutoring should be more effective than the group instruction of classrooms (Chipman, 1992). Teachers' attitudes toward parents helping at home may vary; some teachers may encourage and support parental helping, whereas others may prefer to maintain control over the learning process children experience (Ginsburg et al., 1992). Teacher efficacy—that is, teachers' belief in their own effectiveness—was a significant predictor of parents' tutoring in the home and parents' involvement in home instructional programs in schools including kindergarten through fourth grades; the socioeconomic status of families served by the school was not related to parents' tutoring in the home or involvement in home instructional programs (Hoover-Dempsey, Bassler, & Brissie, 1987). The majority of parents want to know how to help their children at home, as indicated in Epstein and Herrick's (1991) telephone survey of families of sixth, seventh, and eighth graders. There may be limits, however, on the extent to which parents can help directly with school skills. One obvious limit is the academic skills of the parent in relation to the academic skills of the child. As children progress through school, parents' academic skills may not be adequate for the level of work required.

In a theoretical formulation advanced by Wertsch (1979; Wertsch, McNamee, McLane, & Budwig, 1980), based on the work of the Soviet psychologist Vygotsky (1978), parents serve as supportive, knowledgeable "others" as children acquire new skills and knowledge. The interactions of children with adults provide "other regulation" needed for the child to perform cognitive tasks. From interactions with adults involving other regulation, children gradually develop the capacity for self-regulation. According to this theory, children's mental activity exists first on a social or interpsychological level. Gradually, after social interactions with parents or other knowledgeable persons, children's mental activity occurs at an individual or intrapsychological level. This model of children learning from a knowledgeable parent in the everyday social context and gradually advancing to independent performance is termed "apprenticeship" in the work of Rogoff (1990).

In small studies of mothers' tutoring their fifth-grade children on long division, the mothers' use of "scaffolding" was assessed (Pratt, Green, MacVicar, & Bountrogianni, 1992). Scaffolding involves the parents' providing assistance in reducing the complexity of a task so that the child can perform it, but also removing the support when the child no longer needs help. In addition, scaffolding includes the provision of extra support following a failure and the reduction of support following success. Parents also would be attentive to the child's skill level and would provide more support to a child with low skills. Pratt et al. (1992) found that mothers' use of scaffolding was positively associated with children's success with difficult long-division problems.

Hess et al. (1984) found that parents' reading with children and interacting with them verbally were related to children's reading performance. The family's provision of a reading environment, assessed by how often parents read to their children, was positively related to the reading performance of 11-year-olds (Marjoribanks, 1988).

Bacon and Ichikawa (1988) found that U.S. mothers were more likely than Japanese mothers to teach their kindergarten children reading and mathematics skills. Almost all U.S. mothers reported they were teaching their kindergartners numbers, the alphabet, and to write their names, whereas approximately one third to one half of Japanese mothers reported such teaching. The teaching of addition was reported by 49% of U.S. mothers but by only 16% of Japanese mothers. Japanese kindergartners scored higher than their U.S. peers on a mathematics achievement test; no differences were found in reading achievement. Although null effects are difficult to interpret, Hannon (1987) also found no differences in reading performance between children whose parents read to them daily and children who did not participate in the intervention.

Chen and Uttal (1988) found that Chinese mothers spent almost twice as much time as U.S. mothers helping their first, third, and fifth graders with homework. On average, Chinese mothers helped 1 hour per day and U.S. mothers, 32 minutes. The Chinese children earned higher mathematics achievement test scores; U.S. children earned higher reading scores in first and third grades, but the difference disappeared by fifth grade. Interestingly, 66% of Chinese mothers believed that teachers were more influential than parents in children's achievement, whereas only 19% of U.S. mothers believed teachers were more influential.

The limits of parents' own academic skills can be seen in research on populations in which literacy and schooling are not as common as in the United States. In a study of 6- to 12-year-olds and their parents in three regions of Peru, about half of the children had not attended school and most of the unschooled children were illiterate. Of children in the three regions, those in Lima—the most urban—performed better on reading and mathematics achievement tests. Their parents were most likely to be literate and their homes had the most resources (e.g., books, electricity). Parents in Lima also were most likely to spend time with the children, read to children, hold high occupational aspirations for their children, teach letters, and teach by verbal explanation instead of nonverbal demonstration. These parental behaviors were positively related to reading and mathematics achievement and a small but significant effect remained after controlling for parental literacy, home resources, and region (Barber, 1988). Clearly, however, parents' lack of academic skills severely limits the extent to which they can help their children directly.

In the United States, the language used in the home has received a great deal of attention as a potential correlate of children's school performance. Parents who cannot speak English would have great difficulty helping their children with English-language school skills. The role of language may be complex, however. The use of English in the home was positively related to achievement test scores and unrelated to grades of Mexican American eighth graders. For Asian American eighth graders, use of English in the home was unrelated to achievement test scores, and surprisingly, was negatively related to mathematics grades (Kennedy & Park, 1994).

In studies that assess the amount of time parents spend helping their children with schoolwork, the direction of effects often is not clear. Parents may spend time helping and parental help may enhance achievement; conversely, parents may help because the child is not performing well in school. In a comparison of parents of high- and low-achieving third graders, parents of high achievers spent less time helping their children with homework. Parents of high achievers, however, were more knowledgeable about how to help their third graders resolve problems with homework (Clark, 1993).

Learning Together

A second model of parental helping is learning together—parents learn about a subject along with their children. In intergenerational literacy programs, both parents and their children learn to read. When parents are not proficient in English, their children may have more advanced English skills; children in these homes may sharpen their skills by helping their parents.

Identifying Other Sources of Help

When parents are unable to help, they may contribute by identifying sources of help for their children. Siblings or other family members may help with schoolwork. Parents may seek tutoring or after-school programs for their children in the school, community, or neighborhood.

Enrollment in after-school programs may enhance academic skills directly or may contribute indirectly by fostering discipline in children. Muller (1993) found that enrollment in after-school music classes was significantly associated with eighth graders' grades and achievement test scores.

Doing

Parents may become overinvolved in helping their children and may take too much responsibility for their children's school performance. Especially as children reach adolescence, there may be a mismatch between young adolescents' needs for autonomy and both home and school environments. Some issues related to parental overinvolvement have been described in the previous sections. Ginsburg and Bronstein (1993) found that parental overcontrol—which the authors term "surveillance"—was negatively related to fifth graders' intrinsic motivation, grades, and achievement.

Future Directions

If we tried to construct a picture of ideal family interactions that are guaranteed to promote children's success in school, we would encounter great difficulty. Families are dynamic and changing. Changes can result from social and economic change in society; from normal, age-graded changes within children and their parents; and from nonnormative life events, such as divorce or parental job loss, within a given family unit. The search for the ideal sometimes has taken the form of oversimplified comparisons of the school performance of children from different kinds of families. Comparisons have been made of families with two biological parents present to other family forms, of affluent families to those living in poverty, of young parents to those who delay childbearing, of white families to those designated as ethnic minorities. The search for the ideal, however, may not be as useful as seeking to describe and understand the range of family interactions that support children's achievement in school. In this chapter, I have proposed a four-level framework to organize our knowledge of the broad and varied ways in which family interactions are related to children's academic achievement. This four-level framework—valuing, monitoring, helping, and doing—encompasses much of what we know about parental interactions and children's school performance.

A number of limitations exist in the literature in this area. In the studies reviewed in this chapter, parental interactions often are operationalized as maternal interactions. Most studies have not included fathers; more attention needs to be given to the role of fathers in their children's education and schooling.

The studies reviewed in this chapter and fit into the framework include both major large-scale surveys and smaller, local studies. Data from both kinds of studies are important and more effort needs to be directed toward the integration of the best of different research traditions in studies of families and school achievement.

An interesting feature of the literature on families and academic achievement is that cross-cultural comparisons of U.S. mothers and mothers from other nations and cultures exist along with studies of ethnic and cultural differences among U.S. mothers. In the cross-cultural comparisons, U.S. mothers generally are judged less favorably than mothers from Asian countries. In comparisons of U.S. ethnic groups, white mothers—who do not fare well in the cross-cultural comparisons—are judged more favorably than are ethnic minority mothers, with the exception of Asian Americans. More attention needs to be given to the grounding of maternal interactions—and paternal interactions as well—in a particular context. Extrafamilial influences on families in different cultures, and on families in different ethnic groups within the United States, need to be acknowledged.

Programs and practices can be established to encourage positive family interactions that lead to high achievement in school. Because of our limited and incomplete knowledge, these programs and practices must be carefully developed, implemented, and evaluated. Programs and practices must be appropriate for a broad range of families and must acknowledge the varied ways in which parents contribute to their children. Examples and guidelines based on the four-level framework are offered in Scott-Jones's (in press) discussion of home activities and school achievement in the middle grades.

References

Abatso, Y. (1985). The coping personality: A study of black community college students. In M. B. Spencer, G. K. Brooklins, & W. R. Allen (Eds.), *Beginnings: The social and affective development of black children* (pp. 131-144). Hillsdale, NJ: Lawrence Erlbaum.

Abraham, K., & Christopherson, V. (1984). Perceived competence among rural middle school children: Parental antecedents and relations to locus of control. *Journal of Early Adolescence, 4*, 343-351.

Ainley, J., Foreman, J., & Sheret, M. (1991) High school factors that influence students to remain in school. *Journal of Educational Research, 85*, 69-80.

Amato, P. R. (1989). Family processes and the competence of adolescents and primary school children. *Journal of Youth and Adolescence, 18*, 39-53.

Astone, N. M., & McLanahan, S. S. (1991). Family structure, parental practices and high school completion. *American Sociological Review, 56*, 309-320.

Bacon, W. F., & Ichikawa, V. (1988). Maternal expectations, classroom experiences, and achievement among kindergartners in the United States and Japan. *Human Development, 31*, 378-383.

Barber, B. L. (1988). The influence of family demographics and parental teaching practices on Peruvian children's academic achievement. *Human Development, 31*, 370-377.

Baumrind, D. (1966). Effects of authoritative parental control on child behavior. *Child Development, 37*, 887-907.

Baumrind, D. (1972). An exploratory study of socialization effects on black children: Some black-white comparisons. *Child Development, 43*, 261-267.

Baumrind, D. (1975). Early socialization and adolescent competence. In S. E. Dragastin & G. H. Elder (Eds.), *Adolescence in the life cycle: Psychological change and social context* (pp. 117-143). Washington, DC: Hemisphere.

Baumrind, D. (1978). Parental disciplinary patterns and social competence in children. *Youth & Society, 9,* 239-276.

Baumrind, D. (1983). Rejoinder to Lewis' reinterpretation of parental firm control effects: Are authoritative families really harmonious? *Psychological Bulletin, 94,* 132-142.

Baumrind, D. (1991). Effective parenting during the early adolescent transition. In P. A. Cowan & M. Hetherington (Eds.), *Family transitions* (pp. 111-163). Hillsdale, NJ: Lawrence Erlbaum.

Benbow, C. P., & Arjmand, O. (1990). Predictors of high academic achievement in mathematics and science by mathematically talented students: A longitudinal study. *Journal of Educational Psychology, 82,* 430-441.

Billingsley, A. (1992). *Climbing Jacob's ladder: The enduring legacy of African-American families.* New York: Simon & Schuster.

Bronfenbrenner, U. (1979). *The ecology of human development.* Cambridge, MA: Harvard University Press.

Bronfenbrenner, U. (1986). Ecology of the family as a context for human development: Research perspectives. *Developmental Psychology, 22,* 723-774.

Bowman, P. J., & Howard, C. (1985). Race-related socialization, motivation, and academic achievement: A study of black youths in three-generation families. *Journal of the American Academy of Child Psychiatry, 24,* 134-141.

Buriel, R., & Cardoza, D. (1988). Sociocultural correlates of achievement among three generations of Mexican American high school seniors. *American Educational Research Journal, 25,* 177-192.

Chen, C., & Uttal, D. H. (1988). Cultural values, parents' beliefs, and children's achievement in the United States and China. *Human Development, 31,* 351-358.

Cherian, V. I. (1992). The relationship between parental aspirations and academic achievement of Xhosa children from monogamous and polygynous families. *Journal of Social Psychology, 132,* 271-273.

Chipman, S. F. (1992). The higher-order cognitive skills: What they are and how they might be transmitted. In T. G. Sticht, B. A. McDonald, & M. J. Beeler (Eds.), *The intergenerational transfer of cognitive skills* (Vol. 2, pp. 128-158). Norwood, NJ: Ablex.

Chung, R., & Walkey, F. H. (1989). Educational and achievement aspirations of New Zealand Chinese and European secondary school students. *Youth & Society, 21,* 139-152.

Clark, R. M. (1993). Homework-focused parenting practices that positively affect student achievement. In N. F. Chavkin (Ed.), *Families and schools in a pluralistic society* (pp. 85-105). Albany: State University of New York Press.

Conklin, M. E., & Dailey, A. R. (1981). Does consistency of parental encouragement matter for secondary school students. *Sociology of Education, 54,* 254-262.

Davey, L. (1993, March). *Developmental implications of shared and divergent perceptions in the parent-adolescent relationship.* Paper presented at the meetings for Research in Child Development, New Orleans, LA.

DeBaryshe, B. D., Patterson, G. R., & Capaldi, D. M. (1993). A performance model for academic achievement in early adolescent boys. *Developmental Psychology, 29,* 795-804.

Dix, T. (1991). The affective organization of parenting: Adaptive and maladaptive processes. *Psychological Bulletin, 110*, 3-25.

Dix, T., & Lochman, J. E. (1990). Social cognition and negative reactions to children: A comparison of mothers of aggressive and nonaggressive boys. *Journal of Social and Clinical Psychology, 9*, 418-438.

Dix, T., & Reinhold, D. P. (1991). Chronic and temporary influences on mothers' attributions for children's disobedience. *Merrill-Palmer Quarterly, 37*, 251-271.

Dix, T., Reinhold, D. P., & Zambarano, R. J. (1990). Mothers' judgements in moments of anger. *Merrill-Palmer Quarterly, 36*, 465-486.

Dix, T., Ruble, D. N., Grusec, J. E., & Nixon, S. (1986). Social cognition in parents: Inferential and affective reactions to children of three age levels. *Child Development, 57*, 879-894.

Dix, T., Ruble, D. N., & Zambarano, R. J. (1989). Mothers' implicit theories of discipline: Child effects, parent effects, and the attribution process. *Child Development, 60*, 1373-1391.

Dornbusch, S. M., Ritter, P. L., Leiderman, P. H., Roberts, D. F., & Fraleigh, M. J. (1987). The relation of parenting style to adolescent school performance. *Child Development, 58*, 1244-1257.

Dornbusch, S. M., Ritter, P. L., Mont-Reynaud, R., & Chen, Z. (1990). Family decision making and academic performance in a diverse high school population. *Journal of Adolescent Research, 5*, 143-160.

Dornbusch, S. M., & Wood, K. (1989). Family processes and educational achievement. In W. J. Weston (Ed.), *Education and the American family: A research synthesis* (pp. 66-95). New York: New York University Press.

Eccles, J. S., Midgley, C., Wigfield, A., Miller-Buchanan, C., Reuman, D., Flanagan, C., & MacIver, D. (1993). Development during adolescence: The impact of stage-environment fit on young adolescents' experiences in schools and in families. *American Psychologist, 48*, 90-101.

Eccles, J. S., & Harold, R. D. (1993). Parent-school involvement during the early adolescent years. *Teachers College Record, 94*, 568-587.

Entwisle, D. R., & Alexander, K. L. (1990). Beginning school math competence: Minority and majority comparisons. *Child Development, 61*, 454-471.

Epstein, J. L. (1987). Toward a theory of family-school connections: Teacher practices and parent involvement. In K. Hurrelman, F. Kaufmann, & F. Losel (Eds.), *Social intervention: Potential and constrains* (pp. 121-136). New York: Aldine de Gruyter.

Epstein, J. L. (1990). School and family connections: Theory, research, and implications for integrating sociologies of education and family. *Marriage and Family Review, 15*, 99-126.

Epstein, J. L., & Connors, L. (1992). School and family partnerships in middle grades and high schools. *NASSP Practitioner, 18*(4), 1-8.

Epstein, J. L., & Herrick, S. C. (1991). *Two reports: Implementation and effects of summer home learning packets in the middle grades* [Report 21 for Center for Research on Effective Schooling for Disadvantaged Students]. Baltimore: Johns Hopkins University.

Farrell, M. P., & Barnes, G. M. (1993). Family systems and social support: A test of the effects of cohesion and adaptability on the functioning of parents and adolescents. *Journal of Marriage and the Family, 55*, 119-132.

Feldman, S. S., & Wentzel, K. R. (1990). Relations among family interaction patterns, classroom self-restraint, and academic achievement in preadolescent boys. *Journal of Educational Psychology, 82,* 813-819.

Forehand, R., Long, N., Brody, G. H., & Fauber R. (1986). Home predictors of young adolescents' school behavior and academic performance. *Child Development, 57,* 1528-1533.

Ginsburg, G. S., & Bronstein, P. (1993). Family factors related to children's intrinsic/extrinsic motivational orientation and academic performance. *Child Development, 64,* 1461-1474.

Ginsburg, H. P., Bempechat, J., & Chung, Y. E. (1992). Parent influences on children's mathematics. In T. G. Sticht, B. A. McDonald, & M. J. Beeler (Eds.), *The intergenerational transfer of cognitive skills* (Vol. 2, pp. 91-121). Norwood, NJ: Ablex.

Gonzales, R. R., & Roll, S. (1985). Relationship between acculturation, cognitive style, and intelligence: A cross-sectional study. *Journal of Cross-Cultural Psychology, 16,* 190-205.

Hannon, P. (1987). A study of the effects of parental involvement in the teaching of reading on children's reading test performance. *British Journal of Educational Psychology, 57,* 56-57.

Hess, R. D., Holloway, S. D., Dickson, W. P., & Price, G. G. (1984). Maternal variables as predictors of children's school readiness and later achievement in vocabulary and mathematics in sixth grade. *Child Development, 55,* 1902-1912.

Hess, R. D., & McDevitt, T. M. (1984). Some cognitive consequences of maternal intervention techniques: A longitudinal study. *Child Development, 55,* 2017-2030.

Hoover-Dempsey, K. V., Bassler, O. C., & Brissie, J. S. (1987). Parent involvement: Contributions of teacher efficacy, school socioeconomic status, and other school characteristics. *American Educational Research Journal, 24,* 417-435.

Keith, T. Z., Keith, P. B., Troutman, G. C., Bickley, P. G., Trivette, P. S., & Singh, K. (1993). Does parental involvement affect eighth-grade student achievement? Structural analysis of national data. *School Psychology Review, 22,* 474-496.

Kennedy, E., & Park, H. (1994). Home language as a predictor of academic achievement: A comparative study of Mexican- and Asian-American youth. *Journal of Research and Development in Education, 27,* 188-194.

Lee, C. C. (1985). Successful rural black adolescents: A psychological profile. *Adolescence, 20,* 129-142.

Lee, C. C. (1989). Rural African-American adolescents: Psychological development in a changing environment. In R. L. Jones (Ed.), *African-American adolescents* (pp. 79-98). Berkeley, CA: Cobb & Henry.

Lin, C. A., & Atkin, D. J. (1989). Parental mediation and rulemaking for adolescent use of television and VCRs. *Journal of Broadcasting and Electronic Media, 33,* 53-67.

Litovsky, V. G., & Dusek, J. B. (1985). Perceptions of child rearing and self-concept development during the early adolescent years. *Journal of Youth and Adolescence, 14,* 373-387.

Manaster, G. J., Chan, J. C., & Safady, R. (1992). Mexican-American migrant students' academic success: Sociological and psychological acculturation. *Adolescence, 27,* 123-136.

Marjoribanks, K. (1987). Ability and attitude correlates of academic achievement: Family-group differences. *Journal of Educational Psychology, 79,* 171-178.

Marjoribanks, K. (1988). Individual-environment correlates of children's reading performance. *Perceptual and Motor Skills, 67,* 323-332.

Marshall, S. P. (1992). What mathematical cognitive skills do parents offer children? In T. G. Sticht, B. A. McDonald, & M. J. Beeler (Eds.), *The intergenerational transfer of cognitive skills* (Vol. 2, pp. 122-127). Norwood, NJ: Ablex.

Matute-Bianchi, M. E. (1986). Ethnic identities and patterns of school success and failure among Mexican-descent and Japanese-American students in a California high school: An ethnographic analysis. *American Journal of Education, 95,* 233-255.

Mickelson, R. A. (1990). The attitude-achievement paradox among black adolescents. *Sociology of Education, 63,* 44-61.

Muller, C. (1993). Parental involvement and academic achievement: An analysis of family resources available to the child. In B. Schneider & J. S. Coleman (Eds.), *Parents, their children, and schools* (pp. 77-113). Boulder, CO: Westview.

Muller, C., & Kerbow, D. (1993). Parent involvement in the home, school, and community. In B. Schneider & J. S. Coleman (Eds.), *Parents, their children, and schools* (pp. 13-39). Boulder, CO: Westview.

Nickerson, R. S. (1992). On the intergenerational transfer of high-order skills. In T. G. Sticht, B. A. McDonald, & M. J. Beeler (Eds.), *The intergenerational transfer of cognitive skills* (Vol. 2, pp. 159-171). Norwood, NJ: Ablex.

Ogbu, J. U. (1978). *Minority education and caste.* New York: Academic Press.

Ogbu, J. U. (1981). Origins of human competence: A cultural-ecological perspective. *Child Development, 52,* 413-429.

Ogbu, J. U. (1986). The consequences of the American caste system. In U. Neisser (Ed.), *The school achievement of minority children* (pp. 19-56). Hillsdale, NJ: Lawrence Erlbaum.

Portes, P. R., Dunham, R. M., & Williams, S. (1986). Assessing child-rearing style in ecological settings: Its relation to culture, social class, early age intervention and scholastic achievement. *Adolescence, 21,* 723-735.

Pratt, M. W., Green, D., MacVicar, J., & Bountrogianni, M. (1992). The mathematical parent: Parental scaffolding, parenting style, and learning outcomes in long-division mathematics homework. *Journal of Applied Developmental Psychology, 13,* 17-34.

Prom-Jackson, S. (1987). Home environment, talented minority youth, and school achievement. *Journal of Negro Education, 56,* 111-121.

Reynolds, A. J., & Walberg, H. J. (1991). A structural model of science achievement. *Journal of Educational Psychology, 83,* 97-107.

Reynolds, A. J., & Walberg, H. J. (1992). A structural model of science achievement and attitude: An extension to high school. *Journal of Educational Psychology, 84,* 371-382.

Rogoff, B. (1990). *Apprenticeship in thinking: Cognitive development in social context.* New York: Oxford University Press.

Rumberger, R. W., Ghatak, R., Poulos, G., Ritter, P. L., & Dornbusch, S. M. (1990). Family influences on dropout behavior in one California high school. *Sociology of Education, 63,* 283-299.

Scott-Jones, D. (1984). Family influence on cognitive development and school achievement. *Review of Research in Education, 11,* 259-304.

Scott-Jones, D. (in press). Activities in the home that support school learning in the middle grades. In B. Rutherford (Ed.), *Creating family/school partnership* (pp. 161-181). Columbus, OH: National Middle School Association.

Seaborn-Thompson, M., Alexander, K. L., & Entwisle, D. R. (1988). Household composition, parental expectations, and school achievement. *Social Forces, 67,* 424-451.

Seginer, R. (1983). Parents' educational expectations and children's academic achievements: A literature review. *Merrill-Palmer Quarterly, 29,* 1-23.

Siu, S. (1992). How do family and community characteristics affect children's educational achievement? The Chinese-American experience. *Equity and Choice, 8,* 46-49.

Slaughter, D. T. (1987). The home environment and academic achievement of black American children and youth: An overview. *Journal of Negro Education, 56,* 3-20.

Steinberg, L. (1989). Communities of families and education. In W. J. Weston (Ed.), *Education and the American family: A research synthesis* (pp. 138-185). New York: New York University Press.

Steinberg, L., Dornbusch, S. M., & Brown, B. B. (1992). Ethnic differences in adolescent achievement. *American Psychologist, 47,* 723-729.

Steinberg, L., Mounts, N. S., Lamborn, D., & Dornbusch, S. M. (1991). Authoritative parenting and adolescent adjustment across varied ecological niches. *Journal of Research on Adolescence, 1,* 19-36.

Talton, E. L., & Simpson, R. D. (1986). Relationships of attitudes toward self, family and school with attitude toward science among adolescents. *Science Education, 70,* 365-374.

Taylor, R. D., Casten, R., & Flickinger, S. M. (1993). Influence of kinship social support on the parenting experiences and psychosocial adjustment of African-American adolescents. *Developmental Psychology, 29,* 382-388.

Taylor, R. D., Casten, R., Flickinger, S. M., Roberts, D., & Fulmore, C. D. (1994). Explaining the school performance of African-American adolescents. *Journal of Research on Adolescents, 4,* 21-44.

Thompson, M. S., Entwisle, D. R., Alexander, K. L., & Sundius, M. J. (1992). The influence of family composition on children's conformity to the student role. *American Educational Research Journal, 29,* 405-424.

Velez, W. (1989). High school attrition among Hispanic and non-Hispanic white youths. *Sociology of Education, 62,* 119-133.

Visser, D. (1987). The relationship of parental attitudes and expectations to children's mathematics achievement behavior. *Journal of Early Adolescence, 7,* 1-12.

Vygotsky, L. S. (1978). *Mind in society.* Cambridge, MA: Harvard University Press.

Walberg, H. J. (1984, May). Improving the productivity of America's schools. *Educational Leadership,* pp. 19-27.

Weishew, N. L., & Peng, S. S. (1993). Variables predicting students' problem behaviors. *Journal of Educational Research, 87,* 5-17.

Wentzel, K. R., Feldman, S. S., & Weinberger, D. A. (1991). Parent child rearing and academic achievement in boys: The mediational role of socio-emotional adjustment. *Journal of Early Adolescence, 11,* 321-339.

Wentzel, K. R., Weinberger, D. A., Ford, M. E., & Feldman, S. S. (1990). Academic achievement in preadolescence: The role of motivational, affective, and self-regulatory processes. *Journal of Applied Developmental Psychology, 11,* 179-193.

Wertsch, J. V. (1979). From social interaction to higher psychological processes: A clarification and application to Vygotsky's theory. *Human Development, 22,* 1-22.

Wertsch, J. V., McNamee, G. D., McLane, J. B., & Budwig, N. A. (1980). The adult-child dyad as a problem-solving system. *Child Development, 51,* 1215-1221.

Whang, P. A., & Hancock, G. R. (1994). Motivation and mathematics achievement: Comparisons between Asian-American and non-Asian students. *Contemporary Educational Psychology, 19,* 302-322.

Wood, J., Chapin, K., & Hannah, M. E. (1988). Family environment and its relationship to underachievement. *Adolescence, 23,* 283-290.

Zimmerman, B. J., Bandura, A., & Martinez-Pons, M. (1992). Self-motivation for academic achievement: The role of self-efficacy beliefs and personal goal setting. *American Educational Research Journal, 29,* 663-676.

CHAPTER 4

National Patterns of School and Family Connections in the Middle Grades

JOYCE L. EPSTEIN

SEYONG LEE

Research on school, family, and community partnerships in the middle grades has been given a boost by a national study of eighth graders—the National Educational Longitudinal Study of 1988 (NELS:88), conducted by the National Center for Educational Statistics (NCES) (Ingels et al., 1990). In this chapter, we describe the schools, families, and students in the NELS:88 base year to introduce researchers and educators to the richness of the data; to cast the data in terms of a theoretical model for understanding partnerships of schools, families, and communities; and to provide the background needed for empirical analyses on the effects of family and school connections in the middle grades. Researchers will use the NELS:88 surveys for many years to study issues of education and should consider whether and how these data can be used to explore and explain processes and effects of family involvement, school and family connections, and community participation.

AUTHORS' NOTE: This research was supported by the U.S. Department of Education (R117Q00031) in cooperation with the U.S. Department of Health and Human Services. The opinions expressed are those of the authors and do not necessarily represent OERI or HHS positions or policies. An earlier version of this chapter was presented in March 1992, at the annual meeting of the Society for Research on Adolescence, Washington D.C.

The NELS:88 data include items that represent the components of the theoretical perspective of overlapping spheres of influence to study school, family, community, and peer group connections (Epstein, 1987a, 1988). Pictorially, this social-organizational model can be shown as spheres of influence that can, by design, be pushed together to overlap or pulled apart, based on forces that operate in each environment. The model identifies an *external structure* of movable spheres and an *internal structure* of interpersonal exchanges and interactions of the members in the influential contexts.

The external structure of the model shows that the extent of overlap is affected by forces of *behavior*—to account for the background characteristics, philosophies, and practices of each environment—and *time*—to account for changes in the ages and grade levels of students, and the influence of historic or periodic conditions. The external model recognizes that there are some practices that schools and families conduct separately and others that are conducted jointly, in partnership. The NELS:88 data can be used to identify and characterize the school, family, and community contexts in the middle grades. The surveys of principals, parents, and students include information on the background characteristics, attitudes and behaviors, and perspectives on and experiences with the major types of involvement.

The internal structure of the model depicts the interrelationships of the participants in the family, school, and community contexts who work in partnership. It represents *institutional* connections that involve all families, educators, and students (such as a back-to-school night to which all are invited, or attendance or report card policies that apply to all students) and *individual* connections that involve one parent, teacher, and student (such as a parent-teacher conference about an individual student's grades or behavior). The internal structure identifies *the central role of the child* as the focal point for the interactions of school, family, and community in partnerships. NELS:88 data include reports from principals, parents, and students about their interactions with each other.

Thus, the NELS:88 base-year data describe the nation's middle grades schools, eighth-grade students, and their families with information that can be used to represent the components of the theory of overlapping spheres of influence.

Questions for Research

The survey data encourage the development of measurement models to study the processes of partnership and the effects on students, families, and the schools. Researchers using NELS:88 will explore how to best use the data. For example: What variables should be included in well-specified measurement models to represent the forces and processes in the model of overlapping spheres to study the effects of school and family partnerships? What methods of analyses should be used to address selected questions?

The external structure of the theory of overlapping spheres model raises questions that can be addressed with NELS:88 data. For example: What practices—how many and what type—fall within the overlapping sections of the spheres of influence where school and family responsibilities for children intersect? How should these practices change across the grades or from one level of schooling to the next in order to benefit students? Other questions are raised by the internal structure of the model. For example: How do specific practices of partnership affect the interpersonal contacts, attitudes, and behaviors of parents with educators? parents with other parents? parents with children? What practices promote productive relationships between schools and all families, and between teachers and parents about individual children at each grade level? How do these interactions affect youngsters' motivation to learn and their successful development?

The Importance of Developmental Patterns

The theory of overlapping spheres of influence identifies *time* as a force that affects the nature and extent of practices of partnership; that is, the age or grade levels of students, the life stage of families, and the experiences of educators are assumed to affect how, when, and why educators, families, and students communicate and interact. NELS:88 base year is the first in a series of surveys in a longitudinal study that follows eighth graders from the middle grades in 1988 to their high schools in Grades 10 and 12 in 1990 and 1992, and periodically thereafter. The surveys also follow a dropout sample from Grade 8 to Grades 10 to 12, and parents from Grades 8 to 12. Thus, the base-year data establish the foundation for understanding students' school experiences across the grades and the continuity or change of partnerships of schools, families, and communities.

Research shows that practices of partnership decline dramatically from the elementary to middle grades, even though families may need more information and guidance from the schools in order to monitor and assist their early adolescents in the middle grades (Baker & Stevenson, 1986; Dauber & Epstein, 1993; Epstein & Dauber, 1991; Epstein & Herrick, 1991; Leitch & Tangri, 1988; Stevenson & Baker, 1987; Useem, 1991, 1992). Involvement declines further in high schools, although the school organization is more complex, and life-course decisions are made by and with students that affect them and their families (Bauch, 1988; Brian, 1994; Clark, 1983; Connors & Epstein, 1994; Dornbusch & Ritter, 1988; Dornbusch, Ritter, Liederman, Roberts, & Fraleigh, 1987; Keith, Reimers, Fehrmann, Pottebaum, & Aubey, 1986). Most previous studies of family involvement in the middle and high school grades were based on state, local, or regional samples, or national surveys with scant coverage of the complexities of home and school relations. The NELS:88 base-year and follow-up surveys provide a new source of information about the involvement of families in the middle and high school grades with large, national samples of schools, students, and families and improved coverage of practices of partnerships.

Data

The National Educational Longitudinal Study of 1988 (NELS:88) includes information from a national sample of more than 1,000 public and private secular and religious schools in the United States that contain Grade 8. Surveys were administered in the spring of the school year to obtain information from principals about their middle grades schools (Hoachlander, 1991), and from more than 24,000 eighth-grade students on their attitudes and experiences in school, along with short achievement tests in four subjects (Haffner, Ingels, Schneider, Stevenson, & Owings, 1990). Surveys also were administered to two teachers for each student and to a total of more than 20,000 parents (Horn & West, 1992). The surveys of parents and students include questions on how families are involved at school and at home.

Because NELS:88 did not include much information on middle grades school reform, the Hopkins Enhancement Survey (HES) of NELS:88 Middle Grades Practices (Epstein, McPartland, & MacIver,

1991) obtained additional information from the principals on school organization, guidance and advisory periods, rewards and evaluations, curriculum and instruction, interdisciplinary teams of teachers, transitions and articulation activities, involvement of parents, and other recommended middle grades reforms. Of the original 1,036 schools in the NELS:88 spring sample, 1,025 still contained Grade 8 in fall 1988 when the HES was conducted. Information was obtained by mail on self-administered questionnaires (822 schools) and by telephone on shorter follow-up interviews (189 schools) for a completion rate of 99% of the eligible schools (Ingels, 1989). HES data are available from NCES for use by researchers in conjunction with the NELS:88 school surveys.

Types of Involvement

School and family partnerships include practices that are *initiated by parents* and *initiated by schools,* that occur *at school* or *at home,* and that demonstrate six major types of involvement (Epstein, 1992). The types of involvement that create a comprehensive program of partnerships include: Type 1—basic obligations of families for parenting and establishing home conditions that support learning; Type 2—basic obligations of schools to communicate with families about school programs and student progress; Type 3—volunteers and audiences at school; Type 4—learning activities at home, including interactive homework to inform families about curricula and school decisions, and to motivate student learning; Type 5—parent representation and participation in school decision making and governance, including parent organizations, school councils, and other committees; and Type 6—collaboration and exchanges with community organizations to increase family and student access to community resources and services, and participation in the community. Schools with comprehensive programs assist families to become informed and involved in these ways. (For discussion and examples of the types of involvement see Epstein, 1987b, 1992; Epstein & Connors, 1994a, 1994b.)

The NELS:88 and HES data include items that should be useful for studying how the major types of involvement affect student achievements, behaviors, and attitudes in the middle grades. Based on previous studies, we expect, for example, that the different types of school and family connections influence various outcomes for students, parents, and school practice and that activities that involve all families will have greater impact on students and on families than activities that include only selected (often self-selected) families and students (Brandt, 1989; Dauber & Epstein, 1993; Epstein, 1991, in press-a, in press-b; Muller, 1993).

To proceed with analyses of the influence of family background variables on patterns of involvement or the effects of family involvement, it is necessary for researchers to know something about the samples of students, families, and schools in NELS:88. Also, educators, policy leaders, and the public should have a picture of the nation's schools, their eighth graders, and their families. This chapter presents descriptive summaries of the data from the three main reporters in the NELS:88 and HES surveys on the involvement of families in their children's education. The summary statistics reported differ slightly from the NELS:88 code book due to recodings and selection decisions about the samples for later analyses of the schools, families, and students. The data include what *parents* report they experience directly as contacts from the schools and their own involvement with their children; what *principals* believe their schools are doing to involve families and the general participation levels of their families; and what *students* report as ties between school and home, and their achievements, attitudes, and behaviors that may be affected by their families' connections with education. The next sections report each of these perspectives with attention to the six types of involvement.

Data From Parents

The data from parents in the NELS:88 surveys include the characteristics, perspectives, and experiences of families of eighth graders in the United States. Who are they? What do they think of their children's schools? How are they involved in their children's education in the middle grades? In this chapter, *parent* refers to the adult who has the main responsibility at home for the student and the most contact with the school. This individual—parent, stepparent, guardian, or other relative—was asked to respond to the NELS:88 survey.

The Families of Eighth Graders

Popular reports often portray families in the United States as broken, dysfunctional, and uncaring, but this is not the case for most students in the NELS:88 national sample of eighth graders in public, private, and Catholic and other religious schools. Eighth graders in the United States in this national sample have families whose survey responses, on average, indicate caring and responsive attitudes and behaviors. Although there are important exceptions of students and families with serious problems, the average student is a member of a family that appears to be working at least modestly well, perhaps as well as families ever worked.

The families of the nation's eighth graders are variously structured. About 78% of the respondents in the survey of parents have a spouse or partner at home; about 20% are single parents (mainly mothers) with no other adult present; about 2% are other relatives or adults (see also Zill, in press, for analyses of these data).

The parents of students in the NELS:88 sample are educated, with most having more than a high school education. About 14% of the survey respondents did not complete high school. The rest completed high school or obtained a GED (26%), went further with some training or some college (41%), or finished a 4-year college program or more (19%). The parents' education is, however, lower than their expectations for their children, as 58.3% expect their teens to complete 4 years of college or more. Families of middle grades students in the United States value education and have high hopes for their children.

The families of students in NELS:88 are working to support themselves and their children. About 69% of the mothers or female guardians responding to the survey work full time (51%) or part time (17%), and 90% of the fathers or male guardians work full time (87%) or part time (3%). Most parents are therefore busy during the school day. The family work schedules have implications for the number of reasonable demands schools can make for parents to meet or participate at the school building on weekdays. Almost one third of the mothers do not work outside the home, however, and about 10% of fathers are unemployed. These facts also have implications for the potential involvement of volunteers who have various talents and skills that could help schools and students.

Parents' Reports About Their Middle Grades Schools

Parents were asked for their opinions about the schools that their children attend. Families generally support their children's middle grades schools. About 90% of the families agree or agree strongly that the schools place a high priority on learning. Although this items suggests a too-easily convinced public, other items permit a deeper look into families' opinions of their schools. For example, fewer say that their own child is challenged at school (78%) or is working hard (74%). Combining three survey items shows that only about one fourth of the parents *strongly agree* that their middle schools are of high quality *and* are challenging their child *and* are preparing their child well for high school. Thus, the data from parents show no ceiling effect for their evaluations of their schools and considerable room to improve the school programs and their children's successes. Families also indicate that there is room to improve school communications and connections with families.

The Involvement of Families in the Middle Grades

Using the data from parents, we address two questions: How do families report the *schools'* practices to involve them in their children's education? And how do families report their *own* practices to become or remain involved at school or at home? We combine these responses to identify patterns of *partnership* that result when schools and families contact each other, work separately, or avoid each other in the middle grades.

Parents' Reports of How Often the School Contacts Them

Parents were asked how often the school contacts them about different types of involvement, including whether the school gathers information from parents (Type 1); provides information to parents about students' programs, performance, and behavior (Type 2); recruits parent volunteers (Type 3); contacts families about students' options for high school courses and programs (Type 4); and asks for help with fund-raising (Type 5). There are no items representing Type 6 contacts from the school. The responses reveal a serious lack of contact from the schools to most families.

Type 1: Parenting and Child Rearing. School contacts to involve families in workshops about early adolescent development or other topics (typical Type 1 activities) were not included in the NELS:88 survey of parents, but another aspect of Type 1 was represented on gathering information from and about the family. About 60% of the families report that the school never contacts them for information about the student or family for school records, and only about 5% report three or more such contacts.

Type 2: Communications About School Programs and Student Progress. Two thirds (65%) of the parents report that the school never contacts them about their child's academic program. Nearly half say that they are never contacted about their child's academic performance (45%), and many more have no contacts from the school about student behavior (69%). About 25% of the families report three or more contacts about their child's academic performance, and about 10% were contacted three or more times about their child's behavior. About one fourth (23%) were contacted about both performance and behavior.

The latter contacts may have been about problems that schools wanted families to know about and help solve. Although virtually all students receive report cards, some families were not counting these routine communications as school contacts about performance. Conceivably, some did not receive the report cards, but, more likely, parents are reporting the personal contacts they receive from the school about their own child's academic and behavioral problems.

Type 3: Volunteers at School or in Class. Most parents (70%) say they are never asked to volunteer at the school.

Type 4: School Contacts About Learning or Curriculum. School contacts about learning or curriculum were limited to survey questions concerning contacts by the school about high school courses and programs. About 60% of families report no contacts from the school about their child's curricular options or plans for high school.

Type 5: Decision Making, Governance, Committees. Most families (59%) are never invited to participate in fund-raising.

Type 6: Collaborations With Community. Community collaboration was not represented in questions about whether or how schools contacted parents about programs or services in the community (but see parents' reports of their own and their students' involvement in the community in the following section).

What the Contacts From School May Mean. Overall, contacts from schools to parents of eighth graders are selective (only for some parents) and infrequent. Most contacts from schools identify problems, and few are designed for continuous, positive communications or interactions with all families.

Presently, *no contacts* may be viewed by parents as *no problems*— a good thing. In some schools, however, programs of partnership have been designed that include many types of communications from school to home about student programs, performance, and accomplishments. These schools may reach more families with more positive contacts. (For further analyses of the data from parents on the variation and results of school contacts, see Epstein & Jacobsen, 1994; Schneider & Coleman, 1993.)

Parents' Reports of How Often They Contact the School

Parents were asked how often they contacted the school or became involved with their eighth grader at home.

Type 1: Parenting and Child Rearing. One aspect of parenting concerns family rules and supervision at home. Most families, however structured, report that they are guiding their early adolescents. Most have rules for their eighth graders about homework (92%), chores (90%), and maintaining grades (73%). Most families also place limits on TV viewing (84%). The general limits may help explain why fewer families (42%) have specific rules of how many hours of TV children may watch.

These simple percentages hide the complexities of parenting early adolescents. For example, some families may set no rules or few rules for students who have high academic performance and good behavior because these students may not need formal rules to guide their behavior. Other families may set no rules or few rules because they do not know how to control their early adolescents' behavior. Also, not all rules are good rules, as some families may set unreasonable or inappropriate guidelines.

Families are more likely to set rules about matters that families traditionally control and feel comfortable about, such as chores, and less likely to set rules about items about which they have little information, such as how to maintain or improve report card grades. The data on family rules suggest that one fourth or more of the nation's eighth graders may not be held to high standards by their families about their report card grades and achievements in school. This may occur in part because of inadequate information for parents from the schools about how to frame and monitor academically oriented rules in the middle grades. Questions like these pose challenges for researchers who want to use NELS:88 to understand parenting skills and results in early adolescence.

On a survey item corresponding to reports of whether the schools contact them for information, about 60% of the families report they never contact the school to give information about the student or family for school records.

Type 2: Communications About School Programs and Student Progress. Most parents of middle grades students never contact their children's schools about children's performance (48%), the academic programs (65%), or children's behavior (71%).

Type 3: Volunteers at School or in Class. Most parents (80%) never serve as volunteers at the school.

Type 4: School Contacts About Learning and Curriculum. One aspect of parent involvement in learning activities at home is represented in questions about parents' discussions with their own children about education. Most families report that they talk "regularly" about middle school with their children (80%); fewer talk regularly about plans for high school (47%) or about the future (38%). The families who rarely or never talk with their children about school (20%) are most at risk of losing touch with their children and the middle grades schools.

Parents' surveys included questions about homework, a Type 4 activity that connects students and families on learning activities at home. Most parents (91%) believe the homework that their children get is valuable, but more than half (56.2%) never, seldom, or infrequently (once or twice a month) help with homework. This is due in part to homework policies and designs that ask middle grades students to do their work on their own and do not request or require conversations or interactions with parents.

In other studies, we found that most early adolescents say that they are willing to interact with their family members (e.g., demonstrate skills, share ideas, interview families) if homework was designed to encourage these interactions (Connors & Epstein, 1994; Epstein, Herrick, & Coates, in press; Epstein, Jackson, & Salinas, 1994). Such practices still are rare in the middle grades.

Type 5: Decision Making, Governance, Committees. About one third of the parents belong to or attend meetings of a parent organization in middle grades schools. Combining their reports on these items shows that almost half (46.4%) neither belong to nor attend or take part in parent organizations or activities. Most families (80%) say that they never participate in fund-raising.

The surveys asked whether parents have "adequate say" in school policy and whether parents "do their part" to support the school. About 63% of the parents agree that they have adequate say in school policy, but only 8% agree strongly with the statement. Slightly more say that parents work together to support their schools. These figures reflect the complex mix of more and less successful programs to involve families in school decision making. Although most families want parents' voices and views represented in school decisions, most families do not get personally involved in these activities.

Type 6: Collaboration and Exchange With Community Organizations. The NELS:88 surveys include items to measure family and student participation in community activities, although these do not necessarily link to the schools. Most of the parents (83%) participate in some community or cultural activities, and 36% take part in four or more community activities. According to the parents, their children are even more involved: 92% participate in at least one community or cultural activity outside of school, and about 45% of the students take part in four or more activities in their communities.

Parents' Involvement in the School Community

In the middle grades, peers become increasingly important, but parents continue their influence (Epstein, 1983; Youniss & Smollar, 1985). Some families in middle grades schools are connected with each other and create social networks of students, their friends, and their families. These interactions represent the connections of family, school, community, and peer group contexts—the four spheres of influence in the full theoretical model (Epstein, 1988). These connections help to produce "social capital" (Coleman,

1987, 1988) or establish social ties or social relationships that may influence parenting approaches and involvement at school or in the community, as well as parents' behaviors and students' attitudes, behaviors, and achievements.

About 35% of the parents in the NELS:88 sample are "well connected," knowing four or five of the parents of their children's five best friends. About 14% are isolated or unconnected, knowing none of their children's friends' families. The rest fall in between. It may be that parents who are well connected work together at school as volunteers, on committees, in meetings, and in fund-raising and develop a sense of community through school activities. Children in these families may experience stronger family control, parenting that is more similar to that of their friends, and parents who are more knowledgeable about school because of their activities and interactions at school and with other families. Conversely, children whose families are unconnected with other students' families may receive weaker support from their families for school-related behaviors and perhaps less encouragement to join other activities in the community. (See Muller, 1994, for analyses of these relationships and effects.)

What Parents' Contacting the School and Involvement at Home May Mean

Overall, families contact their children's schools infrequently. Few families make contact with the school more than once during the year. The most frequent contacts—three or more times—are about children's academic performance by 17% of the families. Other studies also show that parents care more about their own children's success and how they can understand and help their children at home than about contacting the school frequently to volunteer, attend workshops or meetings, or participate in decision making (Dauber & Epstein, 1993; Epstein, 1986).

The NELS:88 data from parents and from students indicate that parents talk to their middle grades children more than they contact or come to their schools, and far more than the schools contact them. The responses contribute to the stance that students play key roles in school and family partnerships in their conversations with their families and in other connections that they help make between home and school (Connors & Epstein, 1994; Epstein, in press-a; Montandon & Perrenoud, 1987).

Table 4.1 Parents' Reports of Partnership, Separate Initiatives, or Isolation From Their Children's Middle Grades Schools (*N*=22,028)

	Percentage of Parents Who Report:		
	Academic Program	Academic Performance	Volunteers
Partnership	21.5	39.1	15.8
School Initiation	13.9	15.9	13.7
Parent Initiation	13.3	13.3	3.4
Isolation	51.3	31.6	67.1

Partnership Variables

When parents' reports of contacts from and to the school are considered together, the data indicate that some family-school connections are stronger than others. To learn more about these patterns, we created variables of partnership to identify the mutual, independent, or neglected connections of schools and families. The relationships range from *partnership* to *isolation,* as schools and families contact each other, work separately, or ignore each other. For example, contacts about students' *academic program* show evidence of:

Partnership: 21.5% of the families reported that both the school and the family contacted each other about the student's academic program.

School initiation: 13.9% of the parents reported the school contacted them, but they did not contact the school about the student's academic program.

Parent initiation: 13.3% of the parents reported that the family contacted the school, but the school did not contact them about the student's academic program.

Isolation: 51.3% of the parents reported no contact by the school or by the family about the student's academic program.

Communications about academic programs differ from the patterns of school and family communications about students' academic performance and volunteering in middle grades, as shown in Table 4.1. The table shows that most partnerships between schools and families are reported about students' *academic performance* (39%), and the fewest partnerships are formed for *volunteers* in middle grades schools (16%). Correspondingly, the least isolation occurs on the topic of communications about their students' *academic performance* in eighth grade, although about one third (32%) of the parents report that neither they nor the schools contact each other about students' performance. By contrast, the most isolation (or lack of communications) is noted by 67% of the parents, who are not contacted by the school and who do not contact the school about becoming volunteers. Patterns of partnership and isolation for topics of student behavior and fund-raising are similar to those shown for academic program and volunteering, respectively.

Overall, the categories of *isolation* and *parent initiation* reflect a lack of school policies and practices to encourage family involvement. Depending on the type of involvement, from one half to more than two thirds of the families of eighth graders are relatively isolated from the school about their children's school programs and progress. These indicators do not tell a simple tale, however. As noted above, a lack of partnership on student behavior may be a good thing, as contacts usually refer to problems. Contacts about behavior and academic performance may imply more serious problems and risks of failure than contacts about academic performance alone.

Overall, middle grades schools are not effectively reaching out to families to organize or guide family involvement in school or at home. Left on their own, few parents of middle grades students make contact with their children's schools. They wait for information that, as shown above, does not always come from the schools. Many families gather what information they can from their children. Most go uninformed.

Summary and Discussion: Data From Parents

Despite parents' overall general satisfaction with the schools and their efforts to continue to supervise their middle grades children at home, the data in NELS:88 reveal some troubling patterns of risk; isolation; and separation of family, school, and students. A sizable portion of families and students—from one third to two thirds or more, depending on the measure—are isolated or unconnected with their schools and uninformed about their students' work, progress, program, or how to assist them.

Although most families say that they discuss school with their children at home, most lack information from the schools about classwork, homework, and curriculum content. Thus, the frequency and quality of their discussions are questionable. Most families are unlikely to have the information they need to motivate their children to work hard in school, challenge their children's thinking, or help their children meet their potential as students in the middle grades.

Many families have limited time together at home, particularly if both parents or single parents work outside the home, or if there are many children in school at different grade levels. To make the best use of their time together, families need good information from the schools and from their children about school if they are to continue to be effective and knowledgeable partners in their children's education through the middle grades and beyond.

Data From Principals

Data from principals in the NELS:88 and HES surveys include the characteristics of their schools and communities, and their views of the nature and extent of practices of partnership at the school level in the middle grades in U.S. schools containing Grade 8. Where are the nation's schools that serve eighth graders? What are they like? How do they involve families, and how do principals assess the present levels of involvement of families on the major types of partnership?

The Schools in the NELS:88 Sample

The schools in NELS:88 base-year survey were selected as a national probability sample of public and private secular and religious eighth-grade schools in 1988. The 1,035 middle grades schools include 609 public schools (58.8%), 187 Catholic schools (18%), 201 other religious schools (19.4%), and 38 private schools (3.7%). One fourth are urban schools, more than one third each are suburban and rural schools. More schools are located in the South and North Central regions of the nation than in the Northeast or West.

Interestingly, more public schools are in rural locations and in the South. Catholic schools are more often in urban or suburban communities and in the Northeast, whereas the other religious schools are more often in the West and Midwest, and in urban locations. More private, secular schools are located in urban areas and in the South.

The schools include numerous grade organizations, including the familiar K-8, 6-8, 7-8, 7-9, 7-12, and K-12 schools that serve eighth graders. As found in other studies (Epstein & MacIver, 1990), there are about 30 grade spans that include Grade 8. Middle grades schools are diverse organizations in many ways, including grade span. K-8 schools are more often Catholic or other religious schools, rural, and not Southern. More 6-8 and 7-8 middle schools are public, suburban, and Southern. More 7-12 schools are public, rural, and Midwestern.

The schools range widely in size. Almost half of the schools (46.1%) have eighth-grade enrollments of 35 or fewer students. About 20% of the schools are more than four times that size, with more than 145 students enrolled the eighth grade. The largest schools serve more than 1,500 students. About one third of the schools have 10 or fewer teachers, and about 10% have 40 or more teachers.

Most schools for eighth graders (67.5%) are organized with departmentalized programs in which students have different teachers for each subject. The others have semidepartmentalized programs (23.1%) with a few different teachers for major subjects or self-contained classes (9.4%) with one teacher for all major subjects. Most self-contained classes for eighth graders are in K-8 or K-12 schools where grade enrollments are small, sometimes with only one class of eighth graders and one teacher per grade level.

Principals' Reports of the Students and Families in Their Schools

The nation's middle grades schools serve students with highly diverse family backgrounds and structures. About half of the schools have 10% or fewer students on free lunch; almost one quarter of the schools have from 10% to 35% on free lunch; and the others have more poor students. There are more schools serving economically disadvantaged students in rural areas, with mixed distributions of poor and wealthy schools in urban areas. Students from professional or managerial families range from 0% to 100%. Most schools (54%) serve mixed populations, with 15% or more professional families. There are dramatically more students on free lunch and many fewer professional and managerial families in public schools than in private or religious schools.

In more than one third of the middle grades schools there are no students from minority groups; about 17% of the schools are attended by more than 40% minority students. Students from racial or cultural minority groups more often attend middle grades schools in urban areas, in the South and West, and in public schools. There are more single parents in urban, public, and Northeastern schools, and in schools serving poor and minority students.

The students in middle grades schools in the United States vary greatly in ability. About 20% of the principals report that most of their entering students are considerably or somewhat below national norms in academic ability. About 44% report that most of their students are above the national norm in ability when they enter the school. Compared to principals in public schools, many more principals of private and Catholic and other religious schools report that their students are above national norms in academic skills and abilities when they enter the middle grades. Correspondingly, more students of urban, public, and Southern schools are in remedial reading, remedial math, and special education. More students in suburban schools are in gifted and talented programs. These distinctions are least often made by principals in schools in the Midwest, where there may be fewer programs within schools for special students (or more separate schools for special education), policies that reject labeling, or other reasons that principals do not report students in these groups (such as greater homogeneity of student populations).

Middle grades schools in the United States differ greatly in the students and families they serve. The public schools on average serve more economically and educationally disadvantaged students and families than schools in other sectors. It will be important to take this into account in studies that compare public and religious or private secular schools and their students, families, or patterns of involvement.

The differences discussed in this section are important for statistical analyses because they show that middle grades schools in this nation are not randomly distributed by sector, region, or urbanization, and that these features are correlated. Similarly, schools are not randomly organized by grade span, size, race and ethnicity, economic background, initial abilities, and other characteristics of the students or families, all of which factors are correlated. Thus, when researchers use NELS:88 and the follow-up surveys they must statistically account for the independent effects of many factors in order to determine which families become involved at school or at home; how they are involved; and the results of their involvement for students, families, or the schools.

These variables have implications for practices of school and family partnerships. Earlier studies have shown, for example, that it is easier for teachers in self-contained classes to make contacts with a few families than for teachers in departmentalized programs to do so (Epstein & Dauber, 1991). These difficulties do not preclude good programs of partnership, but do raise "red flags" that need attention in the design, staffing, and budgeting of such programs.

Principals' Views of Their Schools

The middle grades schools in the nation overall are relatively stable and conventional places. Most principals in this national sample of middle grades schools report that their students attend school regularly. About 80% of the schools report more than 92% average attendance, and more than 65% of them have at least 95% average attendance. Some middle grades schools, however, have serious attendance and behavior problems. Up to one fourth report moderate or serious problems with student absence and lateness. About 15% report high rates of mobility from the start to the end of the school year. Fewer than 10% of the principals report moderate or serious problems with class cutting; fights; or delinquent behavior such as thefts, vandalism, alcohol use, drug use, or verbal abuse of teachers. Fewer than 2% report problems with weapons or physical abuse of teachers. These numbers are, however, more serious than they first appear, because the top 10% of troubled schools are larger and serve more than 10% of the nation's early adolescents.

The reports from principals suggest that attention to attendance and behavior problems must be targeted to specific schools. For example, specific practices of family involvement and strategic use of volunteers may assist schools to improve student attendance and behavior. Initial analyses of school data from NELS and HES surveys show sizable and persistent effects of partnership activities on student attendance in the middle grades (Epstein & Lee, 1993).

School Climate and Parent Involvement

Most principals in the NELS school sample (over 90%) report that their school climate is generally positive, with relatively few conflicts between teachers and administrators, good discipline, structured classroom environments, and teachers' encouragement of students to do their best. Other items in the surveys suggest underlying problems, however. More than one third of the principals, for example, report that most of their students do not place a high priority on learning and one fifth report that most of their teachers do not have high morale. About one fifth of the principals say their teachers have somewhat negative attitudes about students and about one half report that their teachers find it at least somewhat difficult to motivate students.

The survey response categories in NELS:88 are imprecise, suggesting a range from *few* to *many* problems, but the patterns are provocative and will require creative analyses of NELS data to understand the implications of school climate factors for school, family, and community connections, and for student learning and other outcomes. For example, more than other teachers and administrators, those who frequently inform and involve families may get more help from families in motivating students to keep a high priority on schoolwork and learning. Earlier studies show the teachers who involve families in learning activities at home give parents higher ratings on follow through and helpfulness than teachers who do not communicate with and involve families (Becker & Epstein, 1982). If students hear the same messages at home and at school about learning, they may become more self-motivated to attend school and to work hard. Teachers may have fewer problems motivating these students. Teachers' morale also may be boosted if parents recognize and appreciate the teachers' efforts to create partnerships with families. Earlier studies show teachers get higher ratings from parents and from their principals if they work to inform and involve families (Epstein, 1985; Hoover-Dempsey, Bassler, & Brissie, 1987).

Principals' Reports of Family Involvement

The data from principals about how their schools involve parents and how many parents are involved come from the Hopkins Enhancement Survey (HES) of NELS:88 (Epstein et al., 1991). The data on the six major types of involvement include a small number of representative survey items. According to the principals, middle grades schools in the United States vary greatly in even the most basic practices to involve families and in the level of participation by families.

Type 1: Assisting Families With Parenting, Child Rearing, and Establishing Home Conditions for Learning

Type 1 involvement is represented by principals' reports of the percentage of parents who attend workshops and encourage learning at home, and school practices to provide parents with contacts from counselors and opportunities to visit their child's future high school.

Most principals (82.6%) report that fewer than 10% of their families attend workshops to obtain information on school programs, early adolescent development, or other topics to assist in child rearing and improving home conditions for learning. In part, this is because some schools (17%) do not offer any workshops. There is less participation in workshops in rural schools (perhaps because of the greater distance from home to school in rural areas) and less attendance in large schools, public schools, Southern schools, and schools with more minority students.

Low attendance at workshops is a national and international pattern in schools at all educational levels. Some schools, however, attract more parents to workshops than do others. The correlates of higher attendance provide clues about qualities and processes needed to improve attendance. For example, in the NELS:88 sample, there is more participation in workshops in Catholic schools and K-8 schools where parents of middle grades students may also have younger children and where they may have attended some workshops in the early grades. Feelings of attachment to the school and familiarity with the school may help attract parents to workshops. Personal communications about workshops also may increase participation.

There also is more participation of parents in workshops in schools that offer more extracurricular activities for students and in schools where even low-achieving students (the lowest one third) have opportunities to participate in activities and receive school awards and recognition. These correlates suggest that more "participatory" schools involve students *and* their families in many ways. Patterns like these illustrate why analyses must statistically control for the characteristics of families and students and other qualities of the schools in order to understand how families are involved in their children's education.

The NELS and HES surveys do not include information on the topics or quality of the workshops, nor on whether the workshops are scheduled to enable working parents to attend, nor if transportation and child care are available so that parents far from the school or with small children can attend. These features affect attendance at workshops, but require more detailed survey questions than those available in NELS:88.

Type 1 practices of partnership are reflected in home conditions that support students' learning. The NELS:88 school data do not include information on whether middle grades schools provide guidance to parents about this. More than half (57%) of the principals in the HES report that at least half of their families encourage and support learning at home. From the principals' views, this is more true of families in urban and in private schools. The others (43% of the principals) believe that at least half of their families do *not* establish home conditions that support middle grades students' learning. This is particularly true in rural, Southern, and public schools, and in schools serving poor and minority families.

Counselors' Contact With Families. Other items in the HES surveys of principals suggest that most middle grades schools in the United States do not provide parents with much information that will guide them in their interactions with their children at home. For example, there is high variation in whether middle grades school counselors communicate with children's families in ways that could assist parents in establishing positive home conditions for learning. About 80% of the principals report that their counselors spend 10% or less of their time talking with families. Counselors are only one possible contact or source of information for parents about the schools and early adolescence, but counselors may be underutilized in helping middle grades families know what to do to encourage learning at home in age-appropriate ways.

Making the Transition to High School. Middle grades schools vary in how families are helped to make the transition to high school with their early adolescents. Principals reported whether parents visit the high school that their children will attend while the students are still in the middle grades (48.3%) or in the fall after entry to high school (46%). About one third (35%) of the families have no scheduled opportunity to visit their children's high schools either at the end of the middle grades or when the children enter high school in the fall. The percentages add to more than 100% because about one fourth of the schools have orientations for parents both before and after their children enter high school.

Opportunities for parents to visit their children's future high schools are more common in more economically advantaged communities with more professional families and in schools with middle grades students with higher achievement levels. Visits to high school also are more common in middle grades schools that have established other practices of partnership with families, such as providing more types of information to parents on students' report cards. School-family connections about transitions are important because families who understand their children's "next" school should be better prepared to help their children adjust if there are problems, talk more knowledgeably with them about their new experiences, and continue to support their children as they move through the grades.

Type 2: Communications With Families
About School Programs and Children's Progress

Parent-Teacher Conferences. Almost half of the principals report that 50% or fewer parents attend parent-teacher conferences. Although some schools (53%) have high participation at conferences with more than three fourths of their families attending, many other schools have very low rates of attendance at these basic meetings with teachers. Presently, there is higher participation in parent-teacher conferences in small schools, in schools with high-ability students and professional families, and in schools where teachers have self-contained classes. In an earlier study of elementary schools, we estimated that at least one third of all families do not have a conference each year with their children's teachers (Epstein, 1986). The HES survey shows that this number is higher in the middle grades. Face-to-face meetings between parents and teachers at the start of each school year could help to establish positive relationships so that other forms of communication (such as phone calls or notes) could be used through the school year without requiring many meetings at the school.

Information About Test Scores. Most principals (75%) say that they report standardized test scores to parents. This practice is more common in Catholic than in public or other private schools, more common in the South, and more common in schools serving more professional families. More reporting of test scores occurs in schools that have more parent-teacher conferences, suggesting that student tests are one topic of the teachers' meetings with parents or that these are schools that give many kinds of information to parents in various forms.

At least as important as sending test scores home is whether schools explain the scores in words and forms that parents can understand, discuss, and act on with their children. Interestingly, as noted above, almost half the parents say they had no contacts from the school about their children's academic performance. The discrepancy between principals' reports that they give families information on test scores and parents' reports that they receive no contacts from the school is due in part to differently worded survey items, but it also suggests that communications that are sent by schools are not necessarily understood or used by parents.

Information on Report Cards. Schools vary in the kinds of information they give to parents about their children on report cards. Most schools give an average of four items of information about each subject: achievement grades (99%), conduct (70%), attendance (65%), and handwritten (55%) or computer-generated (25%) comments. Some also give effort grades (49%), progress grades (33%), grade point averages (20%), or other information (8.4%). These percentages do not indicate how much of the information is understood by families or how families, students, and teachers work together to help students improve grades that are considered too low.

Type 3: Volunteers at School

Most middle grades principals (71.4%) report that 10% or fewer parents volunteer at their schools. More than half report fewer than 5% volunteering. Volunteers tend to disappear in the middle grades.

Some educators believe that students do not want their parents to come to the middle grades schools, but this is not true in programs that use volunteers productively (Epstein & Dauber, 1995).

Greater percentages of parents volunteer in suburban middle grades schools, small schools, and those with self-contained classes than in other locations. There are proportionally more volunteers in schools with more professional families and with students who enter with higher academic ability. These patterns suggest that there is greater outreach *to* these families or more initiation *by* these families to continue volunteering in the middle grades. The data confirm reports from parents that most middle schools do not actively or effectively recruit them as volunteers.

Type 4: Activities at Home That Support School Curricula and Student Learning

Only about 25% of the principals report that most of their parents regularly receive information on how to help at home. These communications are more frequent in Catholic and private schools, schools with more professional families, and schools in the Northeast and West. Rural schools inform parents about children's work and learning less often than do other schools. Most middle grades principals (75%) report that fewer than half of their parents receive information regularly from teachers on how to help children at home on specific skills or homework.

Other data suggest that there may be consequences of this lack of information to families. For example, more than 85% of the principals report that fewer than half of the parents regularly monitor homework or assist their children with needed skills. If middle grades schools want more families to monitor or discuss homework with their children, teachers will have to increase the amount and kind of clear information that goes to the home.

Type 5: Families in School Decision-Making Roles

More than half of the principals report that 20% or fewer middle grades parents join the PTA or other parent organizations and even fewer participate regularly in these organizations' meetings or events. These estimates are lower than those given by the parents, in part because of inflated self-reports by some parents and in part because the principals may be considering the level of participation by all parents, including those who are not represented in the NELS:88 surveys. More parents are members of these associations in suburban and private schools, in schools with more professional families, and where students have higher achievement levels when they enter the middle grades. A sizable number of middle grades schools in the United States (about 15%) have no parent organizations.

In some schools, dues are required that prevent some families from joining the parent organization. In others, the "regulars" who join and participate in the PTA or other organizations may directly or indirectly dissuade some families from joining or becoming active. These factors are among the "red flags" that need attention in order to improve the participation of all families in parent organizations, committees, councils, or other decision-making groups.

Type 6: Community Collaborations and Connections With Schools, Families, and Students

This type of involvement is not directly measured on the NELS:88 or HES surveys of principals. There are, however, some indirect measures of community connections in the schools. For example, some volunteers come from community or business groups, linking Type 3 activities with Type 6. As reported above, middle grades schools have very few parent or community volunteers.

Also, principals reported another school practice that affects the involvement of families and the community. More than three fourths of the schools (79%) require visitors to sign in at the main office. This policy is more prevalent in public than in other schools and more characteristic of large schools, those in the South, and those with many students in one-parent homes. A sense of community is established if families feel welcome when they arrive at school, and this may be affected by rules about visiting and how those rules are enforced.

Summary of Principals' Reports of the Involvement of Parents

The principals' assessments indicate that few middle grades schools in the nation have comprehensive programs of parent involvement. Most schools have some involvement activities, but do not reach all families, as shown in Table 4.2. In most schools, very few parents

Table 4.2 Principals' Reports of Families Involved in Different Types of
          Partnership in the Middle Grades (N=1,035)

	Percentage of Principals Who Report:		
Type	A Few Parents (0%-10%)	Some Parents (20%-50%)	Most Parents (75%+)
1. Regularly attend workshops about school programs, early adolescence, and so on	82.6	16.0	1.4
2. Attend parent-teacher conferences each year with all academic subject teachers	12.7	33.2	54.1
3. Volunteer time to help in classrooms or school	71.4	24.8	3.8
4. Receive information frequently from academic subject teachers on how to help child at home on specific skills or homework	31.5	42.1	26.4
5. Join PTA or other parent organization	41.4	41.4	17.2

NOTES: Response categories are 0%, 5%, 10%, 20%, 35%, 50%, 75%+. Type 6 activities were
not reported in this form.

come to school for workshops or to volunteer. The only prevalent
practice is attending parent-teacher conferences (more than half the
schools reach 75% or more families), but even for this common
activity nearly half the principals say that fewer than 50% of their
parents participate.

Data From Students

The data from students document the diversity of early adolescents in Grade 8 in the nation's schools. This section summarizes
data that address these questions: Who are the students in Grade 8
in the United States? Where do they go to school? What do they
say about themselves, their families, and their goals? How do they
see the connections between their schools and families?

Of the 24,600 students in the NELS:88 base-year sample, 88%
are in public schools (*n* = 21,638); 7.6% are in Catholic schools (*n*
= 1,867); 2.9% are in other religious schools (*n* = 716); and 1.5%

attend other private schools ($n = 379$). The percentage of schools in each sector differs greatly from the percentage of students served in each sector because public schools tend to be larger than the others. For example, 59% of the schools in the sample are public schools, but they serve 88% of the eighth graders; 18% of the schools are Catholic schools, serving just 7.6% of the students.

There are about equal numbers of males and females in the NELS:88 base-year sample of students. They include 72% white, 13% African American, 10% Hispanic American, 3.5% Asian American, and 1.3% American Indian youngsters. About 3.2% of the students report using only non-English languages at home. One fifth of the students live in the Northeast and West, one fourth in the North Central region, and more than one third live in the South.

Students' Reports About Their Families

The students' reports add to the information from parents, summarized above, about the diversity of families of eighth graders. About 20% and 30% of the students report that their mothers and fathers, respectively, are in professional occupations. The other students' parents or guardians vary across the full range of occupations from service work (24% mothers; 5% fathers) to farmers (0.3% mothers; 2% fathers). Students' reports of mothers' and fathers' employment reveal different patterns from parents' reports. This bears study for those who are going to use NELS:88 surveys. For example, many more students (18%) say their mothers are homemakers than the parents themselves report (under 5%). Other questions for students about parents' employment include homemaker in the "employed" category. The differences are due in part to differently worded questions and in part to other factors, such as the characteristics of the parents who responded to the surveys and students' possible miscategorizations of mother's employment, volunteer work, and other activities. The discrepancies point out the importance for NELS:88 users to choose variables carefully from among the many that are available on closely related topics in the student, parent, and school surveys.

According to students, their fathers and male guardians tended to finish more schooling (at least junior college or 14 years of school) than their mothers (average of 12-13 years of school). Fathers' education also varied more, with more fathers than mothers

dropping out of high school, and many more completing postgradu-
ate college programs.

Students' Achievements in School

Most eighth graders report that they are in a middle or average
group in math (53%). More than one third (38%) say that they are
in a high math group, and only 9.2% report that they are in a low
math group. Nearly 15% believe that there is no ability grouping
in their school. The percentages are similar for the other academic
subjects, although fewer (25%) say that they are in high or advanced
science and social studies classes. These reports are consistent with
earlier surveys of principals that revealed less homogeneous ability
grouping in science and social studies than in math (Epstein &
MacIver, 1990). About 22% of the eighth graders in NELS:88 say
they are in the top groups in all subjects (math, English, science, and
social studies), and 13% say they are in the low groups in all subjects.
The rest have mixed assignments or are grouped heterogeneously
in all academic subjects. These figures suggest that relatively few
students in this sample have labeled themselves as "low" students.

Nevertheless, by their own reports, about 20% of the students
experienced serious failure in school by repeating at least one grade
level by Grade 8, although only about 7% repeated at least one
middle grade (5-8). About 2% skipped a grade, and about 13% are
enrolled in programs for gifted and talented students.

The data from students and parents raise some questions about
whether the NELS:88 base-year sample fully represents the most
unsuccessful students in the middle grades in the United States. The
surveys exclude students who were chronically absent or truant
from school, because these students were not in school on the day
of the survey or on the day of the make-up survey. Also excluded
from the random sample are students with severe disabilities and
students with severely limited English proficiency who could not
understand the survey. Also missing are students who for all practical purposes already dropped out or were "pushed out" of eighth
grade due to attendance, behavior, attitude, academic, or personal
problems. These exclusions mean that the base-year sample may
underrepresent low-ability students who tend to be absent from
school more often than other students, and low-ability non-English-
speaking students who tend to have the highest and earliest dropout

rates of all students. These exclusions and other nonresponse patterns also affect the sample of parents, who were surveyed only if their children were in the student sample.

Despite these possible problems, the NELS:88 base-year sample of students is the best available national data. It shows that, overall, eighth graders in the United States are not a bad lot. Only about 7% report that they smoke cigarettes. Most (91%) report that they never cut classes, although more (37%) are sometimes late to school (i.e., at least once in the past 4 weeks). There are some slackers, however, including 23% who say they usually or often come to class without a pencil or paper and about 20% who usually or often do not complete their homework on time.

Although most students say that they do their homework, most are assigned or do relatively little—an average of about 1 hour of homework per week in math and less in science, English, social students and other subjects, for a total of about 5 hours of homework a week. The range is great, however, from 0 to 21 hours per week, with 10% of the students reporting that they do 10 or more hours of homework across subjects. Part of this variation reflects the students' initiative, part reflects the variation in parents' continuing attention to homework completion in the middle grades, and a large part of the variation in hours students spend on homework reflects teachers' patterns of assigning homework.

In addition to homework, most students spend 1 to 2 hours a week reading on their own, with 21% giving no time to outside reading, and 10% spending 4 or more hours reading for pleasure.

Most students report that they come to school ready to work. About half, however, say that they are bored in school half or more of the time. Other analyses with the NELS:88 data show that most students are not challenged very much or very well by the curricula they are offered or the instruction they experience (Epstein & MacIver, 1992) This also confirms parents' dissatisfaction with the level of challenge to their children.

Based on these indicators of commitment to schoolwork, it is not surprising that the students' grades vary widely, with 32% reporting that they receive mostly As in English, 38% mostly Bs, 23% mostly Cs, and 7% mostly Ds or Fs. The figures are not very different for the other subjects, though there are slightly more Ds and Fs in math and science (i.e., 9% to 12%).

About one third of the students (34%) score at or beyond the highest reading proficiency level on the reading achievement test administered as part of the NELS:88 survey, with 13% at the lowest reading proficiency level. In math, 19% are at the highest proficiency level and 18% are at the lowest level.

Students are at serious risk of failing in or dropping from the middle grades or high school if they score in the bottom 10% to 25% on report card grades and achievement test scores; have high absence, frequent lateness, or low homework completion; are unprepared for class; or report other poor attitudes and behaviors in school.

Students' Attitudes and Aspirations

There are important variations in students' attitudes toward school and teachers. About one third report that they do not receive much praise from their teachers, nor do they feel their teachers listen to what they have to say. About 22% feel "put down" in class. The reports from students may help to explain why some principals reported (see above) that some students in their schools did not place a high priority on learning and that some teachers find it hard to motivate some students to learn.

As in most surveys, these eighth graders have very high aspirations, on average. Most believe they will go on to attend some college (13%), finish college (43%), or go beyond college (23%). They say they will finish high school, with 82% "very sure" and 16% "probably sure" about this. Very few eighth graders (under 2%) *plan* to drop out before high school graduation.

They report that their parents have even higher aspirations for them. About 75% of the students report that their parents want them to graduate from college or go beyond. This is higher than the 60% of parents in the NELS:88 survey who report this goal for their children (see above). Students may be overstating or misunderstanding their parents' expectations, or they may be reporting the goals of the parents (mostly fathers) who did not fill in the NELS:88 questionnaires. In any case, the students want and expect to obtain more formal education than their parents obtained.

There are signs that the students will have difficulty reaching the goals they and their families set. For example, only about 52% of the eighth graders expect to enroll in a college prep or special high school program. Thus, despite high aspirations, there are serious discrepancies between students' and families' educational goals and the students' immediate plans to enroll in a high school program that will help them reach their goals.

There are questions raised by these responses: How do or how should middle grades schools and high schools work together and work with students and parents to enroll students in high school programs that will prepare them to apply to and succeed in college? What information do students and families need *and when do they need it* to fully understand the options and requirements in the middle grades and in high schools that are prerequisites for college admission? Middle and high schools have responsibilities to make programs, student options, and the consequences of choices understandable to all families and all students. The NELS:88 base-year and follow-up surveys will make it possible for researchers to follow the paths of students from the middle grades to postsecondary school placements in college, other training, or work, and to study the effects of the involvement of families on the choices and programs the students selected. The patterns in the NELS:88 data that show discrepant goals and plans also raise questions for research or for interventions and evaluations of programs to help students and their families make better choices to meet their aspirations.

The students in NELS:88 range widely in the families they return to each day; in their abilities, interests, aspirations, attitudes, and behaviors; and in the middle grades schools they attend and the courses they take. (See also Haffner et al., 1990, for an overview of the base year data from students and Epstein & MacIver, 1992, for other descriptions and analyses of the curriculum and instruction in middle grades schools.)

Students' Reports of Parents' Involvement

The NELS:88 surveys of eighth graders included representative items on the six types of school and family connections. In most of their reports, students reinforced the conclusions drawn from data from parents and principals. Most eighth graders respond that their parents are minimally involved, with most communication between parent and child at home.

*Type 1: Parenting and Child Rearing
and a Supportive Environment at Home*

Family Rules. Most early adolescents recognize and report that their families continue to supervise and guide them at home. Although there are exceptions—families who never require chores (7.4%) or never set curfews (11.3%)—most students report that their families set guidelines about chores, schoolwork, and time to stay out with friends. About 68% of the students report that their parents *often* require chores. There is more variability in student reports of curfews and limits on TV than about chores. According to students, about 43% of their families often limit the time they may stay out with friends, but only 14% of the families often limit TV (compare with parents' reports, above, on TV rules and limits). Students indicate that parents vary widely in their regulations for chores, homework, TV, and curfews, ranging from 0.5% of eighth graders who have no rules for any of these behaviors to 5.8% whose parents highly control all four categories.

Few controls at this age level may mean that few rules are needed or that parents are appropriately helping their children move toward coregulation of their behavior. Or, few controls may indicate laissez-faire parenting, which may shortchange early adolescents on the guidance they need in the middle grades. When most students say that their parents do not limit TV, for example, it may be because most parents have set rules and the students are following them (or that the students are ignoring them). These are interesting questions that may be pursued with NELS:88 and the follow-up surveys with more complete measurement models. (See S. Lee, 1994, for analyses of data from students that explore the antecedents and consequences from Grade 8 to 10 of family involvement on each of the six types discussed here.) But these also are questions that may need new and more focused studies of TV rules, limits, habits, and consequences in adolescence and for other age groups.

Reports from students and parents on family regulations differ because parents were asked whether they set any rules and students were asked about the frequency of the enforcement of parents' rules. Thus, more parents say they set rules for chores (90%) than students report they are often required to do them, and more parents report rules for TV (84%) than students say they experience frequent limits (14%). These discrepancies may reflect some students' overstatements of their independence from their family, but are more likely to indicate how one or two differently worded items may clarify some things and confuse other things about complex parenting behaviors and parent-child relationships. One or two items in a general survey are not enough to fully understand important topics of adolescent development, schooling, and family involvement. Focused and detailed studies will be needed to delve more deeply into the provocative issues that are raised by patterns of responses in large, national sample surveys like NELS:88.

Type 2: Communications With the School

According to the students, some of their parents are contacted by their middle grades schools about problems with attendance, grades, and behavior. About 12% say their parents "received a warning" about poor student attendance; 22%, about misbehavior; and 37%, about poor grades.

About one third of the students report that their parents did not talk to a teacher or counselor by phone or in person that school year. This figure confirms information from parents in NELS:88 (see above) and conforms with earlier surveys indicating that more than one third of the parents of elementary students did not have a conference with a teacher during the school year (Epstein, 1986).

Type 3: Attend School Events or Volunteer

Most students (63%) report that their families attended some events in which they participated at the school, although about one third say their families never came to an event at school that year. Most students (70%) report their parents did not visit their classes.

Type 4: Learning Activities at Home and Homework

Homework. Just under half of the students (44.5%) say that their parents often check whether they have done their homework. Of the rest, about 10% say their families never check, and the others (45.5%) report that their families rarely or sometimes check homework. Without guidance from the school about how and when to check that homework is done or how to discuss this work at home, most families do not regularly initiate procedures to check, follow-up, or discuss homework with their children in the middle grades (as reported by parents, above) and most students do not expect them to do so.

Discussions About School, Courses, Classwork, and the Future. Students reported the number of times since the beginning of the school year that they talked with either or both parents about courses, school programs, activities or events, and topics studied in class. According to the students, just more than one third (38.9%) talked with a parent more than twice about their courses or programs; just more than half discussed activities or events (56.9%) or classwork (52%). About 27% discussed all three topics—courses, events, classwork—three or more times with their parents; and only a few (2.2%) never talked together about any of these topics.

Although most students know their families' expectations, students infrequently talk with their families about their future programs and plans. About half of the students (52%) reported that they talked with their mother three or more times about planning their high school programs; about one third talked about this often with their father. Most discussed their plans at least once, but 10% did not do so at all.

Behind these estimates of one or more conversations are questions of whether students understand that their teachers want them to discuss school, decisions, and activities at home and whether students and families have enough information from the schools to make their discussions meaningful.

Evidence from other studies help to explain why some middle grades students do not often discuss school with their families. For example, about half of the students in one middle grades school believed that their teachers did not want them to talk about school at home (Epstein et al., in press). Without explicit and frequent directions from their teachers to share ideas or progress at home, some students will not raise topics about school or homework in conversations at home.

Type 5: Participation in Decision Making, Committees, and Governance

About half of the students (55.9%) report that their parents attend a school meeting. This may refer to a PTA meeting, back-to-school night, meeting about their future high school, or other meeting. More students do not know whether their parents attended meetings in school or talked to their teachers (11%) than do not know whether their parents visited their classrooms or attended an event at school (3% to 5%). Students may pay more attention to family visits that occur when the students are present (in class or at an event) than to meetings or conversations that parents and teachers have without the students.

Type 6: Collaboration, Exchanges With Community Organizations, and Participation in the Community

Eighth graders participate in many ways at school and in the community. Students in NELS:88 report that they are members and officers of 21 organizations, groups, or clubs at their school (Braddock, 1992). The greatest proportions of students are in varsity (44%) and intramural (40%) sports, band (22%), chorus (23%), dance (25%), or one of several subject clubs (over 20%). Most of these activities include opportunities for connecting with the broader community.

Similarly, many eighth graders are involved in community organizations, clubs, and activities. The most prominent activities are nonschool team sports (35%), religious youth groups (31%), and summer programs (18%). Fewer participate in scouts or neighborhood or hobby clubs, but many say they are in other (unnamed) community activities (40%).

The numbers exceed 100% because some students participate in several activities at school and in the community. A small percentage are nonparticipants. Because of distance, transportation, costs, and other factors, not all students have access to extracurricular school or community activities. These activities establish natural, positive connections for families to share the students' accomplishments, performances, awards, demonstrations, and to discuss their interests and ideas.

Summary: Data From Students

Combining the students' reports across the various types of involvement, about 19% say that their parents are actively involved in various types of *partnership* activities with their schools, whereas about 27% report that their parents operate in relative *isolation* from their schools, involved in few or no communications or activities. The rest (54%) report that their parents are involved with their schools in limited ways, mainly at home. Thus, even on basic indicators—attend meetings, phone teachers, visit classes, or attend events—more than three fourths of the eighth graders in the United States report that their families are far from experiencing or exercising strong partnerships with their middle grades schools. These estimates based on student data correspond closely with the conclusions drawn from the data from parents in Table 4.1 and are in concert with the patterns of data from principals in Table 4.2.

Summary and Discussion

It is important for researchers who want to use NELS:88 data and related surveys such as the Hopkins Enhancement Survey (HES) of NELS:88 schools to have a profile of the participants. It also is important for the public to have a good picture of the nation's schools, students, and families in the middle grades. These samples are sometimes prejudged by the characteristics of the most troubled subsamples of schools, students, or families. Although it is important not to minimize the problems that exist for some middle grades schools, some early adolescents, and some families, it also is important to understand the broad context in which these problems are set.

The three sections of this chapter address the following questions: Who are the families in the NELS:88 base-year survey, and how are they involved in middle grades schools and in their children's education? Which schools are in NELS:88 base year, and what are they doing in partnerships with families? Who are the students in NELS:88, and what do they say about family, school, and community partnerships?

The descriptive data yield two topics for summary and discussion: *comparisons and contrasts* in NELS:88 on school and family connections, and *controls and extensions* of NELS:88 that are needed to study the nature and effects of school, family, and community partnerships.

Comparisons and Contrasts: Patterns of School, Family, and Community Connections in the Middle Grades

The NELS:88 data present a national picture of families, students, and schools that overall evokes neither Norman Rockwell nor

Oliver Twist. Rather, the data reveal a mix of strengths and weaknesses in the connections of schools, families, and students in the middle grades.

Most *families* in the NELS:88 base-year sample are functioning, but struggling. Most parents are trying to monitor and guide their early adolescents, but they receive relatively little assistance from middle grades schools about how to do this. A portion of the families (up to one fourth) are relatively isolated from their children's middle grades schools and may have a hard time understanding, supporting, and guiding their children as students. Despite general satisfaction with their middle grades schools, many families believe the schools could challenge their children more and prepare them better for high school, and most receive little information or direct guidance from the schools to enable them to stay involved in their children's education.

Most *middle grades schools* are operating conventionally with few major conflicts, but the principals indicate that teachers have difficulty motivating many students and that teachers and students often have difficulty relating to each other. Few principals report that their middle grades schools conduct comprehensive programs to involve all families in the education of early adolescents. Most schools have some practices, but do not reach all families. Most do not systematically organize their involvement activities around student development or learning.

Most *students* recognize their families' efforts to guide them at home, but report few deep connections between home and school. Many middle grades students are bored in school and many are not assisted to take steps that will help them meet their long-term goals.

The major results are confirmed across reporters; that is, students, parents, and principals in NELS:88 surveys agree that most families are poorly informed and weakly involved in their children's education in the middle grades. There are important correspondences by at least two of the groups of reporters on items that represent the six major types of involvement:

- In their reports about sample Type 1 activities, about 90% of the students and parents agree that families set some rules for early adolescents. Parents and students recognize that families are trying to maintain influence in their children's lives at home in the middle grades.

- In reports of Type 2 examples, parents and principals report that only about one half of the parents attend parent-teacher conferences at the school.

- On Type 3 sample items, all respondents agree that, presently, few parents are volunteers in the middle grades. The schools do not call for volunteers, and families do not offer their services.

- On Type 4 activities, parents and students report that more than half of the families monitor homework. The principals reveal, however, that most parents do not receive much information or guidance from middle grades schools on how to help at home in specific ways. Thus, few parents are well informed about how to interact with their early adolescents on homework. This is important because other studies indicate that parents at the elementary and middle levels are most interested in knowing how to help their own child each year at home (Dauber & Epstein, 1993; Epstein, 1986). A majority of families and students say they talk about school at home, but fewer talk frequently about plans for high school, and fewer still discuss the future. Only about one fourth of the students and parents indicate that they talk together frequently about all of the basic sample topics in the survey items.

- On Type 5 items, about one half of the principals say that fewer than 20% of the parents participate in PTA or parent association meetings. This perception is substantiated by one half of the parents reporting that they do not belong to these associations, and about one half of the students thinking their families attend meetings at school. Overall, more than one half of the families of middle grades students are not involved in school decisions, even on the most ordinary Type 5 activities such as joining the PTA or attending meetings

- Reports on Type 6 sample items suggest that in contrast to a general lack of involvement at school, large numbers of parents and students report being involved in community activities. These reports either overstate connections in the community (e.g., if parents *ever* participate in one activity) or indicate a real contrast in where parents invest their time and attention. These questions need to be followed in focused studies that include more pointed questions about community participation than are available in NELS:88. On another measure of community, about one third of the families are well connected to the families of their children's school friends. Analyses are needed to determine whether this is a good estimate of family interconnections, whether it is sufficient to be linked with one or two (not five) families of children's friends, whether parents may be tied to families of children's friends made outside of school, and the implications of these ties. These issues, too, will require detailed data on children, friends, and family ties.

The national patterns in the NELS:88 data from students, parents, and principals are in accord with local and regional studies that suggest that about 20% of families remain active and knowledgeable partners with their children's schools, and that many more (up to 70% to 75%) could be. Most middle grades schools in the nation give little information to families, and most families give little assistance about school to their children in the middle grades. Without adequate communications *from* the school, many families may not fully understand their early adolescent's potential or options in school, or may be accepting too little from the schools and from their children. Importantly, studies with these and other data confirm that when middle grades schools create programs to encourage partnerships, give information to families, and guide their interactions, more families participate in the schools and with their children and guide or discuss homework (Dauber & Epstein, 1993; Epstein, 1986; Epstein & Jacobsen, 1994).

Despite the agreed-on weakness in partnerships, the three groups of reporters in NELS:88 also agree that there is a base of communication on which to build better partnerships in middle grades schools. Parents and children are trying to communicate at home; schools communicate with some families, and although this is often about students' problems, these communications are a base on which to build more positive linkages; and students are aware of their families efforts and share their families' and schools' goals for education and high aspirations. All of these factors are important for understanding the potential for more welcoming programs and more informative exchanges and interactions of schools, families, and communities to assist more students to succeed in school.

Controls and Extensions: Using NELS:88 to Study School, Family, and Community Partnerships and Their Effects

One goal of this chapter is to describe NELS:88 and HES so that researchers will be attracted to the data. The NELS:88 surveys provide true longitudinal data that enable researchers to ask many questions about school, family, and community connections. The students are followed from Grade 8 through high school and beyond, with information about their schools and teachers in each survey, and with information from families in Grades 8 and 12.

The surveys reveal vast and intriguing variation in schools, families, and students in the middle grades on factors that may influence involvement or that may affect outcomes for students, families, and for school practice. With an understanding of the basic features of the samples, fuller and better analyses of these data can be conducted that account for the important variables that have been noted in each section in this chapter. The descriptive data identify many characteristics of middle grades schools, students, and families that must be considered in studies that aim to explain the following: Which families become involved in their children's education? How do family background characteristics influence different types of involvement? How do school, family, and community connections influence student learning and development?

For example, the descriptive analyses in this chapter suggest that school, family, and community partnerships vary in schools by sector, size, urbanization, grade organization, and population of families and students. Involvement may be explained by parental education, aspirations for children, and other family background variables as well as family experiences with partnerships. Family involvement may be influenced by the characteristics of the middle grades students themselves, including their attitudes toward school, ability levels, goals, and other experiences in school. These variables must be considered as statistical controls, as mediating variables, and in other ways (e.g., as interaction variables) in full measurement models.

Indeed, many of the patterns suggested by the percentages reported here will change when full statistical controls are applied to learn whether schools that serve similar students (e.g., highly educated families, or predominantly Latino families) involve families in similar ways or involve equal numbers of families. Patterns reported in this chapter will change when analyses are conducted with appropriate statistical controls to determine whether families in similar communities (e.g., urban or rural, in the West or South, in areas serving families with low income, in public schools), with similar educational backgrounds, or with children who are similarly successful in school get involved in similar or different ways. Studies may ask, for example, whether there are fewer workshops in public schools (as reported above) after statistically controlling on the size of schools, urbanization, or other theoretically linked variables. Researchers will need to control students' prior skills, achievements, or other outcomes to fully understand whether and how family involvement in the middle grades or in high school affect present outcomes. The picture of family involvement and the results of partnerships will be redrawn more than once as researchers build on each others' work to improve their measurement models to represent the causal paths between background factors, motivational forces, and effects.

Questions about the nature and effects of family involvement (and many other topics of student development and learning across the grades) may be asked about the full sample or selected subsamples of students (e.g., students placed at risk); subsamples of families (e.g., families with low income, as explored by Tienda & Kao, 1994); changes over time in family involvement as viewed by students (e.g., S. Lee, 1994) or by families; or the influence of school level, student level, or hierarchically nested variables of students in families in schools with different characteristics and programs (Epstein & Jacobsen, 1994; Epstein & Lee, 1993; S. Lee, 1994; V. E. Lee & Croninger, 1994; Schneider & Coleman, 1993).

The variations in involvement described in this chapter show that school, family, and community partnerships are *alterable* variables. Some schools, families, and students presently do better than others in how they connect and communicate about middle grades education. Some schools' and families' practices produce greater overlap of the spheres of family, school, and community influence and more shared responsibilities and interactions among teachers, parents, students, other families in the school, and other groups in the broader community. With planning and work, all schools could do the same. Other analyses with NELS:88 and with other data are needed to determine which practices are worth the time and effort by schools, by families, and by the students themselves. As one example, data similar to NELS:88 school surveys show that schools that invest in transitional activities to inform families in the elementary grades about the middle schools their children will attend continue to conduct more activities to inform and involve families through the middle grades and have fewer students who fail in the year of that transition (Epstein & MacIver, 1990; MacIver & Epstein, 1991). Many other effects of partnership have been reported and summarized (Epstein, 1992; Epstein & Connors, 1994a; Henderson & Berla, 1994).

The diversity of middle grades students' families, test scores, attitudes, behaviors, and other characteristics means that school programs of partnership need to include some common and some different contacts with families. That is, schools need practices that provide all families with good information, useful communications, feelings of welcome at the school, a sense of community, ways to help children at home, and opportunities to participate in school decisions. In addition, schools must tailor practices to meet children's and families' special needs, interests, talents, and requirements. Studies are needed on the optimal mix of common and different practices to involve all families.

These and many other questions can be generated and studied with NELS:88 in cross-sectional studies of each grade level in the surveys; in longitudinal studies across the grades from middle to high school to postsecondary activities; in studies of all or subsamples of students, families, or schools. Indeed, data as rich as the NELS surveys prompt countless questions on the causes and consequences of student, family, and school experiences.

Limitations

Despite its richness and scope, there are limitations to the NELS:88 data. Some of these are raised in the earlier sections of the text, such as the question about the representation in the sample of the lowest-achieving or absent students and their families. There are other questions about the adequacy of coverage of topics. As with all large scale surveys, the NELS:88 data tend to be broader than they are deep, with only a few items to explore each of the many facets of school and family life that are addressed in the surveys. Though an improvement over earlier national data on school and family partnerships, the NELS:88 data do not adequately represent the six types of involvement. Thus, parents could be involved in other ways that are not measured, and schools could conduct other practices to involve families. However, the representative items in NELS:88 are strengthened by the inclusion of the same or similar items on the three surveys for parents, principals, and students and by the same or similar questions in the follow-up surveys. Even so, the slightly-to-substantially different wording across surveys of similar items raises problems for comparing the views across reporters and across survey waves.

Another limitation is the lack of detailed information from teachers about their attitudes and practices of involving families in children's education in the middle grades. NELS base-year and follow-up surveys include two teachers per sampled student but focus mainly on academic classroom issues and ratings of the students. This is a serious limitation in the NELS surveys, because other studies have shown how important teachers' views and practices are for understanding family involvement and its impact on students, families, and teaching practice (Becker & Epstein, 1982; Epstein & Dauber, 1991; Hoover-Dempsey et al., 1987).

Thus, despite their immense potential, the NELS surveys cannot be used to address all questions about family involvement in the middle and high school grades. There are reasons for researchers to explore other national surveys (such as the U.S. Department of Education's new Prospects Surveys of principals, teachers, parents, and students in the elementary, middle, and high school grades, and the future National Household Education Survey, NHES, of families) to study practices of partnership. Also, researchers need to collect other, focused data in local, state, and regional surveys or in field studies in order to assess the effects on students, families, and schools of particular practices of partnership over time and in order to explore in greater detail questions that are raised by results of analyses of NELS:88 data.

The richness and problems in longitudinal data with multiple reporters pose enormous challenges to researchers to analyze and interpret the data. This chapter contributes a base on which to build a better understanding of school, family, and community connections and their effects in the middle grades.

References

Baker, D. P., & Stevenson, D. L. (1986). Mothers' strategies for children's school achievement: Managing the transition to high school. *Sociology of Education, 59,* 156-166.

Bauch, P. A. (1988). Is parent involvement different in private schools? *Educational Horizons, 66,* 78-82.

Becker, H. J., & Epstein, J. L. (1982). Parent involvement: A study of teacher practices. *Elementary School Journal, 83,* 85-102.

Braddock, J. H., II. (1992). *Students' extra-curricular activities in NELS:88* (Informal seminar at Center for Research on Effective Schooling for Disadvantaged Students [mimeo]). Baltimore: Johns Hopkins University.

Brandt, R. (1989). On parents and schools: A conversation with Joyce Epstein. *Educational Leadership, 47,* 24-27.

Brian, D. (1994, April). *Parental involvement in high schools*. Paper presented at the annual meeting of the American Educational Research Association, New Orleans, LA.

Clark, R. M. (1983). *Family life and school achievement: Why poor black children succeed or fail*. Chicago: University of Chicago Press.

Coleman, J. S. (1987). Families and schools. *Educational Researcher, 16,* 32-38.

Coleman, J. S. (1988). Social capital in the creation of human capital. *American Journal of Sociology, 94,* 95-120.

Connors, L. J., & Epstein, J. L. (1994). *Taking stock: The views of teachers, parents, and students on school, family, and community partnerships in high schools* (Report No. 25). Baltimore: Center on Families, Communities, Schools and Children's Learning, Johns Hopkins University.

Dauber, S. L., & Epstein, J. L. (1993). Parents' attitudes and practices of involvement in inner-city elementary and middle schools. In N. Chavkin (Ed.), *Families and schools in a pluralistic society* (pp. 53-71). Albany: SUNY Press.

Dornbusch, S. M., & Ritter, P. L. (1988). Parents of high school students: A neglected resource. *Educational Horizons, 66,* 75-77.

Dornbusch, S. M., Ritter, P. L., Liederman, D. F., Roberts, D. F., & Fraleigh, M. J. (1987). The relation of parenting style to adolescent school performance. *Child Development, 58,* 1244-1257.

Epstein, J. L. (1983). Longitudinal effects of family-school-person interactions on student outcomes. In A. Kerckhoff (Ed.), *Research in sociology of education and socialization* (Vol. 4, pp. 101-128). Greenwich, CT: JAI.

Epstein, J. E. (1985). A question of merit: Principals' and parents' evaluations of teachers. *Educational Researcher, 14*(7), 6-10.

Epstein, J. L. (1986). Parents' reactions to teacher practices of parent involvement. *Elementary School Journal, 86,* 277-294.

Epstein, J. L. (1987a). Toward a theory of family-school connections: Teacher practices and parent involvement. In K. Hurrelmann, F. Kaufmann, & F. Losel (Eds.), *Social intervention: Potential and constraints* (pp. 121-136). New York: Aldine de Gruyter.

Epstein, J. L. (1987b). What principals should know about parent involvement. *Principal, 66,* 6-9.

Epstein, J. L. (1988, June). *Schools in the center: School, family, peer, and community connections for more effective middle grades schools and students* [mimeo]. Paper prepared for the Carnegie Task Force on Education of Young Adolescents, Johns Hopkins University Center for Research on Elementary and Middle Schools, Baltimore.

Epstein, J. L. (1991). Effects on student achievement of teacher practices of parent involvement. In S. Silvern (Ed.), *Literacy through family, community, and school interaction* (pp. 261-276). Greenwich CT: JAI.

Epstein, J. L. (1992). School and family partnerships. In M. Alkin (Ed.), *Encyclopedia of educational research* (6th ed., pp. 1139-1151). New York: Macmillan.

Epstein, J. L. (in press-a). Perspectives and previews on research and policy for school, family, and community partnerships. In A. Booth & R. Dunn (Eds.), *Family-school links: How do they affect educational outcomes?* Hillsdale, NJ: Lawrence Erlbaum.

Epstein, J. L. (in press-b). *School and family partnerships: Preparing educators and improving schools*. Boulder, CO: Westview.

Epstein, J. L., & Connors, L. J. (1994a). School and family partnerships in the middle grades. In B. Rutherford (Ed.), *Creating family/school partnerships*. Columbus, OH: National Middle School Association.

Epstein, J. L., & Connors, L. J. (1994b). *Trust fund: School, family, and community partnerships in high schools* (Report No. 24). Baltimore: Center on Families, Communities, Schools and Children's Learning, Johns Hopkins University.

Epstein, J. L., & Dauber, S. L. (1991). School programs and teacher practices of parent involvement in inner-city elementary and middle schools. *Elementary School Journal, 91*(3), 289-303.

Epstein, J. L., & Dauber, S. L. (1995). Effects on students of an interdisciplinary program linking social studies, art and family volunteers in the middle grades. *Journal of Early Adolescence, 15*(1), 114-144.

Epstein, J. L., & Herrick, S. C. (1991). *Improving school and family partnerships in urban middle grades schools: Orientation days and school newsletters* (Report No. 20). Baltimore: Johns Hopkins University Center for Research on Effective Schooling for Disadvantaged Students.

Epstein, J. L., Herrick, S. C., & Coates, L. (in press). Effects of summer home learning packets on student achievement in language arts in the middle grades. *School Effectiveness and School Improvement.*

Epstein, J. L., Jackson, V., & Salinas, K. C. (1994). *Manual for teachers: Teachers Involve Parents in Schoolwork (TIPS) language arts and science/health interactive homework in the middle grades* (rev.). Baltimore: Center on Families, Communities, Schools and Children's Learning, Johns Hopkins University.

Epstein, J. L., & Jacobsen, J. M. (1994, August). *Effects of school practices to involve families in the middle grades: Parents' perspectives.* Paper presented at the annual meeting of the American Sociological Association, Los Angeles.

Epstein, J. L., & Lee, S. (1993, August). *Effects of school practices to involve families on parents and students in the middle grades: A view from the schools.* Paper presented at the annual meeting of the American Sociological Association, Miami, FL.

Epstein, J. L., & MacIver, D. J. (1990). *Education in the middle grades: National practices and trends.* Columbus, OH: National Middle School Association.

Epstein, J. L., & MacIver, D. J. (1992). *Opportunities to learn: Effects on eighth graders of curriculum offerings and instructional approaches* (Report No. 34). Baltimore: Center for Research on Effective Schooling for Disadvantaged Students, Johns Hopkins University.

Epstein, J. L., McPartland, J. M., & MacIver, D. J. (1991). *Hopkins Enhancement Survey (HES) of NELS:88 Middle Grades Practices: Codebook and data collection instruments.* Baltimore: Johns Hopkins University Center for Research on Effective Schooling for Disadvantaged Students. (Available from U.S. Department of Education, National Center for Education Statistics, with NELS:88 and follow-up surveys).

Haffner, A., Ingels, S., Schneider, B., Stevenson, D., & Owings, J. (1990). *A profile of American eighth graders: NELS:88 student descriptive summary.* Washington, DC: U.S. Department of Education, OERI/NCES.

Henderson, A. T., & Berla, N. (1994). *A new generation of evidence: The family is critical to student achievement.* Washington, DC: National Committee for Citizens in Education.

Hoachlander, E. G. (1991). *A profile of schools attended by eighth graders in 1988* (NCES 91-129). Washington, DC: U.S. Department of Education, OERI/NCES.

Hoover-Dempsey, K. V., Bassler, O. C., & Brissie, J. S. (1987). Parent involvement: Contributions of teacher efficacy, school socioeconomic status, and other school characteristics. *American Education Research Journal, 24*(3), 417-435.

Horn, L., & West, J. (1992). *A profile of parents of eighth graders* (NCES 92-488). Washington, DC: U.S. Department of Education, OERI/NCES.

Ingels, S. J. (1989). *CREMS NELS:88 enhancement survey of middle grades practices* (Final technical report). Chicago: University of Chicago/NORC.

Ingels, S. J., Abraham, S., Rasinski, K. A., Karr, R., Spencer, B. D., & Frankel, M. R. (1990). *NELS:88 base-year data file user's manuals* (Student Component, 90-464; Parent Component, 90-466; School Component, 90-482; Teacher Component, 90-484). Washington, DC: U.S. Department of Education, OERI/NCES.

Keith, T. Z., Reimers, T. M., Fehrmann, P. G., Pottebaum, S. M., & Aubey, L. W. (1986). Parental involvement, homework, and TV time: Direct and indirect effects on high school achievement. *Journal of Educational Psychology, 78,* 373-380.

Lee, S. (1994). *Family-school connections and students' education: Continuity and change of family involvement from the middle grades to high school.* Unpublished doctoral dissertation, Johns Hopkins University, Baltimore.

Lee, V. E., & Croninger R. G. (1994). The relative importance of home and school in the development of literacy skills for middle grade students. *American Journal of Education, 102,* 286-329.

Leitch, M. L., & Tangri, S. S. (1988). Barriers to home-school collaboration. *Educational Horizons, 66,* 70-74.

MacIver, D. J., & Epstein, J. L. (1991). Responsive practice in the middle grades: Teacher teams, advisory groups, remedial instruction and school transition programs. *American Journal of Education, 99,* 587-622.

Montandon, C., & Perrenoud, P. (1987). *Entre parents et ensignants un dialogue impossible?* Berne, Switzerland: P. Lang.

Muller, C. (1993). Parent involvement and academic achievement. In B. Schneider & J. S. Coleman (Eds.), *Parents, their children, and schools.* Boulder, CO: Westview.

Muller, C. (1994, August). *Intergenerational networks and academic behavior among adolescents: The role of parent friendships in the lives of teens.* Paper presented at the annual meeting of the American Sociological Association, Los Angeles.

Schneider, B., & Coleman, J. S. (Eds.). (1993). *Parents, their children, and schools.* Boulder CO: Westview.

Stevenson, D., & Baker, D. (1987). The family-school relation and the child's school performance. *Child Development, 58,* 1348-1357.

Tienda, M., & Kao, G. (1994, August). *Parental behavior and the odds of success among students at risk of failure.* Paper presented at the annual meeting of the American Sociological Association, Los Angeles.

Useem, E. L. (1991). Student selection into course selection sequences in mathematics: The impact of parent involvement and school policies. *Journal of Research on Adolescence, 1,* 231-250.

Useem, E. L. (1992). Middle schools and math groups: Parents' involvement in children's placement. *Sociology of Education, 65,* 263-279.

Youniss, J., & Smollar, J. (1985). *Adolescent relations with mothers, fathers, and friends.* Chicago: University of Chicago Press.

Zill, N. (in press). Family change and student achievement: What we learned, and what it means for schools. In A. Booth & R. Dunn (Eds.), *Family-school links: How do they affect educational outcomes?* Hillsdale, NJ: Lawrence Erlbaum.

CHAPTER 5

The Impact of Family Environment on Educational Attainment: Do Families Make a Difference?

JAY D. TEACHMAN

RANDAL D. DAY

KAREN PRICE CARVER

There is a certain opposition between the ideal of equal opportunity and that of family responsibility. Responsibility involves autonomy, which will produce divergence among families, which, in turn, will mean divergent conditions for the children; that is, unequal opportunities.

—*Charles Horton Cooley*
(quoted in Blau & Duncan, 1967, p. vii)

The real explanation of why the poor are where they are is that they make the mistake of being born to the wrong parents, in the wrong section of the country, in the wrong industry, or in the wrong racial or ethnic group. Once that mistake has been made, they could have been paragons of will and morality, but most of them would never have had a chance to get out of the other America.

—*Michael Harrington (quoted in Solon,*
Corcoran, Gordon, & Laren, 1991, p. 510)

AUTHORS' NOTE: This research was supported by grant HD 31723 from the National Institute of Child Health and Human Development.

These quotes, the first from a sociologist and the second from an economist, reflect the importance social scientists place on the family as an agent in the intergenerational transmission of social and economic well-being. Perhaps one of the most commonly accepted facts in the social sciences is that what goes on in the family is important for understanding the opportunities and constraints children face as they grow into adults. Indeed, a substantial body of literature has evolved through attempts to measure the impact of family background, broadly conceived, on subsequent attainment and well-being.

Our purpose in this chapter is to examine how family environment influences educational and subsequent attainment. We argue that the effects of families and surrounding environment on the attainments of children are widely accepted in both lay and professional audiences, but our understanding of the characteristics of families that are important in generating differences between children is not well developed. As one means of expanding our knowledge of the impact of families on children, we suggest the use of data on siblings. The methodological advantages of using sibling data are considerable, allowing researchers to better measure family environment and its effect on subsequent attainment. We explicate the use of sibling data by reference to a simple ANCOVA model and briefly review attempts at using such data to measure the effects of family on child outcomes. We then review the growing literature attempting to define important components of family environment. Finally, we provide an empirical illustration of the power of sibling data by examining the effect of family environment on mental ability and grades using a sample of siblings taken from the 1980 High School and Beyond (HSB) Study.

The Problem

Seminal work in economics on the effects of family background includes that of Becker (1964, 1981), Behrman, Hrubec, Taubman, and Wales (1980), Bowles and Gintis (1976), Brittain (1977), and Harrington (1962). In sociology, Blau and Duncan (1967), Jencks et al. (1972, 1979), Featherman and Hauser (1978), Hauser and Featherman (1977), and Sewell and Hauser (1975, 1993) have all made significant contributions to our understanding of the role families play in determining success in the United States. However, it remains the case that the effects of family background on social and economic well-being remain poorly specified by the parental and familial variables that ordinarily appear in multivariate models of the status attainment process (i.e., mother's and father's education, father's occupation, parental income, mother's employment, family intact or not, and number of siblings).

Consider the sources of variation between children in different families that may be attributed to family background. These include, but are not limited to, genetic heritage; parental financial and human resources; parental standards and forms of parent-child interaction; and a common social environment involving neighborhoods, schools, and time-specific historical conditions (wars, business cycles, local labor market conditions). Even this limited list indicates the diversity of sources of variation in child well-being that can be attributed to families. Indeed, many of these factors may not represent what some researchers would ordinarily consider to be direct influences of the family, but are, rather, more indirect effects operating through accidents of history or the decisions families make concerning residential mobility and so on. It remains true, though, that each of these sources of variation are tied to membership in a family.[1] To avoid confusion with prior research on the status attainment process, we will use the term family environment to reference broader sources of variation between families that accrue simply by sharing membership in a family. Family background will be used in its more limited sense as a measure of sociodemographic characteristics of parents and family composition.

As noted, attempts to control for differences in family environment using variables such as parental education and income are obviously imperfect. Accordingly, to better account for the influence of family environment on child outcomes, a small but important body of research has pursued data on siblings. The earliest use of sibling data to address this question (as noted by Griliches, 1979) appears to be Gorseline's (1932) dissertation. Using a sample of 156 pairs of brothers from Indiana, Gorseline (1932) attempted to ascertain the impact of education on income, net of any biasing influence of family environment. The question he addressed is central to economics—what are the "pure" economic returns to education and does family environment bias estimates of the pure economic effects of education on income? Gorseline (1932) found that families do not alter the rate of return to education.

Although his statistical approach to the problem was rudimentary by today's standards, Gorseline (1932) was innovative in that he argued that siblings share a common family environment. By the dint of sharing a common family environment, differences between siblings in education and income should reflect the pure economic impact of education on income (what is known as the within-family effect), because the effects of common family environment are subtracted out of the model. It is exactly this insight to which we now turn our attention.[2]

A Methodological Approach to the Problem

To better understand the value of sibling data, consider the following simple ANCOVA model.[3] Although simple ANCOVA models are generally unwieldy, they allow the problem to be presented in a very straightforward fashion. Let y_{ij} be the dependent variable of interest (say, grades received in school) for individual i from family j. Let x_{ij} be the independent variable of interest (say, mental ability) for individual i from family j. Let $y._j$ be the mean of the dependent variable for the jth family. Let $x._j$ be the mean of the independent variable for the jth family. Thus, if two siblings are sampled from 100 families, there will be 200 individual-level measures of grades and mental ability (one for each sibling), and 100 family-level measures of each variable (one for each family that is composed of the average of the two siblings' values for mental ability and grades).

Further assume that y_{ij} and x_{ij} have been deviated from their respective overall means so that one can ignore intercepts. The regression of y_{ij} on x_{ij} is

$$y_{ij} = \beta_t x_{ij} + \varepsilon_{ij} \tag{1}$$

where β_t is the "naive" or total regression slope. Note that

$$y_{ij} = y._j + (y_{ij} - y._j) \tag{2}$$

and

$$x_{ij} = x._j + (x_{ij} - x._j). \tag{3}$$

That is, the measures for each sibling can be thought of as being a function of the family-level value and a component that indicates sibling-specific deviations from that family-level value.

Now consider two regressions of y on x, the regression of family means or the *between*-family regression (which in our example would be based on 100 observations), representing variation that occurs between families:

$$y_{.j} = \beta_b x_{.j} + \varepsilon_{.j} \qquad (4)$$

and the *within*-family regression (which in our example would be based on 200 observations), representing variation that occurs within families:

$$y_{ij} - y_{.j} = \beta_w(x_{ij} - x_{.j}) + \varepsilon_{ij}. \qquad (5)$$

Note that this is equivalent to subtracting out the impact of family environment ($y_{.j}$ and $x_{.j}$), thus yielding an estimate of the "pure" return to mental ability.

Adding Equations (4) and (5), one arrives at

$$y_{ij} = \beta_b x_{.j} + \beta_w(x_{ij} - x_{.j}) + \varepsilon_{ij} \qquad (6)$$

where the error term in Equation (6) is a combination of error terms in Equations (4) and (5). By grouping coefficients, Equation (6) can be rewritten as

$$y_{ij} = \beta_w x_{ij} + (\beta_b - \beta_w)x_{.j} + \varepsilon_{ij}. \qquad (7)$$

If one ignores family effects (by including them in the error term), one can rewrite Equation (7) as

$$y_{ij} = \beta_t x_{ij} + [(\beta_b - \beta_w)x_{.j} + \varepsilon_{ij}]$$

$$= \beta_t x_{ij} + \varepsilon^*_{ij} \qquad (8)$$

Equation (8) shows that Equation (1) may be subject to omitted variable bias. In the current context, the naive regression of grades on mental ability may yield a biased slope estimate if families use resources other than income to influence the achievement of their children. No bias will result if $\beta_b = \beta_w$. Thus, we use the term *family bias* to indicate an omission of one or more variables associated with membership in a family that are important determinants of the outcome in question.

If β_b is not equal to β_w, then two scenarios are possible. If $\beta_b > \beta_w$, this indicates that families increase the returns to mental ability over that expected on "purely" economic terms. If $\beta_b < \beta_w$, this indicates that families decrease the returns to mental ability over that otherwise expected.

Prior Studies

Many economists assume that families act in a fashion that will increase β_b relative to β_w. This conclusion is based on the assumption that families seek to decrease innate differences that occur between siblings. As Griliches (1979) argues, "families . . . act as (potential) . . . equalizers. They try to both allocate resources equally between their children and to compensate, to some extent, for the handicaps of the children with lower natural endowments" (p. S61). A similar position is taken by Becker (1964, 1981), although he argues that parents seek to both augment the strengths (by investing more human capital) of particular children and to compensate (by investing more nonhuman resources) for the weaknesses of others. Again, the basic assumption is that parents seek both to minimize the likelihood that any of their children will encounter negative outcomes and maximize the well-being of all children. In terms of the ANCOVA model, the result of parental actions to diminish variation between siblings is that the within-family regression slope will decrease relative to the between-family regression slope.

For example, using a more appropriate statistical approach, Gorseline's (1932) data were reanalyzed by Chamberlain and Griliches (1975). They estimated that $\beta_t = .082$ and that $\beta_w = .080$. In other words, the Indiana data indicate that family environment is not a source of bias in estimating the effect of years of schooling on subsequent income. Because, as discussed above, this is a some-what counterintuitive finding, a number of other scholars have used sibling data to examine the schooling-income achievement nexus. (A review of previous studies—prior to about 1970—on siblings is provided by Jencks et al., 1972.)

In the 1970s, a number of new sibling samples were identified and analyzed. Brittain (1977) analyzed 60 pairs of brothers from Cleveland; Chamberlain and Griliches (1977) examined 292 pairs of brothers from the National Longitudinal Survey of Young Men; Corcoran, Jencks, and Olneck (1976) analyzed data from 150 pairs of brothers collected by the National Opinion Research Center (NORC) and 99 pairs of brothers from Project Talent data; Olneck (1976) analyzed data from 346 pairs of brothers from Kalamazoo, Michigan; Taubman and associates (Behrman, Taubman, & Wales, 1977) analyzed a set of about 1,000 monozygotic (MZ) twin pairs and 900 dizygotic (DZ) twin pairs taken from records on veterans; Hauser and colleagues (Hauser, 1984, 1988; Hauser & Mossel, 1985; Hauser & Sewell, 1986) examined data from the Wisconsin Longitudinal Survey.[4]

The results of these studies are summarized in Table 5.1. Shown in the table are the samples used by the various researchers, the primary dependent and independent variables investigated, and estimated slopes. The slopes reported in Table 5.1 correspond to the relationship between the independent and dependent variable listed. In most cases, years of schooling is the primary independent variable of interest. For economists, income has been the primary dependent variable. For sociologists, occupational status has been the primary dependent variable.

Two slopes are reported for most studies. The first slope, β_t, is the slope that results when regressing the dependent variable of interest on education using all siblings as unique observations. The second slope, β_w, is the slope that results when controlling for family environment effects. In this case, at least conceptually, differences between siblings on the dependent variable in question are regressed on differences between siblings on years of schooling.[5] The difference between the total slope and the within-family slope represents family bias—bias that results from ignoring unmeasured components of family environment.

The slopes shown in Table 5.1 indicate no basis for supposing that families act to decrease returns to years of schooling. There is some evidence to suggest, however, that families may act to increase the income returns to years of schooling over that based on purely economic terms. The Olneck (1977), Behrman et al. (1977), and Brittain (1977) results all support this notion. The Behrman et al. results based on sets of twins are particularly strong in this direction.

Table 5.1 Summary of Results From Studies That Have Used Siblings to Measure the Effect of Families on Child Attainments

Author	Sample Size	Independent Variable	Dependent Variable	Total Effect	Between Effect	Within Effect
Chamberlain & Griliches[a] (1975)	156	Schooling	Earnings	.082		.080
Chamberlain & Griliches[b] (1977)	292	Schooling	Earnings	.074		.069
Olneck[c] (1977)	346	Schooling	Earnings	.067		.049
Corcoran et al.[d] (1976)	99	Schooling	Earnings	.060		.057
Corcoran et al.[e] (1976)	150	Schooling	Earnings	.100		.110
Behrman et al.[f] (1977)	Mz 1,022	Schooling	Earnings	.077		.027
	Dz 914	Schooling	Earnings	.080		.059
Brittain[g] (1977)	52	Schooling	Earnings	.078		.050
Hauser[h] (1984)	518	Schooling	Occupational Status		.066	.066
	1,623	Schooling	Occupational Status		.053	.053
	598	Schooling	Occupational Status		.049	.049
	346	Schooling	Occupational Status		.050	.050
Hauser & Mossel[h] (1985)	518	Schooling	Occupational Status		.071	.071
Hauser & Sewell[h] (1986)	532	Mental Ability	Schooling		.081	.081
	928	Mental Ability	Occupational Status		.032	.032
		Schooling	Occupational Status		.053	.053
		Mental Ability	Earnings		.036	.036
		Schooling	Earnings		.044	.044
	164	Schooling	Earnings		.063	.063
	151	Schooling	Earnings		.066	.066

NOTES: a. Gorseline data on Indiana Brothers; b. 1966 NLSY-M Brothers; c. Kalamazoo Brothers; d. Project Talent Brothers; e. NORC Brothers; f. NRC Twins; g. Cleveland Brothers; h. Wisconsin Longitudinal Study Siblings; Mz=Monozygotic twins; Dz=Dizygotic twins

It is tempting to interpret the slopes in Table 5.1 as providing support for the notion that family environment biases the estimated effect of education on earnings, but two other results call this conclusion into question. First, in an important methodological observation, Griliches (1979) notes that measurement errors affect estimates of the within-family slope much more than the total slope. And the effect of measurement error is to depress the estimate of the within-family slope. Thus, the extent to which the independent variable of interest is measured with error, the within-family slope is biased downward relative to the between-family slope—and the amount of bias is greater for twins than other siblings. In reviewing the studies cited in Table 5.1 (with the exception of the research by Hauser, 1984; Hauser & Mossel, 1985; and Hauser & Sewell, 1986, which came later), Griliches (1979) concludes that there is little firm evidence for a difference in the total and within-regression slopes, although his conclusions are largely based on "back of the envelope" corrections for measurement error.

Second, the importance of this caution is reflected in the results shown from the Hauser (1984), Hauser and Mossel (1985), and Hauser and Sewell (1986) studies. Using a LISREL model that corrected for measurement error, Hauser and colleagues (Hauser 1984; Hauser & Mossel, 1985; Hauser & Sewell, 1986) found that they could not reject a model in which the effects of years of schooling on occupational status and earnings are the same both within families and between families (which is equivalent to equating the total regression slope to the within families regression slope). Although Hauser and colleagues (Hauser 1984; Hauser & Mossel, 1985; Hauser & Sewell, 1986) mainly relied on data from the Wisconsin Longitudinal Study, they also reanalyzed Olneck's (1977) Kalamazoo data using occupational status as the dependent variable. Without a control for measurement error, the Kalamazoo data indicate different within- versus between-family regression slopes. When measurement error is taken into account, the equality of within- and between-family regression slopes presents an acceptable fit to the data. It appears, therefore, that when the biasing effect of measurement error is taken into account there is little evidence for family bias in the effect of years of schooling on either earnings or occupational status.

As noted above, though, lack of evidence for family bias does not mean that family environmental factors do not affect socioeconomic attainment. This is clear from the information presented in Table 5.2, where the proportion of variance in various outcomes attributable to family environment (between-family variance) is reported for several studies. As shown in Table 5.2, a substantial

Table 5.2 Summary of Results From Studies That Have Used Siblings to Measure the Proportion of Variance in Child Attainments Attributable to Family Environment

Author	Dependent Variable	Proportion of Variance Between Families
Hauser & Featherman[a] (1977)	Education	66% between; one half explained by socio-economic variables
Olneck[b] (1977)	Mental Ability	52% between
	Education	59% between
	Occupational Status[i]	49% between
	Occupational Status[j]	37% between
	Earnings	27% between
Hauser & Sewell[c] (1986)	Mental Ability	49% between
	Education	46% between
	Occupational Status[i]	41% between
	Occupational Status[j]	38% between
	Earnings	27% between
Chamberlain & Griliches[a] (1975)	Education	24% between
	Earnings	37% between
Chamberlain & Griliches[d] (1977)	Education	51% between
	Earnings	11% between
Corcoran et al.[e] (1976)	Education	55% between
	Earnings	21% between
Corcoran et al.[f] (1976)	Education	53% between
	Earnings	13% between
Behrman et al.[g] (1977)	Education (Mz)	76% between
	Earnings (Mz)	54% between
	Education (Dz)	54% between
	Earnings (Dz)	30% between
Brittain[h] (1977)	Education	38% between
	Earnings	40% between

NOTES: a. OCG II Data; b. Kalamazoo Brothers; c. Wisconsin Longitudinal Study Siblings; d. 1066 NLSY-M Brothers; e. Project Talent Brothers; f. NORC Brothers; g. NRC Twins; h. Cleveland Brothers; i. Occupational status—1st Job; j. Occupational status—2nd Job; Mz=Monozygotic twins; Dz=Dizygotic twins

proportion of the variance in various socioeconomic outcomes can be attributed to family environment. For education, estimates for the proportion of variance ascribed to family environment varies from about .25 to .75, with an estimate of about .5 being most common. For occupational status, the proportion of variance accounted for by family environment is about .4 to .5. The figure for earnings varies from about .1 to .4, with a figure around .3 being most common.

The studies represented in Tables 5.1 and 5.2 suggest, therefore, that unmeasured family environment is an important determinant of occupational status and earnings, but that omitting family environment likely does not bias the effect of years of schooling (or mental ability) on these outcomes. This is not to say, however, that family environment does not have a biasing effect on other outcomes. Both occupational status and earnings are outcomes relatively distant from family of orientation. Once siblings leave their parent's household, exogenous sources of variation such as accumulated experience in the workforce might weaken the ability of parents to influence variation between siblings. It is more likely that families will bias outcomes that are more proximate to their influence. This is a supposition that we test below. Our empirical example seeks to ascertain the effect of mental ability on grades received in high school. Grades are an outcome more proximate to family influence than subsequent socioeconomic attainment and therefore may be more subject to family bias. To our knowledge, sibling models have yet to be used to examine the effect of family environment on grades.

Our empirical example also seeks to better specify the content of the family environment. As shown in Table 5.2, family environment affects even relatively distant outcomes. However, our understanding of the composition of the family environment effect is meager. Standard measures of family background explain only a fraction of the effect of family environment on education, income, and occupational status. The most common estimates of the proportion of variance in family environment that can be explained by the most common measures of family background range from about .25 to .50 (Hauser & Featherman, 1976; Hauser & Sewell, 1986; Olneck, 1976, 1977). With this in mind, we turn to a consideration of the content of family environment.

Specifying the Content of Family Environment

The content of the family environment effect remains relatively poorly specified. Standard measures of family background explain only a fraction of the effect of family environment on observable outcomes such as years of schooling, occupational status and earnings, for example, in Hauser & Featherman (1977), shown in Table 5.2, only one half of the between-family variance in education is explained by measured parental background characteristics. Thus, a search for variables that help us to better specify the content of family environment remains an essential task.

Several bodies of research suggest directions in which the search for a better specification of family-environment effects might proceed.[6] One research tradition stresses the importance of home environment (as distinct from the more inclusive concept of family environment), especially with respect to outcomes such as mental ability and years of schooling. This literature is largely rooted in efforts to explain how children from otherwise disadvantaged backgrounds (in terms of parental characteristics) become successful in school. Ethnographic evidence from poor black families indicates the importance of efforts on the part of parents to stress the value of education and to provide children with resources in the home in order to do well in school (Clark, 1983). Support for this argument is provided by Baker and Mott (1989), Bradley and Caldwell (1984), Elardo and Bradley (1981), Entwistle and Alexander (1992), Leibowitz (1974, 1977), Menaghan and Parcel (1991), Murnane, Maynard, and Ohls (1981), and Teachman (1987). Net of parental background characteristics, children who come from more intellectually stimulating home environments (as measured by indicators such as the presence of books and magazines, a place to study, and so on) do better in school.

A number of studies have documented the negative consequences for subsequent well-being of growing up in a single-parent family (Astone & McLanahan, 1991; Garfinkel & McLanahan, 1986; Krein & Beller, 1988; McLanahan, 1985; McLanahan & Bumpass, 1988; Sandefur, McLanahan, & Wojtkiewicz, 1992). These studies have found that measures of parental characteristics such as mother's income and education do not fully explain why children who grow up in single-parent families are less likely to graduate from high school, less likely to attend college, more likely to receive lower wages, more likely to marry early and subsequently divorce, and more likely to rely on welfare when they are adults.

In an attempt to explain the residual effects of experiencing life in a single-parent family, a number of researchers have turned their attention to research conducted in developmental psychology. A wide body of literature in this field identifies reasons why child outcomes in single-parent families should differ from two-parent families. This literature also suggests that stepparent families will differ from biological-parent families. For example, this literature indicates that children in single-parent families are subject to more permissive parenting standards for obedience, dating, and sex (Furstenberg & Nord, 1985; Morgan, Alwin, & Griffin, 1979; Thornton & Camburn, 1987), as well as generally less consistent parental expectations (Baumrind, 1966; Dornbusch et al., 1985; Hetherington, Cox, & Cox, 1978; Nock, 1988; Steinberg, 1987; Wallerstein & Kelly, 1979). In turn, children who grow up in families with more permissive and less consistent parenting styles have lower self-esteem and are generally less successful in school (Astone & McLanahan, 1991; Maccoby & Martin, 1983).

As another example, results from child development research suggest that children in stepparent families are less likely than children in other family types to enjoy warm, supportive relationships with their parents, especially with stepfathers (Amato, 1987; Bray, 1988; Clingempeel, Brand, & Ievoli, 1984; Furstenberg & Nord, 1985; Furstenberg, Nord, Peterson, & Zill, 1983; Peek, Bell, Waldren, & Sorell, 1988; Santrock & Sitterele, 1987; White, Brinkerhoff, & Booth, 1985). In turn, children who have warm and supportive parents have higher cognitive ability (Bradley et al., 1988; Estrada, Arsenio, Hess, & Holloway, 1987; Radin, 1971; Steinberg, Elmen, & Mounts, 1989), are more task oriented and more willing to accept challenges in school (Bradley, Caldwell, & Rock, 1988; Estrada, Arsenio, Hess, & Holloway, 1987), and have more positive attitudes toward school (Steinberg, Elmen, & Mounts, 1989).

A useful framework for synthesizing these sometimes disparate findings is provided by Coleman (1988), who argues that family environment is analytically separable into three separate (although empirically related) components: financial capital, human capital, and social capital (p. 109). Financial capital is approximately measured by the family's wealth or income, whereas human capital is approximately measured by parent's education. Financial and human capital correspond to the most commonly used conceptualizations of family background. A central characteristic of both human and financial capital is that they are largely indivisible—that is, they are equally available to all children in a family. Thus, one can subsume parental characteristics, as well as elements of the home environment (i.e., availability of books and magazines), under financial and human capital. In our empirical example, a wide variety of factors that can be thought of as financial and/or human capital are examined (see the discussion below) for their contributions to family environment.

According to Coleman (1988), social capital in the family is measured, in part, by patterns of social interaction, particularly parent-child interaction. Although Coleman (1988) does not define what he means by the nature of relations between parents and children, the child development literature cited above indicates some important dimensions of the concept of social capital—consistency, discipline, warmth. In addition, as distinguished from financial and human capital, social capital is not necessarily indivisible. The nature of relations between parents and particular children can be variable. Age, gender, and biological relationship are all characteristics of parents and children that might influence the nature of parent-child relationships and thus alter subsequent outcomes. For example, a variety of evidence suggests that fathers interact differently with their sons compared to their daughters—the evidence suggests that fathers are more involved with their sons (Barnett & Baruch, 1987; Belsky, 1979; Lamb, 1981; Marsiglio, 1991; Morgan, Lye, & Condran, 1988).

Recent work by Plomin and colleagues (Cyphers, Fulker, Plomin, & DeFries, 1989; Dunn & Plomin, 1991; Plomin, DeFries, & McClearn, 1990; Thompson, Detterman, & Plomin, 1991) indicates that children who grow up in the same family differ substantially in personality and psychopathology. It is suggested that the source of such differences is the differential experience of family environment by siblings. This situation can occur either because children have different relationships with their parents or because siblings experience the relationship between themselves differently. For example, age differences between siblings can pattern the nature of their interaction with themselves and others.

Hauser and Wong (1989), in an analysis of the relationship between measured family background factors (father's occupation and education, mother's education) and a latent common factor for education, found that the effect of parental characteristics on older children was greater than for younger children. Although the evidence is indirect, because Hauser and Wong (1989) lacked measures of parental-child interaction, it is possible that age patterning of such interaction could have produced such a result. Coleman (1988) also argues that due to differences in developmental capabilities younger children are less likely than older children to benefit from interactions with adults. In our empirical example, we examine the effect of family background on both older and younger siblings.

The Surrounding Environment

Coleman's (1988) framework also recognizes the role that social capital outside the family can play. Consistent with the notion raised above that family environment encompasses a broad array of opportunities and constraints both within and outside individual families, Coleman (1988) emphasizes the impact of schools and neighborhoods in the development of relationships that foster social capital. Basically, he argues that the density of social interactions between parents and between parents and institutions in the community that serve to increase closure in intergenerational relations are positively correlated with social capital.

This perspective is consistent with a wide body of literature that theorizes an effect of schools on children's academic performance (Barr & Dreeben, 1983; Bidwell & Kasarda, 1980; Lee & Bryk, 1988; Oakes, 1985). This perspective suggests that characteristics of schools, above and beyond the characteristics of individuals, are important in determining academic success (and by implication, other outcomes dependent on academic success). Findings indicating that the relationship between social class background and academic achievement is weaker in Catholic than public schools are consistent with this position (Coleman, Hoffer, & Kilgore, 1982; Hoffer, Greeley, & Coleman, 1985). Consistent with Coleman's (1988) argument about social capital, Rutter, Mortimore, Ouston, and Smith (1979) and Lightfoot (1983) argue that good schools share a strong sense of community. Other authors suggest that successful schools are those in which teachers are able to create an environment of commitment and consistent social interaction supporting academic achievement.

Efforts to quantify the components of schools that make them successful have not always been successful (e.g., Gamoran, 1987), but Lee and Bryk (1989) found that the normative environment and academic organization of schools significantly affected differences in academic achievement according to social class and academic background. Thus, schools with less variability in curriculum tracking, schools with motivated and committed teachers, and schools with an orderly and effective disciplinary climate encouraged higher academic achievement and smaller differences in achievement according to social class and academic background. It is suggested here that to properly begin the task of measuring such indicators one would need to use a broad spectrum of measures similar to those used by Lee and Bryk (1989) and Coleman (1988).

In addition to school effects, there is a small literature on the effects of neighborhoods on academic and socioeconomic performance. The theoretical impact of neighborhoods is less well defined, but a number of observers have noted that the larger social environment should affect well-being (Jencks & Mayer, 1990; Wilson, 1987). Empirical estimates of neighborhood effects are more difficult to find (perhaps due to the difficulty of defining a neighborhood), although a few exist. Hogan and Kitagawa (1985) found that neighborhood quality (based on a factor analysis of census tract social, economic, and demographic data) predicted adolescent pregnancy, with adolescent girls in higher-quality neighborhoods being less likely to become pregnant. Datcher (1982) found that neighborhood quality, as measured by the average neighborhood income and the percentage of the neighborhood that was white, was important in generating differences in education and income both within and between race groups. A similar conclusion was reached by Corcoran, Gordon, Laren, and Solon (1992), who found that economic attainment was lower for men who came from communities with a higher proportion of families receiving welfare benefits. Garner and Raudenbush (1991), using data from Scotland, report that educational attainment is lower for individuals who come from economically deprived neighborhoods (as defined by a factor analysis of social, economic, and housing indicators of enumeration districts in the 1981 Scottish Census of Population).

Although the literature on neighborhood effects is minimal and empirical results are not well developed, once again one can interpret the evidence as being consistent with the notion of social capital—that is, better-integrated communities with greater inter-generational closure provide an environment conducive to the well-being of children.

The Influence of Genetic Heritage

We noted earlier that our conceptualization of family environment is broad. We have in mind factors like genetic heritage as well as socioeconomic status and patterns of social interaction. Yet, we have not discussed the importance of genetic background. The omission is deliberate, but not because we do not believe in the importance of genetic sources of variation. Prior research indicates that both genetic and nongenetic forces are at work in shaping a wide variety of child outcomes (Plomin, 1986; Plomin et al., 1988; Plomin et al., 1990; Rowe, 1994). Unfortunately, we do not possess the data necessary to clearly separate genetic from nongenetic sources of variation in child outcomes. Thus, the influence of any measured or unmeasured components of family environment that we identify is likely to include variation associated with genetic inheritance. We return to the influence of genetic heritage at the conclusion of the chapter.

Data

The High School and Beyond (HSB) Study gathered base-year data on more than 58,000 high school seniors and sophomores, using a stratified random sample of public, private and church-affiliated schools (National Center for Education Statistics [NCES], 1982). Schools with large proportions of Hispanics, blacks, and disadvantaged whites were oversampled. Following a complex sampling strategy, 1,122 schools were selected into the first stage of the sample in 1980 from a sampling frame of 24,725 schools. Of the 1,122 schools selected for the sample, 1,015 participated. In the second stage of the sample, 36 sophomores and 36 seniors in each school were selected for interviewing. Of the 70,704 students in the second stage sampling frame, 58,270 (82%) completed the interview (12% were absent, 3.1% refused, and 3% had unusable questionnaires). In addition to the basic data files for students responding to the questionnaires, the HSB contains several ancillary files.

The critical file for the proposed research is a twin and siblings file. NCES, recognizing the value of sibling data for sorting through the impact of family environment on child outcomes, sought to identify twins, triplets, and nontwin siblings in the HSB (NCES, 1982). Because the first-stage sampling frame of the HSB consisted of schools, it was likely that siblings attending the same school could be identified. NCES used surname and other items in the student identification section of the HSB questionnaire to determine whether students with the same surname lived at the same address. If the birth dates were at least 9 months apart and the students had the same surname and street address, they were considered to be nontwin siblings. In a few instances, other corroborative information was used to identify nontwin siblings, including a telephone call to the students' home. A total of 810 nontwin sibling pairs were identified. A majority of these cases (704) consist of one sophomore and one senior—the remainder are about equally split between two seniors and two sophomores.[7]

A number of twins (74 pairs) were identified in the HSB sample (i.e., students sharing the same address with the same surname and identical birth date). However, most twin pairs resulted from a special effort to identify twins. Prior to the HSB survey, newsletters were distributed to encourage twins to identify their co-twin and participate in the study. The newsletter was followed by a similar appeal on orientation day for the survey (usually held about a week before the actual survey). School personnel were also asked to help identify twins. A total of 519 twin pairs were identified (445 pairs consist of one sampled twin and one augmented twin, 74 are sampled twin pairs). Approximately equal numbers of senior and sophomore twins were identified.

In all, 1,329 sibling pairs (twins and nontwins) were identified by NCES. A separate twin and sibling file was prepared by NCES. The twin and sibling file contains all of the information contained on the base year file for all respondents to the HSB questionnaire. Two additional items, a variable that identifies type of sibling (twin, nontwin, and so on) and family ID, are contained on the twin and sibling file. Data on the twin and sibling file can be matched to any other HSB file NCES has made available. For this chapter, the school indicator file is matched to the twin and sibling file. We do not make use of a local labor market indicators file due to the limited nature of the indicators available and the difficulty in adequately defining the boundaries of a neighborhood.[8]

The twin and sibling file contains extensive information about parental characteristics, resources in the home, patterns of parent-child interaction, school performance, life-course attitudes and expectations, mental ability, and so on. This information allows detailed analysis of the effects of family environment on child outcomes occurring prior to or during high school. We selected mental ability and grades as our outcomes of interest.

We based our choice of outcomes on the importance of each in the development of educational attainment. Prior literature consistently shows mental ability to be an important element of educational attainment, quite often mediated through achievement (grades) in school (Featherman & Hauser, 1978; Hauser & Featherman, 1976, 1977; Sewell & Hauser, 1972, 1975; Sewell, Hauser, & Wolf, 1980)—that is, individuals with greater mental ability tend to receive higher grades and subsequently more education. However, this body of research has not made use of sibling data and models to examine the influence of families on mental ability and grades.

For our analyses, we made use of the 704 sibling pairs where there is one sophomore and one senior present. We excluded twins and siblings in the same grade in order to examine the effect of age differences between siblings in modifying the relationships between family environment, mental ability, and grades. Although the sex of siblings was available, we did not consider sex differences. Thus, any age patterning we report may be mitigated by the sex composition of the sibling pairs we considered for the analyses presented here.

We also note that the age difference between siblings was limited (on average, about 2 years). This precludes full consideration of the effects of age variation between siblings. However, the 2-year age difference ensured that siblings had not experienced developmental components of family environment at substantially different developmental stages. In addition, assuming that families can more easily compensate for differences between siblings close in age, the likelihood of finding evidence for family bias in regression slopes was maximized.

Measurement and Structural Model

Figure 5.1 represents a basic measurement and structural model for mental ability using sibling pairs as the unit of analysis. It corresponds closely to commonly used multiple-indicator, multiple-outcome

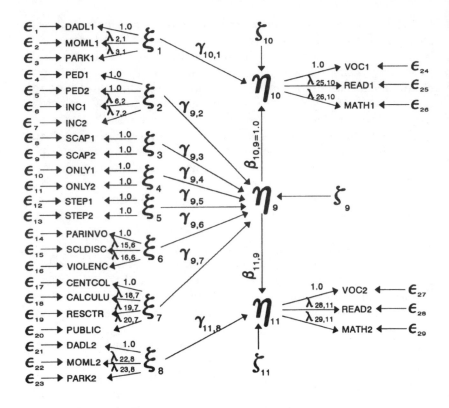

Figure 5.1. A Sibling Model for Mental Ability

models (Dunn, Everitt, & Pickles, 1993; Jöreskog & Goldberger, 1975). EQS (Bentler, 1992) is used to estimate the model in Figure 5.1 and all subsequent models. The structural model in Figure 5.1 can be written as

$$\eta = \beta\eta + \Gamma\xi + \zeta$$

where η is a vector of endogenous latent variables, ξ is a vector of exogenous latent concepts, ζ is a vector of disturbances, and β and Γ are parameter matrices. β is a square matrix of parameters with zero entries along the main diagonal to indicate which is the left-hand variable. The variance-covariance matrix of the ζ is denoted by Ψ. Two measurement models specify the dependence of measured exogenous and endogenous variables on latent constructs:

$$X = \Lambda_x \xi + \delta$$

$$Y = \Lambda_y \eta + \varepsilon$$

where X and Y are a vectors of observed indicators of exogenous and endogenous variables, respectively. Λ_y and Λ_x are parameter matrices, and ε and δ are vectors of identically distributed errors in variables. The variance-covariance matrices of ε and δ are denoted by θ^ε and θ^δ, respectively.

The correspondence between the model outlined in Figure 5.1 and an ANCOVA model is provided by Bielby (1981). In essence, η_9 replaces a set of J dummy variables (one for each of the J sibling pairs in the sample) and acts like a normalized linear contrast representing the influence of the J dummies. As Bielby (1981) notes, a sheaf coefficient for the J dummy variables would serve the same purpose as η_9. By design, the upper half of Figure 5.1 refers to older siblings (seniors); the lower half of the model refers to younger siblings (sophomores).

The model postulates a common family factor (η_9) for mental ability that is a function of measured and unmeasured family environment. Thus, η_9 represents all elements of common family environment specific to mental ability. The most proximate components of measured family environment are parental socioeconomic status (ξ_2), educational resources in the home (ξ_3), household structure (ζ_4 and ζ_5), and school characteristics (ξ_6 and ξ_7) [9] Unmeasured components of family environment are captured by the disturbance term (ζ_9). ξ_2 through ξ_7 represent measured elements of financial capital, human capital, and social capital that are largely indivisible between siblings in a family. The variables (and their definitions) used to measure each of these constructs are shown in Table 5.3. Also shown in Table 5.3 are the means and standard deviations of the variables used. The correlations between these variables are shown in the Appendix.

Parental socioeconomic status is a standard measure of the financial and human resources available to children (Featherman & Hauser, 1978; Hauser & Featherman, 1976, 1977; Jencks et al., 1972, 1979; Sewell & Hauser, 1975). Household structure is a proxy measure of variations in parental interaction associated with absence of a biological father. Educational resources in the home measures attempts by parents to provide a nondivisible intellectually stimulating environment for their children.

School characteristics are included as more distal components of family environment and represent measures of the day-to-day social environment associated with years of schooling and thus the nature of social relationships involving educational expectations and accomplishments. Two constructs are proposed. The first construct corresponds to the degree of discipline and conformity expected of students. The second construct corresponds to the degree of academic excellence associated with the school.[10]

Three measures of mental ability for each sibling are used. These indicators are summary scores on an 8-item vocabulary test, an 8-item reading test, and an 18-item mathematics test. These tests are all subsets of more inclusive tests in both the sophomore and senior questionnaires. Although the more inclusive tests are designed to ascertain the impact of curriculum on learning, the shorter tests are designed to measure ability (Heyns & Hilton, 1982). Moreover, the short tests are designed to be comparable for both sophomores and seniors.

The common family factor, η_9, affects the mental ability of both siblings (η_{10} and η_{11}). Mental ability is also affected by a factor specific to each sibling, ξ_1 and ξ_8. ξ_1 and ξ_8 represent inputs on the part of parents specific to each child. Thus, η_9 represents the indivisible components of family environment, and ξ_1 and ξ_8 represent sibling-specific components of family environment as measured by sibling reports of the degree of parental assistance with homework and general supervision.

There are at least two indicators of each latent construct. In some cases, the indicators correspond to reports of the same variable by each sibling (i.e., variables used to measure the constructs for parental socioeconomic status, household structure, and educational resources in the home). Each of these constructs possesses considerable face validity. In other cases, the indicators correspond to different variables tapping the same construct and reported by the same entity (i.e., variables used to measure parental assistance and supervision, characteristics of schools, and mental ability). In either case, though, the model corrects for measurement error through the use of multiple indicators, addressing Griliches's (1979) methodological concern.

Table 5.3 Means, Standard Deviations, and Definitions of Variables Used in Analysis

Variable	Mean	Standard Deviation
DADL1	0.760	0.427
MOML1	0.893	0.309
PARK1	0.826	0.380
DADL2	0.749	0.434
MOML2	0.848	0.360
PARK2	0.818	0.386
PED1	12.695	2.477
PED2	12.680	2.442
INC1	4.178	1.746
INC2	4.347	1.702
SCAP1	4.396	1.299
SCAP2	4.453	1.321
ONLY1	0.079	0.270
ONLY2	0.067	0.251
STEP1	0.059	0.237
STEP2	0.061	0.240
PARINVO	0.990	0.927
SCLDISC	3.345	0.729
VIOLENC	1.059	1.185
CENTCOL	0.463	0.220
CALCULU	0.501	0.500
RESCTR	0.194	0.396
PUBLIC	0.834	0.373
VOC1	4.822	0.900
READ1	4.846	0.934
MATH1	4.927	0.951
VOC2	5.148	0.977
READ2	5.270	0.975
MATH2	5.181	0.015
GRADES1	5.657	1.521
GRADES2	5.964	1.388

DADL1	Older sib reports father monitors school work (0=no, 1=yes)
MOML1	Older sib reports mother monitors school work (0=no, 1=yes)
PARK1	Older sib reports parents always know where I am (0=no, 1=yes)
DADL2	Same as DADL1 but report from younger sib
MOML2	Same as MOML1 but report from younger sib
PARK2	Same as PARK1 but report from younger sib
PED1	Average of parents' education reported by older sib (less than high school=11, high school graduate=12, vocational/trade/business school after high school=13, less than 2 years of college=13, 2 years of college=14, college graduate=16, MA=18, PhD or professional degree=18)

(continued)

Table 5.3 Continued

PED2	Same as PED1 but report from younger sib
INC1	Family income reported by older sib (less than $6,999=1, $7,000-11,999=2, $12,000-15,999=3, $16,000-19,999=4, $20,000-24,999=5, $25,000-37,999=6, $38,000+=7)[a]
INC2	Same as INC1 but report from younger sib
SCAP1	School capital reported by older sib—Sum of binary variables indicating presence of place to study, newspaper, encyclopedia, typewriter, books, calculator
SCAP2	Same as SCAP1 but for younger sib
ONLY1	Older sibling lives with mother only (0=no, 1=yes)
ONLY2	Same as ONLY1 but for younger sib
STEP1	Older sib lives with stepdad (0=no, 1=yes)
STEP2	Same as STEP1 but for younger sib
PARINVO	School report of parental involvement school—Sum of binary variables indication serious-to-moderate lack of attention to student progress and serious-to-moderate lack of attention to student matters in school
SCLDISC	School report of rules applying to students—Sum of binary variables indicating rules about paying for property damage, hall pass, smoking, and proper dress
VIOLENC	School report of disciplinary problems in school—Sum of binary variables indicating whether there is a serious problem with physical aggression between students, physical aggression between students and teachers, robbery/theft, vandalism, drugs and alcohol, rape and attempted rape, weapons possession, and verbal abuse of teachers
CENTCOL	Percentage of 1978-1979 class now in college
CALCULU	Calculus taught in school (0=no, 1=yes)
RESCTR	School has educational resource center (0=no, 1=yes)
PUBLIC	Public school (0=no, 1=yes)
VOC1	8-Item Vocabulary test score older sib
READ1	8-Item Reading test score older sib
MATH1	18-Item Math test score older sib
VOC2	8-Item Vocabulary test score younger sib
READ2	8-Item Reading test score younger sib
MATH2	18-Item Math test score younger sib
GRADES1	Older sib's report of grades in high school—Mostly As=8 to mostly Fs=1
GRADES2	Same as GRADES1 but report from younger sib

NOTE: a. Students were asked to respond to a question that listed seven categories of income (in 1980 dollars). We simply use the ordinal response indicated by the respondent.

Identification of the measurement model is attained through the use of several proportionality constraints. The loadings, λ, for indicators of the same construct that have the same metric are all set equal to 1.0 (parental income and education, household structure). For the indicators of school characteristics, child-specific social capital and mental ability, only one parameter is set equal to 1.0 due to the different metrics involved. As the model is shown in Figure 5.1, there is no correlation between errors in variables. However, when fitting the model to the data, we relaxed this assumption and found considerable evidence of correlation between errors. We address this point in greater detail below.

The structural component of the model is also identified through a proportionality constraint. As indicated, the slope of the older sibling's mental ability on the common family factor is set equal to 1.0. The result of this constraint is to make the effects of family environment on the younger sibling's mental ability proportional to those for the older sibling.

The information provided by estimating the model implied by Figure 5.1 is considerable, extending beyond a simple consideration of bias in regression slopes. First, the proportion of variance in the mental ability of each sibling accounted for by family environment can be ascertained. Second, the share of variance in each sibling's mental ability accounted for by family environment can be partitioned into a component due to the common family factor and a component due to sibling-specific factors. Third, the variance in the common family factor can be partitioned into an explained and an unexplained component. The explained component can be further subdivided into parts attributable to parental socioeconomic characteristics, educational resources in the home, and school characteristics.

Fourth, the estimated slopes provide important information about the symmetry of intrafamilial processes determining mental ability. By using equality constraints it is possible to determine whether the impact of sibling-specific parental inputs on mental ability is equal for each sibling ($\gamma_{10,1} = \gamma_{11,8}$) and whether the impact of the common family factor on mental ability is equal for each sibling ($\beta_{10,9} = \beta_{11,9} = 1.0$). Finally, the relative impact on the common family factor for mental ability of parental socioeconomic characteristics, educational resources in the home, and school characteristics can be ascertained.

The elaboration of the model in Figure 5.1 to include grades as an outcome variable is shown in Figure 5.2. Because of the complexity

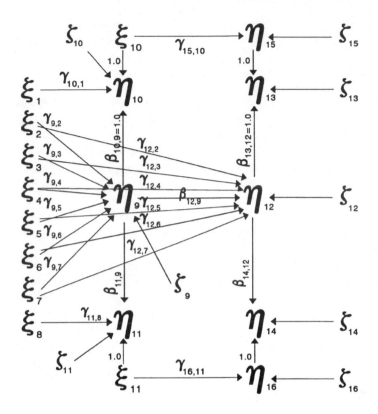

Figure 5.2. A Sibling Model for Mental Ability and Grades

of the model, most of the measurement portion of this model is not shown. Emphasis is placed on the structural relationships. In essence, the model simply adds an additional endogenous variable to the model. As indicated by the measurement portion of the model that is shown, the additional variable is grades (with one indicator of grades for each sibling).

The model in Figure 5.2 specifies a common family factor for mental ability and a common family factor for grades. The common family factor for grades (η_{12}) is affected by the common family factor for mental ability (η_9) and the measured elements of the common family environment ($\xi_2 - \xi_7$). In the upper portion of the figure, the within-family component of grades for the older sibling is regressed on his or her within-family component for mental ability. In the bottom portion of the figure, the within-family component of grades for the younger sibling is regressed on his or her within-family component for mental ability.

The model presented may look somewhat strange in that it appears that disturbances in siblings' grades (η_{15} and η_{16}) are being regressed on disturbances in siblings' mental ability (ξ_{10} and ξ_{11}). This is not strictly the case, though, because the within-family components of both mental ability and grades pertain to true deviations from family levels of these variables (i.e., they are neither errors in variables nor errors in equations). One might ask, though, why not estimate an alternative specification of the model and regress 15 on 10 and 16 on 11? In the special case where the two within-family regressions of grades on mental ability are equal (in terms of the alternative specification, $\beta_{13,10} = \beta_{14,11}$), there is no distinction between the two specifications. However, in the case where these regressions are not equivalent, the alternative specification implies that there are two between-family regressions. We can think of no reason why such a specification would make sense. The specification shown in Figure 5.2 implies only one between-family regression, even when the within-family slopes are different. For a full discussion of both model specifications, see Hauser (1988).

Again, much useful information is obtained from estimating the model represented in Figure 5.2. For example, the variance in grades can be decomposed into within-family and between-family components. In addition, the between-family variance can be decomposed into explained and unexplained components, with the explained component disaggregated further into parts due to the common family factor, sibling specific family factors, and mental ability.

The major extension in the model associated with Figure 5.2 is that family bias in the slope of grades regressed on mental ability can be assessed. The slope, $\beta_{12,9}$, represents the between-family regression of grades on mental ability. The slopes, $\gamma_{15,10}$ and $\gamma_{16,11}$, represent the within-family regression of grades on mental ability. Family bias is indicated when $\beta_{12,9}$ is not equal to $\gamma_{15,10} = \gamma_{16,11}$.

If the within-family slopes are not equivalent (i.e., $\gamma_{15,10}$ is not equal to $\gamma_{16,11}$) then a more complex set of possibilities exist. The relative values of the within-family slopes indicate the extent to which the within-family effect of mental ability on grades depends on the ordinal position of the sibling. The complexity of the comparisons is increased when the between-family slope is taken into account. Possibilities include a between-family slope that is greater than both within-family slopes, a between-family slope that is less than both within-family slopes, or a between-family slope that is intermediate between the within-family slopes.

Results

We began the analysis by estimating a measurement model for mental ability corresponding to Figure 5.1 with covariances between latent constructs and measurement errors constrained to equal zero. Not surprisingly, this model fitted the data poorly. We have no reason to expect that we measured all the influences (random or nonrandom) that would lead the latent constructs to be related. Similarly, by the force of propinquity, it is logical to expect that siblings' reports of parental behaviors and characteristics would be related. Thus, we sought to improve the model first by including covariances between each of the exogenous latent constructs (those for measured family environment), as well as between selected errors in measurement. The nonzero covariances between latent constructs have no theoretical import for our study and simply allow for relationships that might occur without imposing a causal structure.

With respect to errors in measurement, we allowed nonzero covariances between older and younger siblings' reports of each of the indicators of parental supervision and assistance with homework ($\theta^{\varepsilon}_{1,21}$, $\theta^{\varepsilon}_{2,22}$, $\theta^{\varepsilon}_{3,23} \neq 0$). We also allowed nonzero covariances between siblings' reports of parental education and income ($\theta^{\varepsilon}_{8,7}$, $\theta^{\varepsilon}_{10,9} \neq 0$) and between siblings' scores on each of the three indicators of mental ability ($\theta^{\varepsilon}_{24,27}$, $\theta^{\varepsilon}_{25,28}$, $\theta^{\varepsilon}_{26,29} \neq 0$). Finally, nonzero covariances were permitted between the construct for a mother-only family and the error in each sibling's report of father assistance with homework, $Cov(\varepsilon_1, \xi_4)$, $Cov(\varepsilon_{21}, \xi_4) \neq 0$.

The resulting model fitted well, but before proceeding, we tested whether selected equality constraints could be imposed on the parameters of the measurement model without leading to a signifi-

Table 5.4 Summary of Model Selection Criteria for High School and Beyond Siblings: Mental Ability

Model	L^2	df	L^2/df	Comparative Fit Index	Contrast	L^2	df
A. Basic model plus covariances	634.5	339	1.87	.95			
B. A plus $\beta_{11,9} = \beta_{10,9}$	636.2	340	1.87	.95	B − A	1.70	1
C. A plus $\gamma_{10,1} = \gamma_{11,8}$	637.6	341	1.87	.95	C − B	1.40	1

cant decrease in model fit. Specifically, we constrained the measurement parameters for siblings' reports of parental supervision and assistance to be equal ($\lambda_{2,1} = \lambda_{22,8}$ and $\lambda_{3,1} = \lambda_{23,8}$). Similarly, we constrained the measurement parameters for siblings' reports of parental income to be equal ($\lambda_{6,2} = \lambda_{7,2}$; the parameters for siblings' reports of parental education were already set equal to each other for purposes of identification). We also constrained the error variances of siblings' reports of parental supervision and assistance to be equal ($\theta^\varepsilon_{2,2} = \theta^\varepsilon_{22,22}$ and $\theta^\varepsilon_{3,3} = \theta^\varepsilon_{23,23}$). Finally, the covariances between the construct for a mother-only family and each sibling's report of father assistance with homework were constrained to be equal, $Cov(\varepsilon_1, \xi_4) = Cov(\varepsilon_{21}, \xi_4)$.

These restrictions did not lead to a significant deterioration in model fit. Accordingly, we use this model as the baseline from which we begin our consideration of the structural portion of the model. The fit of this model is presented in Row A of Table 5.4. The model chi-square is 634.5 with 339 degrees of freedom. Strictly speaking, the model does not fit the data at the .05 level. However, the sample size is quite large, and it is well known that small differences between observed and expected covariance matrices become significant as sample size increases. With larger samples, such as ours, Carmines and McIver (1981; see also Hayduk, 1987) suggest the use of the ratio of chi-square to degrees of freedom as an indictor of model fit. A model that fits well should have values less than 2.0 for this ratio. For the model shown in Row A, the ratio is 1.87. Also shown is the Comparative Fit Index (Bentler, 1992). For well-fitting models, this index should be greater than .90. We judge from these criteria that the fit of the model represented in Row A is acceptable.

Although not the focus of our investigation, the covariances between error terms appear to be patterned logically. We anticipate most of these covariances would be positive, assuming that family-specific factors associated with propinquity generate the bulk of the discrepancies between true and observed values. Indeed, all but one of the covariances are positive (the covariance between siblings' scores on the vocabulary test is negative, but not significant) and significant (results not shown).

The next model estimated constrains two structural parameters, $\beta_{11,9}$ and $\beta_{10,9}$, to be equivalent. This constraint tests whether the effect of the common family factor on the mental ability of each sibling is equivalent. By way of this constraint, the effects of common family environment on each sibling's mental ability are also equated. Thus, this model imposes considerable symmetry on the process by which mental ability in siblings is determined.

The model chi-square values shown in Row B indicate that equality of these slopes yields an acceptable model (contrasts refer to tests that are conducted by subtracting chi-square values for nested models). Although we have no rationale for expecting returns to common family environment to vary according to ordinal position of sibling (an asymmetrical model), we note that a similar model for educational attainment estimated on sibling data from Wisconsin found that the effect of the common factor (and thus measured family environment) on the years of schooling of younger siblings was only about three quarters of the effect found for older siblings (Hauser & Wong, 1989). Our findings for mental ability suggest that the lesser impact of the common family factor on the educational attainment of younger siblings is not attributable to differences in processes determining mental ability.

The last model estimated constrains two additional parameters, $\gamma_{11,8}$ and $\gamma_{10,1}$, to be equivalent. This constraint tests whether the effect of parental involvement with children on mental ability is the same for older and younger siblings. The model chi-square values shown in Row B indicate that the equality of these slopes cannot be rejected. The equality of these slopes indicates that unique components of family environment have similar effects on mental ability. Thus, although siblings may vary in the amount of unique parental interaction they experience, the returns to such interaction in terms of developed mental ability do not vary according to ordinal position of the sibling.

Table 5.5 Summary of Parameter Estimates for High School and Beyond Siblings: Structural Model for Mental Ability

Concept	Metric Values			Standardized Values		
	η_9	η_{10}	η_{11}	η_9	η_{10}	η_{11}
ξ_1		.001 (.076)		.001		
ξ_2	.201* (.048)			.664		
ξ_3	.016 (.057)			.030		
ξ_4	.017 (.119)			.008		
ξ_5	−.104 (.150)			.040		
ξ_6	−.423 (.510)			−.098		
ξ_7	.139* (.312)			.051		
ξ_8			.001 (.076)			.001
η_9		1.000	1.000		.815	.739
ζ_9	1.000			.642		
ζ_{10}		1.000			.579	
ζ_{11}			1.000			.674

NOTES: Values in parentheses are standard errors.
* Fixed or constrained coefficients.

Overall, the results presented in Table 5.4 indicate considerable symmetry in the effects of unique and common family environment on the mental ability of siblings. There is no evidence to suggest that ordinal position of siblings influences the process by which family environment affects mental ability. With this point in mind, we turn our attention to a discussion of the structural parameters corresponding to the model represented in Row C of Table 5.4.

These parameters are presented in Table 5.5. Shown in the table are the metric and standardized solutions, including error terms. For the standardized solutions, the error terms can be used to determine the amount of variance explained by the model. Explained variance is equal to $1 - \zeta^2$. The model explains about 41% of the variance in the common family factor for mental ability (between-family variance) and 34% to 45% of the variance in the mental ability of each sibling (within-family variance).

It is clear from the parameter estimates shown in Table 5.5 that parental socioeconomic status is the most important predictor of mental ability. Indeed, the parameter for parental socioeconomic status is the only coefficient that reaches statistical significance. Parents with greater financial and human resources produce children with higher scores on our measure of mental ability. Household structure, educational resources in the home, and characteristics of schools do not witness an independent effect on mental ability. In the conclusion to this chapter, we suggest genetic heritage as one explanation for the general lack of effects for our measured components of family environment.

The equations for each sibling's mental ability indicate that the divisible components of family environment (parental supervision and assistance) are not important predictors. Indeed, results not shown here indicate that ξ_1 and ξ_8 can be eliminated from the model without reducing fit substantially. The results also show that the metric coefficients for the common family factor are equivalent and set equal to 1.0.

There is a substantial proportion of the overall variation in mental ability that occurs between families—about 45% for older siblings and 33% for younger siblings. Thus, families are important in determining mental ability, despite our inability to specify the components of family environment that are important predictors. Substantially less than half the variance in the between-family component of mental ability is explained by our measures of family environment.

We now turn our attention to a model that incorporates grades as an outcome. Our point of departure was the measurement and structural model for mental ability represented in Row C of Table 5.4. To this model, we added a very simple measurement component for grades and a series of additional structural parameters. The measurement component is simple in that we have only one measure of grades for each sibling, and we assume that grades are measured perfectly. The initial structural component includes parameters for the effects of a common family factor (η_{12}) for grades on each sibling's grades (η_{13} and η_{14}), the effects of measured family environment and the common family factor for mental ability on the common family factor for grades (between-family slope), and

Table 5.6 Summary of Model Selection Criteria for High School and Beyond Siblings: Grades

Model	L^2	df	L^2/df	Comparative Fit Index	Contrast	L^2	df
A. Basic model plus covariances	747.9	389	1.92	.937			
B. A plus $\gamma_{15,10} = \gamma_{16,11}$	748.1	390	1.92	.937	B – A	.20	1
C. B plus $\beta_{14,12} = \beta_{13,12}$	763.3	391	1.95	.935	C – B	15.20	1
D. B plus $\gamma_{15,10} = \gamma_{16,11} = \beta_{12,9}$	748.3	391	1.92	.938	D – B	.20	1

the effects of each sibling's mental ability on their grades (within-family slopes). Note that we are assuming distinct common family environments for mental ability (η_9) and grades (η_{12}). In results not shown here, we determined that a model with a single common family factor for both mental ability and grades fitted the data poorly.

The fit of this first model is indicated in Row A of Table 5.6. Even though the model chi-square is large, we judge this model to be an acceptable fit given the ratio of model chi-square to degrees of freedom (1.92) and the comparative fit index of .937. In Row B, we added the restriction that $\gamma_{15,10} = \gamma_{16,11}$; that is, the effect of older sibling's mental ability on grades is equivalent to the effect of younger sibling's mental ability on grades (equivalent within-family slopes). According to the contrast in chi-square values between Row A and Row B, this restriction cannot be rejected.

The next model fitted added the constraint $\beta_{14,12} = \beta_{13,12}$. This constraint holds that the effect of the common family factor is the same for older and younger siblings' grades. The chi-square value shown in Table 5.6 indicates a substantial deterioration in fit ($\chi^2 = 15.20, df = 1$). Thus, we reject the equivalency of these slopes. The effect of the common family factor on grades (and of all preceding constructs) is not equal for older and younger siblings. This finding may be useful in explaining why Hauser and Wong (1989) found the effect of parental characteristics on the educational attainment of older children to be greater than for younger children.

Finally, we tested whether the between-family and within-family slopes for the regression of grades on mental ability were equivalent ($\gamma_{15,10} = \gamma_{16,11} = \beta_{12,9}$). Using the model in Row B as the baseline, the contrast in chi-square values indicates that the equivalency of these slopes can be accepted, that is, there is no evidence to support the notion that there is family bias in the regression of grades on mental ability. Families do not alter the basic relationship between mental ability and grades. As indicated below, this does not mean that families are not important in determining grades. However, they do not alter the mechanism by which mental ability affects grades.

We now turn our attention to the structural parameters corresponding to the model represented in Row D. These parameters are shown in Table 5.7. There is little change in the parameters for the model of mental ability. Parental socioeconomic status remains the sole predictor of siblings' mental ability, and there is no difference in the effect of the common family factor on the mental ability of older and younger siblings.

The coefficients indicate that the impact of family characteristics on the grades of younger siblings is only about 40% of the effect of family characteristics for older siblings. In turn, the only significant predictor of the common family factor for grades is the common family factor for mental ability. The effects of the measured components of family environment on the common family factor for grades are indirect through the common family factor for mental ability. It remains the case, though, that for whatever reason, older siblings are more successful than younger siblings in translating parental resources into better grades.

The residuals shown for the standardized estimates indicate that the model explains 50% of the variance in the common family factor for grades and 31% to 34% of the variance in the grades of each sibling. Thus, the model does somewhat better in explaining the between-family component for grades than it does the within-family components. The explained component for the between-family component for grades is slightly more than observed for mental ability, whereas the values for the within-family components for grades are a bit lower than the value for the within-family components for mental ability.

A substantial proportion of the overall variance in grades lies between families—39% in the case of older siblings and 33% in the case of younger siblings—that is, as discussed above, families are important in determining grades. Moreover, only half of the between-family component of variance in grades can be explained by the various components of family environment included in the model. Clearly, therefore, families are important sources of variation in grades, just as they are important sources of variation in mental ability.

Summary and Discussion

We have striven to meet several goals in this chapter. First, we have sought to review some of the literature pertaining to the influence of families on the educational and subsequent outcomes of siblings. Second, we have described the use of sibling-resemblance models for evaluating the effect of family environment on educational and subsequent attainment. Third, we have illustrated the use of sibling-resemblance models using data on 704 nontwin sibling pairs taken from the High School and Beyond Study.

We believe that sibling-resemblance models allow for fuller consideration of the impact of family environment on child outcomes than do more conventional sibling-specific models. Our illustration of sibling-resemblance models focused on two outcomes: mental ability and grades. For mental ability, our goals were to specify several different dimensions of the concept of family environment and consider whether family environment had similar effects on the mental ability of older and younger siblings. For grades, we had the same general goals but also considered whether family environment biased the regression of grades on mental ability.

The results for mental ability suggest considerable symmetry in the effects of family environment for older and younger siblings. That symmetry should occur in the model for mental ability is perhaps not surprising. A wide range of literature indicates a strong genetic basis for determining mental ability, at least under normal child-rearing conditions (Plomin, 1986; Plomin & Loehlin, 1989; Plomin et al., 1988; Rowe, 1994; Scarr & Weinberg, 1978; Thompson et al., 1991). Because the extent to which siblings share genetic heritage (on average, about 50%), and mental ability is at least partly genetically determined, one might expect symmetry in underlying processes. The available literature is also devoid of findings that

Table 5.7 Summary of Parameter Estimates for High School and Beyond Siblings: Structural Model for Mental Ability and Grades

Con-	Metric Values								Standardized Values							
cept	η_9	η_{10}	η_{11}	η_{12}	η_{13}	η_{14}	η_{15}	η_{16}	η_9	η_{10}	η_{11}	η_{12}	η_{13}	η_{14}	η_{15}	η_{16}
ξ_1		-.073* (.063)								-.036						
ξ_2	.199* (.046)			.016 (.095)					.692			.026				
ξ_3	.017 (.054)			-.188* (.115)					.035			-.177				
ξ_4	.032 (.111)			.089 (.255)					.016			.020				
ξ_5	-.115 (.141)			.167 (.319)					-.048			.032				
ξ_6	-.356 (.468)			.741 (1.069)					-.088			.084				
ξ_7	.125 (.291)			.010 (.629)					.049			.002				
ξ_8			-.073* (.063)								-.041					

	ξ10	ξ11	η9	η12	ζ9	ζ10	ζ11	ζ12	ζ13	ζ14	ζ15	ζ16
ξ10												.553
ξ11												.583
η9	1.000	1.000	1.737* (.143)							.813	.743	.800
η12			1.000	.422* (.105)						.688	.319	
ζ9					1.000						.611	
ζ10						1.000				.593		
ζ11							1.000			.679		
ζ12								1.000		.726		
ζ13									1.000	.948		
ζ14										1.000	.709	
ζ15											.833	
ζ16												.812

NOTES: Values in parentheses are standard errors.
* Fixed or constrained coefficients.

191

would indicate a genetic-environment interaction that would lead to asymmetry in the development of mental ability in siblings.

Genetic heritage may also be used to explain our inability to identify and measure components of family environment other than parental socioeconomic status that affect mental ability. If socioeconomic status is positively correlated with the mental ability of parents (see Scarr & Weinberg, 1978), then genetic heritability would lead one to expect a positive relationship between parental socioeconomic attainments and the mental ability of offspring. With parental socioeconomic status controlled, one would not anticipate our other measures of family environment (household structure, educational resources in the home, and characteristics of schools) to be related to mental ability, to the extent to which they do not represent sources of genetic covariation.

This is not to say that family environment, separate from its covariation with genetic heritage, does not affect mental ability. Prior research is clear in noting that the relationship between genetic heritage and mental ability is far from perfect. Clearly, nongenetic factors are at work. However, the components of family environment we have succeeded in measuring do not contribute independently to the development of mental ability. This point is consistent with a substantial body of literature that has found few environmental predictors of mental ability beyond parental socioeconomic status (Sewell & Hauser, 1972, 1975; Sewell et al., 1980).

We also hasten to add that positing a strong, symmetrical influence of genetic heritage is speculative. Although our results may be consistent with such an interpretation, they are also consistent with alternative interpretations. For example, it may be the case that parents, using means that we have not identified, make every effort to equalize the intellectual environment in which each sibling is raised. Or we may have misspecified the nature of the underlying causal relationships involving our measured components of family environment. Unfortunately, we do not have data that can provide a stronger test of the influence of genetic heritage on the processes determining mental ability (see Rowe, 1994, for a discussion of appropriate research designs for doing so). We encourage subsequent research to provide an answer to this question. For now, we remain impressed by the similarity in the processes determining the mental ability of siblings.

The results pertaining to grades indicate that only mental ability witnessed a statistically significant effect. None of the other measured components of family environment had a statistically significant effect (although parental socioeconomic status has an indirect effect through mental ability). This finding is consistent with prior literature that finds a substantial effect of mental ability and nonexistent-to-weak effects of family background (Sewell & Hauser, 1972, 1975; Sewell et al., 1980). It appears that grades are largely dependent on mental ability and not other components of family environment that have been identified to date.

The model for grades also showed less symmetry than for mental ability. Compared to older siblings, family environment is less important in determining the grades of younger siblings. And the difference is substantial. The effect of family environment on the grades of younger siblings is only about 40% of that for older siblings. Why this should be the case is not immediately clear. However, we do not believe that genetic heritability is the source of the difference. If genetic heritability was the primary source of the relationship between mental ability and grades, we would anticipate greater symmetry between older and younger siblings. It is much more likely that nongenetic sources of variation are responsible for the difference in effects by ordinal position of siblings.

Again, we do not possess the data necessary to ascertain the source of asymmetry in the effects of mental ability on grades. However, we can rely on prior literature to suggest that patterns of sibling interaction may provide part of the answer. A growing body of literature indicates that siblings exert considerable influence on each other, especially if relatively close in age. Of importance here is the fact that younger children often imitate and model older siblings, and older siblings are more likely to teach analytical and physical skills to younger siblings (Azmitia & Hesser, 1993; Cicirelli, 1974; Dunn, 1983; Weisner, 1989). Although most of the research in this area refers to sibling interaction that occurs in early childhood, it may be hypothesized that analytical skills learned in tutoring younger siblings, especially those relatively close in age, increase the older sibling's ability to translate available resources into achievement in school. This hypothesis is theoretically consistent with the confluence model associated with Zajonc (Zajonc, 1983, 1986; Zajonc & Markus, 1975). It may also be the case that the process of instructing younger siblings increases interest in and appreciation for formal learning that occurs in school.

Finally, we note that the regression of grades on mental ability does not yield evidence of family bias—that is, the within-family regression slopes (for younger and older siblings) are equal to the between-family regression slope. Thus, the slopes reported may be interpreted as closely approximating the true returns to mental ability.

We close with confidence in the ability of sibling-resemblance models to better answer questions about the impact of families on educational and subsequent outcomes. Databases containing information on multiple members of families are becoming increasingly available. Moreover, many of these databases are nationally representative and include a wide variety of indicators that may be used to measure the components of family environment. We look forward to continued research efforts that will merge methodological and theoretical developments to answer questions about the processes through which families influence the life chances of their offspring.

Appendix Correlation Matrix Used in Analysis

	V1	V2	V3	V4	V5	V6	V7	V8	V9	V10	V11	V12	V13	V14	V15	V16
V1	1.000															
V2	.451	1.000														
V3	.109	.096	1.000													
V4	.295	.080	.107	1.000												
V5	-.019	.138	.096	.567	1.000											
V6	-.001	.038	.067	.235	.228	1.000										
V7	.205	.083	.032	.231	.132	-.041	1.000									
V8	.192	.073	.050	.211	.132	-.029	.945	1.000								
V9	.289	.068	-.073	.206	.034	-.069	.403	.384	1.000							
V10	.224	.055	-.054	.258	.096	-.064	.381	.365	.643	1.000						
V11	.150	.135	.100	.135	.066	-.046	.324	.311	.278	.301	1.000					
V12	.123	.085	.039	.210	.171	.007	.335	.334	.267	.363	.568	1.000				
V13	-.316	.007	-.020	-.337	.043	-.033	-.130	-.128	-.200	-.249	-.022	-.101	1.000			
V14	-.293	.042	-.002	-.336	.026	-.016	-.063	-.068	-.103	-.245	-.039	-.068	.858	1.000		
V15	-.134	.060	-.017	-.028	.083	.119	-.074	-.067	-.088	-.032	-.070	-.010	-.074	-.068	1.000	
V16	-.127	.008	-.122	-.061	.040	.078	-.053	-.048	-.088	-.057	-.053	-.019	-.014	-.069	.704	1.000
V17	.009	.017	-.061	-.100	-.028	.073	-.165	-.185	-.134	-.212	-.180	-.215	.027	.046	.030	.083
V18	-.034	-.074	.017	-.077	-.049	-.009	-.075	-.071	-.095	-.104	-.109	-.097	.042	.046	-.119	-.098
V19	-.019	-.015	-.034	-.006	.012	-.006	.028	.029	-.027	-.041	-.019	.051	.078	.093	.065	.043
V20	.083	.009	.059	.097	.089	-.011	.345	.345	.243	.312	.261	.229	-.048	-.032	-.025	-.071
V21	-.041	-.025	-.083	.051	.017	-.091	.077	.079	.147	.185	.100	.079	-.001	-.001	.033	-.025
V22	-.053	.024	-.025	-.073	-.029	-.080	.011	.019	.033	.035	.082	.093	.004	-.012	-.017	.021
V23	-.051	-.051	-.023	-.038	-.027	.078	-.298	-.297	-.220	-.250	-.265	-.197	.013	.014	.022	.003
V24	.040	-.004	.022	.126	.102	-.008	.326	.318	.207	.170	.180	.241	-.033	-.001	-.089	-.075
V25	.110	-.001	.055	.107	.014	-.059	.362	.355	.183	.195	.222	.225	-.111	-.114	-.089	-.100
V26	.102	.067	.121	.100	.042	.009	.314	.328	.245	.238	.197	.248	-.121	-.070	-.059	-.087
V27	.102	-.002	.068	.121	.096	-.014	.312	.336	.237	.264	.314	.275	-.144	-.113	-.002	.003
V28	.040	.059	.006	.092	.075	.033	.265	.277	.155	.187	.173	.182	-.049	-.019	-.037	-.005
V29	.081	.014	.066	.146	.123	.062	.356	.351	.241	.273	.257	.282	-.097	-.042	-.116	-.084
V30	.075	.061	.144	.068	.024	.032	.275	.282	.154	.083	.109	.131	-.083	-.028	-.059	-.040
V31	.006	.050	.124	.136	.116	.099	.159	.162	.058	.062	.055	.074	-.040	-.016	-.006	.013

(continued)

195

Appendix Correlation Matrix Used in Analysis—Continued

	V17	V18	V19	V20	V21	V22	V23	V24	V25	V26	V27	V28	V29	V30	V31
V17	1.000														
V18	.152	1.000													
V19	.203	.066	1.000												
V20	-.368	-.023	-.067	1.000											
V21	-.195	-.104	-.020	.216	1.000										
V22	-.173	-.081	.022	.165	.209	1.000									
V23	.317	-.059	.180	-.645	-.052	-.157	1.000								
V24	-.229	-.013	-.025	.278	.102	.068	-.312	1.000							
V25	-.124	.044	-.099	.161	.117	-.011	-.218	.514	1.000						
V26	-.162	-.044	-.027	.237	.078	-.001	-.202	.436	.543	1.000					
V27	-.169	-.073	.013	.300	.135	.048	-.277	.359	.358	.375	1.000				
V28	-.138	-.064	.011	.221	.090	.019	-.150	.266	.248	.289	.574	1.000			
V29	-.163	.009	-.001	.318	.084	.012	-.244	.317	.316	.404	.513	.590	1.000		
V30	-.073	-.044	-.078	.154	-.035	.012	-.209	.309	.406	.548	.274	.217	.258	1.000	
V31	-.043	.061	.037	.068	-.094	-.045	-.107	.103	.106	.180	.307	.366	.479	.215	1.000

V1=DADL1
V2=MOML1
V3=PARK1
V4=DADL2
V5=MOML2
V6=PARK2
V7=PED1
V8=PED2
V9=INC1
V10=INC2
V11=SCAP1

V12=SCAP2
V13=ONLY1
V14=ONLY2
V15=STEP1
V16=STEP2
V17=PARINVO
V18=SCLDISC
V19=VIOLENC
V20=CENTCOL
V21=CALCULU
V22=RESCTR

V23=PUBLIC
V24=VOC1
V25=READ1
V26=MATH1
V27=VOC2
V28=READ2
V29=MATH2
V30=GRADES1
V31=GRADES2

Notes

1. Longitudinally, family environment for different siblings is complicated by changes in household structure. Divorce and remarriage can substantially alter family environment. More important for sibling-resemblance models, divorce and remarriage mean that siblings in the same household at time $t+1$ may have experienced substantially different family conditions at time t. Although less common, adoption can play the same role as divorce and remarriage.

2. This insight is not unique to economists. Behavioral geneticists have long known of the value of sibling data to help decompose the sources of variation in human behavior (Rowe, 1994).

3. This illustration corresponds to a fixed effects model for sibling differences. One could also postulate a random effects model (see Madalla, 1981, for a discussion of both fixed effects and random effects models).

4. The work by Taubman and associates (Taubman, 1976, 1977; see also Behrman et al., 1977; Behrman et al., 1980) constitutes one of two distinct bodies of literature dealing with twins. The other body of literature is associated with the research of Plomin and colleagues (Cardon, DiLalla, Plomin, DeFries, & Fulker, 1990; Chipuer, Rovine, & Plomin, 1990; Cyphers et al., 1989; Plomin, 1986; Plomin et al., 1988; Plomin et al., 1990; Thompson et al., 1991). The focus in this proposal is on Taubman's work because it is more central to the concerns of this proposal. Plomin's research is more concerned with establishing the heritability of IQ and its linkages to cognitive achievement.

5. The statistical procedures used to control for family background are varied. However, the analogy that holds in all cases is one where differences between siblings on the dependent variable are regressed on differences between siblings on the independent variable. Note that this is equivalent to the ANCOVA procedure described previously, that is, deviating each sibling's score from the mean value for their family

6. For the purposes of this chapter, we opt for an inclusive list of the components of family environment. For the sake of policy, however, one would want to sort variables according to their degree of tractability.

7. Unfortunately, we are unable to determine from the data available whether one or more of the siblings was adopted, or if they are stepsiblings.

8. The labor market data refers either to counties or to SMSAs. We are hesitant to believe that either geographic boundary corresponds closely to our concept of neighborhood. Moreover, in results not reported here, we were unable to empirically separate the effects of neighborhoods (defined as counties or SMSAs) from schools due to collinearity.

9. Our original formulation of the model included race as a predictor. However, race was never a significant predictor in any of the models we estimated, and we dropped it from further consideration.

10. We began our consideration of school characteristics by including school size and the racial composition of the school as measured components of school characteristics. However, these variables never witnessed a significant relationship to school characteristics and were subsequently dropped.

References

Amato, P. (1987). Family processes in one-parent, stepparent and intact families: The child's point of view. *Journal of Marriage and the Family, 49,* 327-337.

Astone, N., & McLanahan, S. (1991). Family structure, parental practices and high school graduation. *American Sociological Review, 56,* 309-320.

Azmitia, M., & Hesser, J. (1993). Why siblings are important agents of cognitive development: A comparison of siblings and peers. *Child Development, 64,* 430-444.

Baker, P., & Mott, F. (1989). *NLSY child handbook, 1989.* Columbus: Center for Human Resource Research, Ohio State University.

Barnett, R., & Baruch, G. (1987). Determinants of father's participation in family work. *Journal of Marriage and the Family, 49,* 29-40.

Barr, R., & Dreeben, R. (1983). *How schools work.* Chicago: University of Chicago Press.

Baumrind, D. (1966). Effects of authoritative parental control on child behavior. *Child Development, 37,* 887-907.

Becker, G. (1964). *Human capital.* New York: Columbia University Press.

Becker, G. (1981). *A treatise on the family.* Cambridge, MA: Harvard University Press.

Behrman, J., Hrubec, Z., Taubman, P., & Wales, T. (1980). *Socioeconomic success: A study of the effects of genetic endowments, family environment and schooling.* Amsterdam, The Netherlands: North Holland.

Behrman, J., Taubman, P., & Wales, T. (1977). Controlling for and measuring the effects of genetics and family environment in equations for schooling and labor market success. In P. Taubman (Ed.), *Kinometrics: Determinants of socioeconomic success within and between families* (pp. 35-98). New York: North-Holland.

Belsky, J. (1979). Mother-father-infant interaction: A naturalistic observation study. *Developmental Psychology, 15,* 601-607.

Bentler, P. (1992). *EQS: Structural equations program manual.* Los Angeles: BMDP Statistical Software.

Bidwell, C., & Kasarda, J. (1980). Conceptualizing and measuring the effects of schools and schooling. *American Journal of Education, 88,* 401-430.

Bielby, W. (1981). Neighborhood effects: A LISREL model for clustered samples. *Sociological Methods and Research, 10,* 82-111.

Blau, P., & Duncan, O. D. (1967). *The American occupational structure.* New York: John Wiley.

Bowles, S., & Gintis, H. (1976). *Schooling in capitalist America: Education reform and the contradictions of economic life.* New York: Basic Books.

Bradley, R., & Caldwell, B. (1984). The relation of infant's home environments to achievement test performance in first grade: A follow-up study. *Child Development, 55,* 803-809.

Bradley, R., Caldwell, B., & Rock, S. (1988). Home environment and school performance: A ten-year follow-up and examination of three models of environmental action. *Child Development, 59,* 852-867.

Bray, J. (1988). Children's development during early remarriage. In E. M. Hetherington & J. Aresteh (Eds.), *Impact of divorce, single parenting, and stepparenting on children* (pp. 279-298). Hillsdale, NJ: Lawrence Erlbaum.

Brittain, J. (1977). *The inheritance of economic status.* Washington, DC: Brookings Institute.

Cardon, L., DiLalla, L., Plomin, R., DeFries, J. C., & Fulker, D. (1990). Genetic correlations between reading performance and IQ in the Colorado adoption project. *Intelligence, 14,* 245-257.

Carmines, E., & McIver, J. (1981). Analyzing models with unobserved variables: Analysis of covariance structures. In G. Bohrnstedt & E. Borgatta (Eds.), *Social measurement: Current issues* (pp. 65-115). Beverly Hills, CA: Sage.

Chamberlain, G., & Griliches, Z. (1975). Unobservables with a variance-components structure: Ability, schooling and the economic success of brothers. *International Economic Review, 16,* 422-449.

Chamberlain, G., & Griliches, Z. (1977). More on brothers. In P. Taubman (Ed.), *Kinometrics: Determinants of socioeconomic success within and between families* (pp. 97-124). New York: North-Holland.

Chipuer, H., Rovine, M., & Plomin, R. (1990). LISREL modeling: Genetic and environmental influences on IQ revisited. *Intelligence, 14,* 11-29.

Cicirelli, V. (1974). Relation of sibling structure and interaction to younger siblings' style. *Journal of Genetic Psychology, 125,* 37-49.

Clark, R. (1983). *Family life and social achievement: Why poor black children succeed in school.* Chicago: University of Chicago Press.

Clingempeel, W. G., Brand, E., & Ievoli, R. (1984). Stepparent-step child relationships in stepmother and stepfather families: A multimethod study. *Family Relations, 33,* 465-473.

Coleman, J. (1988). Social capital in the creation of human capital. *American Journal of Sociology, 94,* S94-S120.

Coleman, J., Hoffer, T., & Kilgore, S. (1982). *High school achievement: Public, Catholic, and private schools compared.* New York: Basic Books.

Corcoran, M., Gordon, R., Laren, D., & Solon, G. (1992). The association between men's economic status and their family and community origins. *Journal of Human Resources, 27,* 575-601.

Corcoran, M., Jencks, C., & Olneck, M. (1976). The effects of family background on earnings. *American Economic Review, Papers and Proceedings, 66,* 430-435.

Cyphers, L., Fulker, D., Plomin, R., & DeFries, J. C. (1989). Cognitive abilities in the early school years: No effects of shared environment between parents and offspring. *Intelligence, 13,* 369-386.

Datcher, L. (1982). Effects of community and family background on achievement. *Review of Economics and Statistics, 64,* 32-41.

Dornbusch, S., Carlsmith, J. M., Bushwall, S., Ritter, P., Leiderman, H., Hastorf, A., & Gross, R. (1985). Single parents, extended households and the control of adolescents. *Child Development, 56,* 326-341.

Dunn, G., Everitt, E., & Pickles, A. (1993). *Modelling covariances and latent variables using EQS.* London: Chapman & Hall.

Dunn, J. (1983). Sibling relationships in early childhood. *Child Development, 54,* 787-811.

Dunn, J., & Plomin, R. (1991). Why are siblings so different? The significance of differences in sibling experience within the family. *Family Process, 30,* 271-283.

Elardo, R., & Bradley, R. (1981). The home observation for measurement of the environment (HOME) scale: A review of research. *Developmental Review, 1,* 113-145.

Entwistle, D., & Alexander, K. (1992). Summer setback: Race, poverty, school composition and mathematics achievement in the first two years of school. *American Sociological Review, 57,* 72-84.

Estrada, P., Arsenio, W., Hess, R., & Holloway, S. (1987). Affective quality of the mother-child relationship: Longitudinal consequences for children's school-relevant cognitive functioning. *Developmental Psychology, 23,* 210-215.

Featherman, D., & Hauser, R. (1978). *Opportunity and change.* New York: Academic Press.

Furstenberg, F., & Nord, C. (1985). Parenting apart: Patterns of childrearing after marital disruption. *Journal of Marriage and the Family, 47,* 893-904.

Furstenberg, F., Nord, C., Peterson, J., & Zill, N. (1983). The life course of children of divorce: Marital disruption and parental contact. *American Sociological Review, 48,* 656-668.

Gamoran, A. (1987). The stratification of high school learning opportunities. *Sociology of Education, 60,* 135-155.

Garfinkel, I., & McLanahan, S. (1986). *Single mothers and their children.* Washington, DC: Urban Institute Press.

Garner, C., & Raudenbush, S. (1991). Neighborhood effects on educational attainment: A multilevel analysis. *Sociology of Education, 64,* 251-262.

Gorseline, D. (1932). *The effect of schooling upon income.* Bloomington: Indiana University Press.

Griliches, Z. (1979). Sibling models and data in economics: Beginning of a survey. *Journal of Political Economy, 87,* S37-S64.

Harrington, M. (1962). *The other America: Poverty in the United States.* Baltimore: Penguin.

Hauser, R. (1984). Some cross-population comparisons of family bias in the effects of schooling on occupational success. *Social Science Research, 13,* 159-187.

Hauser, R. (1988). A note on two models of sibling resemblance. *American Journal of Sociology, 93,* 1401-1423.

Hauser, R., & Featherman, D. (1976). Equality of schooling: Trends and prospects. *Sociology of Education, 49,* 99-120.

Hauser, R., & Featherman, D. (1977). *The process of stratification.* New York: Academic Press.

Hauser, R., & Mossel, P. (1985). Fraternal resemblance in educational attainment and occupational status. *American Journal of Sociology, 91,* 650-671.

Hauser, R., & Sewell, W. (1986). Family effects in simple models of education, occupational status and earnings: Findings from the Wisconsin and Kalamazoo studies. *Journal of Labor Economics, 4,* S83-S115.

Hauser, R., & Wong, R. S.-K. (1989). Sibling resemblance and intersibling effects in educational attainment. *Sociology of Education, 62,* 149-171.

Hayduk, L. (1987). *Structural equation modelling with LISREL.* Baltimore: Johns Hopkins University Press.

Hetherington, E. M., Cox, M., & Cox, R. (1978). The aftermath of divorce. In J. Stevens & M. Matthews (Eds.), *Mother-child father-child relationships* (pp. 149-176). Washington, DC: National Association for the Education of Young People.

Heyns, B., & Hilton, T. (1982). The cognitive tests for High School and Beyond: An assessment. *Sociology of Education, 55,* 89-102.

Hoffer, T., Greeley, A., & Coleman, J. (1985). Achievement growth in public and Catholic school. *Sociology of Education, 58,* 74-97.

Hogan, D., & Kitagawa, E. (1985). The impact of social status, family structure and neighborhood on the fertility of black adolescents. *American Journal of Sociology, 90,* 825-855.

Jencks, C., Bartlett, S., Corcoran, M., Crouse, J., Eaglesfield, D., Jackson, G., McClelland, K., Mueser, P., Olneck, M., Swartz, J., Ward, S., & Williams, J. (1979). *Who gets ahead? The determinants of economic success in America.* New York: Basic Books.

Jencks, C., & Mayer, S. (1990). The social consequences of growing up in a poor neighborhood. In L. Lynn & M. McGeary (Eds.), *Inner-city poverty in the United States* (pp. 91-117). Washington, DC: National Academy Press.

Jencks, C., Smith, M., Acland, H., Bane, M., Cohen, D., Gintis, H., Heyns, B., & Michelson, S. (1972). *Inequality: A reassessment of family and schooling in America.* New York: Basic Books.

Jöreskog, K., & Goldberger, A. (1975). Estimation of a model with multiple indicators and multiple causes of a single latent variable. *Journal of the American Statistical Association, 70,* 631-639.

Krein, S., & Beller, A. (1988). Educational attainment of children from single parent families: Differences by exposure, gender and race. *Demography, 25,* 221-234.

Lamb, M. (1981). Fathers and child development: An integrative overview. In M. Lamb (Ed.), *The role of the father in child development* (pp. 1-70). New York: John Wiley.

Lee, V., & Bryk, A. (1988). Curriculum tracking as mediating the social distribution of high school achievement. *Sociology of Education, 61,* 78-94.

Lee, V., & Bryk, A. (1989). A multilevel model of the social distribution of high school achievement. *Sociology of Education, 62,* 172-192.

Leibowitz, A. (1974). Home investments in children. *Journal of Political Economy, 82,* S111-S131.

Leibowitz, A. (1977). Parental inputs and children's achievement. *Journal of Human Resources, 12,* 242-251.

Lightfoot, S. (1983). *The good high school: Portraits of character and culture.* New York: Basic Books.

Madalla, G. (1981). *Limited dependent and qualitative variables in econometrics.* Cambridge, UK: Cambridge University Press

Maccoby, E., & Martin, J. (1983). Socialization in the context of the family: Parent-child interaction. In E. M. Hetherington (Ed.), *Handbook of child psychology* (pp. 1-101). New York: John Wiley.

Marsiglio, W. (1991). Paternal engagement activities with minor children. *Journal of Marriage and the Family, 53,* 973-986.

McLanahan, S. (1985). Family structure and the intergenerational transmission of poverty. *American Journal of Sociology, 90,* 873-901.

McLanahan, S., & Bumpass, L. (1988). Intergenerational consequences of family disruption. *American Journal of Sociology, 94,* 130-152.

Menaghan, E., & Parcel, T. (1991). Determining children's home environments: The impact of maternal characteristics and current occupational and family conditions. *Journal of Marriage and the Family, 53,* 417-431.

Morgan, S. P., Lye, D., & Condran, G. (1988). Sons, daughters and the risk of marital dissolution. *American Journal of Sociology, 94,* 110-129.

Morgan, W., Alwin, D., & Griffin, L. (1979). Social origins, parental values and the transmission of inequality. *American Journal of Sociology, 85,* 156-166.

Murnane, R., Maynard, R., & Ohls, J. (1981). Home resources and children's achievement. *Review of Economics and Statistics, 63,* 369-377.

National Center for Education Statistics (NCES). (1982). *High school and beyond: Twins and siblings' file users' manual.* Washington, DC: U.S. Department of Education.

Nock, S. (1988). The family and hierarchy. *Journal of Marriage and the Family, 50,* 957-966.

Oakes, J. (1985). *Keeping track: How schools structure inequality.* New Haven, CT: Yale University Press.

Olneck, M. (1976). *The determinants of educational attainment and adult status among brothers: The Kalamazoo study.* Unpublished doctoral dissertation, Harvard University.

Olneck, M. (1977). On the use of sibling data to estimate the effects of family background, cognitive skills and schooling: Results from the Kalamazoo brothers study. In P. Taubman (Ed.), *Kinometrics: Determinants of socioeconomic success within and between families* (pp. 125-168). New York: North-Holland.

Peek, C., Bell, N., Waldren, T., & Sorell, G. (1988). Patterns of functioning in families of remarried and first-married couples. *Journal of Marriage and the Family, 50,* 699-708.

Plomin, R. (1986). *Development, genetics, and psychology.* Hillsdale, NJ: Lawrence Erlbaum.

Plomin, R., DeFries, J. C., & Fulker, D. (1988). *Nature and nurture during infancy and early childhood.* New York: Cambridge University Press.

Plomin, R., DeFries, J. C., & McClearn, G. E. (1990). *Behavioral genetics: A primer.* New York: W. H. Freeman.

Plomin, R., & Loehlin, J. C. (1989). Direct and indirect IQ heritability estimates: A puzzle. *Behavior Genetics, 19,* 331-342.

Radin, N. (1971). Maternal warmth, achievement motivation and cognitive functioning in lower-class pre-school children. *Child Development, 42,* 1560-1565.

Rowe, David. (1994). *The limits of family influence.* New York: Guilford.

Rutter, M., Mortimore, P., Ouston, J., & Smith, A. (1979). *Fifteen thousand hours.* Cambridge, MA: Harvard University Press.

Sandefur, G., McLanahan, S., & Wojtkiewicz, R. (1992). The effects of parental marital status during adolescence on high school graduation. *Social Forces, 71,* 103-122.

Santrock, J., & Sitterele, K. (1987). Parent-child relationships in stepmother families. In K. Pasley & M. Ihinger-Tallman (Eds.), *Remarriage and stepparenting: Current research and theory* (pp. 273-299). New York: Guilford.

Scarr, S., & Weinberg, R. (1978). The influence of "family background" on intellectual attainment. *American Sociological Review, 43,* 674-692.

Sewell, W., & Hauser, R. (1972). Causes and consequences of higher education: Models of the status attainment process. *American Journal of Agricultural Economics, 54,* 851-861.

Sewell, W., & Hauser, R. (1975). *Education, occupation, and earnings: Achievement in the early career.* New York: Academic Press.

Sewell, W., & Hauser, R. (1993). *A review of the Wisconsin Longitudinal Study of Social and Psychological Factors in Aspirations and Achievements, 1963-1993* (CDE Working Paper, 92-1). Madison: University of Wisconsin.

Sewell, W., Hauser, R., & Wolf, W. (1980). Sex, schooling, and occupational status. *American Journal of Sociology, 86,* 551-861.

Solon, G., Corcoran, M., Gordon, R., & Laren, D. (1991). A longitudinal analysis of sibling correlations in economic status. *Journal of Human Resources, 26,* 509-534.

Steinberg, L. (1987). Single parents, stepparents, and the susceptibility of adolescents to antisocial peer pressure. *Child Development, 58,* 269-275.

Steinberg, L., Elmen, J., & Mounts, N. (1989). Authoritative parenting, psychosocial maturity, and academic success among adolescents. *Child Development, 60,* 1424-1436.

Taubman, P. (1976). The determinants of earnings: Genetics, family, and other environments—A study of white male twins. *American Economic Review, 66,* 858-870.

Taubman, P. (Ed.). (1977). *Kinometrics: Determinants of socioeconomic success within and between families.* New York: North-Holland.

Teachman, J. (1987). Family background, educational resources, and educational attainment. *American Sociological Review, 52,* 548-557.

Thompson, L., Detterman, D., & Plomin, R. (1991). Associations between cognitive abilities and scholastic achievement: Genetic overlap but environmental differences. *Psychological Science, 2,* 158-165.

Thornton, A., & Camburn, D. (1987). The influence of the family on premarital sexual attitudes and behavior. *Demography, 24,* 323-340.

Wallerstein, J., & Kelly, J. (1979). *Surviving the break-up: How children and parents cope with divorce.* New York: Basic Books.

Weisner, T. (1989). Comparing sibling relationships across cultures. In P. Zukow (Ed.), *Sibling interaction across cultures: Theoretical and methodological issues* (pp. 11-25). New York: Springer-Verlag.

White, L., Brinkerhoff, D., & Booth, A. (1985). The effect of marital disruption on children's attachment to parents. *Journal of Family Issues, 6,* 5-22.

Wilson, W. (1987). *The truly disadvantaged: The inner city, the underclass, and public policy.* Chicago: University of Chicago Press.

Zajonc, R. (1983). Validating the confluence model. *Psychological Review, 82,* 74-84.

Zajonc, R. (1986). Family configuration and intelligence. *Science, 192,* 227-236.

Zajonc, R., & Markus, G. (1975). Birth order and intellectual development. *Psychological Review, 82,* 74-88.

PART II

Issues

High Achievement, Underachievement, and Learning Disabilities: A Family Systems Model

ROBERT-JAY GREEN

In this chapter, I present an ecosystemic model of children's academic achievement that addresses the entire achievement continuum (from high to low), including "nonspecific" underachievement as well as specific learning disabilities (LD). In this model, achievement-related actions of the child, the family, and the community are viewed as interacting elements that can amplify one another's effects for better or worse.

The model is focused on four main dimensions of a family's learning environment that may influence the child's achievement in school: (a) family communication deviances, (b) family structure, (c) family attributions, and (d) family intellectual/achievement orientation. In addition, these four dimensions of family interaction

AUTHOR'S NOTE: Over the last 10 years, many colleagues and doctoral students have contributed to the research reviewed here. I especially would like to acknowledge the efforts of Jeanne Xena Brenna, Patricia Ditton, Julie Hagmann-Lasher, Jennifer Moore-McDowell, Patricia Mittelstadt, Roxanne Okun, Paul Richard Perkins, Uma Ratnam, John M. Shields, Margaret T. Singer, Gerald Whitmore, and Marilyn Commerford Wilts. Also, I am grateful to the following colleagues who served as members and consultants on various students' dissertation projects: Patricia Ditton, Margaret T. Singer, Bruce Cooper, Valata Jenkins-Monroe, Josephine Arasteh, Pat Canson, Harriet Curtis Boles, Yvette Flores-Ortiz, Dianne Adams, Daniel Taube, Cheryl Polk, and Christopher Tori.

are embedded in, and partially determined by, larger sociocultural and community patterns related to academic achievement.

In what follows, theory and research related to each of these family dimensions are reviewed, including studies of African American inner-city families, white middle-class suburban families, and families in Finland. At the end of the chapter, treatment guidelines are suggested. The main question before us is: What aspects of family interaction are likely to cocreate, comaintain, or coamplify a child's achievement behaviors in school?

Points of Departure

All of the theory and research reviewed in this chapter draws on three underlying ideas or basic premises. The first is that the family is the *original and primary classroom experience* in a child's life. A child's cognitive functioning and behavior in school reflect family interaction patterns—especially family interaction in task-oriented, instructional, and intellectual/achievement situations at home.

The second premise is that diagnostic categories such as *underachievement* and *specific learning disabilities* (and criteria for their application) are socially constructed within families, school districts, communities, professional organizations, and subcultures within the larger society. In particular, the assignment of the label learning disability frequently requires a high level of causal inference, depends a great deal on the practitioner's clinical judgment, and relies heavily on local customs and resources. The biomedical way in which LD has been defined often obscures its substantial areas of overlap with nonspecific underachievement. The unfortunate consequence of this medicalization is that theory and research about LD have become too restricted in focus and separated too exclusively from general theories about achievement. In this chapter, I argue for a broadened multidimensional approach to all forms of underachievement rather than a narrow search for indicators of biomedical malfunction.

Third, the work reported in this chapter begins with the view that achievement does not occur in a social vacuum. Rather, it is inseparable from patterns of interaction in larger social systems. An adequate theory of achievement—one that could serve as a basis for comprehensive intervention programs—would use at least three interrelated levels of analysis: (a) *individual* (genetic, psychophysiological, cognitive, emotional, motivational, behavioral), (b) *social network* (nuclear families, extended families, peer relations, school classrooms, neighborhoods, parents' work setting), and (c) *sociocultural/political/economic* (particularly social class, race, gender, and intergroup relations within the society at large).

In the remainder of this section, these three "great notions" will be explored further. Subsequently, a specific application of these basic ideas will be presented in a model connecting processes of family interaction to academic achievement.

A Guiding Metaphor

The theoretical model presented later in this chapter has been guided by a single organizing metaphor—the *family as the primary classroom* in a child's education. This metaphor underscores aspects of family interaction that may contribute to a child's level of achievement in school. Using this metaphor, parents are viewed as the child's primary *teachers,* and siblings are viewed as *primary classmates.* Questions to consider include:

- What is the family "classroom's" composition? How many "teachers" and "teacher's aides" (parents and other adult caregivers) are involved in teaching the "students" (siblings)? What is the "classroom size" (number of siblings), and what is the age/ability range of the "student group"?
- What has been the parents' preparation for "teaching" children and for modeling an achievement orientation? What was the academic achievement orientation in each parent's own family-of-origin, and what has been the parent's own educational/occupational success?
- What are the parents' "instructional methods" (styles and clarity of communication in instructional situations at home)?
- What are the parent's "classroom management techniques" (family structure, parental authority)?
- What are the parents' beliefs about the causes of their children's academic successes or failures (causal attributions)?
- What are the parents' achievement expectations for their "students' " performance?
- How actively do parents monitor, socially reinforce, and engage with "students' " intellectual/achievement interests?

- What are the content areas ("subjects") in the family's "curriculum" (such as recurrent topics of conversation and shared activities)?
- What "educational materials" in the home are provided to enrich the "classroom" learning environment (toys, books, chemistry sets, pets, magazines, computers, television)?
- How is this particular family "classroom" affected by the characteristics of the larger "educational institutions" in which it is embedded (e.g., the surrounding community's and culture's achievement norms, social stability, economic resources, leadership, prescribed "curricula")?

The family-as-classroom metaphor helps clarify how the child's cognitive style and behavior at school may be coherent with family and community patterns, and it highlights areas for possible intervention.[1]

The Social Construction of Underachievement and Learning Disabilities (LD)

To familiarize readers with the central ideas in the field of underachievement, the major definitional issues and controversies in this field are described below. Since the passage of Public Law 94-142, the Education for All Handicapped Children Act (Office of Education, 1976), the emphasis of much theory and research in the area of academic underachievement has been on children's learning disabilities. Therefore, basic notions of LD, as a subtype of underachievement, are reviewed and critiqued here.

Underachievement may be defined as a significant discrepancy between the child's apparent *potential to achieve* in school ("intelligence") and his or her *actual achievement*. Underachievement can result from any one, or a combination, of the following four child variables: (a) lack of effort, (b) performance anxiety, (c) attention deficits, or (d) information-processing deficits (difficulties in perceiving, comprehending, storing, categorizing, retrieving, or coordinating information).

LD is a subcategory of underachievement in which the child's less-than-expected academic performance is attributed to attention deficits and/or information-processing deficits that interfere with the child's use of language, whether written, spoken, or received. LD includes diagnostic labels such as perceptual handicaps, minimal brain dysfunction, dyslexia, developmental speech disorders, and developmental coordination disorders. The causes of LD are presumed to be genetic, neurological, or biochemical (rather than environmental, emotional, motivational, cultural, economic, or educational). By contrast, underachievement *not* related to LD typically is attributed to the child's lack of effort or to performance anxiety.

The ultimate decision to place children into LD classes is made by a school committee on the handicapped, which usually is composed of a school administrator, a school psychologist, a special education teacher, a speech pathologist, and one or both of the particular child's parents. Many of the tests used to assess LD are unstandardized, and no typical battery of tests has won the allegiance of the field at large. To receive LD class placement, a child must show a "significant discrepancy" between scores on tests of intelligence (IQ) and achievement tests. Keogh (1982) reports that out of 408 studies, more than 1,400 different diagnostic methods had been used to select LD children (including 40 different IQ tests and 79 different achievement tests). Only a small minority (estimated at about 5%) of LD cases show demonstrable neurological dysfunction, although LD theories usually presume some underlying neurological deficit (Hagin, Beecher, & Silver, 1982).

LD has been attributed to genetic, biochemical, neurological, behavioral, motivational, attributional, and information-processing deficits (Das, Mulcahy, & Wall, 1982; Kavanagh & Truss, 1988; Kolligian & Sternberg, 1986). This theoretical heterogeneity creates lack of consensus on definitional criteria, even though all of the definitions share the premise that LD is caused by factors *intrinsic* to the child. The case-by-case determination of LD and special education class placement frequently involve considerable subjective judgment and school politics.

It is important to keep in mind that the criteria for achievement (or underachievement) are *socially defined and labeled* by actual persons who base their judgments on cultural standards and values within a given family, classroom, school, school district, and community. Thus, performance defined as underachievement by some parents and school systems would not be considered problematic or seriously so in other contexts. Many children fitting the diagnostic criteria for LD class placement come from economically deprived backgrounds and have had inadequate schooling, and the LD exclusionary criterion "not due to environmental/economic disadvantage" is impossible to rule out in these cases.

Moreover, the field of LD remains uniquely wedded to intraindividual conceptual models. Yet almost everywhere else one looks, behavioral genetics and family systems research are demonstrating that both individual heredity *and* family environment play significant roles in the development of both cognitive abilities and emotional disorders (Plomin, 1989; Tienari et al., 1987). There is no reason to expect otherwise for LD. One needs to keep in mind that broad diagnostic categories such as learning disability encompass a wider variety of persons and symptoms than single labels imply. Although most cases of LD may be a complex function of biological *and* environmental factors, some subtypes may be nearly exclusively the result of biological *or* environmental factors (Green, 1988, 1990).

For these reasons, it seems premature to create artificial boundaries around information-processing, neurological, motivational, emotional, and socioeconomic components of underachievement. These four aspects (or a subset) seem so intertwined in the majority of cases that a multiaxial approach to definitional criteria seems most appropriate at this time. Except for cases of measurable neurological impairment, mental retardation, pervasive developmental disorders (e.g., autism), visual or hearing handicaps, and other measurable organic dysfunctions, it is arbitrary to assume that the causes of underachievement are purely intrinsic to the child and due solely to neurological dysfunction (Coles, 1988; Green, 1990).

An Ecosystemic Perspective

From a systems point of view, child, family, and community are conceptualized as overlapping components of a single evolving ecosystem. The most useful framework for understanding achievement or its lack (whether due to LD or otherwise) is a general ecological-somatic model, which takes into account the child's presumed genetic vulnerability and response proclivities and places them within an interactional framework. Examples pertinent to this model include Wynne and Cole's (1983) framework for schizophrenia spectrum disorders; Thomas, Chess, and Birch's (1968) concept of fit between children's genetically based temperament and the child-rearing environment; Sameroff's (1979) transactional/cognitive framework for infants at risk; and Minuchin, Rosman, and Baker's (1978) framework for psychosomatic disorders.

Especially relevant here is Feldman's (1986) genetic/familial/cultural theory for understanding the phenomenon of child prodigies and the development of human abilities (based on an intensive study of six prodigies and their ecosystems). Feldman's (1986) ideas regarding the developmental process he calls *co-incidence* can be extrapolated to apply equally well to underachievers, LD children, average achievers, and above average students:

> It is the fortuitous convergence of highly specific individual proclivities with specific environmental receptivity that allows a prodigy to emerge. This is an infrequent and unlikely event. The convergence is not simply between two unitary, looming giants—an individual and an environment—but between a number of elements in a very delicate interplay: it includes a cultural milieu; the presence of a particular domain [of achievement] which is itself at a particular level of development; the availability of master teachers; family recognition of extreme talent and commitment to support it; large doses of encouragement and understanding; and other features. (p. 12)

As Howard Gardner (1983) has illustrated, family/cultural factors determine which out of many "multiple intelligences" will be valued and amplified and which will be left to lie dormant. He cites an example from the Caroline Islands where a 12-year-old boy is selected by the community on the basis of talent to become a master sailor—an unlikely event in the United States. By contrast, persons with the potential to become nuclear physicists or psychologists are unlikely to fulfill that potential in the Caroline Islands.

This ecosystemic model points to processes of mutual amplification (for better or worse) between genetic talent or vulnerabilities on the one hand and social factors on the other. In such a process, biological, psychological, familial, and social network factors are in a process of changing one another such that characteristics at all levels are affected (to varying degrees) by changes in any one level. The whole suprasystem induces and responds to changes in its parts.

In this sense, one may speak of *vicious interactional spirals* that lead toward deterioration of academic performance, *virtuous interactional spirals* that lead toward improvement of academic performance, and *maintenance cycles* that perpetuate academic performance at a given level over time. This general framework can encompass such diverse phenomena as children's underachievement, LD, general "giftedness," special learning abilities, and high achievements in the lives of eminent adults.

Achievement problems are best conceptualized as being on a continuum—from those subtypes that are exclusively biologically caused and only marginally responsive to environmental factors, to those subtypes that seem more purely socially determined and shaped (Owen, Adams, Forrest, Stolz, & Fisher, 1971). Between these two extremes are the bulk of cases in which presumed polygenetic factors (attentional predispositions, perceptual styles, memory, temperament) may show a wide range of outcomes depending on the constraints they impose and depending on characteristics of the interactional milieu. Given varying degrees of genetic vulnerability, and depending on the unique characteristics of the "achievement ecology," some potentially problematic genetic tendencies may remain inconsequential. In other cases, they may emerge as problems that endure at relatively fixed levels over time through a symptom maintenance cycle. Or their manifestations in the academic sphere may progressively improve or deteriorate over time through virtuous or vicious interactional spirals. Improvement, deterioration, or stability of achievement problems are a function of the whole ecological context of which the child's mind-body is a part.

A Conceptual Model
for Achievement and Family Interaction

In this section, I apply the general ecosystemic perspective to the domain of achievement. In a following section, I review research related to the model. Toward the end of the chapter, this model is used to formulate clinical and research hypotheses that link the four dimensions of family interaction (family communication deviances, family structure, family attributions, and family intellectual/achievement orientation) to the four possible causes of child underachievement (information-processing deficits, attention deficits, performance anxiety, and lack of effort). Readers are referred to an earlier presentation of this model, which more comprehensively reviewed previous research related to these family dimensions (Green, 1989).

Family Communication Deviances

Beginning in the early 1960s at the National Institutes of Mental Health, the concept of *communication deviance* was developed by Wynne and Singer based on extensive research into the relationship between parental communication and the thought disorders of schizophrenic offspring (see Singer, Wynne, & Toohey, 1978, for a summary). Their studies highlighted a fundamental aspect of parent/child communication—the parent's ability to name, explain, categorize, and direct shared focal attention to aspects of the world for the child. Because reality frequently is ambiguous—and language by nature is imprecise—instances of blurred meaning, bewilderment, and attentional misdirection occur from time to time in all families. However, temporary deviances in family communication have minimal long-range effects.

By contrast, in a family environment saturated with amorphous and fragmented styles of parental communication, children may experience a persistent state of cognitive confusion and disorientation. Over time, such children may develop an overall inability to name, categorize, explain, and direct focal attention to relevant aspects of a new situation or to retrieve relevant stored information from past experience. In this way, pervasive disorder at the level of interpersonal communication in the family may impair a child's ability to process and retain new information outside the family.

The scoring manual designed to measure communication deviance (Singer, 1977; Singer & Wynne, 1966) lists the kinds of speech acts that are likely to blur a listener's focus of attention, impede the transmission of meaning, or otherwise induce confusion in the listener. The following clusters of items are listed: (a) *commitment problems*—the speaker fails to commit to a definite idea, (b) *referent problems*—the speaker leaves one wondering what is being talked about, (c) *language anomalies*—the speaker constructs sentences or uses words oddly, (d) *disruptions*—speeches or nonverbal behaviors that are irrelevant or tangential to the topic under discussion and therefore disrupt the task focus of the conversation, and (e) *contradictory, arbitrary sequences*—the speaker gives incompatible ideas, retracts or denies ideas given, or uses peculiar logic (see Ditton, Green, & Singer, 1987, for a summary listing of specific items).

In the original research studies and numerous replications conducted by Singer, Wynne, and associates (Doane, 1978, 1985;

Singer et al., 1978), these forms of parental communication deviance showed a strong and consistent relationship with offsprings' diagnoses of schizophrenic and borderline conditions. This link was particularly strong for families of the most thought-disordered, cognitively confused schizophrenic offspring. Put simply, confusing and disorienting styles of parental communication were reflected in the confused and disoriented thought processes of schizophrenic offspring.

Based on this earlier theory and research, Ditton et al. (1987) theorized that high parental communication deviance would be present whenever offspring exhibit persistent problems in information processing, language usage, and/or focusing attention—including cases of childhood LD:

> Learning disabled students may find it difficult to attend to, focus on, or complete tasks in school partly because they have not learned these basic cognitive skills in the family setting. Some parents may fail to orient the child to the task, or may not maintain a shared focus of attention long enough for the youngster to understand the relevant aspects of the task. Over time, the parents' inability to teach the child how to focus and how to attend may affect the child's [cognitive] development. (p. 78)

Thus, a child's ability to orient to and grasp school tasks may be developed and maintained in the family setting where the child "learns how to learn." To the degree that the family is characterized by confusing and disorienting communication (communication deviances), the child's ability to think and perform in the school setting may be compromised.

Family Structure

Family structure can be defined by two dimensions: *patterns of proximity* (closeness) and *patterns of hierarchy* (authority) among family members (Wood, 1985). At the extremes, family dyads may be either too close (emotionally overinvolved, intrusively enmeshed, fused) or too distant (disengaged) (Werner & Green, 1993). Also, families may have either too little hierarchy (chaotic, laissez-faire, permissive) or too much hierarchy (rigid, authoritarian). At moderate levels, families are characterized by "flexible connectedness"

(Olson, Russell, & Sprenkle, 1983) and democratic (rather than authoritarian or permissive) styles of control (Dornbusch, Ritter, Leiderman, Roberts, & Fraleigh, 1987; Steinberg, Dornbusch, & Brown, 1992). In particular, there are two types of family structures that seem to be associated with children's achievement difficulties: the *underorganized* family and the *overorganized* family.

The Underorganized Family. Over 25 years ago, in studies of delinquent boys, Minuchin and colleagues (Minuchin, Chamberlin, & Graubard, 1967; Minuchin, Montalvo, Guerney, Rosman, & Schumer, 1967) described the socialization processes in the underorganized family and related these processes to the child's academic difficulties. These clinical researchers described the following characteristics of the underorganized family's structure: (a) parental styles of control that are global and erratic such that clear and consistent behavioral contingencies (rules) for rewards and punishments are lacking; (b) disciplinary responses based on the parent's moods; (c) resolution of conflict by escalating threats and counterthreats rather than discussions leading to closure; (d) an overall deficit of communication through words and logic, which are replaced by intensity of physical action and sound; (e) a communication style in which members do not expect to be listened to, so resort to yelling; (f) an emphasis on hierarchical relatedness and immediate/temporary compliance by the use of force, rather than long-term solutions and cognitively mediated responses; and (g) communication filled with disconnected interruptions and abrupt topic changes.

In school, these delinquent children showed an inability to focus their attention, a disruptive communication style that precluded taking in new information, and behavior focused on eliciting authoritarian/proximal control by the teacher rather than on classroom tasks. The results of several empirically controlled studies have been consistent with Minuchin et al.'s clinical findings (see the citations in Green, 1989).

The Overorganized Family. In contrast to the tendency toward chaotic disengagement in the underorganized family, the polar-opposite family structure (overorganized, tending toward rigid enmeshment) may sometimes contribute to another set of achievement problems. Whereas the underorganized structure seems to be associated with child attention deficits and conduct disorders that interfere with learning, the overorganized structure is sometimes associated with symptoms of obsessional worry, performance anxiety, procrastination, passive-negativism, or overtly oppositional behavior in reference to academic tasks.

The overorganized family is characterized by parental intrusiveness, overinvolvement, and overprotective restrictiveness (Werner & Green, 1993). In these families, the parents tend to be too involved and too controlling of the child's school performance—taking over, cajoling, pressuring, demanding, dominating. The child may be perceived as "lazy" or as "weak and incompetent." Parental attempts to control these problems (especially if these attempts are punitive and escalating) tend to backfire and to maintain or exacerbate the problem. In many cases, the parents are unified and overly involved in the child's school performance. However, in other cases, one parent seems too involved and the second parent is peripheral.

Various other clinicians and researchers have described similar patterns of overinvolvement and overprotectiveness in some of the families of underachievers or LD children (see the review in Green, 1989). Some overorganized, rigid families have an overprotective parental style, but others seem to have a more authoritarian-punitive style. In either case, the parents take too much responsibility for the child's school performance and, complementarily, the child rebels, takes on too little responsibility for achievement, and may be riddled with performance anxiety in achievement situations.

Family Attributions

Interpersonal Perceptions and Attributions. Family members attribute varying degrees of intelligence, inability, laziness, industry, and creativity to one another in particular areas (Laing, Phillipson, & Lee, 1966). Interpersonal attribution theory looks at how *interpersonal perceptions* and consequent *interpersonal attributions* affect child performance. Labels such as "stupid," "bright," "musical," and so on may be applied to a child. Similarities with other successful or unsuccessful family members or extrafamilial persons may be ascribed.

Such attributions may undermine or support the child's achievement by creating a self-fulfilling prophecy (Rosenthal & Jacobson, 1968; Watzlawick, 1984). In this process, the child enacts and embodies those characteristics that are attributed to him or her by others. Through positive feedback loops, a cycle is created whereby parental attributions and child characteristics are reciprocally amplified (Alexander & Dibb, 1977; Stierlin, Levi, & Savard, 1971).

Such attributions may or may not be in accord with test data (e.g., IQ), actual performance (school grades) or the views of others (e.g., school personnel, therapists) (Pollner & McDonald-Wikler, 1985; Shapiro, Fisher, & Gayton, 1974). Inappropriately negative family attributions and low expectations in the achievement area seem associated with lowered motivation in the child at school. Inappropriately positive attributions and excessively high expectations may equally undermine a child's achievement motivation. Unable to live up to such expectations, the child may rebel or give up altogether.

The Source of Attributions and the Systemic Function of the Child's Underachievement. The source of distorted interpersonal attributions has not been studied experimentally. However, there is a large clinical literature suggesting that parents' conflicts in the area of achievement may fuel inappropriately negative parental attributions (projections) and the child's identification with those attributions (Vogel & Bell, 1981).

Stierlin (1974) describes how such unresolved parental conflicts may be conveyed to the child as parental pressure to fulfill the parents' own unrealized aspirations. Or a child may be given the mission to fail in school in order to protect a parent from feeling competitively inadequate. Finally, a child may be given an impossible mission in which a parent, or two conflicting parents, convey incompatible directives about achievement. In this last situation, the child may be pressured to fulfill vicariously the parents' own unrealized ambitions, but simultaneously, the parents may undermine the child's efforts.

These theories about the source of negative attributions sometimes propose that the child's school failure serves a homeostatic (morphostatic) function for the family—that is, the child's underachievement has positive stabilizing effects on the family (Klein, Altman, Dreizen, Friedman, & Powers, 1981a, 1981b; Miller & Westman, 1964). Recently, Johnson (1988) and Colapinto (1988) have criticized the notion of an *identified patient* whose school failure serves a homeostatic, myth-preserving, positive function for the family. Johnson (1988) believes that the idea of a family-created,

LD-identified patient implicitly blames the family for causing a symptom that is actually biologically caused. However, based on an ecological-somatic model, LD is hypothesized to have both biological *and* interactional roots. The lessening of LD symptoms could have destabilizing effects on the family, regardless of its partly biological origins (Green, 1988). Thus, for example, a parent who has organized his or her life meaningfully around the care of a child with LD, may unwittingly participate in problem-maintenance simply out of habit or out of an unconscious fear that change will leave a void or create new problems.

Causal Attributions in Families. Extensive research has been done on the topic of causal attributions, that is, how individuals *explain the causes of their own successes or failures* in the domain of achievement (Seligman, 1991). Such causal attributions vary along continua such as (a) *internal versus external* locus of the cause (Is the causal factor viewed as residing in the self or in something external to the self?), (b) *stability versus instability* of the causal factor (What impact will the causal factor have in terms of the individual's future success or failure?), and (c) *global versus specific* influence of the causal factor (How many different kinds of performance situations might be similarly affected?). Studies have shown that children who attribute their successes to external/unstable/specific causes and attribute their failures to internal/stable/global factors are more likely to be depressed and to show lower achievement effort in academics (Dweck, 1990; Dweck & Leggett, 1988; Seligman, 1991).

In addition, the manner in which parents generally explain the causes of their children's performance may influence a child's tendency to persist or give up on academic tasks. An investigation of childhood depression showed that children's causal attributional styles converged with their parents' (Seligman et al., 1984). Thus, in the area of achievement, parents' feelings of helplessness and sense of failure in their own lives may be reflected in children's passivity and perceived helplessness in the face of achievement demands in school (Campis, Lyman, & Prentice-Dunn, 1986; Dweck & Licht, 1980). In these situations, both parent and child may view the child's failures as being caused by internal/stable/global factors, whereas they may view the child's successes as being caused by external/unstable/specific factors (Kistner, White, Haskett, & Robbins,

1985; Klein et al., 1981a). In a vicious interactional spiral, such parental styles of explaining failure may contribute to a child's learned helplessness, diminished sense of efficacy, lack of effort, and eventual failure, which in turn may reinforce the parent's failure-inducing attributions.

Family Intellectual/Achievement Orientation

Families differ in the extent to which they value education and educational institutions. Parents may devalue academic achievement explicitly in words or implicitly by example. They model a set of achievement values through their own work successes and failures; intellectual, cultural, and recreational activities; relations with school authorities; and level of involvement with school activities (Freund & Cardwell, 1977; Henderson, 1987; Klein et al., 1981a, 1981b; Wynne & Green, 1985).

For example, Klein et al. (1981a, 1981b) discuss how parental values based on subcultural factors, such as ethnicity or socioeconomic status (SES), may negatively affect the child's motivation in school by undervaluing or overvaluing school achievement. In this regard, McGoldrick and Rohrbaugh (1987) found that U.S. ethnic subcultures differentially valued success and education—Irish American, African American, Italian American, Greek American, Latino, and WASP families tended to place less emphasis on success than Asian American and Jewish families. O'Connor and Spreen (1988) found that LD children from lower SES families had poorer occupational and educational achievement in adulthood compared with LD children from higher SES families (in which high achievement presumably was emphasized to a greater degree).

Klein et al. (1981a, 1981b) also note the frequency with which underachievers' parents disparage education and show disregard for school authority, often unfairly blaming the teachers and school system for the child's learning difficulties. The child is sometimes encouraged to defy school teachers and ignore assignments. Thus, parents may model an anticonformist/antischool rebelliousness that their children then imitate (Wynne & Green, 1985). Moreover, in the fields of early childhood and school-age education, there is substantial evidence of a strong association between supportive/active parental involvement in the child's school-related activities (a sign of placing high value on education and achievement) and higher levels of child school performance (Epstein, 1990; Henderson, 1987).

Finally, in studies of creativity and achievement motivation, individuals who are oriented toward extrinsic rewards and performance goals (avoidance of failure and disapproval) in achievement situations show less motivation (exert less effort when faced with difficult tasks or obstacles) than individuals who are oriented toward intrinsic rewards and mastery goals (Amabile & Tighe, 1993; Dweck, 1990; Dweck & Leggett, 1988). It is possible that children learn these different achievement orientations (extrinsic-performance vs. intrinsic-mastery) from their parents, who for example, may emphasize "achievement as a means to gain status and income" versus "learning for the love and enjoyment of the process itself."

Research on the Model

In this section, I review some research that bears most directly on the model presented above. Four of these studies were conducted by members of a research team at the California School of Professional Psychology. The other study—a replication and extension of our work on parental communication deviances—was conducted independently by a research group in Finland.[2]

Study 1: Parental Communication Deviances in the Families of Learning-Disabled and Normally Achieving Adolescents

The first study in this series was conducted by Ditton et al. (1987), comparing two demographically matched groups of families of junior high school students: 30 families of average IQ children placed in special education classes for reading and language skill disabilities and 30 families of average IQ children in regular classes. The sample consisted of middle-class families drawn from a predominantly white suburban school district in California. The primary caregiving parents (almost all were mothers) and their male or female adolescents in Grade 7 or 8 participated together in the communication portion of the study.

Parents in the study were asked to teach their children an experimental task over a one-way telephone. In a monologue, the parent

explained to the child how to arrange five black-and-white reproductions of Rorschach Ink Blot cards into a specific design (the
Rorschach Arrangement Task; see Green et al., 1993). The parents'
communication was tape-recorded and transcribed. Trained research assistants ("blind" to the child's learning status) were asked
to rate these parental communication transcripts as having either
high or low levels of communication deviance.

Analyses revealed that 87% of LD students' parents were rated
high in communication deviance. By contrast, 77% of average-
achieving students' parents were rated low in communication deviance. Thus, we discovered a significant association between parental
communication deviance and child LD.

Study 2: Parental Communication Clarity
in the Families of High-Achieving, Average-
Achieving, and Learning-Disabled Adolescents

In an extension of Study 1, Perkins, Green, Ditton, and Singer
(1994) added a third comparison group (30 high-achieving children
and their parents) to the sample from Study 1. Thus, Perkins et al.'s
(1994) entire sample contained 90 parents and their children (all
of whom had scored in the average range on IQ tests): 30 high-
achieving children (mean achievement test score at the 91st percentile), 30 average-achieving children (mean achievement score at the
66th percentile), and 30 children diagnosed as LD and placed in
special education classes (mean achievement score at the 31st
percentile). The new comparison group (high achievers) also consisted of 7th- and 8th-grade, male and female students drawn from
the same suburban school district.

As was done with the original LD and average groups in Study 1,
we administered the Rorschach Arrangement Task to parent-and-
child dyads from the new high-achieving group. However, to assess
parental communication, we used a new rating system derived from
communication deviance concepts (the Clear Communication Rating Scale; see Green et al., 1993). This five-part rating system
evaluates: (a) how well parents orient the child to the Rorschach
Arrangement Task; (b) how "visualizable" their descriptions of the
cards are; (c) how specific their card placement instructions are; (d)
how thoroughly they summarize/end the task; and (e) in a global
clarity rating, how likely the parents' speech is to facilitate the

child's successful completion of the task. New raters, blind to the child's achievement status, rated all 90 transcripts using the Clear Communication Rating Scale.

Data analyses showed a significant linear relationship between all five parental clarity variables and students' achievement group. On the global ratings, for example, parents of high-achieving students were significantly clearer in their communication than parents of average-achieving students, who, in turn, were significantly clearer than parents of LD children. Thus, we discovered that the significant link between parental communication and child achievement was not confined to children with an LD diagnosis, but also extended to comparisons between children performing in the average and high ranges on achievement tests.

Study 3: The Effects of Adult Communication Clarity Versus Unclarity on the Task Performance and Abstract Thinking of Learning-Disabled Adolescents

For this study, Shields, Green, Ditton, and Cooper (in press) recruited a new sample of 61 LD adolescents. The subjects were middle class, in Grades 6 through 9, and drawn from predominantly white suburban schools throughout northern California. These LD adolescents were randomly assigned to complete the Rorschach Arrangement Task under conditions of either clear ($n = 30$) or unclear ($n = 31$) verbal instructions delivered on audiotapes.

To develop these audiotapes, we utilized the transcripts of 15 parents who were rated as showing the most communication clarity and 15 parents who were rated as showing the least communication clarity on the Rorschach Arrangement Task from the Perkins et al. (1994) sample (Study 2). Graduate students were asked to read these clear and unclear communication transcripts onto audiotapes. The two experimental conditions were implemented by playing either a clear or unclear communication audiotape for each adolescent LD subject.

After an audiotape was played for an LD subject, his or her arrangement of the ink blots was scored for correct placement. Then, immediately following the Rorschach Arrangement Task, each subject was administered three trials of a test of abstract thinking (the Twenty Questions Task). This experiment thus constituted a short-term analogue study of the immediate and subsequent impacts of parental communication deviances on the cognitive functioning of children with LD.

Results supported the hypotheses that LD adolescents who experienced the clear communication condition would perform significantly better than LD students who experienced the unclear communication condition, in terms of correct card placement and in terms of subsequent abstract thinking. Students who received the clear communication on the Rorschach Arrangement Task later used more efficient cognitive strategies on the Twenty Questions Task.

These findings were consistent with the theory that adult communication deviance induces cognitive confusion in the LD child and has a "lasting" negative effect on the LD child's abstract thinking. By contrast, adult communication clarity induces better cognitive functioning in LD children. These results also highlight the potential importance of clear communication for all adults who have an instructional role with LD students (e.g., special education teachers).

Study 4: Parental Communication Deviances in the Families of Learning-Disabled and Normally Achieving Boys (the Finnish study)

Rasku-Puttonen, Lyytinen, Poikkeus, Laakso, and Ahonen (1994) undertook a study in Finland of a younger age group (Grades 2-4) that constituted an independent replication and extension of the Ditton et al. (1987) research (Study 1). Subjects were 60 mother-son pairs in which half of the children had LD and the other half were normally achieving children matched for SES and age. These subjects were white and middle class and spoke Finnish as their native language.

The Rorschach Arrangement Task was extended to include two parts. The first part was identical to the Rorschach Arrangement Task administered in all of the California studies above (i.e., a one-way, parent-to-child monologue). The second part allowed two-way communication between parent and child (a dialogue portion of the task). Transcriptions of the monologue and dialogue were rated "blind" using a new scoring system developed by these investigators. The monologue rating categories focused on both communication deviances and communication clarity and were strikingly similar to those used in Studies 1 and 2, respectively. For example, much like Perkins et al. (1994) in Study 2, the Finnish investigators' Communication Clarity Scale rated the parent's monologue for (a) orientation to the task, (b) accuracy of card description, (c) specification of card location, (d) specification of card direction, and (e) overall amount of information conveyed. The rating categories for the new dialogue portion of their Rorschach Arrangement Task included parents' verifying questions and children's clarifying questions.

Similar to our findings in the California studies, the mothers of LD children in the Finnish study showed significantly higher communication deviances and less communication clarity than did mothers of the normally achieving children. In spite of their mothers' less clear communication in the monologue instructions, LD students did not ask for more clarification than did normally achieving children during the dialogue portion. As expected, the less clear instructions given by LD students' parents were associated significantly with the child's poorer performance on the card arrangement task.

The results of the study by Rasku-Puttonen et al. (1994) suggest that the link between parental communication clarity and offspring achievement found in the studies of U.S. adolescents extends also to children raised in a different culture (Finland), speaking a different language (Finnish), and in a younger age group (Grades 2-4). Also, given that this replication was conducted entirely without our knowledge or involvement, it suggests that the earlier findings in California were not an artifact of idiosyncracies in our research group or our samples.

Study 5: Family Interaction Correlates of Academic Achievement in a Community Sample

The most recent collaborative study from our research group was an attempt to test all four parts of the theoretical model (family communication deviances, family structure, family attributions, and family intellectual/achievement orientation).[3] For this correlational study, we recruited a community sample of 95 African American primary caregivers (86% mothers) and their male or female child. The children were in regular classes (Grades 4-6) of Oakland's Chapter I inner-city schools (predominantly working-class and poor families).

Achievement was measured by children's scores on a standardized achievement test, the Comprehensive Test of Basic Skills (CTBS), and by parent report of child's grades in school (Child Behavior Checklist—School Competence scores). Methods and results pertaining to each of the four separate domains are summarized below:

Family Communication Deviances. Hagmann (1993) administered a two-part Rorschach Arrangement Task to the primary caregivers and index children. Part I consisted of parent's instructions delivered over a one-way intercom (an adult-to-child monologue). Part II consisted of a dialogue in which the child and parent conversed together over the telephone to assist the child in completing the card arrangement correctly. Transcripts of parent-and-child communication were rated for clarity after the monologue portion and again after the dialogue portion, using the Clear Communication Rating Scale (Green et al., 1993). Also, parent and child clarifying questions and comments were tallied from transcripts of the dialogue portion.

As hypothesized, children's scores on the standardized achievement test (CTBS) correlated significantly with communication clarity in both the monologue and dialogue portions of the Rorschach Arrangement Task. Children's grades in school correlated significantly with parents' communication clarity in the monologue portion. Number of cards correctly placed by the child correlated significantly with communication clarity of the monologue and of the dialogue. Parent global clarity and SES together were the best predictors of achievement test scores, and both of these variables remained individually significant as predictors in the presence of each other.

These results pertaining to parental communication clarity in an African American inner-city sample are consistent with all the prior results on white middle-class samples in the United States and Finland. Together, these findings suggest that the link between parental communication clarity and child achievement is generalizable across different social classes, races, cultures, languages, and children's ages.

Family Structure. Ratnam (1994) administered to the primary caregivers a 75-item questionnaire about whole-family functioning and a new 5-minute speech sample (caregiver's monologue about the child and his or her relationship with the child). The 5-minute speech sample was rated for "expressed emotion" (parental criticism and emotional overinvolvement). Also pertinent to family structure, Whitmore (1994) administered a 37-item questionnaire to the child, which assessed the child's closeness with his or her biological father (regardless of whether the father resided in the home). Where applicable, child's closeness with other male parenting figures residing in the home (e.g., stepfather, grandfather) also was assessed.

Data analyses revealed that child achievement test scores were significantly related to higher scores on whole-family cohesiveness (closeness) and expressiveness (freedom to express feelings and opinions), higher scores on closeness with male parenting figures living in the home, and lower scores on whole-family enmeshment and permissiveness. School grades were positively associated with child's closeness to biological father and negatively related to primary caregiver's emotional overinvolvement with child. This set of findings suggests that a family structure that is both cohesive and allows for open individual expression—but is not overly permissive (underorganized) or intrusively enmeshed (emotionally overinvolved)— is optimal for children's academic achievement. These results were consistent with the ideas about family structure and achievement proposed earlier in this chapter.

Family Attributions. Wilts (1994) administered an attributional style questionnaire to the primary caregiver (how she or he explains positive and negative events *that happen in the child's life*) and separately administered a parallel form of the questionnaire to the child (how the child explains positive and negative events *that happen to self*). Also, as part of a 75-item questionnaire, Ratnam (1994) administered 5 items pertaining to family external locus of control (the family's belief that outcomes in their lives are beyond their control).

As expected, Wilts (1994) found that parents' more pessimistic attributional style for negative events in the child's life (attributing them to internal/stable/global causes) correlated significantly with children's poorer achievement test scores and poorer grades in school. By contrast, parents' more optimistic attributional style (for combined positive and negative events in child's life) correlated significantly with children's higher achievement test scores and higher grades. In addition, Ratnam (1994) found that whole-family external locus of control was related significantly to children's lower achievement test scores (accounting for 14% of the variance).

These results were consistent with the theory proposed earlier in this chapter, namely that family attributional styles affect children's academic achievement. In particular, parents' pessimistic attributions about negative events in the child's life—and the whole family's general external locus of control—seem to be associated with poorer academic achievement in a child.

Family Intellectual/Achievement Orientation. Moore-McDowell (1993) administered a questionnaire about "family achievement practices" to the primary caregivers and children in the study. Ratnam (1994), as part of her 75-item questionnaire, administered 5 items pertaining to family intellectual orientation.

Moore-McDowell (1993) found that the following family variables were significantly and positively related to achievement test scores: caregiver and child college aspirations, child reports of caregiver PTA attendance, child report of family's involvement in supervising/helping with homework, child and caregiver reports of family's encouragement and offers of help in response to the child's poor grades, and child reports of family's overall involvement in intellectual/achievement activities at home and school. On the other hand, the following two family variables were significantly and negatively related to child achievement test scores: family's "ineffective" responses to child's good grades (especially, making demands for even better grades in this or other subjects) and family's "ineffective" responses to poor grades (criticism, love withdrawn, punishment). In addition, Ratnam (1994) found that family intellectual orientation was significantly related both to children's achievement test scores and to their grades.

These findings are consistent with the theory proposed earlier in this chapter that family intellectual/achievement orientation is related to the child's academic success.

Case Examples

To bring the data alive for readers, four case examples of Rorschach Arrangement Task instructions are presented verbatim. These case illustrations, taken from research for Study 2, conducted by

Perkins and others in 1994, represent extremes examples of unclear versus clear communication from the sample of 90 parents.

In the Rorschach Arrangement Task, the parent was given five black-and-white reproductions of Rorschach Ink Blot cards arranged in a specific design—a rectangle with one extra card. Starting clockwise from the upper left-hand corner, Rorschach Cards I, III, VII, and IV were affixed adjacent to one another to form the rectangle, and the fifth blot (Card VI) was placed above and away from the rectangle. In another room, the child was given the same five cards, but in a randomly ordered stack. The parent's task was to instruct the child (over a one-way telephone) how to place the five cards into the same arrangement as the parent's. There was no time limit set for this task.

The first two case examples below (Parent A and Parent B) are parents of low-achieving LD students:

Parent A: OK, we have five pictures, ah, that we want, ah, sort out, four of them are similar looking at least, ah, to a degree and one is, ah, completely different, the way I see it, ah that we want, ah, put together. So, what we want to do first is take, go, lay all five of them out so that we can take a look at all of them together, and we want to put, ah, four of them in a stack, ah, we want to take the ones that look like Halloween masks and, and take those two, there's two of those that look like Halloween masks, and we'll put those two in the stack, and then we have three more left, and we want to put two more in that stack, so we'll take, take the one that is completely different from the last two that are left, and that one has, ah, oh, it looks like, ah, a skinned cat, is what it looks like. A cat skin with a paw sticking out of it and a head coming up off of it, and that's different than the other two. So we're going to put that one aside and that's going to be the one that will not be with the other four. So, we have two that look like a Halloween mask, and two other ones that are different than the other third one, and we will put those four together.

Parent B: Tell him to put the picture that looked like a bat with a little bit of hair on him, to his left, and below that what looks like a bat with a lot of hair on it, under it. Next to the first one, put down, put down the one that looks like maybe the skeleton of a bat, and underneath that put the one that looks like the skeleton of a bat only a little bit more bone around it or something. Am I supposed to do something with this one? Then put the last one under it, OK.

It is noteworthy that neither of these parents begins by orienting the child to the complete task (i.e., arranging four cards into a rectangle and placing the fifth card above and away from the others). In addition, the parents' descriptions of the cards do not provide enough visualizable and distinctive information about each card for the child to be able to select the right card at the right time. For example, Parent A gives the global-undifferentiated description, "There's two of those that look like Halloween masks," and later makes the amorphous statement, "The one that is completely different from the last two." Parent B's "two bats," one of which has more hair on it, are impossible to distinguish from one another based on this limited description, as are the "two skeletons of bats," one of which has a little more "bone around it or something." Furthermore, the correct reference points for card placement are impossible to decipher. Parent A describes the arrangement simply as "a stack" and instructs the child to put one of the cards "aside." Parent B advises the child to put the first card "to his left," never clarifies that the cards are to be touching one another to form a cohesive rectangle, and instructs the child to put the final card "under it" (under what?) rather than above and away from the other four cards. Thus, the card descriptions and card placement instructions in these parental monologues are likely to leave the child feeling both confused and helpless. Finally, both transcripts seem to end too quickly, almost abruptly, leaving the listener "hanging," with no sense of closure. Based on these transcripts, the child has virtually no chance of getting the cards arranged correctly.

The next two examples (Parent C and Parent D) are parents of high-achieving children. Parent D's instructions were very long, so only an excerpt is reproduced here.

Parent C: Hi. I know you can't uh, you can't talk to me, so uh, what you need to do is, you've got those cards there with the ink blots on 'em. And what I'm gonna do is, you need to put 'em in order for me, in a rectangle form, OK?, four of 'em. And then the last one I'll describe to you, put up above it, aside from it, OK? Let's see, the first one that I've got here that I want to place, will be like in the upper left-hand corner, OK, of your square. It looks like, let's see, how can I say this? It's a lil, it, it looks pretty thick, and it's got like four, four holes in the center. Well, four holes on each side, and it's like a little hole in the center of it. Looks almost like it could be uh, two bats or something, side by side. So, if you can do that. So right next to that, to the right of it, if you could find one, looks almost like two people, like two people on ah, ah, teeter-totter type thing. And, let's see, I'm trying to see if there's like two little blots on, behind their heads on the side, like off to the side, not connected to them. So, if you could place that next to that. OK? And then underneath the first one to make your bottom of the square, that rectangle, the next one, it's like a real thick, thick blot. And it's got [parent clears voice] it, it almost looks like somebody, trying to see if it, it almost looks like the back end of maybe a dog on a motorcycle maybe, with it's little feet sticking out of the side, and little handle bars up on the side. And, the fourth one, it looks like two, to me it looks like two ladies looking at each other with an Indian feather in their head. And they're facing each other. And, I hope I'm not going too fast. OK. And the la, then the extra one would be, it almost looks like a, I don't know, almost looks like one of those skins. You know like when you go to somebody's house and they have it on the wall hanging, one of those bear skins or something. Almost looks like that. OK? Now what do I do? Just say good-bye? OK, good-bye.

Parent D: OK, you have, you're holding five cards in your hand. And I want you to try and put them in the order umm, that I tell you to put them in. Four of the cards are in a rectangle shape. When you get done the four cards will be, will make the shape of a rectangle. And then you'll have one card that is left over, and that'll be placed above and away from the rectangle. OK, umm, the first card that I'm gonna describe, in the rectangle, uh, when you're facing, when you're sitting and you're facing the rectangle, OK the first card is the one on the left, and it's the top part of the rectangle. Uhh, OK, it looks uh, like a butterfly and it has uh, let's say this was the body of the butterfly in the middle, it has two little uh, small like humps on the top, and like two little antenna. They look like little, almost like uh, a mouth with a little thing on the side. And as you, and then it has two wings on the side. In the middle, by the body, there's a circle, then there's two like, almost like triangles on each side, and on the bottom there's two triangles. So there's like four triangles in the middle part of the body, and the small little circle. And it's the largest of the ink blots. And that's goin to be your first, your first card. And it's going to be on the left-hand side, on the top. Ahh, OK, now the next card, which is going to be right next to the first card, on your right-hand side. Uh, OK, this one has like two desi, it has uh, like a picture in the middle. And it looks like there's a little tiny butterfly, a small butterfly right in the middle. Then there's ah, kindda of a design on both sides of this. Then in each corner, there's a little design that has kindda like a long line and then ah, body attached to it. So, the second card has a little butterfly that's like in the middle, and then a uh, design going around that, and then up in each little corner there's two other designs on each side. And it sorta resembles ah, kindda like a skeleton effect, of uh, like a hip, hip area or pelvic area. Uh, OK, the third card which is going to make up our rectangle, is going to be on the left-hand side right below your first card. So, it's going to be on the left-hand side below the first card, on the bottom. [Parent describes remaining cards in rectangle.] And once you have those cards placed, that will make up a rectangle. [clears throat] The extra card that you have left should be placed above your rectangle and away from it. It should not be touching the edge of your rectangle, it should be above it, and away from it. OK, uh, this card also uh, to me resembles some kindda an animal, but it's, the head and like neck part are like very thin. And it has like little things coming off of it. So you would have the head, with kindda a long neck, with things coming to, almost like two fins coming off each side. Then as it comes down, it gets larger, and it has like two points on each side, which could be like front paws, and then two feet below that, which are longer than the front ones. And it doesn't have, this particular uh, animal, if that's what it was, wouldn't have a tail. So, it has like a small head, a long neck, and a body, without any tail. But, you could see like the four feet. And the bottom legs, or feet, are longer than the top ones. Ummm, I can't think of anything else to say. I guess we're done.

Parents C and D give excellent initial orientations to the task, both of them specifically mentioning the rectangle made up of four cards and the fifth card being placed "above it, aside from it" (Parent C) or "above and away" from the rectangle (Parent D). Although in each of these transcripts there are brief moments of unclarity in the card descriptions (Parent C's "four holes in the center. Well, four holes on each side, and it's like a little hole in the center of it"), the listener eventually is given enough distinctive and visualizable information about each card to be able to select the correct card in sequence. Likewise for the card placement instructions, which contain some temporary deviances (Parent C's "if you could place that next to that"), but ultimately contain enough specific information so that the child would stand a fair chance of completing the arrangement correctly. Both Parent C and Parent D clearly signal the end of their instructions (Parent C by literally saying "Good-bye," Parent D by stating "I can't think of anything more to say. I guess we're done"). The child is not left in limbo as to whether the parent has finished the instructions.

Future Research Directions

Etiology of Learning Disabilities

It is important to emphasize that the positive associations between LD and family variables found in Studies 1 through 4—all of which used concurrent rather than longitudinal designs—do not answer two very important questions: What is the causal relationship (direction of effects) between child and parent factors? And what roles do heredity and environment play in the development of these family patterns? Thus, the existing findings on communication deviance and LD are consistent with, but can neither fully support nor disconfirm, any of five competing etiological theories:

The Pure Genetic Theory. A parent's deviant communication could be a sign that the parent also has a learning disability (or subclinical LD). The association between parent communication deviance and child LD would then signify genetic concordance and hereditary transmission of LD phenomena across two generations in families.

The Unidirectional Child-to-Parent Environmental Theory. Children's LD could be a necessary and sufficient cause of parents' communication deviance.

The Unidirectional Parent-to-Child Environmental Theory. Parents' communication deviance could be a necessary and sufficient cause of children's LD.

The Vulnerability/Stress Theory. Parents' communication deviance could be a specific stressor that amplifies (to clinical proportions) a given child's inherited potential (genetic vulnerability) for LD.

The Ecosystemic Theory. Parent and child cognitive and behavioral factors (any of which may be partially genetically based) could reciprocally amplify one another in a *vicious interactional spiral* over time. This spiral eventually would yield a family learning environment higher in communication deviances and associated with more severe LD in the child. A communicationally deviant family environment and the child's LD each could be part of mutual amplification processes in family members' other social networks (e.g., extended family, work, classroom) (Shields & Green, in press; Shields et al., in press).

Because of the great heterogeneity of LD cases (Owen et al., 1971), our research group believes that each causal theory may fit only certain subtypes of LD (Green, 1988). Thus, some subtypes may arise solely from hereditary or nongenetic central nervous system deficits, whereas other subtypes may stem from environmental factors alone. Still other families may be in "double jeopardy"—both parent and child inheriting information-processing or attention deficits that manifest as family communication deviances, which in turn exacerbate each party's information-processing or attention deficits.

Only large-scale, longitudinal family studies of children at high genetic risk (by virtue of a biological parent being diagnosed as LD) could answer these important "nature/nurture" and "direction of effects" questions more definitively. An optimal longitudinal research strategy would involve comparing four cohorts of children: genetically high-risk children raised by adoptive parents; genetically high-risk children raised by their biological parents; genetically low-risk children raised by adoptive parents; and genetically low-risk children raised by their biological parents. Repeated assessments would need to be made of each family's communication deviances and clarity, and each child's achievement status, over time. Obviously, the difficulties in identification, recruitment, and retention of suitable subjects for such a longitudinal study, as well as the financial and human resources needed to carry it out, would be formidable. Nevertheless, such a strategy is the only way to answer this important etiological question.

Sociocultural and Community Factors

Although our studies have focused primarily on families, our research group is beginning to explore the impact of sociocultural and community factors on family relations and achievement. In the study of 95 inner-city African American families (Study 5), many important interconnections between family, community, and achievement variables were revealed. Okun (1994), in qualitative interviews with parents of high-achieving and low-achieving children from the larger sample, examined aspects of family-community relations that affected children's achievement. She found that violence and drug abuse in the community severely impacted the stability and membership of many families, which contributed to their children's poorer achievement. Also, parents of very high achievers intentionally started preparing their children—well in advance of adolescence—to make independent choices, to select friends wisely, to cope with dangers in the community, and to form a positive racial identity as African Americans. Whitmore (1994) used qualitative interviews to assess children's relations with nonfamilial, male father-figures outside the home. He found that many children had ongoing relationships with several such men, all of whom took an active role in advising and helping the children with educational and psychosocial matters. Moore-McDowell (1993) found that higher achievement was associated significantly with children's experience of less racial prejudice from teachers and other children in the neighborhood. Green and Cooper (1994) found that children's achievement was related significantly to the amount of social support their parents received from friends.

All of these results suggest that an exclusive focus on the family— especially the nuclear family as defined by blood or adoptive relations—obscures other important social factors. Just as children's achievement is intertwined with family processes, family achievement-related interaction patterns are intertwined with processes in the larger community and society. The most obvious example of these multiple layers of reciprocal influence is the consistent association found between SES, family interaction patterns, and children's achievement.

Also in this context, the work of John Ogbu (Ogbu, 1978, 1989; see also Fordham & Ogbu, 1986), an educational anthropologist at the University of California at Berkeley, is relevant. In a review of cross-national studies of immigrants and colonized peoples, he has shown that the social position of a minority group (i.e., the extent to which its opportunities are limited by the larger society) is the major determinant of that minority group's educational attainment.

In particular, Ogbu (1978, 1989) distinguishes between two types of minority groups. The first type are called *voluntary, immigrant* minority groups. These groups voluntarily came to the new country seeking a better life, sometimes to escape intolerable conditions in their countries of origin. Most European and Asian ethnics in the United States would be considered voluntary immigrants.[4] The second type Ogbu (1978, 1989) calls *involuntary, castelike* minority groups. These groups have a history of being enslaved or colonized by the dominant cultural group. For example, African Americans, Native Hawaiians, Puerto Ricans, Native Americans, and Mexican Americans would be considered involuntary, castelike minorities in the United States.

In Ogbu's (1978, 1989) cross-national review, voluntary, immigrant minority groups did as well or better academically than the majority group in any given country. However, the involuntary, castelike minority groups tended to do more poorly in school. To illustrate, let us consider a few examples from Ogbu's (1989) review.

Koreans have been studied in three locations: Korea, Japan, and the United States. In Korea and the United States, Korean children are achieving very well in school. In Japan, however—where there is a long history of discrimination against Koreans—Korean children are performing poorly in school. Clearly, this implies that there is not something intrinsic to being Korean (such as higher IQ) or Korean culture (such as placing a higher value on education) that leads to Koreans' higher achievement in the United States. Rather, there must be something in how Koreans are being treated in the United States versus in Japan, or how Koreans view their situation in the two countries that accounts for their better school performance in the United States than in Japan.

Similarly, the academic achievement of Finns has been studied in two locations: Sweden and Australia. In Sweden, which colonized Finland for hundreds of years, Finns are performing very poorly in school. However, Finns who voluntarily immigrated to Australia are doing quite well in school. Again the culture of origin does not, in and of itself, predict school achievement in these cross-national immigration comparisons.

Nor does dissimilarity between the culture-of-origin and culture-of-immigration predict poorer school achievement. If cultural differences (e.g., between home and school) were the key, why would Koreans be doing more poorly in Japan (a more similar Buddhist culture) than in the United States (a more different Judeo-Christian culture)? Or why would Finns be doing more poorly in Sweden (a more similar Scandinavian culture) than in Australia (a more different Anglo-Saxon British culture)?

As a final example here, West Indians have been studied in Great Britain, Canada, and the United States. In Great Britain, which colonized the West Indies, West Indians are the *least* academically successful minority group, whereas in Canada and the United States, West Indians are doing well academically.

These and other cross-national immigration studies imply that language differences, economic differences, and culture-of-origin differences are *not* the primary determinants of differential school achievement by minority groups. Rather, a minority group's relative academic success seems related to its immigration history (voluntary versus involuntary) and current status in relation to the dominant group. In particular, children from a given subcultural group will achieve more poorly if their group was colonized or enslaved historically by the dominant group (as was the case for African Americans, Native Americans, Puerto Ricans, and Mexican Americans in the United States; Koreans in Japan; Finns in Sweden; and West Indians in Great Britain).

From his review, Ogbu (1989) concludes that a minority group's pattern of incorporation within a given society is more important to its academic success than are its *intra*cultural patterns, language differences, or other cultural differences from the majority. Extrapolating from Ogbu's work, family researchers might conclude that issues of *inter*cultural oppression, racial discrimination, and their psychological effects (rather than *intra*group cultural traditions) should be emphasized in our attempts to understand the long-term, multigenerational functioning of racial minority families and their children's achievement in the United States (Kozol, 1991).

Although I am stressing the profound influences of racial stratification and social class stratification in U.S. society here, families still are partially autonomous systems and have a major role to play in children's educational attainment and psychosocial functioning. Thus, given that racial discrimination is an important determinant of a minority group's relative achievement as a *group,* families and individuals within a given racial minority group still show great variability in their academic performance. In sum, although the amount of societal discrimination may determine the relative academic performance of one ethnic/racial group compared to other ethnic/racial groups, the family also makes a significant contribution to individual children's academic performance within each ethnic/racial group and within each social class.

Therefore, in the area of academic achievement, family researchers and clinicians should focus on three distinct community/sociocultural issues:

1. How do sociocultural factors influence the four family processes that are associated with children's achievement (family communication deviances, structure, attributions, and intellectual/achievement orientation)?

2. How do families from involuntary minority groups help their members acquire a positive ethnic/racial identity, cope with specific acts of racial discrimination, and deal with institutionalized oppression of their group generally within U.S. society (i.e., what is the relationship between academic achievement and racial socialization processes in families and peer groups)? (Fordham & Ogbu, 1986)

3. In what ways are patterns of family interaction differentially related to achievement within each specific ethnic/racial group (e.g., do the same family patterns predict to the achievement of African American, Asian American, Latino, and European American children)? (Steinberg et al., 1992)

Summary: Hypotheses Linking Achievement to Family Interaction

The ecosystemic family model assumes that the vast majority of achievement problems are at least partially caused or maintained by factors in the family context, as well as by characteristics of the school and larger social systems. A number of hypotheses, connecting characteristics of the underachieving child to characteristics of the family, can be derived from this review. These hypotheses can be used as a guide by clinicians (in assessing academic problems presented for treatment) as well as by researchers (in designing formal empirical investigations):

1. *Information-processing deficits of the child* may be maintained or amplified by high levels of family communication deviances.

2. *Child attention deficits* in school may be maintained or amplified by an underorganized/chaotic family structure with a disruptive, interruptive style of communication.

3. A *child's performance anxiety* and anxiety-based procrastination in relation to school tasks may be maintained or amplified by an overorganized, rigid family structure in which parents intrusively pressure the child to perform, frequently combined with inappropriately high parental expectations about the child's ability to perform.

4. A *child's lack of effort* in academic situations may be maintained or amplified by the family's (a) inappropriately negative interpersonal attributions about the child's ability and motivation; (b) attributions that view the child's academic failures as being caused by internal/stable/global factors and view the child's academic successes as being caused by external/unstable/specific factors; (c) an overorganized, authoritarian family structure that elicits from the child passive-negativism or oppositional behavior toward academic tasks; (d) overt values, or parental modeling of values, that minimize the importance of education, school authorities, achievement, and intellectual pursuits; (e) lack of parental involvement in helping with and monitoring the child's homework and school performance; and (f) family emphasis on extrinsic rewards and performance goals versus intrinsic rewards and mastery goals in the learning process.

These hypotheses should be held open to confirmation or disconfirmation as data in a case warrant. Not all subtypes of underachievement can be traced to these patterns alone. Neurological, nutritional, socioeconomic, school-related, peer-related, drug-related, or transitional (e.g., parental divorce) factors can be prepotent.

In many cases, the symptom picture is mixed. A child labeled LD may show information-processing, attentional, behavioral, and motivational problems. In such a case, one might find high family communication deviance, an underorganized structure, and a focus on performance goals (avoidance of negative external judgments) in the learning process. In addition, such a child may have a genetic predisposition to the information-processing and attentional aspects of the problem. Thus, the assessment of underachievement and family interaction always must be multidimensional in order to grasp adequately the complexity of these phenomena.

Treatment Implications

All poorly achieving children should undergo a complete psychoeducational and neurological assessment at the outset of treatment. Likewise, in all cases, the clinician *must* work closely with school personnel and parents in developing, implementing, and maintaining a suitable educational plan at school, or the treatment may be doomed (Shields & Green, in press; Wynne & Green, 1985). Conjoint family/school consultation sessions are sometimes useful in working out a cooperative educational plan (Aponte, 1976). However, sometimes it is best for the therapist to play a go-between role, meeting with members of the school and family separately and coaching them to support each other's efforts (Colapinto, 1988). Although traditional family therapy can be used alone in some rare cases, neglecting the family/school interface is usually a fatal error for the treatment (Fine & Carlson, 1992).

For underachieving children (especially in the elementary school years), our findings on communication deviances suggest some innovative methods of family evaluation and intervention. However, we have done only very limited exploration of these methods (with a few cases). The ideas are presented here in the hopes that others will develop them further.

Based on our research, I suggest directly observing the parents' teaching skills and the child's learning skills as enacted in *family learning tasks,* which can be observed and/or taped for review in the clinic. This method can be presented to the family as a way to assess the child's "thinking style" and "how best to help the child learn."

First, without the child present in the room, the clinician explains to the parental couple, or the primary caregiving parent, the nature of the tasks they will be participating in with the child. Then, when the child is brought into the room, the parents' role is to explain and carry out a sequence of tasks with the child. Tasks might include:

- Supervising the completion of a grade-level homework assignment in a specific subject
- Instructing the child verbally in how to recreate an "etch-a-sketch" design that the parent has been given (but cannot show to the child)
- Helping the child make up a verbal or written story "with a beginning, middle, and end, being sure to describe what the characters are thinking and feeling and how it will all turn out" (TAT or CAT cards may be used as stimuli, and the task may be repeated with several cards, requiring 5 minutes of interaction per card)

- A Rorschach Arrangement Task (with parent and child sitting at opposite ends of the room and facing away from each other so that child cannot see the parents' card arrangement)
- A Consensus Rorschach Task in which family members are instructed to look together at an ink blot and "in 5 minutes of discussion, come up with as many *agreements* as possible about what the ink blot looks like to you" (this may be repeated with several blots)
- Playing board games that require the parent to teach game rules to the child
- 10-minute discussion tasks such as "plan a daylong trip together" or "discuss together your child's progress in school and how to improve it"

While observing the parents and child interacting, the clinician assesses:

- How well parents orient the child to each task and maintain the task set during the interaction
- How clearly they convey information via language during the instruction period, including their ability to assume the child's frame of reference
- How they structure, set limits for, reinforce, and correct the child, including how they respond to the child's mistakes
- How well they acknowledge the child's communications and clarify misunderstandings in communication
- How they balance initiative, effort, and verbal participation between themselves and the child during the tasks
- How they summarize and end the learning interactions
- How the child derails the instructional process (e.g., by not paying attention visually or auditorially, by starting the task without understanding the instructions, by not asking for clarification when the parent's communication is confusing, by disrupting the task with extraneous remarks or behaviors, by seeking excessive help from the parent without sufficient independent effort first, by giving up or exerting less effort after an error)
- How the parent responds when the child derails the instructional process

The goal is to assess in vivo the family's communication patterns, structure, attributions, and achievement motivations in a teaching/learning interaction. Then, based on this assessment of how a family's teaching/learning style could be improved, parents (especially of younger children) can be asked to start tutoring their child in specific subjects at home because of their child's special learning needs. This framing seeks to remove all blame from parents, who could not have acquired these "remedial teacher" skills previously (Steinert, Campbell, & Kiely, 1981). In the clinic, parents can be helped to become better tutors through observing a professional demonstrate the tutor role with their child in front of a one-way mirror, role-play practice, review and feedback (using audiotapes or verbal report) of the parent's tutoring at home, and immediate intervention during *tutoring enactments* between parent and child in the clinic.

These parent training techniques are didactic-experiential, somewhat similar in form to filial therapy techniques with parents and young children, and could be used in a group format like filial therapy (Guerney, 1964, 1977; Stollak, 1981). Similar to Minuchin et al.'s (1978) *family lunch sessions,* tutoring enactments bring the problems directly into clinic sessions so that new behaviors can be practiced by parents and children together.

Of course, not all parents are able to function as home tutors; they may lack personal organization or basic academic skills (e.g., English literacy) or already be too enmeshed with the child. In some cases, a peripheral parent can do the tutoring to rebalance the system, or a parent can enlist the help of a member of the extended family or social network to do the tutoring. In such cases, the primary caregiving parent should be empowered as much as possible in selecting and monitoring the child's tutor.

In addition to these psychoeducational approaches with the families of underachieving children, our research findings support the idea of *family-school collaboration programs that involve entire school communities.* In recent years, outstanding examples of such programs have been developed at the Ackerman Institute for Family Therapy in New York City (Weiss & Edwards, 1992) and at Yale University (Comer, 1980, 1985). These community-oriented prevention programs are fully in accord with our latest findings about the importance of parents' active involvement in children's homework and school-based activities (Moore-McDowell, 1993; Okun, 1994). Family-school collaboration programs render the school climate more "user friendly" to all parents. This new climate increases the likelihood that parents of underachieving children will participate actively in special programs to help their children.

Notes

1. A useful exercise is for readers to apply this metaphor of "the family as primary classroom" to their own family systems (past and present) and their own achievement histories.

2. Whenever warranted in the studies reviewed in this section, statistical tests of the hypotheses partialed out the effects of social class or parent educational level (e.g., by using analysis of covariance, partial correlations, or logistic regression procedures). Thus, the results reported here are not artifacts of, or inflated by, differences in families' SES or Parent Education. All results reported in the text were statistically significant at $p \leq .05$ level.

3. As of this writing, many of the results of Study 5 are contained in the form of six separate doctoral dissertations completed in the past year at the California School of Professional Psychology, Alameda (Hagmann, 1993; Moore-McDowell, 1993; Okun, 1994; Ratnam, 1994; Whitmore, 1994; Wilts, 1994). These six dissertations shared a common subject pool and were supported in part by the 1993 Graduate Student Research Grant Award from the American Association for Marriage and Family Therapy (AAMFT). The dissertations by Hagmann, Moore-McDowell, Okun, and Wilts also were supported in part by dissertation research grants from the Fahs-Beck Fund for Research and Experimentation, administered by the New York Community Trust. Additional data from this study were collected by Green and Cooper (1994). We are still in the process of doing secondary analyses of the data (multiple regressions) to determine the relative contributions of each of the four family dimensions and various community factors to the joint prediction of the child's achievement test scores and school competence (grades).

4. Recent illustrations occurred on both the East and West Coasts of the United States during 1993 when ships carrying illegal immigrants from mainland China were intercepted. It was discovered that many families had saved for years and paid $30,000 for the voyage to the United States.

References

Alexander, B. K., & Dibb, G. S. (1977). Interpersonal perception in addict families. *Family Process, 16,* 17-28.

Amabile, T. M., & Tighe, E. (1993). Questions of creativity. In J. Brockman (Ed.), *Creativity.* New York: Simon & Schuster.

Aponte, H. (1976). The family-school interview: An eco-structural approach. *Family Process, 15,* 303-311.

Campis, L. K., Lyman, R. D., & Prentice-Dunn, S. (1986). The parental locus of control scales: Development and validation. *Journal of Clinical Child Psychology, 15,* 260-267.

Colapinto, J. (1988). Avoiding a common pitfall in compulsory school referrals. *Journal of Marital and Family Therapy, 14,* 89-96.

Coles, G. (1988). *The learning mystique: A critical look at "learning disabilities."* New York: Pantheon.

Comer, J. P. (1980). *School power.* New York: Free Press.

Comer, J. P. (1985). The Yale-New Haven primary prevention project: A follow-up study. *Journal of the American Academy of Child Psychiatry, 24,* 154-160.

Das, J. P., Mulcahy, R. F., & Wall, A. E. (Eds.). (1982). *Theory and research in learning disabilities.* New York: Plenum.

Ditton, P., Green, R.-J., & Singer, M. T. (1987). Communication deviances: A comparison between parents of learning disabled and normally achieving students. *Family Process, 26,* 75-87.

Doane, J. A. (1978). Family interaction and communication deviance in disturbed and normal families: A review of research. *Family Process, 17,* 357-376.

Doane, J. A. (1985). Parental communication deviance and offspring psychopathology. In L. L'Abate (Ed.), *Handbook of family psychology and therapy* (Vol. 2). Homewood, IL: Dorsey.

Dornbusch, S. M., Ritter, P. L., Leiderman, P. H., Roberts, D. F., & Fraleigh, M. J. (1987). The relation of parenting style to adolescent school performance. *Child Development, 58,* 1244-1257.

Dweck, C. S. (1990). Self-theories and goals: Their role in motivation, personality, and development. In R. A. Dienstabler (Ed.), *Nebraska symposium on motivation.* Lincoln: University of Nebraska Press.

Dweck, C. S., & Leggett, E. L. (1988). A social-cognitive approach to motivation and personality. *Psychological Review, 2,* 256-273.

Dweck, C. S., & Licht, B. (1980). Learned helplessness and intellectual achievement. In J. Garber & M. E. P. Seligman (Eds.), *Human helplessness.* New York: Academic Press.

Epstein, J. L. (1990). School and family connections: Theory, research and implications for integrating sociologies of education and the family. In D. G. Unger & M. B. Sussman (Eds.), *Families in community settings: Interdisciplinary perspectives.* Binghamton, NY: Haworth.

Feldman, D. H. (1986). *Nature's gambit: Child prodigies and the development of human potential.* New York: Basic Books.

Fine, M. J., & Carlson, C. (Eds.). (1992). *The handbook of family-school intervention: A systems perspective.* Needham Heights, MA: Allyn & Bacon.

Fordham, S., & Ogbu, J. U. (1986). Black students' school success: Coping with the burden of "acting white." *Urban Review, 18,* 176-206.

Freund, J. D., & Cardwell, G. F. (1977). A multi-faceted response to an adolescent's school failure. *Journal of Marital and Family Therapy, 3*(2), 49-57.

Gardner, H. (1983). *Frames of mind: The theory of multiple intelligences.* New York: Basic Books.

Green, R.-J. (1988). The "biological reframe": A response to Johnson's views on psychoeducation. *Journal of Marital and Family Therapy, 14,* 433-434.

Green, R.-J. (1989). "Learning to learn" and the family system: New perspectives on underachievement and learning disorders. *Journal of Marital and Family Therapy, 15,* 187-203.

Green, R.-J. (1990). Family communication and children's learning disabilities: Evidence for Coles's theory of interactivity. *Journal of Learning Disabilities, 23,* 145-148.

Green, R.-J., & Cooper B. C. (1994). [Unpublished data]. California School of Professional Psychology, Alameda.

Green, R.-J., Ditton, P., Singer, M. T., Perkins, P. R., Shields, J. M., & Hagmann, J. (1993). *The Rorschach Arrangement Task (RorAT) and the clear communication rating scale (CCRS)*. Unpublished manuscript, California School of Professional Psychology, Alameda.

Guerney, B. G. (1964). Filial therapy: Description and rationale. *Journal of Consulting Psychology, 28,* 304-310.

Guerney, B. G. (1977). *Relationship enhancement: Skill-training programs for therapy, problem prevention, and enrichment.* San Francisco: Jossey-Bass.

Hagin, R. A., Beecher, R., & Silver, A. A. (1982). Definition of learning disabilities: A Clinical approach. In J. P. Das, R. F. Mulcahy, & A. E. Wall (Eds.), *Theory and research in learning disabilities.* New York: Plenum.

Hagmann, J. (1993). *Parent-child communication clarity, children's academic achievement, and psychosocial functioning: A study of inner-city African-American families.* Unpublished doctoral dissertation, California School of Professional Psychology, Alameda.

Henderson, A. (1987). *The evidence continues to grow: Parent involvement improves student achievement* [an annotated bibliography]. Columbia, MD: National Committee for Citizens in Education.

Johnson, H. (1988). Biologically based deficit in the identified patient: Indications for psychoeducational strategies. *Journal of Marital and Family Therapy, 13,* 337-348.

Kavanagh, J. G., & Truss, T. J. (Eds.). (1988). *Learning disabilities: Proceedings of the national conference.* Parkton, MD: York.

Keogh, B. K. (1982). Research in learning disabilities: A view of status and need. In J. P. Das, R. F. Mulcahy, & A. E. Wall (Eds.), *Theory and research in learning disabilities.* New York: Plenum.

Kistner, J., White, K., Haskett, M., & Robbins, F. (1985). Development of learning-disabled and normally achieving children's causal attributions. *Journal of Abnormal Child Psychology, 13,* 639-647.

Klein, R. S., Altman, S. D., Dreizen, K., Friedman, R., & Powers, L. (1981a). Restructuring dysfunctional parental attitudes toward children's learning and behavior in school: Family oriented psychoeducational therapy (Part 1). *Journal of Learning Disabilities, 14,* 15-19.

Klein, R. S., Altman, S. D., Dreizen, K., Friedman, R., & Powers, L. (1981b). Restructuring dysfunctional parental attitudes toward children's learning and behavior in school: Family-oriented psychoeducational therapy (Part 2). *Journal of Learning Disabilities, 14,* 99-100.

Kolligian, J., & Sternberg, R. J. (1986). Intelligence, information processing and specific learning disabilities: A triarchic synthesis. *Journal of Learning Disabilities, 20,* 8-11.

Kozol, J. (1991). *Savage inequalities: Children in America's schools.* New York: HarperCollins.

Laing, R. D., Phillipson, H., & Lee, A. R. (1966). *Interpersonal perception.* New York: Springer.

McGoldrick, M., & Rohrbaugh, M. (1987). Researching ethnic family stereotypes. *Family Process, 26,* 89-99.

Miller, D. R., & Westman, J. C. (1964). Reading disability as a condition of family stability. *Family Process, 3,* 66-76.

Minuchin, S., Chamberlin, P., & Graubard, P. (1967). A project to teach learning skills to disturbed, delinquent children. *American Journal of Orthopsychiatry, 37,* 558-567.

Minuchin, S., Montalvo, B., Guerney, B., Rosman, B., & Schumer, F. (1967). *Families of the slums.* New York: Basic Books.

Minuchin, S., Rosman, B. L., & Baker, L. (1978). *Psychosomatic families.* Cambridge, MA: Harvard University Press.

Moore-McDowell, J. (1993). *Inner-city African-American families' achievement practices and children's experienced prejudice: Correlates of children's academic achievement and psychosocial competence.* Unpublished doctoral dissertation, California School of Professional Psychology, Alameda.

O'Connor, S. C., & Spreen, O. (1988). The relationship between parents' socioeconomic status and education level, and adult occupational and educational achievement of children with learning disabilities. *Journal of Learning Disabilities, 21,* 148-153.

Office of Education. (1976). Assistance to states for education of handicapped children, notice of proposed rulemaking. *Federal Register, 41*(230), 52404-52407. Washington, DC: Government Printing Office.

Ogbu, J. U. (1978). *Minority education and caste: The American system in cross-cultural perspective.* New York: Academic Press.

Ogbu, J. U. (1989). *Cultural models and educational strategies of non-dominant peoples* [1989 Catherine Molony Memorial Lecture]. New York: City College Workshop Center.

Okun, R. (1995). *Family and community factors in the lives of high-achieving and low-achieving African-American inner-city children: A qualitative study.* Unpublished doctoral dissertation, California School of Professional Psychology, Alameda.

Olson, D. H., Russell, C. S., & Sprenkle, D. H. (1983). Circumplex model of marital and family systems: 6. Theoretical update. *Family Process, 22,* 69-83.

Owen, F. W., Adams, P. A., Forrest, T., Stolz, L. M., & Fisher, S. (1971). *Learning disorders in children: Sibling studies.* (Monographs of the Society for Research in Child Development, Vol. 36, No. 4, Serial No. 144).

Perkins, P. R., Green, R.-J., Ditton, P., & Singer, M. T. (1994). *High-achieving, average-achieving, and learning disabled adolescents: A comparison of their parents' communication clarity.* Unpublished manuscript, California School of Professional Psychology, Alameda.

Plomin, R. (1989). Environment and genes: Determinants of behavior. *American Psychologist, 44,* 105-111.

Pollner, M., & McDonald-Wikler, L. (1985). The social construction of unreality: A case study of a family's attribution of competence to a severely retarded child. *Family Process, 24,* 241-254.

Rasku-Puttonen, H., Lyytinen, P., Poikkeus, A. M., Laakso, M. L., & Ahonen, T. (1994). Communication deviances and clarity among the mothers of normally achieving and learning-disabled boys. *Family Process, 33,* 71-80.

Ratnam, U. (1994). *Whole family functioning and parental expressed emotion in inner-city African-American families: Correlates of children's academic achievement and psychosocial functioning.* Unpublished doctoral dissertation, California School of Professional Psychology, Alameda.

Rosenthal, R., & Jacobson, L. (1968). *Pygmalion in the classroom: Teacher expectations and pupil's intellectual development.* New York: Holt, Rinehart & Winston.

Sameroff, A. J. (1979). The etiology of cognitive competence: A systems perspective. In R. G. Kearsley & I. E. Sigel (Eds.), *Infants at risk: Assessment of cognitive functioning.* Hillsdale, NJ: Lawrence Erlbaum.

Seligman, M. E. P. (1991). *Learned optimism.* New York: Knopf.

Seligman, M. E. P., Peterson, C., Kaslow, N. J., Tanenbaum, R. L., Alloy, L. B., & Abramson, L. Y. (1984). Attributional style and depressive symptoms among children. *Journal of Abnormal Psychology, 93,* 235-238.

Shapiro, R. J., Fisher, L., & Gayton, W. F. (1974). Perception of cognitive ability in families of adolescents. *Family Process, 13,* 239-252.

Shields, J. D., & Green, R.-J. (in press). P.O.E.T.I.C.S.: A model for conceptualizing problem behavior in classroom systems. *Elementary School Guidance and Counseling.*

Shields, J. D., Green, R.-J., Ditton, P., & Cooper, B. C. (in press). The impact of adults' communication clarity versus communication deviance on adolescents with learning disabilities. *Journal of Learning Disabilities.*

Singer, M. T. (1977). The Rorschach as a transaction. In M. A. Rickers-Ovsiankina (Ed.), *Rorschach psychology.* Huntington, NY: Krieger.

Singer, M. T., & Wynne, L. C. (1966). Principles for scoring communication defects and deviances in parents of schizophrenics: Rorschach and TAT scoring manuals. *Psychiatry, 29,* 260-288.

Singer, M. T., Wynne, L. C., & Toohey, M. L. (1978). Communication disorders and the families of schizophrenics. In L. C. Wynne, R. L. Cromwell, & S. Matthysse (Eds.), *The nature of schizophrenia.* New York: John Wiley.

Steinberg, L., Dornbusch, S. M., & Brown, B. B. (1992). Ethnic differences in adolescent achievement: An ecological perspective. *American Psychologist, 47,* 723-729.

Steinert, Y. E., Campbell, S. B., & Kiely, M. (1981). A comparison of maternal and remedial teacher teaching styles with good and poor readers. *Journal of Learning Disabilities, 14,* 38-42.

Stierlin, H. (1974). *Separating parents and adolescents.* New York: Quadrangle.

Stierlin, H., Levi, L. D., & Savard, R. J. (1971). Parental perceptions of separating children. *Family Process, 10,* 411-427.

Stollak, G. E. (1981). Variations and extensions of filial therapy. *Family Process, 20,* 305-309.

Tienari, P., Lahti, I., Sorri, A., Naarala, M., Moring, J., Wahlberg, K. E., & Wynne, L. C. (1987). The Finnish adoptive family study of schizophrenia. *Journal of Psychiatric Research, 21,* 437-445.

Thomas, A., Chess, S., & Birch, H. (1968). *Temperament and behavior disorders in children.* New York: New York University Press.

Vogel, E. G., & Bell, N. W. (1981). The emotionally disturbed child as the family scapegoat. In R.-J. Green & J. L. Framo (Eds.), *Family therapy: Major contributions.* New York: International Universities Press.

Watzlawick, P. (1984). Self-fulfilling prophecies. In P. Watzlawick (Ed.), *The invented reality.* New York: Norton.

Weiss, H. M., & Edwards, M. E. (1992). The family-school collaboration project: Systemic interventions for school improvement. In S. L. Christenson & J. C. Conoley (Eds.), *Home-school collaboration: Enhancing children's academic and social competence.* Silver Spring, MD: National Association of School Psychologists.

Werner, P. D., & Green, R.-J. (1993). *The California Inventory for Family Assessment (CIFA): Users' manual.* Unpublished manuscript, California School of Professional Psychology, Alameda.

Whitmore, G. P. (1994). *Closeness between African-American father-figures and children as correlates of the children's achievement and psychosocial functioning: An African psychology perspective.* Unpublished doctoral dissertation, California School of Professional Psychology, Alameda.

Wilts, M. C. (1994). *Parent and child attributional style: Correlates of academic achievement and psychosocial competence among African-American inner-city children.* Unpublished doctoral dissertation, California School of Professional Psychology, Alameda.

Wood, B. (1985). Proximity and hierarchy: Orthogonal dimensions of family interconnectedness. *Family Process, 24,* 487-507.

Wynne, L. C., & Cole, R. E. (1983). The Rochester risk research program: A new look at parental diagnoses and family relationships. In H. Stierlin, L. C. Wynne & M. Wirsching (Eds.), *Psychosocial intervention in schizophrenia.* New York: Springer-Verlag.

Wynne, L. C., & Green, R.-J. (1985). A truant family. In S. Coleman (Ed.), *Failures in family therapy.* New York: Guilford.

CHAPTER 7

Children's School Performance: The Roles of Interparental Conflict and Divorce

REX FOREHAND

LISA ARMISTEAD

KARLA KLEIN

> Most of what we really need to know about how to live, and what to do, and how to be, we should learn in kindergarten. Wisdom is not at the top of the graduate school mountain but there in the sand box and nursery school.
>
> And it is still true, no matter how old we are, when we go out into the world, it is best to hold hands and stick together.
>
> —*Robert Fulghum (1993, pp. 6-7)*

The above quotes from Robert Fulghum's well-known *All I Really Need to Know, I Learned in Kindergarten* appear relevant for a chapter dealing with the relationship between home and school and, in particular, how family processes can

---

AUTHORS' NOTE: The preparation of this chapter was supported, in part, by the William T. Grant Foundation and the University of Georgia's Institute for Behavioral Research. The assistance of Corinne David and Nancy Woodall is gratefully acknowledged.

disrupt school functioning. Fulghum's primary point is that the important things in life are learned on a simple level in our early years. In contrast to his emphasis on nursery school and kindergarten, our view is that the most important early beginnings to knowledge originate in the home and are then built on in the school setting. The skills learned in the home environment prepare a child to play appropriately in the sandbox at nursery school, to learn simple skills in kindergarten, and to set out on life's journey. However, as noted by Fulghum in the second quote, holding hands and sticking together is important for our development and our learning. Unfortunately, holding hands and sticking together does not occur in increasing numbers of families in our society, which are characterized by divorce and/or conflict between parents. We propose in this chapter to examine the extent to which such family disruption influences children when they are in the sandbox at nursery school, learning elementary but important facts of life in kindergarten, and later learning interpersonal and academic skills in the school setting. We touch on the mechanisms that explain how divorce and interparental conflict disrupt children's functioning in the school. And perhaps most important, we identify buffering factors and methods of intervention that can protect children's school performance from the negative effects of disruption in the home environment.

It is important to consider the relative contributions of the home and school to a child's development within an appropriate context. In some of our earlier writings, (e.g., Forehand & Wierson, 1993), we have delineated how the home sets the stage for interaction and learning within the school. Behavior learned in the home is used with peers and teachers within the school. If problematic behaviors are learned, this can then produce difficulties in a child's functioning within the school setting.

An emerging literature supports the importance of family life for school achievement and behavior. These studies have used children from preschool through middle school, and in all cases, aspects of family life serve as predictors of school performance (e.g., Bierman & Smoot, 1991; Forehand, Long, Brody, & Fauber, 1986; Hess & McDevitt, 1984; Pettit, Dodge, & Brown, 1988; Stevenson & Baker, 1987). The data are clear: When considering how children perform academically and behaviorally in school, the role of a family cannot be ignored.

The primary issue to be entertained in this chapter focuses on two particular aspects of family life and their influence on children in the school. These two aspects are parental divorce and interparental conflict, which clearly are not independent from one another. Nevertheless, we will begin by considering each separately, as they have been treated in the literature. Let us now turn our attention to the first of these two family disruptors.

Divorce

A substantial literature now addresses the issue of the effects of divorce on children. This is not surprising, as many of our children face family disruptions through parental divorce. Each year 2% of children in the United States experience divorce of their parents; 40% of children live in a divorced family by age 16 (Emery & Forehand, 1994). Such high percentages mandate studying, understanding, and identifying the extent to which parental divorce is detrimental for children. Of particular importance are the mechanisms by which divorce affects children and the buffers that can protect children from the possible negative effects of parental divorce.

To what extent are children scarred by divorce? If one reads the lay literature, the effects appear to be dramatic. In a recent paper, Forehand (1992) identified 29 articles that appeared during a 27-month period in magazines and newspapers such as *Newsweek,* *Parent's Magazine,* and the *New York Times.* Typical titles from these articles included "Children From Divorce: Wounds That Do Not Heal," "Children of the Aftershock," and "The Lasting Wounds of Divorce." These titles, as well as the anecdotal and nonscientific accounts of the effects of parental divorce on children in the articles, portray parental divorce as a traumatic and painful event.

Fortunately, the scientific data, although confirming that there is a negative effect of parental divorce on children, fail to support the traumatic conclusions often portrayed in the lay literature. Perhaps the best synopsis of the literature is presented by Amato and Keith (1991a, 1991b) in their recently published meta-analyses of the effects of parental divorce on children during childhood and subsequently in adulthood. The results indicated that parental divorce was associated with difficulties in functioning during childhood and subsequently during adulthood. These difficulties were revealed in multiple areas, including school behavior and achievement. However, the magnitude of the effect was quite small. In fact, Amato and Keith (1991b) noted that it would be considered trivial by many scientists.

Thus, the effects of parental divorce on children are open to interpretation. If one looks only at whether children from divorced versus intact homes differ on various measures of adjustment, the answer is, "Yes, divorce is detrimental." Alternately, if one looks at the magnitude of those effects, as Forehand (1992, 1993a) and Amato and Keith (1991a, 1991b), among others, have done, the conclusion is, "Yes, but the magnitude and perhaps the meaningfulness of the effect is relatively minor."

If the latter conclusion is accepted, should one conclude from the scientific data that parental divorce is harmless for children? Recently, Forehand (1993a) indicated that there are three other feasible and more appropriate interpretations. First, divorce may be a painful and long-remembered *subjective* experience, but the pain may not interfere with functioning in school or elsewhere to any great extent (Emery & Forehand, 1994). Such an interpretation could explain the incongruence between the lay and scientific literatures. Second, although some children are probably negatively influenced by divorce, others probably are not. Therefore, one should not conclude that divorce is harmless—or that it is so harmful that all children should automatically receive psychological treatment. The third point, which is related to the preceding one, is that it is not divorce per se that primarily determines a child's functioning, but rather variables that frequently accompany family disruption (Amato, 1993; Emery & Forehand, 1994; Rutter, in press). These are factors to which we return later.

Within the context of the impact of parental divorce on children delineated thus far, the most pertinent question for our purposes is: What do the data say about the effects of divorce on school-related behavior and academic functioning? The most efficient way to address this question is to return to the analyses performed by Amato and Keith (1991a, 1991b). When these investigators, using 39 studies, examined the effects of parental divorce on school achievement during childhood, they found a mean effect size of .16 (Amato & Keith, 1991a). In 19 studies examining adults whose parents divorced when they were children, Amato and Keith (1991b) found a lower level of educational attainment than in individuals from intact families. The mean effect size was .28. Basically, these effect sizes indicate that individuals from divorced families function, in terms of school achievement, about one sixth and one fourth of a standard deviation worse than individuals from intact families during childhood and adulthood, respectively. Interestingly, these effect sizes approximated the mean effect sizes found across all areas of functioning that were examined (e.g., psychological adjustment, social adjustment, mother-child relationships, conduct problems). School functioning, at least in terms of academic achievement, appears to be influenced by divorce to a similar extent as other areas of functioning. Although the effect size is statistically significant, the magnitude of the effect, as we have already emphasized, is quite small and may even be considered trivial.

Turning from academic achievement to school behavior (e.g., disruption in the classroom), it is not possible from the Amato and Keith (1991a, 1991b) reviews to partial out behavior in school versus in another settings. These investigators examined various domains of functioning, such as psychological and behavioral adjustment, conduct problems, and social adjustment, but these were not examined independently in the school environment. Therefore, it is necessary to turn to two projects with this specific focus to ascertain the extent to which divorce impacts the behavior of children in school.

One of these projects, the National Association of School Psychologists-Kent State University (NASP-KSU) project, was a nationwide study of children in schools conducted by Guidubaldi and his colleagues (Guidubaldi & Perry, 1985; Guidubaldi, Perry, & Cleminshaw, 1984; Guidubaldi, Perry, & Nastasi, 1987). Data were obtained from 144 psychologists from 38 states, each of whom assessed six children: two first graders, two third graders, and two fifth graders. One child from each grade level was from an intact family and the other was from a divorced single-parent family. The mean time since divorce in the latter group was approximately 4 years. The results indicated that children from divorced families were functioning significantly more poorly than those from intact families in a number of social-emotional areas. These included conduct grades and scores on a number of teacher-completed scales reflecting domains such as blaming, withdrawal, negative feelings, and inattention. Academic and intellectual functioning (e.g., achievement scores, IQ scores) was also lower for children from divorced homes than for those from intact homes. However, amplifying the argument raised earlier about the magnitude of the effect, the mean differences between children from divorced and intact families were relatively small. For example, boys' conduct grades were 2.04 versus 2.09 for those from married versus divorced families, respectively. Similarly, the means for inattention were 5.00 and 6.19 for children from married and divorced homes, respectively. And the mean differences in the IQ scores were 105 (divorced) versus 108 (intact) (Guidubaldi et al., 1984). Thus, although the differences are significant, the magnitude of the effects is relatively small.

A second project focusing on school behavior, the Parent-Adolescent Project, has involved approximately 140 young adolescents (mean age, 13.5 years) from recently divorced homes (less than one year since divorce) and approximately 140 adolescents from intact homes. Assessments consisted of mothers and adolescents completing measures, as well as teachers completing measures about academic progress and behavior in school. The sample was followed over a 4-year period.

Early studies from this project, with small sample sizes, suggested that divorce did not exert an influence on adolescent functioning in the school (e.g., Forehand, McCombs, Long, Brody, & Fauber, 1988; Long, Forehand, Fauber, & Brody, 1987). However, more recent analyses conducted with most of the full sample suggest that teachers do report more difficulties in various areas for adolescents from divorced homes during the first year following the divorce. Compared to adolescents from intact homes, those from divorced homes evidenced more internalizing problems and less social competence and cognitive competence (Forehand, Neighbors, Devine, & Armistead, 1994; Forehand, Thomas, Wierson, Brody, & Fauber, 1990). Differences also were manifested in the area of externalizing problems (e.g., acting out, disrupting classroom) in one study (Forehand et al., 1990), but not the second study (Forehand et al., 1994). Differences in internalizing problems, social competence, and cognitive competence between adolescents from intact and divorced families were observed in at least 1 of the 3 years subsequent to the first assessment. However, as in Amato and Keith (1991a, 1991b) and Guidubaldi et al. (Guidubaldi & Perry, 1985; Guidubaldi et al., 1984, 1987), the absolute magnitude of the differences between adolescents from divorced and intact homes was quite small (Forehand et al., 1994).

In conclusion, parental divorce is related to multiple areas of children's school performance. However, contrary to the image portrayed in the public media, the scientific data suggest that the magnitude of these effects, as well as effects in settings other than school, is relatively small. As previously noted, it is our opinion that divorce per se does not determine a child's school functioning. Instead, some children are immensely affected by divorce and others are not, resulting in a small, but statistically significant, mean group difference between children from intact and divorced families. One needs to explore factors that frequently accompany divorce to best understand its relationship to a child's performance in school. One of these factors, interparental conflict, can influence children in both intact and divorced families. Let us now turn our attention to this aspect of the family.

Interparental Conflict

Early reviews indicated that conflict between parents, whether in divorced homes or intact homes, has a detrimental effect for children (see Emery, 1982, 1988). In fact, Amato and Keith (1991a) found that conflict between parents from intact families is more detrimental than parental divorce. Conflict that occurs in front of children appears to be particularly detrimental (e.g., Forehand et al., 1990). The impact of such conflict is observable in multiple areas of functioning, including social and cognitive competence, as well as internalizing and externalizing problems (e.g., Forehand et al., 1994).

Two recent reviews support the hypothesis that conflict between parents is detrimental for children; however, both reviews suggest that the relationship is more modest than previously proposed. Grych and Fincham (1990) reported that 79% of the 19 studies they reviewed found an association between interparental conflict and child functioning. They concluded that "recent research documents a modest but consistent relationship between interparental conflict and children's adjustment" (p. 269). Reid and Crisafulli (1990) conducted a meta-analysis of 33 studies and found an effect size of .16 between marital conflict and child behavior problems. Interestingly, this effect size is identical to that found between parental divorce and child functioning by Amato and Keith (1991a). Thus, the more recent reviews indicate that conflict between parents may not be as detrimental as earlier reviews suggested (e.g., Emery, 1982).

In their review, Grych and Fincham (1990) point out that interparental conflict has various dimensions, each of which may influence the relationship of the conflict to child functioning. They concluded that more frequent and intense conflict (e.g., physical aggression), as well as conflict that pertains to the child, is associated with poorer functioning. Resolution of conflict (Camara & Resnick, 1989) and children's appraisal of the meaning of the conflict (Grych & Fincham, 1993) appear to be important dimensions in the relationship of interparental disputes to child functioning. Finally, recent work by Jaycox and Repetti (1993) indicates that family conflict (i.e., a pervasive climate of anger in the family) is more strongly associated with child adjustment than is conflict that occurs strictly between parents. Our point here is that research on interparental conflict is moving beyond broad generalizations reached in earlier work to a more refined analysis of its effects, its critical dimensions, and its role within the family environment in general. Within this movement, the understanding of the relationship between conflict and child functioning will be enhanced.

Of importance for this chapter is the influence of interparental conflict on school performance. The recent reviews did not differentiate school functioning from the functioning of children in other areas of life. Thus, we return to the Parent-Adolescent Project data to reach conclusions about school performance. Research from this project suggests that interparental conflict has detrimental effects on multiple areas of school performance: internalizing behavior problems, externalizing problems, social competence, and cognitive competence (Forehand et al., 1994). As long as the interparental conflict persists, in either married or divorced families, it appears to have negative effects. For example, Forehand et al. (1994) found a relation between such conflict and adolescent functioning over a 4-year period. Interparental conflict appears to be a family process variable of importance when one considers how children function, including in school.

Work from the Parent-Adolescent Project also provides information regarding another interesting question: What are the relative influences of *interparental conflict* and *divorce* on child functioning? The former variable appears to exert more of a detrimental influence than the latter, at least in some areas of school functioning (e.g., Forehand et al., 1988, 1994). In reality, however, interparental conflict and divorce are overlapping events in the lives of many children. Divorce is frequently surrounded by conflict, and thus children are potentially exposed to both variables concurrently. As we alluded to earlier, many investigators (e.g., Emery, 1982; Forehand, 1993a) have concluded that interparental conflict is a major component of divorce that separates children who fare well from those who fare poorly when their parents' marriage dissolves. Let us now turn to a more systematic examination of the mechanisms that may influence children's school performance when parents divorce and/or engage in conflict.

Mechanisms of Operation

Five primary mechanisms have been proposed to explain the variability between children whose parents divorce. These include loss of a parent, compromised adjustment and/or parenting of the custodial parent, interparental conflict, economic hardship, and stressful life changes (Amato, 1993; Emery & Forehand, 1994). Some evidence exists to support each of these potential explanations. For example, the average family incomes of women decline from $26,000 to $15,000 (in 1981 dollars) during the first year following divorce (Emery & Forehand, 1994). This income loss is frequently associated with other difficult changes for families (e.g., living with the mother's parents, the mother working more hours or receiving public assistance).

Amato (1993) derived hypotheses from each of the five mechanisms and then examined available studies to determine the degree of support for each. He concluded that the most consistent and convincing evidence supported the mechanism of interparental conflict. Amato (1993) noted that from this perspective, the relationship between parental divorce and children's well-being may actually be spurious in that interparental conflict produces both child problems and marital disruption. Nevertheless, although the strongest support was generated for interparental conflict in Amato's (1993) review, he proposed that a model combining all five explanations will be necessary to account fully for research findings regarding why children react differently to parental divorce.

Clearly, children's adjustment to parental divorce is a complex issue that varies for different children, depending on factors such as how much conflict exists between parents, how much contact the child has with a noncustodial parent and the quality of that relationship, the adjustment of the custodial parent, the economic hardship imposed by the divorce, and how many stressful life changes occur with marital disruption. Data are not available specifically addressing whether these various mechanisms are influential on children's school behavior, but there is no reason to assume that the outcome for school behavior is different from that for child behavior in general. We feel it can be concluded with some confidence that all five mechanisms operate in parental divorce to influence school behavior, but interparental conflict appears to play the most important role.

A logical next question concerns the mechanisms by which interparental conflict operates to disrupt children's behavior. Several different mechanisms have been proposed, including modeling of aggression and poor interpersonal skills, disruption of the parent-child relationship and/or parenting skills, and induction of emotional distress by exposure to a stressor (e.g., the conflict) (Emery, 1982, 1988; Fauber, Forehand, McCombs, & Wierson, 1990). However, as both Grych and Fincham (1990) and Forehand (1993a) have indicated, the exact mechanism that is detrimental for a child is, for the most part, still unknown. For our purposes, when school behavior is considered, each of the mechanisms proposed above could obviously influence children's behavior and academic performance in the school setting. For example, Fauber et al. (1990) found that interparental conflict influenced parenting behavior, which then predicted children's functioning, including school performance.

Protective Factors for School Performance

Although the magnitude of the effects may be in question, the existing data do indicate that divorce, at least under certain conditions (e.g., high interparental conflict), and conflict between parents are associated with difficulties in school, both in terms of academic performance and behavior. In a recent comprehensive review, Emery and Forehand (1994) identified protective and risk factors in divorce research with children. Three categories emerged: *individual, family,* and *extrafamilial* support factors. When children's school performance is considered, there may be factors within the individual child, within the family, or within the school itself that may promote academic performance and prosocial behavior during the stresses of parental divorce and/or during high levels of interparental conflict.

Other than demographic characteristics such as gender that cannot be modified, a *child's coping style* is the most salient protective factor within the individual. Several studies (Armistead et al., 1990; Kliewer & Sandler, 1993; Radovanovic, 1993) have examined the relationship between coping style and functioning in children whose parents are divorcing or already have divorced. Although the results are not always consistent across or within studies, it would appear that active coping (e.g., planning how to solve problems by generating solutions and implementing them) promotes competence in school. Interventions (e.g., Alpert-Gillis, Pedro-Carroll, & Cowen, 1989; Pedro-Carroll & Cowen, 1985, 1987) that include problem-solving strategies may facilitate children's functioning in the school setting during and after parental divorce.

A second factor within the child that has emerged as important in differentiating children who function well versus poorly cognitively in school during periods of high interparental conflict is *self-esteem.* Neighbors, Forehand, and McVicar (1993) found that among adolescents whose parents reported engaging in high levels of conflict, those who were viewed as cognitively competent by teachers reported higher self-esteem than less cognitively competent adolescents. Interventions (Alpert-Gillis et al., 1989) that include building self-esteem may well facilitate school performance during times of family stress.

Turning to family factors that may serve as buffers for functioning in the school, *reduced interparental conflict* emerges again as a variable that appears to be important. For example, Long, Slater, Forehand, and Fauber (1988) found that parents whose conflict level was reduced following divorce, relative to those who continued a high level of conflict after divorce, had adolescents with higher grade point averages and fewer internalizing and externalizing problems. Teachers, school counselors, and therapists need to emphasize to parents, whether married or divorced, that engaging in high levels of interparental conflict in front of a child or directly involving a child in the conflict (e.g., as a messenger between parents or as an ally with one parent) is detrimental for a child and his or her school performance. However, if such conflict does occur, research indicates that parents should explain the meaning of the conflict to a school-aged child, particularly when the explanation absolves the child of blame for the conflict (Grych & Fincham, 1993).

A second buffering factor within the home when parents are divorcing or engaging in high levels of conflict is a good *parent-child relationship* (Emery & Forehand, 1994). For example, Wierson, Forehand, Fauber, and McCombs (1989) assigned adolescents to one of three groups: parents divorced/adolescent has good relationship with both parents; parents divorced/adolescent has poor relationship with both parents; and parents married/adolescent has a good relationship with both parents. The results indicated that in several areas of school functioning, including cognitive competence and externalizing problems, adolescents in the "parents divorced/ good relationship" group were functioning significantly better than those in the "parents divorced/poor relationship" group. Further and of primary importance, the adolescents in the "parents divorced/good relationship" group did *not* differ significantly in school functioning from those in the "parents married/ good relationship group." This provides strong support for the idea that a good parent-adolescent relationship can promote a child's school performance following parental divorce. Thomas and Forehand (1993) suggest that in divorced families, the adolescent's relationship with the noncustodial parent can make an important and unique contribution to school functioning. Neighbors et al. (1993) indicate that a good parent-adolescent relationship is also important for school functioning during times of high interparental conflict, regardless of whether the adolescent is from an intact or divorced family. During times of family stress (divorce or interparental conflict), parents should be encouraged to focus on their relationship with their child. Obviously, in times of stress, this is a difficult task; nevertheless, by facilitating this relationship, parents can prevent compromised or disrupted school functioning.

The final potential buffer within the family that can influence child functioning in the school is *parenting skills*. Obviously, the parent-child relationship and the parenting skills displayed by the parent are likely to be closely related. Parents who display good parenting skills will establish a good relationship with their child. Thus, one way to promote a good parent-child relationship *and* facilitate school performance during times of family stress may be to teach parenting skills.

A number of investigators (e.g., Capaldi & Patterson, 1991; Hetherington, 1993) have found that the functioning of children in divorced homes is related to parenting skills. Recent studies from the Parent-Adolescent Project (Fauber et al., 1990; Forehand et al., 1990) have reported that the functioning of children in school is related to the quality of parenting skills displayed by parents in homes disrupted by divorce. The parenting skills that have proven to be important include good communication, problem solving, monitoring, acceptance, and involvement with the child. Fortunately, programs for parents of preadolescent (Forehand & McMahon, 1981) and adolescent (Robin & Foster, 1989) children are available to teach such skills and thereby improve the parent-child relationship and ideally the child's functioning in school.

Fauber et al. (1990) suggest not only that parenting skills can buffer children in divorced families, but also may serve as a mediator between interparental conflict and children's behavior problems, including those in the school. These investigators found that lower levels of interparental conflict were associated with an accepting style of parenting, which was associated with fewer internalizing and externalizing problems in adolescents. As was noted by Emery and Forehand (1994), parenting does not stand alone as a protective factor for children. Rather, it is related to other protective or risk factors, such as interparental conflict, and may qualify the influence of these other factors.

Protective factors for children's school performance can also exist outside the home. For example, Cowen, Pedro-Carroll, and Alpert-Gillis (1990) found that *social support* received by children of divorce from adults other than parents was associated with higher teacher ratings of competence and lower teacher ratings of problem behavior. The adults were unspecified, but could be teachers, grandparents, or friends of a parent. In any case, the results suggest that in terms of promoting school functioning (e.g., grades, social competence), adults from outside the home can play an important role following parental divorce.

Protective factors for promoting school performance also can be present in the school itself. For example, Hetherington, Cox, and

Cox (1979) and Kelly and Wallerstein (1977) found that attention and warmth showed by teachers was associated with positive child adjustment following divorce. More recently, Hetherington (1993) has classified schools into four categories: authoritative, authoritarian, permissive, and chaotic/neglecting. For our purposes, the *authoritative school environment* is most important and will be delineated here in more detail. According to Hetherington (1993), authoritative schools provide a predictable environment with clear standards, expectations for responsible behavior, and nurturance. Within such an environment, Hetherington (1993) found adolescents from divorced homes demonstrated higher achievement levels and fewer behavior problems than those from other types of school environments. This enhanced effect of the school environment on performance within the school setting occurred for children regardless of whether their mothers were or were not authoritative at home. However, the protective effects of an authoritative school were most pronounced when the custodial mother was not authoritative. These findings not only point to the importance of the school environment in facilitating school performance for children whose parents divorce, but also emphasize the interplay of protective factors across settings (i.e., home and school). When attempting to promote school performance, mental health professionals need to consider interventions not only with the child (e.g., teaching effective coping strategies), but also across the various environments within which the child spends her or his time.

Direct interventions within the school setting also have been developed for children of divorce. Many of these school-based programs are designed to alleviate misconceptions, negative feelings, and practical problems experienced by children after divorce (Grych & Fincham, 1992). As noted by Emery and Forehand (1994), components of such interventions include support, providing information, discussing feelings, and social-skills training. According to Grych and Fincham (1992), the program with the most empirical support is one developed by Pedro-Carroll and Cowen (1985, 1987). This program consists of a structured 12-session group intervention for four to six children in the fourth to sixth grade. The program involves a number of components, including teaching children how to understand changes in families, how to cope with changes, social problem-solving skills, understanding and dealing with anger, acceptance of diverse family forms, and identification of positive postdivorce changes. The program has been systematically evaluated, and relative to a control group, participants' school problem behaviors (i.e., aggression, shyness, and learning problems) decreased and school competence (e.g., following rules and adaptive assertiveness) increased (Pedro-Carroll & Cowen, 1985).

More recently, Alpert-Gillis et al. (1989) have slightly modified the program intervention for use with urban second- and third-grade children. The format was extended to 16 sessions and program books and exercises were modified to fit the children's developmental skills (e.g., greater use of visual aids for the younger children). Relative to control children from both divorced and intact families, teachers rated those children from divorced families who participated in the program as demonstrating greater increases in competence from pre- to posttreatment. Thus, standardized, well-validated intervention programs exist for improving the school functioning of children, Grades 2 through 6, from divorced homes.

To summarize across studies that examine protective factors for parental divorce, it is evident that there are multiple levels on which we can intervene to reduce children's problem behaviors in school. These can involve working individually with children to teach them better coping skills; working with parents to improve their relationship with their child, to improve their parenting skills, and to reduce interparental conflict; working directly with teachers and schools to help them provide an authoritative environment; and providing children with group intervention programs within the school context. Determining which of these avenues would be best for a particular child depends on an assessment including the child, parents, and teachers.

The effects of parental divorce on school performance are variable across children, probably because the various protective factors just delineated are operating at different levels for different children. Making parents, teachers, school administrators, children, and mental health experts aware of the importance of the protective factors is an initial step toward facilitating the school performance of children from divorced homes. Then, as Pedro-Carroll and Cowen (1985) have done with their program for children, systematic interventions at each level should be developed.

When interparental conflict is considered separately, the literature is not as rich as the literature on divorce in terms of potential buffers for children's school performance. Considering our view that interparental conflict is at least equally, and probably more, detrimental for children than is divorce (Forehand et al., 1994), the absence of research on buffers is surprising. As we indicated above when discussing interparental conflict within the context of divorce, there are practical steps that can be taken by parents to promote better school performance. Not engaging in interparental conflict in front of the child, keeping the children out of the conflict, agreeing about disciplinary procedures, and simply being aware of the harmful effects of interparental conflict on children have been recommended (e.g., Emery, 1982; Forehand, 1993b). Attempting to improve the relationship between each parent and the child in the midst of interparental conflict has the potential to be an important protective factor for school performance (Neighbors et al., 1993).

Conclusions

For children living in stressful home environments, such as those often characterized by high levels of interparental conflict and divorce, it would be comforting for us as educators and mental health professionals to assume that the two worlds of children, the home and the school, are independent of one another. However, the empirical data reviewed in this chapter, as well as data delineated in other chapters in this book and the theoretical formulations by individuals such as Bronfenbrenner (1979) and Cairns and Cairns (1991), indicate that the various worlds of a child are intertwined. For many children in our society, living within a stable family environment results in a positive influence of the home on a child's achievement and behavior in school. Unfortunately, this intertwining across environments also occurs for those who must face high levels of interparental conflict and/or parental divorce. Those children's behavior may suffer not only in the home but also in school. We must stress again, as we have done repeatedly, that the magnitude of the effect appears to be modest; nevertheless, there clearly is an association between family stress (divorce and interparental conflict) and school performance of children. As a consequence, it is necessary to identify additional protective factors and design interventions that incorporate those factors.

As our review indicates, a literature already exists suggesting a number of protective factors for children experiencing parental divorce and, to a lesser extent, interparental conflict. Some of these factors have been included in intervention programs with children. It is our hope that by identifying the effects of divorce and interparental conflict, as well as some of the buffers to prevent behavior from deteriorating in school, more elaborate preventive programs can be implemented.

To promote school competence, the family must provide a basic foundation for children prior to and during their school experience. When this does not occur naturally, it becomes necessary to develop policy and implement prevention and intervention efforts to improve the lives of children. Only then will children from these homes be able to learn to the fullest extent possible in the school setting what they "really need to know about how to live, and what to do, and how to be" (Fulghum, 1993, p. 6).

References

Alpert-Gillis, L. J., Pedro-Carroll, J. L., & Cowen, E. L. (1989). The children of divorce intervention program: Development, implementation, and evaluation of a program for young urban children. *Journal of Consulting and Clinical Psychology, 57,* 583-589.

Amato, P. R. (1993). Children's adjustment to divorce: Theories, hypotheses, and empirical support. *Journal of Marriage and the Family, 55,* 23-38.

Amato, P. R., & Keith, B. (1991a). Parental divorce and adult well-being: A meta-analysis. *Journal of Marriage and the Family, 53,* 43-58.

Amato, P. R., & Keith, B. (1991b). Parental divorce and the well-being of children: A meta-analysis. *Psychological Bulletin, 110,* 26-46.

Armistead, L., McCombs, A., Forehand, R., Wierson, M., Long, N., & Fauber, R. (1990). Coping with divorce: A study of young adolescents. *Journal of Clinical Child Psychology, 19,* 79-84.

Bierman, K. L., & Smoot, D. L. (1991). Linking family characteristics with poor peer relations: The mediating role of conduct problems. *Journal of Abnormal Child Psychology, 19,* 341-356.

Bronfenbrenner, U. (1979). *The ecology of human development: Experiments by natural design.* Cambridge, MA: Harvard University Press.

Cairns, R. B., & Cairns, B. D. (1991). Social cognition and social networks: A developmental perspective. In D. J. Pepler & K. H. Rubin (Eds.), *The development and treatment of childhood aggression* (pp. 249-278). Hillsdale, NJ: Lawrence Erlbaum.

Camara, K. A., & Resnick, G. (1989). Styles of conflict resolution and cooperation between divorced parents: Effects on child behavior and adjustment. *American Journal of Orthopsychiatry, 59,* 560-575.

Capaldi, D. M., & Patterson, G. R. (1991). Relation of parental transitions to boys' adjustment problems: 1. A linear hypothesis. 2. Mothers at risk for transitions and unskilled parenting. *Developmental Psychology, 3,* 489-504.

Cowen, E. L., Pedro-Carroll, J. L., & Alpert-Gillis, L. J. (1990). Relationship between support and adjustment among children of divorce. *Journal of Child Psychology and Psychiatry, 31,* 727-735.

Emery, R. E. (1982). Interparental conflict and the children of discord and divorce. *Psychological Bulletin, 92,* 310-330.

Emery, R. E. (1988). *Marriage, divorce, and children's adjustment.* Newbury Park, CA: Sage.

Emery, R. E., & Forehand, R. (1994). Parental divorce and children's well being: A focus on resilience. In R. J. Haggerty, M. Rutter, & L. Sherrod (Eds.), *Stress, coping and development: Risk and resilience in children* (pp. 64-99). London: Cambridge University Press.

Fauber, R., Forehand, R., McCombs, A., & Wierson, M. (1990). A mediational model of the impact of marital conflict on adolescent adjustment: The role of disrupted parenting. *Child Development, 61,* 1112-1123.

Forehand, R. (1992). Parental divorce and adolescent maladjustment: Scientific inquiry versus public opinion. *Behavior Research and Therapy, 30,* 319-327.

Forehand, R. (1993a). Family psychopathology and child functioning. *Journal of Child and Family Studies, 2,* 81-86.

Forehand, R. (1993b). Twenty years of research: Does it have practical implications for clinicians working with parents and children? *Clinical Psychologist, 46,* 169-176.

Forehand, R., Long, N., Brody, G. H., & Fauber, R. (1986). Home predictors of young adolescents' school behavior and academic performance. *Child Development, 57,* 1523-1533.

Forehand, R., McCombs, A., Long, N., Brody, G. H., & Fauber, R. (1988). Early adolescent adjustment to recent parental divorce: The role of interparental conflict and adolescent sex as mediating variables. *Journal of Consulting and Clinical Psychology, 56,* 624-627.

Forehand, R., & McMahon, R. J. (1981). *Helping the noncompliant child: A clinician's guide to parent training.* New York: Guilford.

Forehand, R., Neighbors, B., Devine, D., & Armistead, L. (1994). Interparental conflict and parental divorce: The individual, relative, and interactive effects on adolescents across four years. *Family Relations, 43,* 387-393.

Forehand, R., Thomas, A. M., Wierson, M., Brody, G., & Fauber, R. (1990). Role of maternal functioning and parenting skills in adolescents functioning following parental divorce. *Journal of Abnormal Psychology, 99,* 278-283.

Forehand, R., & Wierson, M. (1993). The role of developmental factors in planning behavioral interventions for children: Disruptive behavior as an example. *Behavior Therapy, 24,* 117-141.

Fulghum, R. (1993). *All I really need to know I learned in kindergarten: Uncommon thoughts on common things.* New York: Fawcett.

Grych, J. H., & Fincham, F. D. (1990). Marital conflict and children's adjustment: A cognitive-contextual framework. *Psychological Bulletin, 108,* 267-290.

Grych, J. H., & Fincham, F. D. (1992). Interventions for children of divorce: Towards greater integration of research and action. *Psychological Bulletin, 111,* 434-454.

Grych, J. H., & Fincham, F. D. (1993). Children's appraisals of marital conflict: Initial investigations of the cognitive-contextual framework. *Child Development*, *64*, 215-230.

Guidubaldi, J., & Perry, J. (1985). Divorce and mental health sequelae for children: A two-year follow-up of a nationwide sample. *Journal of the American Academy of Child Psychiatry*, *24*, 531-537.

Guidubaldi, J., Perry, J. D., & Cleminshaw, H. K. (1984). The legacy of parental divorce: A nationwide study of family status and selected mediating variables on children's academic and social competencies. In B. B. Lahey & A. E. Kazdin (Eds.), *Advances in clinical child psychology* (Vol. 7, pp. 109-151). New York: Plenum.

Guidubaldi, J., Perry, J. D., & Nastasi, B. K. (1987). Assessment and intervention for children of divorce: Implications of the NASP-KSU nationwide study. In J. P. Vincent (Ed.), *Advances in family intervention, assessment and theory: A research annual* (Vol. 4, pp. 33-69). Greenwich, CT: JAI.

Hess, R. D., & McDevitt, T. M. (1984). Some cognitive consequences of maternal intervention techniques: A longitudinal study. *Child Development*, *55*, 2017-2030.

Hetherington, E. M. (1993). An overview of the Virginia longitudinal study of divorce and remarriage with a focus on early adolescence. *Journal of Family Psychology*, *7*, 39-56.

Hetherington, E. M., Cox, M., & Cox, R. (1979). Play and social interaction in children following divorce. *Journal of Social Issues*, *35*, 26-49.

Jaycox, L. H., & Repetti, R. L. (1993). Conflicts in families and the psychological adjustment of preadolescent children. *Journal of Family Psychology*, *7*, 344-355.

Kelly, J. B., & Wallerstein, J. S. (1977). Brief interventions with children in divorcing families. *American Journal of Orthopsychiatry*, *47*, 23-39.

Kliewer, W., & Sandler, I. N. (1993). Social competence and coping among children of divorce. *American Journal of Orthopsychiatry*, *63*, 432-440.

Long, N., Forehand, R., Fauber, R., & Brody, G. H. (1987). Self-perceived and independently observed competence of young adolescents as a function of parental marital conflict and recent divorce. *Journal of Abnormal Child Psychology*, *15*, 15-27.

Long, N., Slater, E., Forehand, R., & Fauber, R. (1988). Continued high or reduced interparental conflict following divorce: Relationship to young adolescent adjustment. *Journal of Consulting and Clinical Psychology*, *56*, 467-469.

Neighbors, B., Forehand, R., & McVicar, D. (1993). Resilient adolescents and interparental conflict. *American Journal of Orthopsychiatry*, *63*, 462-471.

Pedro-Carroll, J. L., & Cowen, E. L. (1985). The children of divorce intervention program: An investigation of the efficacy of a school-based prevention program. *Journal of Consulting and Clinical Psychology*, *53*, 603-611.

Pedro-Carroll, J. L., & Cowen, E. L. (1987). The children of divorce intervention program: Implementation and evaluation of a time limited group approach. In J. P. Vincent (Ed.), *Advances in family intervention, assessment and theory* (Vol. 4, pp. 281-307). Greenwich, CT: JAI.

Pettit, G. S., Dodge, K. A., & Brown, M. M. (1988). Early family experience, social problem solving patterns, and children's social competence. *Child Development*, *59*, 107-120.

Radovanovic, H. (1993). Parental conflict and children's coping styles in litigating separated families: Relationships with children's adjustment. *Journal of Abnormal Child Psychology, 21,* 697-713.

Reid, W. J., & Crisafulli, A. (1990). Marital discord and child behavior problems: A meta-analysis. *Journal of Abnormal Child Psychology, 18,* 105-117.

Robin, A. L., & Foster, S. L. (1989). *Negotiating parent-adolescent conflict.* New York: Guilford.

Rutter, M. (in press). Beyond longitudinal data: Causes, consequences, changes, and continuity. *Journal of Consulting and Clinical Psychology.*

Stevenson, D. L., & Baker, D. P. (1987). The family-school relation and the child's school performance. *Child Development, 58,* 1348-1357.

Thomas, A. M., & Forehand R. (1993). The role of paternal variables in divorced and married families: Prediction of teacher-report of adolescent internalizing and externalizing problems. *American Journal of Orthopsychiatry, 63,* 126-135.

Wierson, M., Forehand, R., Fauber, R., & McCombs, A. (1989). Buffering young male adolescents against negative parental divorce influences: The role of good parent-adolescent relations. *Child Study Journal, 19,* 101-116.

• CHAPTER 8 •

Truancy, Family Processes, and Interventions

JANE CORVILLE-SMITH

Concerns about school absence are often linked to general concerns about its connection to various social problems (Paterson, 1989) and the serious implications that school absence and dropout have for society as a whole (Schultz, 1987). Berg (1992) recently recommended that greater attention be given to understanding school absence disorders because they serve as an indicator of various educational, social, family, legal, medical, and psychiatric problems. School administrators have also expressed concern for school absence (Levanto, 1975; Rood, 1989). Noted are the serious administrative costs (Levine, 1984) as well as the reduction in the quality of educational leadership if considerable time is spent locating students and contacting parents (Duckworth & deJung, 1989).

Evidence of a link between school absence and negative outcomes in adulthood include unstable employment histories (Farrington, 1980; Gray, Smith, & Rutter, 1980; Hibbett, Fogelman, & Manor, 1990), lower income levels (Robins & Ratcliff, 1980), a greater likelihood of involvement in antisocial and deviant behaviors (Farrington, 1980; Hibbett & Fogelman, 1990; Robins & Ratcliff, 1980), and marital breakdown and depression (Hibbett & Fogelman, 1990).

It is also generally agreed that there are two broad types of school absence disorders—truancy and school phobia. Truancy is viewed as a behavioral or conduct disorder; school phobia is considered an emotional or anxiety disorder (Berg, 1992). It is generally acknowl-edged that truancy is the more widespread of the two school absence disorders. Reid (1985) noted that the incidence of school phobia (refusal) is so low that it is unlikely that most teachers and social workers encounter it in their careers. Truancy, on the other hand, is more common. Although both school phobia and truancy are important, it is the latter that is my focus in this chapter. Although often defined as absence from school for the entire school day (Levanto, 1975), truancy has recently come to include students who selectively cut class(es). Duckworth (1988) speculated that when a school reports 1 in 10 students were absent for an entire school day, likely 1 in 3 skipped at least one class that day.

School phobia has captured the strong interest of psychologists and psychiatrists, and numerous theoretical and diagnostic publi-cations have appeared, providing a basis for treatment and inter-vention programs, but truancy has received relatively small amounts of research attention and consequently lacks a scientific back-ground from which to base treatment (Galloway, 1980). Published information on truant behavior, particularly up to the mid-1970s, appeared only intermittently and remained largely the domain of teachers, educational welfare officers, educational social workers, and attendance officers. More recently, however, truancy has come to be considered a major social problem (Brown, 1983), and greater attention has been directed toward identifying the factors precipi-tating its occurrence (Kearney & Silverman, 1990, 1993; Levine, 1984; Murgatroyd, 1987; Reid, 1983, 1985; Taylor & Adelman, 1990; Weinberg & Weinberg, 1992).

Several factors have been linked to school absence. These factors can be classified as child, school, community, and home based. It is important that the relative contribution of each of the factors be considered in developing interventions to treat school absence (Levine, 1984; Weinberg & Weinberg, 1992).

Included among child-based explanations is consideration of children experiencing problems with social and emotional func-tioning, such as poor relations with peers (Billington, 1979; Croft & Grygier, 1956), low self-esteem, low academic self-concept (Reid, 1985; Southworth, 1992), and delinquency (Farrington, 1980; May, 1975; Reid, 1986; Tennent, 1971). Moreover, children may avoid school because they are unable to perform assigned work due to low intelligence or achievement (Billington, 1979; Farrington,

1980; Kavanaugh & Carroll, 1977; Reid, 1982; Sommer & Nagel, 1991), learning disabilities (Levine, 1984; Weinberg & Weinberg, 1992), or learning styles incompatible with classroom instruction (Levine, 1984).

School-based explanations include inadequate monitoring and recording of attendance (Sharples, Loken, Marshall, Whitehead, & Paragg, 1979), failing to distinguish excused from unexcused absences, inconsistent enforcement of school attendance rules (Levine, 1984), student perception of curriculum as irrelevant or boring (Reid, 1984), poor teacher-pupil relations (Bealing, 1990; Buist, 1980; Nielsen & Gerber, 1979; Reynolds, Jones, St. Leger, & Murgatroyd, 1980; Seabrook, 1974; Sullivan & Riches, 1976; Zieman & Benson, 1980, 1981), alleged bullying (Reid, 1983; Sullivan & Riches, 1976), and school transfers and class changes (Buist, 1980; Reid, 1983).

Community-based factors include fear of being harassed by neighborhood gangs and of attending interracial schools in which the child is a member of the minority (Levine, 1984). It has also been suggested that truant behaviors are a product of antisocial values passed on from the truant's parents and reinforced in the wider community or neighborhood (Brown, 1983).

Family-based explanations of school absence can be divided into two categories: those that revolve around family structure and those pertaining to family process. Cooper (1986) noted that because truant behavior has generally been viewed as a social problem, there has been a strong interest in the home background. Family-based explanations suggest truancy is a form of emotional disturbance or maladjustment (Tyerman, 1968), likely precipitated by adversity in the home (Berg, 1992; Hersov, 1960). Wardhaugh (1990) similarly noted that a focus among many writers was on a deviant family believed responsible for the truant behavior either through neglect or deprivation. Some parents are believed to collude in their children's absence by failing to demonstrate an interest in education and not insisting on regular attendance (Galloway, 1976; Tyerman, 1968).

Studies on family structure include its link with family size. Truants are often found to be from large families (Brooks, Buri, Byrne, & Hudson, 1962; Farrington, 1980; Hersov, 1960; Kavanaugh & Carroll, 1977; May, 1975; Mitchell, 1972). The fathers of truants are often unskilled or semiskilled workers (Davie, Butler, & Goldstein,

1972; Fogelman & Richardson, 1974; Fogelman, Tibbenham, & Lambert, 1980; Kavanaugh & Carroll, 1977; May, 1975; Mitchell, 1972; Reid, 1984), unemployed (Farrington, 1980; May, 1975; Reid, 1984), irregularly employed (Blythman, 1975; Farrington, 1980; May, 1975), and overrepresented in lower socioeconomic groups (Cooper, 1966; Davie et al., 1972; Farrington, 1980; Hersov, 1960; Kavanaugh & Carroll, 1977; May, 1975; Mitchell, 1972; Nielsen & Gerber, 1979).

In this chapter, I focus on the link between family process factors and truant behavior, including a discussion of the interventions and treatments involving the truant's family to reduce school absence. In the sections that follow, I review the literature on the above-mentioned family process factors: family interaction, parental rejection, overprotection/overindulgence, parental control and discipline, the mental health of truants' relatives, and the intactness of the truant's family. These factors are not mutually exclusive; all function as indicators of the quality of relations among family members of truants.

Family Interaction. The relationship between parents and their truant children has received little research attention. However, some professionals (Nielsen & Gerber, 1979; Tyerman, 1958) have suggested that the relations of parents to truant children are often distant and negative.

Bernstein, Svingen, and Garfinkel (1990) and Huffington and Sevitt (1989) employed systematic measures in their investigations of the relations of school absentees and their families. Huffington and Sevitt (1989) examined whether features of family interaction distinguished school phobic and truant families from one another. Employing the Summary Format for Family Interaction and the Family Description Form, they found that two items on the Family Description Form significantly distinguished the two groups. The behavior of school phobics within the family was significantly more passive, lacking in initiative, and seeming sad and appearing to have given up. A list of characteristics describing the families of school phobics was compiled, but a similar list could not be generated for truants because no clear pattern of family interaction could be identified. The authors cautioned that because the truants were drawn from a psychiatric agency it was unlikely they were representative of truants in general; they might not even represent a coherent subgroup of psychiatric truants, which could explain why patterns of family interaction were unclear.

Huffington and Sevitt (1989) also employed the Family Health Scale (FHS) to assess the level of health or pathology in the families of truants, school phobics, and nonpsychiatric controls. They noted that although the scores of the absentees (i.e., truants and school phobics) were not significantly different from one another, they scored lower than the nonpsychiatric controls, suggesting that family functioning was less healthy.

Bernstein et al. (1990) used the Family Assessment Measure (FAM) to assess family relations of what they called school phobics and their parents. The children were classified into one of four diagnostic groups: depressive and anxiety disordered, depressive disorder only, anxiety disorder only, and neither depressive or anxiety disordered. The clinical description provided for this latter group (i.e., conduct disordered and oppositionally defiant) suggests that these children may, in fact, have been truants rather than phobics.

Bernstein et al. (1990) reported clinically significant dysfunction on the subscales of the FAM in the areas of role performance and values and norms for all groups except the anxiety group. As Bernstein and colleagues (1990) noted, dysfunction in role performance suggests that boundaries between parental and child roles may be poorly defined, whereas dysfunction of values and norms suggests a conflict between family and cultural values, which often results in the child receiving contradictory messages regarding school attendance, independence, and separation. Moreover, they noted that the most dysfunctional families in the sample had been referred from a social agency rather than a school and a truancy petition had been filed. The diagnosis of these children was likely depressive disorder only or neither depressive or anxiety disorder (i.e., truant type).

Parental Rejection. There is some evidence suggesting that the parents of truants may be more likely to reject their children (Andriola, 1943; Hersov, 1960). Andriola (1943), in a retrospective study of truancy cases, found that almost four fifths, or 18 of a total of 25 cases, had been rejected by one or both parents. Andriola (1943) commented that this finding was particularly notable, as seven of the truants had received little or no treatment, making it impossible to determine whether they too were rejected. More recently, Hersov (1960) noted a pattern of maternal rejection prior to age 5 and paternal rejection after age 5 in a group of truants.

Parental Overprotection/Overindulgence. Although a comparison study of truant and nontruant students suggests that the former are more often overprotected and overindulged (Little & Thompson, 1983), a comparison study of truants and school phobics found that the school phobics were more likely to be overprotected by both mothers and fathers as compared to the truants (51% vs. 15% among mothers and 32% vs. 10%, respectively, among fathers) (Cooper, 1986).

Little and Thompson's (1983) finding that the truants in their sample were more overprotected than the nontruants appears to contradict the findings by Andriola (1943) and Hersov (1960) that truants tend to be rejected by their parents. Andriola (1943), and more recently Blagg (1987), suggested that overprotection may actually be rooted in underlying feelings of rejection for the child. The contradiction thus may be more apparent then real.

Parental Control and Discipline. Inconsistent handling and defective parenting has been reported in families of truants (Cooper, 1966; Cooper, 1986; Tyerman, 1968; Young, 1947). In an early study, Young (1947) compared samples of truants and nontruants and found that the truants were significantly more likely to come from homes where discipline was defective. Tyerman (1968) reported excessive parental control, evidenced by the frequent use of corporal punishment, in the homes of truants.

In a comparison study of truants and school phobics (refusers), Cooper (1986) found the use of corporal punishment was more evident among the truants (28%) versus school phobics (0%). In an earlier comparison study of school phobics, truants, and controls, Cooper (1966) found that "over-anxious discipline administered by a dominant mother" (p. 229) distinguished the school phobics from all other children in the study.

Mental Health. Relatively few researchers have examined the mental health of first-degree relatives of truants (Cooper, 1986; Hersov, 1960; Warren, 1948). Comparing truants and school phobics, Warren (1948) found 7 of the 8 mothers and 4 of the 8 fathers of the school phobics were disturbed; all 12 of the mothers and 9 of the 12 fathers of the truants suffered from a psychiatric illness. Cooper (1986) studied cases of truants and school phobics and noted that 8% of the truants' mothers versus 5% of the school phobics' mothers were anxious, ill, or depressed; 8% of the truants' fathers, compared to 3% of the school phobics' fathers, were similarly described.

Comparing truants, school phobics, and regularly attending controls, Hersov (1960) noted that neurotic illness was more prevalent among parents, parental siblings, and grandparents of children with school phobia as compared to the other two groups.

It would appear that there is some evidence to suggest that first-degree relatives of truants may be likely to suffer from a psychological disorder or mental illness, although it is unclear whether this is more likely the case in the families of truants as compared to school phobics or perhaps characteristic of both types of school avoiders.

Intactness of Family. In an early comparison study of truants and nontruants, Young (1947) did not find a significant difference in the number of truants versus nontruants from nonintact homes. In a more recent comparison study of truants and nontruants, Sommer and Nagel (1991) found that the truants were less likely than the nontruants to live with both parents (8 of 25 vs. 14 of 25, respectively). Tyerman (1968) reported that in one third to one half of all cases of truancy, the child lived in a home disrupted by separation, divorce, desertion, or death. Elliott (1975) reported that more than half (53%) of those charged with school nonattendance in his study were from a home in which at least one parent was absent, compared to 37% of the subjects appearing in court on some other charge. Reid (1984) found that pupils who were persistently absent were more likely to have experienced some form of family disruption (e.g., parental separation, divorce, or death) than a control group of regularly attending students and a second control group of academically superior students (44%, 19%, and 23%, respectively).

In a comparison study of truants and school phobics (refusers), Cooper (1986) reported, based on case study reports, that truants were more likely to come from a divorced or separated home (59%) as compared to school phobics (refusers) (24%).

However, in a more recent study comparing groups of truants, school phobics (refusers), and combined truants and school phobics (refusers), Bools, Foster, Brown, and Berg (1990) found no significant differences between the groups with regard to intactness of their family. Of 100 children, less than half (46 cases) lived with their biological parents; 16 children resided in a stepparent family. This finding also suggested that less than half of the nonattending youth making up the sample resided in homes where both biological parents were present.

In general, the evidence appears to suggest that one third to two thirds of truants, depending on the sample and the study, live in families that have been disrupted through separation or divorce. Significantly, where comparisons have been made between truants and other students, the data (with the exception of Young, 1947) consistently show that truants are more likely to be from nonintact families.

Summary of Family Factors. Because too few empirical investigations have been conducted employing standardized measures, little is currently known of the interactions among family members of truants. Bernstein and colleagues (1990) recently suggested the roles of family members may be poorly defined and absentees' families may be in conflict with society regarding values and norms. Huffington and Sevitt (1989) report being unable to identify patterns of family interaction among the truants in their study. However, they did find evidence that family functioning may be less healthy among absentee students.

Hersov (1960) noted that parental rejection appeared more common in the families of truants, compared with school phobics and a control group of regular attenders. However, others (Little & Thompson, 1983) noted a tendency for the truants to be overprotected and overindulged (possibly a disguised rejection; see Andriola, 1943; Blagg, 1987) when compared to a control group of nontruants.

As to parental discipline, there are so few systematic investigations that it is presently impossible to know whether parents adopt inappropriate discipline strategies to deal with difficult children or ineffective parenting functions as a precursor in the development of school avoidant disorders. Similarly, too little is known of the psychological state or mental health of truants' family members as this too is an area that has received limited research attention. What research is available would suggest that the mental health of first-degree relatives may be an issue of importance.

Intervention and Treatment

Galloway (1980) noted over a decade ago that the scientific literature offered little direction in the treatment of truant behavior. Unfortunately, this situation has not changed significantly. Regardless of the exact procedure used to manage truant behavior, however, Levine (1984) suggests that regular attendance is more likely if the absentees' parents are actively involved in the treatment process. The following sections present a review of the various treatment interventions advanced to reduce truancy. Only the interventions or treatments that engage the truant's family in treatment have been included here. For presentation purposes these interventions are divided into six approaches: therapy/counseling, residential, legal, family therapy, behavioral, and family-school. It should be noted that in many instances more than one approach was adopted in treating the disorder, but usually one strategy dominated.

Therapy/Counseling Interventions. Blagg (1987), reviewing literature on school absence, noted that a psychotherapeutic treatment approach predominated initially. Warren (1948), in an early study of school phobics and truants, employed psychotherapy in treatment. However, limited information was reported regarding the specific procedures used. Andriola (1943) examined cases of truants who had been referred to a children's center for intensive treatment that involved sessions with a psychiatrist. Again, few details were provided regarding the treatment. In both Andriola's (1943) and Warren's (1948) studies, there was, however, reference to including the absentee child's parent(s) in treatment.

Galloway (1986) maintained that although the effectiveness of psychotherapy and counseling approaches has been demonstrated with some school phobics, these approaches have been less amenable to treating truants with disruptive behavioral problems. Reid (1985) noted that we currently know very little about the management of truancy using guidance and counseling, because it has not been widely researched.

Residential Interventions. Warren (1948) was the first to advance hospitalization as a viable treatment measure. Warren supported hospital, hostel, and boarding school placements as an adjunct to psychotherapy, noting that "psychotherapy was easier in the neutral and emotionally uncharged atmosphere away from the home" (p. 268). Andriola (1943) had earlier commented that the success in treating truants had been impeded by a lack of hospital or other detaining facilities for youngsters requiring such treatment. Andriola also advocated hospitalizing truants as an adjunct to psychotherapy, although on the premise that it would prevent truants from running from their problems once therapeutic discussions reached an intense level.

Truant children may also be sent to a boarding home or boarding school to live as evidenced in the study by Andriola. Overlapping with legal interventions, truant children can also be removed from their home and sent to an observation and assessment center on an interim care order (Berg, 1985).

Legal Interventions. The court is often used when the parents of the truant child are seen as either "apathetic or hostile" to their child's schooling (Brown, 1987). Typically, three legal sanctions are available. In the first, solutions revolve around taking the parents to court and imposing fines to encourage them to take greater initiative in ensuring their child's regular attendance at school (Brown, 1987; Desnoyers & Pauker, 1988). Reid (1987) recommended that the fines imposed on parents of truant children be automatic and graduated for repeated offenses. Second, the child's poor attendance may be used as evidence that he or she is in need of care, protection, or control and therefore a care or supervision order may be issued (Galloway, 1986). Wardhaugh (1991) similarly noted that when children fail to attend school, their educational needs are believed neglected, and hence a care order may be issued removing the child from the home to preserve his or her opportunity for an education. Third, an adjournment procedure may be used in which the magistrate suspends the court proceedings for a specified period of time, allowing the child time to resume attending school regularly (Berg, 1985). According to Berg, the adjournment procedure is most effective when supplemented with sessions with a social worker to counsel parents and truant children on problems relating to the school absence.

Family Therapy Interventions. An alternative to the psychoanalytic view focusing on the child's character deficits and the sociological view emphasizing environmental factors is the systems or interactionist view (Compher, 1982). From an interactionist point of view, truancy is believed symptomatic of malfunction among significant persons in the system (i.e., parent[s] and school personnel). Interventions therefore involve all significant persons and not simply the truant child (Compher, 1982).

Compher identified three typologies of parent-school interactional systems. He recommended that therapists learn strategies to work effectively with each to promote the constructive dialogue needed to resolve the child's attendance problem.

Wetchler (1986) similarly suggested that the family and school are interacting systems that often function to maintain the child's problem behavior. Wetchler recommended that the therapist initially treat each system separately and rejoin the two once a cooperative working relationship was established.

According to Wetchler, the families of truants are often disengaged. Consequently, the parents know little about what or how their child is doing in school. In treating the family, he recommended realigning the family hierarchy and developing contingency contracts between the child and his or her parents.

Behavioral Interventions. In reviewing the truancy intervention literature, Schultz (1987) noted that behavioral approaches have been used to improve school attendance. For instance, Brooks (1974), MacDonald, Gallimore, and MacDonald (1970) and Schloss, Kane, and Miller (1981) used contingency and behavioral contracts that included parents and/or grandparents in the treatment of truant children. These interventions were school based, being initiated and monitored by school personnel. They nevertheless actively sought and involved the truant child's parent(s) in treatment.

Family-School Interventions. Wetchler (1986) speculated that possibly the most critical step in treating school-focused problems is developing a working alliance between the family and school. The practice of parents and educators working cooperatively to reduce school absence has been advocated by several educators (Dowdle, 1990; Eastwold, 1989; Miller, 1986; Rood, 1989; Stine, 1989). Duckworth (1988) found in a study of several high schools that most important in reducing absenteeism was the alliance between parents and teachers committed to increasing pupil's attendance. Based on findings from their study, Eggert and Nicholas (1992) recommended that the barriers to communication between the home and school be dismantled.

According to Levine (1984), an initial step in reducing school absenteeism is parental knowledge of the child's whereabouts. Duckworth and deJung (1989) examined, among other things, the effect of parental supervision in inhibiting school absence. They found that parental monitoring exhibited a strong negative correlation with frequency of class cutting as compared to school-based consequences for unexcused absence. Duckworth and deJung's (1989) finding supports the importance of including parents in attempts to reduce student absence, as parents apparently function as inhibitors to truancy.

Eastwold (1989) noted that the most effective attendance policies involve contact by phone with parents regarding unexplained absence. Licht, Gard, and Guardino (1991) reported that students whose parents were contacted when they were absent, compared to a control group whose parents were not contacted, sustained their level of attendance during the period of the study. Sheats and Dunkleberger (1979) found that truancy decreased even if the parents were contacted by someone other than the principal; the school secretary had the same impact. In fact, Helm and Burkett (1989) noted that even computerized phone messages to truants' homes were effective in improving student attendance.

Miller (1986) recommended family school conferences to discuss the child's attendance problem when it becomes more persistent. Dowdle (1990) implemented such a policy where the truant students, their parents, and school counselors come together to discuss the attendance problem. According to Dowdle, this provides an opportunity to discuss the ramifications and consequences of continued absenteeism. According to Stine (1989), one of the benefits of suspending truant pupils from school is the opportunity it provides for a home-school conference to establish consequences for the child's behavior.

Interventions Derived From an Identification of Motives Underlying School Absence. Recent authors have suggested that although the presenting problem is nonattendance, there are various reasons or motives underlying the behavior (Kearney & Silverman, 1990, 1993; Murgatroyd, 1987; Reid, 1983, 1985; Taylor & Adelman, 1990). However, despite growing recognition of these different motives, there is little empirical work on how to assess pupils' motives and select treatments most likely to promote regular attendance.

As recently as 1990, Kearney and Silverman noted that researchers had not examined assigning treatment based on the motivating variables associated with the child's decision not to attend school. Consequently, they employed a measure they developed earlier called the School Refusal Assessment Scale (SRAS). They argued that this measure could be used both to assess the motives behind students school avoidance and in prescribing treatment. For instance, Kearney (1993) suggested that treatment for pupils motivated to absence for tangible rewards (e.g., to watch television) should include parent training in procedures such as shaping and time-out, and contingency contracts to reduce the rewards for staying at home and increase the rewards for school attendance.

Suggestions and Conclusions

A primary aim of this chapter was to review existing literature on the link between family process factors and truancy. It is evident, however, that despite the recurring theme in the literature of the family's influence, there is relatively little well-grounded empirical information on the interactions and relations among family members of truants. For instance, several findings are dated, some are based on case study reports, and most researchers have failed to use systematic measures in their investigations. Huffington and Sevitt (1989) speculated that our ability to describe family interactions of nonattending students has been impeded by an absence of appropriate measures. Such information it is felt would, however, enhance the precision of treatment choice (Hersov, 1977).

A review of literature on the management of truancy is similarly limited, although it appears that legal, and more recently, school-initiated family-school approaches are among the dominant interventions. More promising is the recent literature acknowledging that there are several different motivational bases for not attending school regularly and that these differences must be taken into account when prescribing treatment (Kearney & Silverman, 1990, 1993; Levanto, 1975; Murgatroyd, 1987; Reid, 1983, 1985; Taylor & Adelman, 1990).

Interventions failing to consider the motives that underlie a student's school absence could result in contributing to the problem rather than to the solution (Murgatroyd, 1987). Mulvany (1989) found that various social control agents (i.e., teachers, attendance officers, and counseling and guidance personnel), when questioned about the causes of nonattendance for specific cases, admitted they were unsure and therefore frequently resorted to handling cases on a trial-and-error basis. Other workers admitted to resorting to punitive methods only because other approaches were ineffective and they were uncertain of what else to do. Wardhaugh (1990) suggested that because truancy has typically drawn on criminal models of deviance, treatment or management strategies have tended toward interventions of control aimed to promote change by imposing sanctions. This may explain in part why the successful management of truant behavior continues to elude us—treatments are often simply unrelated to the underlying cause, reason, or motives for the nonattendance in the first place.

Because truants are not necessarily delinquent (May, 1975; Tennent, 1971), future researchers should be encouraged to follow the example of Kearney and Silverman (1990, 1993) in developing systematic measures to permit identifying the underlying motives of school absence and promote the interface of assessment and treatment.

An additional point that should be underscored is that because school-related problems such as absenteeism involve significant persons (i.e., parents and teachers) in two contexts (i.e., home and school), it is likely that treatment success would be strongly influenced by cooperation and commitment between persons within these two systems.

Because school absence serves as an indicator of a variety of problems, it is important that we direct our attention to acquiring a better understanding of the disorder (Berg, 1992). A better understanding of the individual's reasons or motives for not attending (i.e., whether child, school, community, or family based) would facilitate identifying the most effective treatment and thus restore or promote students' regular attendance at school.

References

Andriola, J. (1943). Success and failure in the treatment of 25 truants at a child guidance clinic. *American Journal of Orthopsychiatry, 13,* 691-717.

Bealing, V. (1990). Pupil perception of absenteeism in the secondary school. *Maladjustment and Therapeutic Education, 8,* 19-34.

Berg, I. (1985). Annotation: The management of truancy. *Journal of Child Psychology and Psychiatry and Allied Disciplines, 26,* 325-331.

Berg, I. (1992). Absence from school and mental health. *British Journal of Psychiatry, 161,* 154-166.

Bernstein, G., Svingen, P., & Garfinkel, B. (1990). School phobia: Patterns of family functioning. *Journal of the American Academy of Child and Adolescent Psychiatry, 29,* 24-30.

Billington, B. (1979, Autumn). Truants: Some personality characteristics. *Durham and Newcastle Research Review,* pp. 1-6.

Blagg, N. (1987). *School phobia and its treatment.* London: Billing.

Blythman, M. (1975). Truants suffer more from the disadvantages of life. *Scottish Educational Journal, 58,* 80-84.

Bools, C., Foster, J., Brown, I., & Berg, I. (1990). The identification of psychiatric disorders in children who fail to attend school: A cluster analysis of a non-clinical population. *Psychological Medicine, 20,* 171-181.

Brooks, D. B. (1974). Contingency contracts with truants. *Personnel and Guidance Journal, 52,* 316-320.

Brooks, E., Buri, J., Byrne, E., & Hudson, M. (1962). Socioeconomic factors, parental attitudes, and school attendance. *Social Work, 7,* 103-108.

Brown, D. (1983). Truants, families and schools: A critique of the literature on truancy. *Educational Review, 35,* 225-235.

Brown, D. (1987). The attitudes of parents to education and the school attendance of their children. In K. Reid (Ed.), *Combatting school absenteeism* (pp. 32-44). London: Hodder & Stoughton.

Buist, M. (1980). Truants talking. *Scottish Educational Review, 12,* 40-51.

Compher, J. (1982, September). Parent-School-Child Systems: Triadic assessment and intervention. *Social Casework: The Journal of Contemporary Social Work, 83,* 415-423.

Cooper, M. (1986). A model of persistent school absenteeism. *Educational Research, 28,* 14-20.

Cooper, M. G. (1966). School refusal: An inquiry into the part played by school and home. *Educational Research, 8,* 223-229.

Croft, I., & Grygier, T. (1956). Social relationships of truants and juvenile delinquents. *Human Relations, 9,* 439-466.

Davie, R., Butler, N., & Goldstein, H. (1972). *From birth to seven.* London: Longmans, in association with National Children's Bureau.

Desnoyers, J., & Pauker, J. (1988). *School attendance and non-attendance in Canada and the United States: Survey of methods and programs to increase school attendance, decrease absenteeism, and deal with drop out.* Toronto: MGS Publication Services.

Dowdle, J. M. (1990). Keeping kids in school. *North Central Association Quarterly, 64,* 470-472.

Duckworth, K. (1988). Coping with student absenteeism. *Practitioner, 14*, 3-14.

Duckworth, K., & deJung, J. (1989). Inhibiting class cutting among high school students. *High School Journal, 72*, 188-195.

Eastwold, P. (1989). Attendance is important: Combatting truancy in the secondary school. *NASSP Bulletin, 73*, 28-31.

Eggert, L., & Nicholas, L. (1992). Speaking like a skipper: Skippin' an' gettin' high. *Journal of Language and Social Psychology, 11*, 75-100.

Elliott, R. (1975). Some characteristics of school non-attenders assessed at Lisnevin school. *Community Home Schools Gazette, 69*, 400-403.

Farrington, D. (1980). Truancy, delinquency, the home, and the school. In L. Hersov & I. Berg (Eds.), *Out of school: Modern perspectives in truancy and school refusal* (pp. 49-64). Chichester, UK: John Wiley.

Fogelman, K., & Richardson, K. (1974). School attendance: Some results from the National Child Development Study. In B. Turner (Ed.), *Truancy* (pp. 29-51). London: Ward Lock Educational.

Fogelman, K., Tibbenham, A., & Lambert, L. (1980). Absence from school: Findings from the National Child Development Study. In L. Hersov & I. Berg (Eds.), *Out of school: Modern perspectives in truancy and school refusal* (pp. 25-47). Chichester, UK: John Wiley.

Galloway, D. (1976). Persistent unjustified absence from school. *Trends in Education, 30*, 22-27.

Galloway, D. (1980). Problems in the assessment and management of persistent absenteeism from school. In L. Hersov & I. Berg (Eds.), *Out of school: Modern perspectives in truancy and school refusal* (pp. 149-169). Chichester, UK: John Wiley.

Galloway, D. (1986). Should truants be treated? *Maladjustment and Therapeutic Education, 4*, 18-24.

Gray, G., Smith, A., & Rutter, M. (1980). School attendance and the first year of employment. In L. Hersov & I. Berg (Eds.), *Out of school: Modern perspectives in truancy and school refusal* (pp. 343-370). Chichester, UK: John Wiley.

Helm, C. M., & Burkett, C. W. (1989). Effects of computer-assisted telecommunications on school attendance. *Journal of Educational Research, 82*, 362-365.

Hersov, L. A. (1960). Persistent non-attendance at school. *Journal of Psychology and Psychiatry, 1*, 130-136.

Hersov, L. (1977). School refusal. In M. Rutter & L. Hersov (Eds.), *Child psychiatry: Modern approaches* (pp. 455-486). Oxford, UK: Blackwell Scientific Publications.

Hibbett, A., & Fogelman, K. (1990). Future lives of truants: Family formation and health related behaviour. *British Journal of Educational Psychology, 60*, 171-179.

Hibbett, A., Fogelman, K., & Manor, O. (1990). Occupational outcomes of truancy. *British Journal of Educational Psychology, 60*, 23-36.

Huffington, C., & Sevitt, M. (1989). Family interaction in adolescent school phobia. *Journal of Family Therapy, 11*, 353-375.

Kavanaugh, A., & Carroll, H. C. M. (1977). Pupil attendance in three comprehensive schools: A study of the pupils and their families. In H. C. M. Carroll (Ed.), *Absenteeism in South Wales* (pp. 40-49). Swansea, UK: University College of Swansea Faculty of Education.

Kearney, C. A. (1993). Depression and school refusal: A review with comments on classification and treatment. *Journal of School Psychology, 31*, 267-279.

Kearney, C. A., & Silverman, W. K. (1990). A preliminary analysis of a functional model of assessment and treatment for school refusal behaviour. *Behaviour Modification, 14,* 340-366.

Kearney, C. A., & Silverman, W. (1993). Measuring the function of school refusal behavior: The school refusal assessment scale. *Journal of Clinical Child Psychology, 22,* 85-96.

Levanto, J. (1975). High school absenteeism. *NASSP Bulletin, 59,* 100-104.

Levine, R. (1984). An assessment tool for early intervention in cases of truancy. *Social Work in Education, 6,* 133-150.

Licht, B. G., Gard, T., & Guardino, C. (1991). Modifying school attendance of special education high school students. *Journal of Educational Research, 84,* 368-373.

Little, L. F., & Thompson, R. (1983). Truancy: How parents and teachers contribute. *School Counsellor, 30,* 285-291.

MacDonald, W., Gallimore, R., & MacDonald, G. (1970). Contingency counselling by school personnel: An economical model of intervention. *Journal of Applied Behavior Analysis, 3,* 175-182.

May, D. (1975). Truancy, school absenteeism and delinquency. *Scottish Educational Studies, 7,* 97-106.

Miller, D. (1986). Fifty ways to improve attendance. *NASSP Bulletin, 70,* 74-79.

Mitchell, S. (1972). The absentees. *Education in the North, 9,* 22-28.

Mulvany, J. (1989). Social control processes, activities and ideologies—The case of school non-attendance in Melbourne. *Australian and New Zealand Journal of Sociology, 25,* 222-238.

Murgatroyd, S. (1987). Combatting truancy: A counselling approach. In K. Reid (Ed.), *Combatting school absenteeism* (pp. 121-130). London: Hodder & Stoughton.

Nielsen, A., & Gerber, D. (1979). Psychosocial aspects of truancy in early adolescence. *Adolescence, 14,* 313-326.

Paterson, F. (1989). Introduction: Truancy is normal. In F. Paterson (Ed.), *Out of place: Public policy and the emergence of truancy* (pp. 1-3). London: Falmer.

Reid, K. (1982). The self-concept and persistent school absenteeism. *British Journal of Educational Psychology, 52,* 179-187.

Reid, K. (1983). Retrospection and persistent school absenteeism. *Educational Research, 25,* 110-115.

Reid, K. (1984). Some social, psychological, and educational aspects related to persistent school absenteeism. *Research in Education, 31,* 63-82.

Reid, K. (1985). *Truancy and school absenteeism.* London: Hodder & Stoughton.

Reid, K. (1986). Truancy and school absenteeism: The state of the art. *Maladjustment and Therapeutic Education, 4,* 4-17.

Reid, K. (1987). Combatting school absenteeism: Main conclusions. In K. Reid (Ed.), *Combatting school absenteeism* (pp. 208-212). London: Hodder & Stoughton.

Reynolds, D., Jones, D., St. Leger, S., & Murgatroyd, S. (1980). School factors and truancy. In L. Hersov & I. Berg (Eds.), *Out of school: Modern perspectives in truancy and school refusal* (pp. 85-110). Chichester, UK: John Wiley.

Robins, L. M., & Ratcliff, K. S. (1980). The long-term outcome of truancy. In L. Hersov & I. Berg (Eds.), *Out of school: Modern perspectives on truancy and school refusal* (pp. 65-83). Chichester, UK: John Wiley.

Rood, R. E. (1989). Advice for administrators: Writing the attendance policy. *NASSP Bulletin, 73,* 21-25.

Schloss, P. J., Kane, M. S., & Miller, S. (1981). Truancy intervention with behavior disordered adolescents. *Behavioral Disorders, 6,* 175-179.

Schultz, R. M. (1987). Truancy: Issues and interventions. *Behavioral Disorders, 12,* 117-130.

Seabrook, J. (1974). Talking to truants. In B. Turner (Ed.), *Truancy* (pp. 70-78). London: Ward Lock Educational.

Sharples, B., Loken, J., Marshall, A., Whitehead, L., & Paragg, R. (1979). *Patterns of school attendance in Ontario elementary and secondary schools.* Toronto: Ontario Ministry of Education.

Sheats, D., & Dunkleberger, G. (1979). A determination of the principal's effect in school-initiated home contacts concerning attendance of elementary school students. *Journal of Educational Research, 72,* 310-312.

Sommer, B., & Nagel, S. (1991). Ecological and typological characteristics in early adolescent truancy. *Journal of Early Adolescence, 11,* 379-392.

Southworth, P. (1992). Psychological and social characteristics associated with persistent absence among secondary aged school children with special reference to different categories of persistent absence. *Personality and Individual Differences, 13,* 367-376.

Stine, M. P. (1989). Why suspend students for truancy? A principal responds. *NASSP Bulletin, 73,* 45-47.

Sullivan, R., & Riches, S. (1976). On your marks: Interviews with truants in East London. *Youth Social Work Bulletin, 3,* 8-10.

Taylor, L., & Adelman, H. (1990). School avoidance behaviour: Motivational bases and implications for intervention. *Child Psychiatry and Human Development, 20,* 219-232.

Tennent, T. G. (1971). School non-attendance and delinquency. *Educational Research, 13,* 185-190.

Tyerman, M. J. (1958). A research into truancy. *British Journal of Educational Psychology, 28,* 217-225.

Tyerman, M. J. (1968). *Truancy.* London: University of London Press.

Wardhaugh, J. (1990). Regulating truancy: The role of the education welfare service. *Sociological Review, 38,* 735-764.

Wardhaugh, J. (1991). Absent without leave: State responses to school non-attendance. *International Studies in Sociology of Education, 1,* 209-223.

Warren, W. (1948). Acute neurotic breakdown in children with refusal to go to school. *Archives of Disease in Childhood, 23,* 266-272.

Weinberg, C., & Weinberg, L. (1992). Multiple perspectives on the labelling, treatment and disciplining of at-risk students. *Journal of Humanistic Education and Development, 30,* 146-156.

Wetchler, J. (1986). Family therapy of school-focused problems: A macrosystemic perspective. *Contemporary Family Therapy: An International Journal, 8,* 224-240.

Young, A. J. (1947). Truancy: A study of mental, scholastic, and social conditions in the problem of non-attendance at school. *British Journal of Educational Psychology, 17,* 50-51.

Zieman, G. L., & Benson, G. P. (1980). School perceptions of truant adolescent boys. *Behavioral Disorders, 5,* 212-222.

Zieman, G. L., & Benson, G. P. (1981). School perceptions of truant adolescent girls. *Behavioral Disorders, 6,* 197-205.

CHAPTER 9

The Family Resource Center: A Community-Based System of Family Support Services

ROBERT W. PLANT

PATRICIA A. KING

Over the past 30 years the nature of family life in the United States has undergone tremendous change. Increased mobility has reduced the influence and availability of the extended family (Zigler & Finn-Stevenson, 1990). Increases in the divorce rate and the number of children born out of wedlock have swelled the ranks of single-parent families (U.S. Bureau of the Census, 1987). Social and economic forces have contributed to a dramatic increase in the percentage of women working outside the home (U.S. Department of Labor, 1987), which in turn has created a shortage of affordable high-quality child care and a growing number of latchkey children. These and other social changes have significantly hindered family efforts to nurture and promote the positive development of children (Zigler & Finn-Stevenson, 1990). This increased stress on the family unit has been implicated as a contributing factor in a whole host of societal ills, including child abuse, school failure, adolescent suicide, teenage pregnancy, violence, and drug addiction.

In response to increased family stress and the simultaneous erosion of stress-buffering family structures, a wide range of programs and services have been developed to empower, educate, and support the family unit. These *family support programs* share the common goals of enhancing family functioning and supporting effective parenting. A variety of programs and services have been developed, particularly in the last 6 to 8 years (National Resource Center for Family Support Programs [NRCFSP], 1993). These programs differ in many ways, including the setting, funding source, organizational structure, target population, specific goals, and the number and nature of services offered. In this chapter, we describe one model of family support service delivery—the *family resource center.*

Family Resource Centers

A family resource center (FRC) is a prevention-oriented, family-focused, community-based system of supportive and educational services provided to children and families. FRCs are community based to improve access to services and increase family involvement and community ownership. Their orientation is preventive rather than remedial. In general, FRCs attempt to build strengths and enhance competencies rather than identify and correct defects. FRCs differ from other community-based support programs focused on children in their emphasis on the family unit, rather than the individual child as the focus of supportive efforts. FRCs are based on the philosophy that "parents who are confident and competent in their parenting roles are more likely to raise healthy, productive children" (NRCFSP, 1993, p. 1).

FRCs are often located in schools, although they may also be based in community centers, churches, hospitals, or free-standing centers. Most important, an FRC is accessible to the community group it is designed to serve and should be placed in a setting that is relatively free of cultural, political, geographic, or practical barriers to utilization.

Although there are numerous FRC models, many in the field believe it is too early to promote a single, or even several, models (Gomby & Larson, 1992). Most FRC programs are relatively new and there is insufficient research to endorse any particular model or to determine which program elements are most successful. Also, it is arguable that successful programs need to be tailored to the specific needs of the community and should facilitate community ownership through community input into program design. A program that comes prepackaged may not have the flexibility to adapt to specific needs.

Rationale

FRCs are based on the concept that the family is the primary social unit and that there is a reciprocal relationship between family problems and social problems. Family problems, such as absent fathers; child abuse; and the lack of positive, nurturing, parent-child interactions, contribute to the inability to maintain economic self-sufficiency, incidence of violence, and other social problems. Unemployment, racial prejudice, illiteracy, and other social problems often have a direct, negative impact on the quality of family life. To many, the current system of social programs is inadequate primarily because it does not offer the services families need or provide them in a manner that families can easily access. For the most part, the system of care is crisis oriented and offers too little, too late. Service coordination is fragmented and communication between agencies and programs is too often poor or nonexistent. Families who often lack transportation must contact multiple agencies and tell their story over and over to access needed services. Coordination is lacking and a tangled web of inconsistent and confusing bureaucratic rules create sizable roadblocks, particularly for families and children with multiple needs (Larson, Gomby, Shiono, Lewit, & Behrman, 1992). Bureaucratic offices are typically not user friendly and focus on processing cases rather than serving families.

FRCs aim to improve on previous efforts by providing multiple services under a single roof; placing the services in a familiar, accessible, and user-friendly site; and focusing solutions on the family rather than on individuals or specific problems.

History

School-linked and school-based services are not new ideas. As early as the 1890s, school-based health clinics were operating in urban communities and offering medical exams, vaccinations, and hygiene instruction (Tyack, 1992). Beginning around and shortly after the turn of the century, philanthropic groups introduced school-based programs of free and subsidized meals, before- and after-school child care, summer programs, and social workers who functioned as advocates for poverty-stricken families. Some of these programs took hold and were incorporated into standard school operation (e.g., school social workers), some took many years before they were regularly implemented (subsidized school lunches did not become common until the late 1940s), and some programs faded out altogether despite significant community support and satisfaction (most child care programs and school-based health clinics were defunded or removed from the schools). We hope that analysis of what has been attempted in the past and of the reasons for success and failure can assist current efforts to establish school-based programs of family support.

According to a review of school-linked health and social services by the historian David Tyack (1992), there are four major lessons that we can learn from history regarding the implementation of programs in the schools. First, attempts to integrate successful programs into the school administrative structure have been hindered by *goal displacement,* where the initial aim and purpose of a program is shifted toward one that is more closely aligned with the primary educational goal of the system. Tyack (1992) cites the example of the school social worker. Initially, school social workers were not paid employees of the school, but were supported by outside philanthropic organizations. Their initial role was to be a family advocate who linked families with needed services and championed their rights in disputes with large institutions, including at times the school system itself. As schools began hiring social workers, the social workers' role shifted toward monitoring and ensuring attendance and providing counseling services. Their ability to advocate for the family in disputes with the school system was compromised by their position within the school bureaucracy. Tyack recommends that the goals and procedures of any program be spelled out clearly to avoid goal displacement.

Second, Tyack cites several examples in which well-meaning philanthropists have instituted programs based on their beliefs about what families need rather than what families ask for. It is important to recognize that communities have different needs and that what is needed in one community may not be needed in another. Elitist approaches can miss the true needs of communities and lead to programs based on a deficit model that result in stigmatizing and a rejection of the program. Tyack recommends *involving prospective clients* early in the planning stages to ascertain their particular needs and facilitate community ownership of the project.

Third, Tyack notes how *funding issues* play a major part in the acceptance of new programs and their likelihood of surviving in the long term. According to Tyack, "School leaders are understandably wary of new mandates with inadequate funding" (p. 30). Too often, school systems have been left "holding the bag" when outside funding has been pulled but they remain obligated to continue to provide services. It is wise to secure a wide base of community support and multiple funding options so programs are not axed during periods of retrenchment.

Fourth, Tyack emphasizes the danger of hype based on a history of *overselling social programs* with the inevitable result of disappointed, disillusioned, and mistrustful schools and communities. The hyperbole associated with school health programs at the beginning of this century contributed to an attitude of suspicion and mistrust toward subsequent efforts to bring services into the schools.

The war on poverty begun in the 1960s taught us that although the schools may not be the ideal setting for family support programs, they do offer a stability that cannot be matched by government-funded community centers (Jehl & Kirst, 1992). Many programs established during the war on poverty avoided placement in the schools due to a mistrust of institutions and a concern that they were not the best place to reach the community. Unfortunately, many of these programs were defunded when government policies and priorities shifted. We will revisit the pros and cons of placement of FRCs in the schools later in this chapter.

Models of Service Delivery

Over the past 5 years, many models of family support have been promoted and hundreds of programs have been initiated. Many programs are now in the process of being evaluated, either formally or informally. According to Levy and Shepardson (1992), the field is in its early formative stages and lacks clear guidelines regarding which programs and services are most effective. They argue that "distillation and promotion of models seems premature" (p. 46). We would argue that a wide variety of programs is preferable to the proliferation of a single, or even several, models. Variety allows for the best match between community needs and program services, and makes room for community input and creative, innovative solutions to family problems (Chaskin & Richman, 1992).

It is beyond the scope of this chapter to review all family support programs. We have selected a handful of programs to illustrate the variety of approaches and philosophical orientations. We conclude our discussion of models of services delivery with a detailed description of FRCs in Connecticut. The Connecticut model was selected for extensive review based on the second author's firsthand experience in administering an FRC; this does not represent an endorsement of this model over others reviewed.

Family Focus Inc. of Chicago. Family Focus emphasizes the creation of linkages between schools, health care, and social services. The program offers a drop-in center, parent-child activities, parent education, child health and developmental screenings, literacy programs, and job skills training (National Commission on Children, 1993).

Kentucky's Family Resource and Youth Service Centers. Kentucky has launched an ambitious statewide program designed to integrate social and educational services. Rather than targeting students, the Kentucky program targets the schools with the greatest need. Initial legislation provided for centers to be located in all public schools where 20% or more of the population qualifies for free or reduced-price lunches. Kentucky's FRCs provide child care, parent and child education, parent-child activities, and support and training for child care providers. The youth service centers emphasize obtaining access to a wide range of services, including health care, job development and employment services, mental health counseling and crisis intervention, substance abuse counseling, transportation, and recreational activities.

Parents Place in San Francisco. The National Commission on Children (1993) Implementation Guide series describes this San Francisco program as offering parent support groups; parenting education; "warmlines"; drop-in playrooms for children, parents, and caregivers; individual and family counseling; and a parenting library.

The Probstfield Elementary School. A program in Moorehead, Minnesota, assists families by consolidating access to services through a single point of entry—the school (Levy & Shepardson, 1992). Elementary schools were selected to better target families, presumed to be more actively involved in children's elementary education than in later grades. The program provides teachers with a comprehensive resource manual and training in how to recognize needs and facilitate referrals. Social service agencies have representatives present on school grounds to facilitate immediate enrollment in recommended services.

The School Based Youth Services Program. A statewide New Jersey program aimed at coordinating educational and human service programs is a hybrid combination of a school-based health center offering physical and mental health services and an FRC with child care (at some locations), services for teen parents, vocational education, and other family support services (NRCFSP, 1993).

The State of Texas—Communities in Schools Program. A Texas program attempts to maximize efforts by targeting services for the students most in need rather than offering services to the general school population (NRCFSP, 1993). Initiated in 1979, the Communities in Schools Program is a comprehensive dropout prevention intervention modeled after the national Cities in Schools Program. The program targets children identified as at risk of dropping out. Program goals are to work with families to increase attendance, academic performance, and graduation rates; develop vocational and employment skills; reduce delinquency; and support personal and social development. Programs vary based on the specific needs of the population served, but most programs provide six core services, including individual and family counseling, tutoring, enrichment activities, parental involvement, referral to health services, and job training and placement.

The Wallbridge Caring Communities Program, St. Louis, Missouri. A collaborative effort by Missouri education, mental health, and social service agencies and the Danforth Foundation offers a combination of school- and home-based services (Levy & Shepardson, 1992). Home-based services include case management and an intensive family stabilization program for families in crisis. Mental

health, substance abuse, and academic counseling services are offered on school grounds, as are child care, tutoring, and nursing.
The program also offers training and job placement services for
parents. To increase community involvement, a substance abuse
task force was organized to develop community-specific solutions
and preventive strategies to combat substance abuse.

Family Resource Centers in Connecticut

In Connecticut, the state Department of Education has funded
18 programs designated as Family Resource Centers (FRCs). Three
of these centers were developed as a pilot project in 1990. Later,
FRC contracts were awarded to six additional communities. In
January 1994, the state was awarded one of four federal 3-year
demonstration grants to more fully articulate the 9 existing centers,
expand the number of sites to 18, and evaluate the implementation
of the model.

FRCs are located in a variety of school districts, including large
and small cities, suburban towns, and rural communities. Connecticut's goal is to locate each FRC in a public elementary school, which
then allows, and sometimes forces, the school toward deinstitution-
alization and further expansion of the facility as a community
resource. However, due to space limitations in public elementary
schools, some FRCs established prior to 1994 are located in community centers or in social service agencies. Location in a public
elementary school was a criterion for funding the most recently
established centers.

Participation in FRC activities is unrestricted, barrier free, and
voluntary. Each family in the FRC district is eligible to take advantage of its services. The intent is to integrate families of diverse
socioeconomic, ethnic, and cultural backgrounds. Each FRC persistently includes all groups and discourages interpretation of the
program as a deficit model, that is, one that strives to correct or
eliminate family- or child-specific risks.

Adapting the Yale Bush Center's model of the Schools of the 21st
Century, Connecticut's FRCs offer seven distinct services to the
communities in which they are located: preschool child care, school-
aged child care, Positive Youth Development, Families in Training,
adult and parenting education, support and training for family day
care providers, and resource and referral (Connecticut Department

of Human Resources, 1991). Each of the seven components is available to all families in the district served by the FRC.

Preschool Child Care. Preschool child care, specific to children ages 3 to 5, must be available from 7 a.m. until 6 p.m., Monday through Friday, 52 weeks a year. Child care centers in Connecticut generally must be licensed by the Department of Public Health and Addiction Services, but those housed in, and operated by a public school system, fall under the supervision of the state Department of Education and are not required to be licensed. However, the state Department of Education encourages quality programming and urges all FRC child care programs to meet license requirements, participate in the licensing process, and maintain a current license.

Although each FRC has the freedom to develop its own curricula, each site must observe developmentally appropriate practices. A nonacademic program provides daily activities in the areas of language; large and small motor skills; and social, emotional, and cognitive development. The primary concern of the curricula is social interaction and the building of an experiential foundation for positive successes in the elementary grades.

Enrollment criteria for children is strict. Parents of children must be working or enrolled in an instructional program. The instructional program may include any adult education program, college course, or technical or career training. Employment may be part time or full time. Each family's child care schedule is determined according to the parents' work schedule. In a two-parent family, both parents must be working or in an instructional program to be eligible to receive child care services. When parents complete their program or their employment is terminated, children may remain in child care through a transitional period enabling the parent to (re)enter the work force. Fees for child care services are charged according to a sliding scale based on income and family size. Transportation to and from the school is not provided for preschool children.

School-Aged Child Care. School-aged child care must be available from 7 a.m. until 6 p.m., Monday through Friday, 52 weeks a year. With the program operating year-round, including during school vacation and holidays, families are provided an opportunity for consistent child care without needing to seek supplemental care or leave children unsupervised when school is not in session.

In school districts where kindergarten operates on a half-day schedule, child care may wrap around the academic class time. The intent of the school-aged program is to offer a safe, nonacademic alternative to inappropriate child care arrangements while parents work. Staff are available to assist with homework and offer social and recreational opportunities.

Ideally, school-aged child care occurs on site in the elementary school and near the preschool child care program. This prevents fragmentation of the day for the family and cultivates parent involvement in the school. Programs housed in the same building where children spend their academic day need to be sensitive to the children's experiences during school hours and their need for a respite from school.

Because children are enrolled in the school-aged program while their parents are working or enrolled in educational programs, child care schedules are designed to meet the individual needs of each family. As in the preschool program, transportation to and from the school is not provided.

Positive Youth Development. Positive Youth Development activities provide opportunities for youth to interact in a positive, prosocial environment while discovering and developing their own interests. The underlying belief is that development of skills and interests and involvement in prosocial activities will inhibit dysfunctional behavior that could lead to pregnancy, substance abuse, violence, or criminal activity.

In each FRC, implementation of Positive Youth Development varies according to the unique needs of the community. FRCs may collaborate with local agencies, the state Health Department, or school-based health centers to implement Positive Youth Development activities. In some communities the FRC administrator works closely with the Department of Youth Services to provide recreational and community service opportunities. The resulting activities may include youth participation in theater, teen dances, and food and clothing drives. Other activities may be coordinated with 4-H clubs; Boy and Girl Scout troops; and after-school activities such as crafts, sports activities, and discussion groups.

Families in Training. The Families in Training component of an FRC is a home-based parent education program using Missouri's

Parents as Teachers curriculum. The curriculum is structured to allow family participation from the third trimester of pregnancy up to the child's third birthday. Families may enter the program at any time during this age span. Parent educators trained to implement the program regularly visit families in their homes.

Throughout the 3-year span, the mission and function of the home visits revolve around developmental and parenting issues. The goal of initial visits is to develop relationships and build trust between the visitors and the parents. Prenatal and developmental information is shared and child-rearing practices are discussed.

Throughout the family's enrollment in the program, parents learn to use their observational skills and become more aware of their child's developmental growth. During home visits, the parent educator works with the family to cultivate an awareness of the language, motor, social, and cognitive stages of child development. The parent educators typically prepare and bring appropriate activities to demonstrate principles of child growth and development. Health education is threaded throughout the enrollment period. As the child grows, developmental issues of self-feeding, toileting, child-proofing the home, discipline, and sibling rivalry are the theme of visits.

In addition, Families in Training participants are invited to monthly group meetings. These group meetings provide opportunities for children to interact with other children and for parents to meet and socialize with other parents. Often part of the group meeting unites parents and children in a play group. Guest speakers or FRC staff may present information to the parents or the parents plan their own group agenda.

Often, parent educators work closely with Young Parent programs, which are available to parenting teens in many school systems. Parent educators may assist with the teaching of parenting classes, the organization of young parent support groups, and the provision of home visits.

Adult and Parenting Education. FRCs collaborate with adult and parent education programs in a variety of ways. The programs offered may include English as a Second Language, adult basic education, basic skills training, adult literacy, GED preparation, and parenting classes.

Adult and parenting education services are offered in a variety of settings within, or outside of the school setting. The school library, unused classroom space, or a specially designed family resource room may serve as the site of educational programs. Where space in the school is not available, FRCs may collaborate with a local adult education program to provide child care and support services for parents enrolled in classes.

Each FRC implements a parent education program that should be tailored to meet the particular needs of the community. Parenting education is implemented through workshops or a prepackaged curriculum. Individual workshops target such topics as anger management and self-esteem, how children learn, and activities for parents to do with their children at home. Programs may be targeted toward FRC participants or the general community.

To maximize the success of parenting education and support services, FRC administrators need to consider scheduling issues, participant motivation, and in some cases, the need for additional supports to increase attendance.

Scheduling of sessions is dependent on the population of the participants. Sessions should be offered in the morning, afternoon, and evening. Employed parents cannot usually participate in morning or early afternoon programs. Student parents can only participate around their educational schedule. The time of day most convenient to employed or to student parents seems to be late afternoon or early evening, around 5:30 p.m. This allows programs to attract parents as they pick up their children from child care arrangements and keep them on site for an informal educational program, support group, or social experience.

FRC administrators report that events are of more interest to parents than are lectures or workshops. Interactive sessions with parents and children are the most successful. Providing dinner for the children and/or parents enables parents to relax and enjoy themselves without worrying about preparing dinner when they get home. The most well attended and successful events occur when parents are encouraged to share a part of themselves, such as food for a potluck supper, musical entertainment for a social event, and participating in a playground cleanup or classroom-painting day. The most successful programs tend to be those sponsored by the parents themselves.

Support and Training for Family Day Care Providers. FRCs in Connecticut are committed to supporting multiple models of child care service delivery. Although FRCs are heavily school focused and school based, the program planners recognize the need for variety in child care options. Some parents prefer to place their children with local, home-based, family day care providers rather than center-based programs. For others, family day care may be more convenient, and in some cases, less expensive than center-based child care. Despite these advantages, there is rightful concern that the typical home day care provider is only minimally trained in child development and may tend to operate in isolation, without access to support or information necessary to provide quality services. To support an array of child care options, FRCs in Connecticut strive to enhance the quality of family day care programs by providing training and support services. As with other FRC components, support and training for providers is managed according to the unique needs of the community.

FRCs allow providers the opportunity to network with each other. This networking may occur through evening or Saturday group meetings, training conferences, and newsletters. Professional relationships are built between the providers and the FRC staff, and also between the individual providers. This encourages mutual support and camaraderie among paraprofessionals who typically function in isolation from each other. Sharing ideas and participating in mutual training builds skills, enhances self-esteem, and elevates the role of the family day care provider.

Some FRCs have designed a program similar to the Families in Training model. An FRC consultant regularly visits providers, offering individual support and guidance along with personal training in child development. These home visits are supplemented with monthly group meetings of the providers and the children they care for. The visits offer the providers an opportunity to network and learn from each other, and for the children to interact with a larger social group.

A few FRCs have established resource lending libraries of toys, books, and reference materials. Other programs routinely invite providers, and the families they serve, to participate in FRC functions, including special events at the child care center, adult and parent education opportunities, and Positive Youth Development activities. Programs may also collaborate with local educational resource centers that provide support and training services to family day care providers.

Resource and Referral. The resource and referral component of an FRC is designed to support family effectiveness, expand parental options, and educate parents about quality child care by functioning as a conduit to a broad range of community services and programs. FRCs make parents aware of local child care options and provide referrals to meet family needs in housing, finances, social services, and physical and mental health.

In Connecticut, FRCs work cooperatively with INFOLINE, a resource and referral agency jointly funded by the state of Connecticut and the United Way. Through toll-free telephone service, IN-FOLINE provides information, referral, and crisis intervention for all human service needs throughout Connecticut. Specific to child care, INFOLINE maintains a database of all licensed family day care providers and early childhood programs.

Once a family becomes a part of the FRC system, resource and referral to family-specific issues becomes more individualized. Through their daily interactions, FRC staff often become aware of family needs before the need reaches crisis proportions. Staff may offer a direct referral or suggest the family contact INFOLINE. Staff also directly provide moral support and guidance for the family. Staff may assist the family by making the initial contact and locating the service, guiding the family through the initial visit and assessing the degree to which the service meets the identified need.

Evaluation of FRCs

FRCs are designed to enhance family functioning, improve parenting skills, and support the growth and development of children and families through the provision of family support services. Those involved in the administration and provision of services within an FRC feel strongly that the services provided are effective and worthwhile. However, in this era of cost containment, shrinking resources, and increased accountability, belief in a program is not enough. We need tangible data that can be used to improve, revise, or expand the services being offered and demonstrate that program goals are being achieved in the most cost-effective manner possible.

There are a number of questions and levels of analysis that can be applied in evaluating FRCs. Evaluations can range from brief process assessments focusing on utilization patterns and internal program dynamics to long-term longitudinal outcome studies with large sample sizes, random assignment, and validated instruments. The more complex and scientifically rigorous the evaluation, the more expensive it tends to be. There is typically a trade-off between the cost of an evaluation and the quality and scope of the information it provides. All evaluations cost money and time, but scientifically rigorous ones tend to cost more. Only well-done scientific studies can definitively answer whether program services produce significant positive outcomes, but process evaluations can provide useful data at lower cost.

An evaluation can address a number of basic questions. Some questions can be answered through process evaluations in which data about utilization or program practices are collected and subjected to descriptive statistical analysis. For example, the demographics of program participants could be analyzed to help identify geographic, cultural, or economic barriers to program access. Internal measures of quality assurance, such as time between referral and program entry, or staff/client ratios, can help to ensure the high quality of services provided. Client and staff surveys regarding program satisfaction can help to determine which program elements are best meeting the needs of the community.

Questions regarding whether program services have produced expected results require outcome assessment. (Questions that lend themselves to outcome or process evaluation are listed in Table 9.1.) An outcome assessment begins with a statement of the hypothesized effects of program participation. For example, program participants who complete job training or adult education should eventually get better jobs with higher pay. Those who complete a Families in Training program should have better relationships with their children and fewer episodes of abuse or maltreatment. After hypothesizing about the expected outcome, a valid and reliable means of measuring outcome needs to be selected. For example, a subjective global rating of parenting effectiveness may not be a very reliable measure, whereas a validated questionnaire with a series of questions about parenting practices that have been empirically explored is likely to be a valid and reliable measure of outcome.

Once a hypothesis has been made and measures have been chosen, a research design is selected. A posttest-only design measures the expected outcome after services have been provided. However, without a baseline for comparison, one cannot reliably determine if the measured outcome represents a positive or negative effect, or if the effect is due to the services having been provided. A repeated measures design takes pre- and postmeasures of the expected outcome. Although this represents an improvement over a posttest-only design, it does not allow the evaluator to reliably conclude that observed changes are due to the intervention.

A truly randomized experimental design is the best method of determining causal relationships between program services and expected outcomes. At the point of application for services, prospective program participants are randomly assigned to a control or an experimental group. Those in the experimental group receive services, but those in the control group do not. At some point in the future, the two groups are compared on the outcome measure using statistical methods to determine if observed differences are significant or due to chance variations. If the study has been done correctly, one can reliably infer that any observed differences between the experimental and control groups is due to the impact of the services provided. More complex factorial designs can help to determine which program elements are most responsible for the observed changes.

Decisions about process evaluations versus outcome evaluations often have as much to do with practical and ethical considerations as scientific ones. Evaluations cost time and money and the more complex the evaluation the more it will cost. Truly randomized designs are often objected to on ethical grounds, as some portion of potential participants could be denied needed services. Matching techniques, waiting-list control groups, and procedures in which the neediest cases are automatically assigned to the experimental group, are all partial solutions to the ethical problems of real-world experimental studies (Gomby & Larson, 1992).

Longitudinal studies help to determine if the effects of program participation are transitory or stable by sampling data at specified intervals over a relatively long period of time. Longitudinal studies may be particularly appropriate in assessing the impact of FRCs, as it may take time for the impact of FRC services to be recognized.

Evaluation strategies are selected based on a variety of scientific, practical and ethical issues, but it is imperative that FRCs include some evaluative component. FRCs are still in the early stages of development and only evaluation will provide the information

Table 9.1 Questions That Lend Themselves to Process or Outcome Evaluations

Process Evaluations	Outcome Evaluations
Are the services being utilized? Who is utilizing them?	If the program is successful, what changes can be expected in program participants or in the community in general?
What is the quality of the services being provided? Are they being provided in a cost-effective manner?	If changes occurred, can they be attributed to the impact of the services being offered?
What services do the staff and the program participants see as most valuable? Least valuable?	Which services produce the greatest change?
What other services, not currently offered, do the staff and program participants feel are most needed?	What is the long-range impact of program services? Do effects last?
What are the costs of providing services?	
Can the program demonstrate cost savings?	

needed to determine which programs work and why. Larson et al. (1992), reporting on initial evaluations of family support programs, have found that successful programs (a) provide comprehensive services, (b) promote increased involvement of parents, and (c) incorporate changes that make schools and agencies more responsive to the needs of children and families. They also report that purely informational programs without a high level of participant involvement are not very effective.

Issues in Design and Implementation

The basic concept driving the FRC movement is that providing family support services reduces the number and severity of social problems and fosters the development of healthy, competent, and productive children. This concept is quite simple, but the real-world implementation of an FRC can be quite complex. FRC administrators are faced with myriad choices and decisions. How these choices and decisions are made can determine the success or failure of the program. In this section, we review some of the major issues involved in the design and implementation of an FRC.

The Setting

FRCs have been located in schools, churches, social service agencies, community centers, health care facilities, and other community settings. The most common setting is a public school facility. Although there are many good reasons for locating FRCs in a school setting, there are also reasonable arguments against doing so. The best setting for an FRC will depend on the particular qualities and character of the community it is designed to serve as well as the resources available.

One argument for school-based FRCs is that schools are typically present in almost every neighborhood and tend to be one of the most enduring and stable institutions in the community. Locating programs in a stable school setting is likely to increase the program's ability to survive periods of retrenchment in the shifting sands of government support. Schools also have natural access to children and families as they are one of the few statutorily mandated programs and tend to see children for more hours than any other institution. In addition to having a captive audience, schools often have facilities available that are not fully utilized due to the limited educational schedule. Placing programs in the schools may also allow for cross-fertilization between educational and family support efforts in that participation in the FRC may increase parental participation in children's education and participation in school activities may lead to enrollment in FRC-sponsored programs. School-based FRCs are also quite convenient and practical, particularly when before- and after-school child care services are offered. Placing child care in the schools is convenient for parents because they do not have to worry about making extra stops to drop their children off or pick them up, or make arrangements for transportation between school and child care settings.

Despite the advantages of school-based FRCs, there are reasonable arguments against considering schools as the setting of choice. Gomby and Larson (1992) argue that the location or administration of FRCs should not be dominated by any one institution. They fear "goal displacement," with the goals of the FRC transformed or subordinated to meet the primary educational goals of the school system. In fact, there is an historical precedent for the likelihood of goal displacement, as reported earlier regarding how the role of school social workers changed once they became school employees (Tyack, 1992).

Although schools are highly accessible within most communities, not all members of the community are positively disposed toward schools. In these cases, location in a school setting may function as a barrier to accessing services. Similarly, the young people who are most in need of FRC services (e.g., teen parents or children with behavior problems) may be alienated or have dropped out. In addition, busing and development of magnet schools may result in the school being located outside of the community. The subjective sense of community may not correspond to the boundaries of the school district.

Gomby and Larson (1992) suggest that political or historical barriers may interfere with the success of programs based in established institutions such as schools. Institutional affiliation may also breed bureaucratic rigidity and reduce the opportunity for the community to contribute to program planning and service delivery.

In selecting a site for FRC implementation, program planners need to consider the individual needs and resources available as well as how community members define their community and the history of community relationships with the schools and other potential sites. In many cases, the school setting may be best suited to offering FRC services, but it appears equally true that to effectively serve all who could benefit, there needs to be a variety of access points and an appreciation of unique community features.

Menu of Services

Our earlier discussion on models of service delivery showed the wide range of services available within programs structured as FRCs. Some programs focus on the provision of health and mental health services (School Based Youth Services Program of New Jersey). Others emphasize use of the school as a community resource (Connecticut FRCs). Still others focus on improving access to existing social services (Probstfield Elementary School) or integrating educational, vocational, health, and social services (Texas—Communities in Schools Program). Which combination of services

Table 9.2 Range of Services Offered Within an FRC

Adult education	Literacy training
Basic medical care	Medical referral and diagnosis
Case management services	Mentoring program
Child care—Infant	Parenting library
Child care—Preschool	Physical exams
Child care—School aged	Positive Youth Development
Crisis intervention	Resource and referral
Dental care	Resource manual development
Developmental screenings	Social service representatives on site
Drop-in center for children and parents	Structured parent-child educational activities
Families in Training	Structured parent-child recreational activities
Family counseling	
Formation of community task forces	Substance abuse counseling
GED preparation	Support groups
Group counseling	Teacher training for social service referral
Health education	
Health screenings	Teen dropout prevention
Hotlines	Teen pregnancy prevention
Immunizations	Training for family day care providers
Improved linkages between schools and social services	Tutoring
	Violence prevention programs
Individual counseling	Vocational counseling
Intensive home-based services	Vocational training
Intergenerational programs	Warmlines
Job bank and employment services	Well child/baby clinics
Job skills training	Young Parents Program

is most needed or most effective has yet to be determined. At this point in the development of FRC models it is probably best to be aware of the range of services that are offered elsewhere and select those that best match the needs of the community. However, there will remain a need for creativity and innovation to design and refine services that grow out of meaningful dialogue with the families to be served. Perhaps the best services have yet to be designed or implemented.

In general, program planners need to strike a balance between comprehensiveness of services, service quality, and the restrictions imposed by limited resources.

Table 9.2 contains a list of services appropriate for an FRC. The list is meant to be suggestive rather than exhaustive.

Standardization of Programmatic Elements

When implementing FRCs on a state or regional basis, it is important to decide whether to require a standard set of services or to allow flexibility in selecting those services most needed in the particular community. From an administrative point of view, standardization helps to streamline implementation, evaluation, and financial accountability. It is easier to compare budgets, expenditures, and the quality of services provided when services are standardized from program to program. Standardization of services also allows for a more clearly defined model of FRCs, in contrast to a host of programs offering a hodgepodge of services and lacking a shared vision or philosophy. For example, in Connecticut, FRCs are based on the School of the 21st Century model (Zigler & Finn-Stevenson, 1990), which requires all programs to provide a core set of seven services. This model emphasizes the value of quality child care services. Other models, such as the Probstfield Elementary School of Moorehead, Minnesota, emphasize resource and referral by training teachers to recognize needs and facilitating access by bringing social service representatives into the school. Purifying and replicating exact models of service delivery may give FRCs a greater probability of being successful. Allowing diversity may dilute program philosophy and obscure the evaluation process, making it difficult to answer questions about what works and why.

There are several arguments against standardizing FRC service offerings. First and foremost, standardization precludes meaningful community participation regarding what services are needed, as the decision about what services to offer has already been made. Past experience teaches that ownership is one of the most important factors in motivating community action and maximizing productive utilization of services.

Standardization also reduces a program's capacity to match services to particular community needs. Problems and solutions may differ across urban, suburban, and rural communities and socioeconomic and cultural groups. A single model cannot address the variety of community needs and existing resources.

It is also true that program standardization across communities can sometimes result in inefficient duplication of services. In Connecticut, one example of duplication of service is the training and support of family day care providers. Both FRCs and early childhood and teacher resource centers are located throughout the state and consider their mission to include training and support for family day care providers. The catchment area for some of the resource centers includes communities in which FRCs are located. In most cases, the FRC and the resource center collaborate to provide services to family day care providers. However, there is a considerable possibility that other, nonduplicated services, may be more useful to the community.

Targeting Subgroups and Specialized Outreach Efforts

One major issue facing FRC program planners is whether to target services to particular populations or subpopulations, or to offer services to all. For example, in Connecticut, FRCs offer services to all families within the school district in which the FRC is located. Their philosophy is against targeting services out of a concern that programs would gravitate toward a deficit model in which program participants could be stigmatized by their deficit status. The Texas—Communities in Schools Program targets services to youth at risk for dropping out, recognizing the devastating outcomes associated with school dropout and attempting to maximize effectiveness by targeting intensive services to those most in need. Although the advocates of the Connecticut program should be commended for their high-minded adherence to the principle of unrestricted access, the fact is that limited resources often force the need to target services. In fact, services in Connecticut are targeted in the sense that grants are awarded by competitive bid and communities with the greatest needs are given priority in allocating funds.

It is also often true that families who need the most support also require specialized outreach efforts that would be wasted on the typical consumer of FRC services. However, one argument against targeting is that it could lead to a homogenization of the population of FRC participants, reducing the opportunity for exposure to individuals of differing background, experiences, and socioeconomic status.

Perhaps the best solution is to hold to the general principle of unrestricted access, but to target some services and outreach efforts to groups of families with special needs. Once again, the most important factors in deciding this crucial philosophical issue are the needs of the community, available resources, and program goals. Program planners should recognize the philosophical and practical implications associated with decisions regarding targeting of services.

Funding

The nature and source of funding for FRCs is likely to vary from state to state, making it difficult to provide generalizable guidelines for funding issues. Potential funding sources include state departments of education, social services, and health services as well as private foundations and charitable organizations such as the United Way (Farrow & Joe, 1992). Many FRCs combine funds from state and local agencies, United Way contributions, and private agency funds. When considering basing an FRC in a school setting, it is unlikely that the school system will be able to provide anything more than in-kind donations of space and utilities. Many school administrators feel that there are so many mandated adjunctive services that what is left over for general educational needs is a relatively small and precious resource that they are unwilling to allocate to other "noneducational" services. The one exception may be in the area of special education funds. Schools may be willing to reallocate special service resources toward preventive efforts such as FRCs if it can be demonstrated that there are cost savings to be realized through reductions of other expenditures, such as expensive out-of-district placements.

Another problem is the categorical nature of most funding sources, which heightens the challenge to provide comprehensive services that cross categorical boundaries (Farrow & Joe, 1992). For instance, a proposed FRC may anticipate providing a combination of medical, mental health, and child care services. In the absence of state or federal grants that cross categorical boundaries, funding a comprehensive FRC could be an administrative nightmare, requiring separate contracts and accountability processes for each service provided. This can certainly hamper collaborative efforts and dramatically increase administrative overhead. The solution to this problem requires action at the state and national level to reconfigure the way funds are allocated. Obviously this is no small task.

FRCs can improve their financial status and increase client commitment to services through optimal utilization of Medicaid billing and a carefully constructed policy regarding client fees. FRCs may provide services that are reimbursable under Medicaid. Program officials may need to negotiate with state Medicaid administrators to obtain the status of approved providers for Medicaid reimbursement. Structuring client fees on a sliding scale can both strengthen the financial viability of programs and enhance client commitment to services.

Larson et al. (1992) argue that school-based family support programs should not rely exclusively on outside grants for funding. They recommend that each agency participating in FRC service provision allocate some of its own funds to reduce the risk of the program dying if grant funds dry up. However, this may not be practical for many agencies who do not have access to funds except through grant initiatives or client fees.

Administrative Issues

Administering an FRC can be an extremely rewarding and frustrating experience. Whether the experience is positive or negative depends on a host of factors, including those reviewed above. In addition, success or failure also hinges on the effective negotiation of several administrative challenges concerning host relations, staffing, and in programs offering child care services, the program's educational philosophy.

Whatever site is selected for FRC implementation, it is critically important to maintain a positive collaborative relationship between the service providers and the host site. Turf and boundary issues naturally arise in such arrangements and are best acknowledged up front, early in the negotiations. It may be necessary to reassure host staff that the proposed FRC does not threaten their job security. FRC administrators may need to relinquish a significant degree of control over their programs in order to foster a strong collaborative relationship. Beyond maintaining civility, host and service provider need to actively seek out means of enhancing collaboration. In the case of school-based FRCs, merely locating a program on school grounds does not guarantee a collaborative or cooperative relationship between host and service provider. FRCs are at risk of remaining isolated from school personnel without active efforts to the contrary. This may include sponsoring joint events, inviting school personnel to participate in programs, or including FRC staff in school meetings and committees where appropriate.

Equity of status and pay of FRC staff is another issue facing program administrators. The qualifications of child care workers, family educators, and FRC administrators are often comparable to their counterparts in the school setting, namely, teachers, school social workers, and administrative staff. FRC staff typically work year-round with fewer vacations and significantly lower salaries than their school-employed counterparts. The discrepancies in pay and status are discouraging to FRC staff. The ramifications can include worker dissatisfaction, staff turnover, and reduced continuity of care. The solution lies in tireless lobbying of funding sources regarding the impact of pay inequities and the need for comparable funding in order to provide quality services.

FRCs that offer child care services need a clear educational philosophy driving program design. A developmentally appropriate child care program emphasizes individual and small-group activity and structures lessons to teach concepts and skills through relevant experience. There should be minimal involvement in structured, teacher-directed pencil-and-paper tasks and frequent, daily opportunities for children to make choices about activities. This is in direct contrast to the academic curricula of most elementary grades. Children need a respite from academic activities. Although child care can assist in the development or enhancement of academic readiness skills, the primary focus needs to be on social and emotional development.

Summary and Conclusions

Increased family stress and the simultaneous erosion of stress-buffering family structures has contributed to many social problems. U.S. society needs a well-organized, comprehensive, and community-based system of family support to combat these disturbing social trends. FRCs, as described in this chapter, offer hope that such a system of family support can succeed where previous efforts have failed. The following conclusions are offered:

1. Previous efforts to provide family support services resulted in a disorganized system of social programs lacking in vision, organization, and coordination. To avoid repeating the same mistakes, support services need to be provided in a manner that is sensitive to the needs

of the entire family. This requires centralizing access to services and focusing interventions on the entire family rather than individual problems.

2. FRCs must remain flexible in order to adapt to community needs and incorporate community input. This argues against the development of a single model with a standardized set of services and supports the creation of a diverse and flexible menu of services.

3. To remain responsive to the diversity of family needs, FRCs must remain flexible regarding the nature of the setting in which the program is based. Although schools are often the best sites to locate programs, limiting programs to school sites may close off access to alienated and disenfranchised groups with the greatest needs.

4. Proponents of FRCs and other family support programs need to lobby at the state and local level to remove the barrier to comprehensive services caused by categorical funding.

5. FRCs must conduct evaluations to demonstrate the effectiveness of their programs and to identify the most effective services. Program evaluators need to strike a balance between maintaining rigorous scientific standards and remaining sensitive to the economic, ethical, and practical aspects of conducting real-world studies.

6. Program planners need to carefully evaluate existing local resources to avoid duplication of services.

7. Proponents of FRCs that offer child care services need to educate funding sources about the impact of pay inequities on FRC staffing and continuity of care.

References

Chaskin, R. J., & Richman, H. A. (1992). Concerns about school-linked services: Institution-based versus community-based models. In R. E. Behrman (Ed.), *The future of children: School-linked services* (pp. 107-117). Los Altos, CA: Center for the Future of Children, the David and Lucile Packard Foundation.

Connecticut Department of Human Resources. (1991). *Family resource center: Program guidelines.* Unpublished manuscript, Connecticut Department of Human Resources, Hartford.

Farrow, F., & Joe, T. (1992). Financing school-linked service efforts. In R. E. Behrman (Ed.), *The future of children: School-linked services* (pp. 56-67). Los Altos, CA: Center for the Future of Children, the David and Lucile Packard Foundation.

Gomby, D. S., & Larson, C. S. (1992). Evaluation of school-linked services. In R. E. Behrman (Ed.), *The future of children: School-linked services* (pp. 68-84). Los Altos, CA: Center for the Future of Children, the David and Lucile Packard Foundation.

Jehl, J., & Kirst, M. (1992). Getting ready to provide school-linked services: What schools must do. In R. E. Behrman (Ed.), *The future of children: School-linked services* (pp. 95-106). Los Altos, CA: Center for the Future of Children, the David and Lucile Packard Foundation.

Larson, C. S., Gomby, D. S., Shiono, P. H., Lewit, E. M., & Behrman, R. E. (1992). Analysis. In R. E. Behrman (Ed.), *The future of children: School-linked services* (pp. 6-18). Los Altos, CA: Center for the Future of Children, the David and Lucile Packard Foundation.

Levy, J. E., & Shepardson, W. (1992). A look at current school-linked service efforts. In R. E. Behrman (Ed.), *The future of children: School-linked services* (pp. 44-55). Los Altos, CA: Center for the Future of Children, the David and Lucile Packard Foundation.

National Commission on Children. (1993). *Strengthening and supporting families.* Washington, DC: Author.

National Resource Center for Family Support Programs (NRCFSP). (1993). *Family support programs and school-linked services.* Chicago, IL: Author.

Tyack, D. (1992). Health and social services in public schools: Historical perspectives. In R. E. Behrman (Ed.), *The future of children: School-linked services* (pp. 19-31). Los Altos, CA: Center for the Future of Children, the David and Lucile Packard Foundation.

U.S. Bureau of Census. (1987). Money, income, and poverty status of families and persons in the United States. *Current population reports* (P-60). Washington, DC: Author.

U.S. Department of Labor. (1987). *Child care: A workforce issue.* Washington, DC: U.S. Department of Labor, Bureau of Labor Statistics.

Zigler, E. F., & Finn-Stevenson, M. (1990). *Child care, family services and the School of the 21st Century.* Hartford: Connecticut Department of Education—Connecticut Leadership Academy.

CHAPTER 10

Intergenerational Influences on Child Outcomes: Implications for Prevention and Intervention

ANNETTE U. RICKEL

EVVIE BECKER-LAUSEN

The Developing Child's Needs

The study of abnormal behavior has occupied psychology and psychiatry throughout history, but factors contributing to healthy behavior have only become a focus of attention in recent years. More recent still is the concept that some "abnormal" behavior may have been an appropriate (or at least expected) response to extreme circumstances, such as child abuse, war, and other traumatic experiences—and that response has been overgeneralized to situations where it is no longer appropriate.

Freud said the healthy person is one who is able "to love and to work." Alfred Adler suggested the concept of prosocial behavior as a marker for psychological well-being—or what he termed the development of "social interest." One group of psychologists attempted to delineate characteristics of the "normal" person (Atkinson, Atkinson, Smith, & Bem, 1990). Such a person, they suggested, would possess realistic perceptions, self-awareness, voluntary control of his or her behavior, a sense of self-worth, and a feeling of acceptance by others, in addition to Freud's criteria, which they called the ability to form affectionate relationships and to be productive.

The concept of psychological resiliency, though flawed (see Anthony & Cohler, 1987; Felsman & Vaillant, 1987), has helped draw attention to the study of factors that allow children to thrive in difficult environments.

Findings from a 30-year study of infants at risk from perinatal stress and poverty suggest that autonomy and a positive social orientation serve as protective factors for children (Werner, 1988). Consistent with the findings of other researchers, Werner also found that children who appear to thrive despite the most difficult circumstances have an established bond with at least one caregiver (see also Anthony & Cohler, 1987; Farber & Egeland, 1987; Field, 1990).

Children and Families

Children usually grow and develop in some type of family. In the contemporary United States, the face of that family has changed dramatically in this century. The motion picture *Avalon* visually depicted some of these changes, showing us a family of immigrants evolving over time from a full, multigenerational household sitting down to a meal at a large table to a time years later when two parents sat with their one child, watching television and eating their meal from TV trays.

The latter scene, depicting the 1950s, emphasized the increasing isolation and alienation of the family unit. Now, 40 years later, we find the family unit still further isolated: a single parent, usually a mother, rearing her children with few supports from family or from society. The popularity of the 1990s sitcom *Grace Under Fire*—a story about just such a struggling, single mother—reflects the fact that one in four children lived in a single-parent family in 1993, a 9% increase since 1985, and most of these families are headed by women (Center for the Study of Social Policy, 1993).

Demographic changes, such as the increase in single-parent families (particularly female-headed households), have been an important factor in the rising numbers of children living in or near poverty: Nearly 20% of all U.S. children lived below the poverty line in 1989, including 44% of African American children and 38% of Hispanic children (Center for the Study of Social Policy, 1993).

Yet two-parent households have also seen economic changes. In 1970, 39% of children had mothers in the workforce; in 1990, 61%

did. In 1987, only 29% of children in two-parent households were in homes with one parent working and one a full-time homemaker. Although many women have entered the workforce by choice, for large numbers of working- and middle-class families, two wage earners are a necessity, not an option (National Research Council, 1993).

Parents who are depressed or overburdened by work, financial problems, lack of social support, and lack of respite from child care activities are more likely to have problems attending to their children's needs. Interactions between high-risk infants and their mothers, as well as between high-risk mothers and their infants, have been found to be characterized by lack of excitement and responsiveness. This interaction pattern, which has been shown to occur when the mother fails to read the infant's signals, has been linked to behavioral and emotional problems when the child reaches school age, problems such as hyperactivity, attentional difficulties, disturbances in peer relations, and childhood depression (Field, 1990).

Fathers likewise can and do play an important role in the developing child's life—both by their presence, and by their absence. Although there has been a striking lack of attention to the father's role in child development, studies that have been conducted suggest that fathers influence children in ways similar to mothers' influences (Lamb, 1986; Phares, 1992).

Preventing Negative Outcomes

Rickel (1989) and others (Field, 1990) have demonstrated that parents can be successfully coached to improve their interactions with infants and young children, and resiliency researchers have stressed the importance of intervention in the first year of a child's life (Felsman & Vaillant, 1987).

Demographic changes indicate that most families are no longer able to provide children with sustained, full-time care in the home. Studies have shown that experience with peers and with day care settings early in life does not interfere with infants' attachment to their parents or primary caregivers. In fact, such experience appears to enhance the child's ability to form multiple attachments and to be a more socially interactive child.

What cannot be provided in the context of home and family must, of necessity, be provided by social systems. Yet the National Research

Council's (NRC) assessment of these systems in 1993 found them woefully lacking:

> The nation's major service institutions and systems—health, academic and vocational education, and employment and training—are not meeting the needs of many young people. . . . Similarly, the child protection and criminal and juvenile justice systems not only are unable to respond to the complex needs of adolescents who come under their care, but in many situations exacerbate the difficulties of young people. (NRC, 1993, p. 237)

Therefore, any discussion of intergenerational influences on children must address the implications for social policy. For example, discussion of welfare reform plans, such as the so-called workfare, too often fail to address the critical question, "Who cares for the children?" Such discussions must address practical realities, such as low pay and status of child care workers (who make less than laundry workers), as well as the broader concerns for quality of programs.

Child Rearing:
Developmental and Parental Influences

In the past 50 years, significant advances have been made in reducing risk factors associated with early growth and development. Nevertheless, children still are exposed to an abundance of conditions hazardous to their healthy development—particularly children of ethnic minorities and those living in poverty. If we are to ameliorate these developmental difficulties, which cost the United States tremendously in human potential and fiscal resources, the first step is to identify risk factors, their nature, and their cause.

Infants and children face risks developmentally from negative reproductive outcomes such as heredity or genetic predispositions, from prenatal and perinatal factors related to fetal growth and delivery of the infant, and from the socioeconomic and environmental aspects of the child's home (Field, 1990).

The influence of genetic factors and the magnitude of their influence on various aspects of individuality are the subject of continued debate. The accumulated evidence indicates that emotional temperament is in part determined at conception. Single gene defects, such as Huntington's chorea and phenylketonuria (PKU), are known to have an impact on emotional adjustment. Thought disorders and emotional disturbances, such as attention deficit disorder, manic depression, and schizophrenia, are also now seen as subject to genetic influence (Plomin, DeFries, & McClearn, 1980; Roberts & Peterson, 1984).

Several prenatal and perinatal factors are known to increase developmental risk in infants and children—factors such as maternal illness and malnutrition as well as alcohol and drug abuse. Prematurity, the most common birth abnormality, may result in inhibited mother-infant responsiveness because of the infant's lack of integrated physiologic and motoric functioning (Rickel, 1986).

Socioeconomic and environmental conditions increasing developmental risk include low socioeconomic status (SES) and ethnicity. For example, women who are poor and black have the highest rates of infant mortality in the United States, twice the rate for the U.S. population as a whole. Furthermore, although the U.S. rate is worse than that in 19 other countries, for black U.S. infants, the rate is worse than in 31 other nations. Likewise, the overall rate of U.S. infants with low birth weight is worse than in 30 other nations, whereas the rate for black U.S. infants is worse than in 73 other countries, including many Third World and Eastern European, formerly Communist countries. Complication rates for white, upper-class U.S. groups are only 5%. (Center for the Study of Social Policy, 1993; Children's Defense Fund, 1992; U.S. Bureau of the Census, 1992).

In addition to these negative biological outcomes, economically disadvantaged children experience environmental hazards such as lead paint and community violence, and they often experience unfavorable emotional outcomes related to the complex interplay of biological and environmental factors.

The Detroit Parent Project

All children are placed at risk for a variety of caretaking casualties when parental behavior fails to meet the minimum requirements for a child's normal healthy development. Parents must be able to provide a protective and nurturing environment for a child's growth and development.

Toward that end, a parent training program was developed in the Detroit public schools preschool and primary grades to improve the home environment of children by enhancing their parents' child-rearing techniques (Rickel, Dudley, & Berman, 1980).

The goals of the Detroit Parent Project were twofold: First, the program sought to develop insight into the relationship between parenting styles to which a child is exposed and the child's adjustment; second, the program endeavored to improve understanding of how best to conduct an effective parenting-technique training program.

To begin to address the first goal, an initial assessment of parenting styles was made in the context of the parenting program. This assessment employed the *Rickel Modified Child Rearing Practices Report* (Rickel & Biasatti, 1982). The original Block Child Rearing Practices Report (CRPR) consisted of 91 statements of self-reported child-rearing practices administered in a Q-sort format (Block, 1965); studies with the CRPR found that it lacked homogeneity from sample to sample, because of the large number of determined factors (28-33).

The modified version of the Block CRPR consists of 40 of the original 91 items presented in the form of a 6-point Likert-type scale questionnaire, which yields scores on two subscales, Restrictiveness and Nurturance. The two subscale factors each have an alpha coefficient of .82 (Rickel & Biasatti, 1982).

The items in Factor 1, Restrictiveness, represent an authoritarian view of child rearing, which includes how a child should behave and how he or she should feel. The items in Factor 2, Nurturance, represent greater flexibility in child-rearing attitudes and practices, and also reflect parents' willingness to listen to their children and to share feelings and experiences with them.

The items making up these factors, Nurturance and Restrictiveness, had high internal consistency and reliability, which held up across different samples. Samples included parents from an urban center city, parents from a middle-to-upper-income community, and college students from a large urban university. Results remained the same, whether the method of CRPR administration was the Likert-type format or the originally designed Q-sort technique, indicating generalizability of results (Rickel & Biasatti, 1982).

In addition, a study by Jones, Rickel, and Smith (1980) demonstrated that responses of children to social problem-solving tasks were related to parents' scores on the factors measured by the Rickel Modified CRPR. Parents with high scores on Restrictiveness had children who more frequently used an evasion strategy for solving parent-child problems, whereas parents who considered themselves high providers of nurturance had children less likely to turn to an authority figure to resolve interpersonal problems. This finding provided evidence of construct validity for the factors developed in these studies.

The existence of a link between parents' self-reported parenting styles used in the home and the social problem-solving strategies used by their children suggested that a complete program to correct maladaptive behavior patterns of parent and child should focus on the home environment as well as the classroom. Thus, the Detroit parent-training program was developed along these lines and evaluated using an experimental versus placebo group comparison.

The experimental group consisted of a behaviorally oriented format compared to a placebo control discussion group format. From pre- to postprogram, experimentally trained parents decreased significantly on self-reports of restrictiveness, compared to controls (Rickel, 1989). Of interest for future research is the determination of whether the training program will have a positive effect on the children's behavior. Longitudinal research is planned to address this issue, focusing on the effect of the parent training on the social-emotional adjustment of children whose parents received the training.

Rickel Modified Child Rearing
Practices Report: Further Developments

Recently, cross-cultural studies have extended the generalizability of the earlier findings regarding the factor structure, reliability and construct validity of the Rickel Modified CRPR. One study, conducted in the Netherlands with 239 Dutch parents, provided successful replication of the two-factor solution; that is, two reliable scales measuring important constructs in socialization, Restrictiveness and Nurturance, were identified (Dekovic, Janssens, & Gerris, 1991). Furthermore, direct observation of parent-child interaction was conducted, and the results indicated that parental self-reports using the Rickel Modified CRPR corresponded to parental behavior in interactions with children.

The Rickel Modified CRPR was also administered to 628 black parents in the Caribbean island of Barbados, providing additional cross-cultural data. Payne and Furnham (1992) found that those items with the highest factor loadings in Rickel and Biassati's (1982) North American study also tended to load heavily on the same Nurturance and Restrictiveness factors in the Caribbean sample. The researchers found that nurturance scores for mothers tended to be higher than those for fathers; however, given the predominance of mother-headed households in this Afro-Caribbean community, these results were anticipated. The data further revealed that parents in nonmanual occupations were less inclined to endorse restrictive parenting styles.

Silverman and Debow (1991) extended work with the Rickel Modified CRPR in a study of 216 unmarried college students. They found that unique predictors of nurturant child-rearing attitudes differed for males and females. For males, experience with children predicted nurturance; for females, psychological well-being was the primary predictor.

Parental Stress

The home environment plays a major role in determining the quality of parent-child relations. Parental stressors can include poverty or financial problems, unemployment, and living in a dangerous neighborhood, as well as psychosocial factors such as marital satisfaction, a parent's childhood history of abuse, the use of alcohol and other drugs by family members, and family violence. All of these factors can be significant detriments to the establishment of a healthy child-rearing atmosphere.

Research has shown that a high level of marital satisfaction leads to effective parenting, whereas marital discord often negatively affects parenting practices. A study conducted by Duvall (1990) examined marital satisfaction, as related to parenting effectiveness, in 72 husband-wife dyads with a preschool child, using the Rickel Modified CRPR. Results showed that marital satisfaction for wives was significantly related to greater nurturance toward their children, greater satisfaction with their own and their husbands' parenting, and greater husband involvement in child care. Husbands' marital satisfaction was related to greater satisfaction with their wives' parenting.

Duvall (1990) reported additional gender differences between fathers and mothers in that husbands were more restrictive in their self-reported parenting style than wives, and wives scored higher on the nurturance dimension than did husbands. Parental agreement on child rearing was not associated with marital satisfaction; therefore, rather than an index of marital functioning, such agreement may only represent concordance with a standard of good parenting.

The abuse of alcohol has been found to correlate with certain parenting styles. The nurturance and restrictiveness of parents toward their children appears to be related to whether the parent is currently abusing alcohol. Packer (1992) administered the Rickel Modified CRPR and a family assessment measure to 26 "prerecovering" alcoholic fathers and 34 recovering alcoholic fathers. He found that prerecovering alcoholic fathers were significantly more restrictive than recovering alcoholic fathers, but he found no differences in nurturance levels. Correlations showed self-reported nurturance was positively related to healthy family functioning, whereas restrictiveness was negatively associated with healthy family functioning.

Among parents who abuse their children, there appears to be a significant probability that these parents were subjected as children to parenting that was high in restriction and low in nurturance. In a study conducted by Wiehe (1992), a group of 153 abusing and 141 nonabusing parents were given the Rickel Modified CRPR. However, instead of answering how they would act in a given situation, participants were instructed to answer how they thought their parents would have reacted in rearing them. Results confirmed that abusive parents rated their own parents as highly restrictive and low on nurturance, compared to nonabusers.

The study provides evidence for a theory of the intergenerational transmission of abuse, as well as a possible explanation of the ways in which it is transmitted and the means to prevent it. Kaufman and Zigler (1987), in their extensive review of the literature on intergenerational abuse, suggest the rate of transmission is about 30%, plus or minus 5%. Thus, among parents who were neglected or physically or sexually abused as children, one third will perpetrate some form of maltreatment on their own children. We discuss this theory in greater detail below.

Family Violence

In the 1990s, violence in the United States reached epidemic proportions. Family violence cuts across all races and classes, and women and children are the most frequent victims (Becker-Lausen, Barkan, & Newberger, 1994).

Ninety-five percent of domestic violence victims are women— 2 to 4 million each year. In fact, battering is the single most common cause of injury to women medical patients, more common than automobile accidents, rapes, and muggings combined, accounting for one third of all women's emergency room visits (Stark & Flitcraft, 1988).

Child fatalities from abuse and neglect have increased by 49% since 1985, and, during that same period, reports of child abuse and neglect rose 50% (McCurdy & Daro, 1993). Researchers and policymakers have in recent years begun to make the connection between assaults on women and the abuse of children. Although the figures vary depending on the population studied, the best estimate is that in about 50% of cases where a woman is a victim of violence from a male partner, children are also being physically abused by the same man (Browne, 1987). In some cases, the child is also being sexually assaulted.

The effects of violence on children, beyond the physical injury, include depression, dissociation, aggression, anxiety, vulnerability to revictimization, developmental delays, substance abuse, and, in some cases, criminal behavior (Becker-Lausen, Sanders, & Chinsky, 1992; Briere, 1992; Browne, 1991; Kolko, 1992; Rickel & Becker-Lausen, 1994; Sanders & Giolas, 1991; Widom, 1989b).

Studies have also suggested that witnessing the abuse of a parent may be as harmful as being the recipient of the abusive behavior (Widom, 1989a). Furthermore, violence within the family has been shown not only to affect individual members, but also to harm the relationships between them; that is, as violence increases in the family, its members' perceptions of family strength are decreased, and the adults report less satisfaction with marriage and with parenting (Meredith, Abbott, & Adams, 1986).

The extensive effects of violence on children should come as no surprise to those familiar with the literature on divorce and family conflict. The finding that children have more behavioral, emotional, and social problems if parents continue to argue in front of the children after a divorce is a long-standing one (Hetherington, Cox, & Cox, 1986; Santrock & Sitterle, 1987). A number of studies have also documented that conflictual intact families are more detrimental to a child's well-being than a stable single-parent family or stepparent family (Block, Block, & Gjerde, 1986; Demo & Acock, 1988).

Intergenerational Transmission

"Do abused children become abusive parents?" Kaufman and Zigler asked in 1987 in their review of the literature on both sides of the question. As mentioned above, they concluded that 30% (plus or minus 5%) of parents with a childhood history of abuse would become perpetrators of child abuse, noting that this rate is six times higher than the base rate for abuse in the general population (5%). They suggested that a better question would be, "Under what conditions is the transmission of abuse most likely to occur?"

Gelles (1987) estimated, similarly to Kaufman and Zigler (1987), that about 39% of child abuse victims go on to become abusers of their own children. Early work on family violence (Straus, Gelles, & Steinmetz, 1980) suggested that men who witnessed their fathers hitting their mothers were three times more likely to hit their wives than those who did not witness marital violence in their childhood (35% compared to 11%). Subsequent research supported this finding by demonstrating that the only variable predicting men's use of violence against female partners was the witnessing of parental violence in their childhood home (Hotaling & Sugarman, 1986).

As the literature on childhood trauma has burgeoned in recent years, so have the attempts to answer Kaufman and Zigler's (1987) question of mediator variables in the intergenerational transmission of abuse. As measurement of childhood trauma and its effects becomes more sophisticated (Briere & Runtz, 1993; Gold, Milan, Mayall, & Johnson, 1994; Sanders & Becker-Lausen, in press), the intervening variables will continue to be identified.

Adult Outcomes

One group of researchers (Kelder, McNamara, Carlson, & Lynn, 1991) argued that the use of severe punishment is passed to the next generation by way of attitudes; that is, the legitimization or normalization of violence by the parents increases the chances that a child will adopt these harsh techniques. Kelder et al. (1991) found that subjects who reported more severe discipline in childhood and adolescence considered physical punishment more appropriate than subjects less severely disciplined. However, those reporting the most abusive experiences in childhood viewed punishment as less appropriate than those without these experiences. On the other hand, those who believed their punishment was deserved, even when it was severe or abusive, considered physical punishment to be more appropriate than those who saw their punishment as undeserved. The authors speculated that the parents' attitude toward their own use of punishment (and what they tell the child about it) may affect the child's belief about culpability. Finally, males in this study rated punishment as more appropriate than females.

Unrealistic expectations of children have also been implicated in child abuse. Such expectations involve a lack of knowledge of developmental capabilities, for example, for self-care, responsibility for others, help and affection toward parents, staying alone, proper behavior, and punishment. Azar, Robinson, Hekimian, and Twentyman (1984) demonstrated that unrealistic expectations distinguished a group of maltreating mothers from a group of demographically matched control mothers with no known abuse in their homes.

To control for the possibility that abuse in the homes affected other variables, Azar and Rohrbeck (1986) compared a sample of child-abusing mothers to mothers whose partners abused their children. Once again, they found that the abusing mothers had significantly more unrealistic expectations of their children than the control mothers. A discriminant function analysis indicated that the measurement of unrealistic expectations correctly classified 83% of the subjects.

Further development of abuse potential models has indicated that child characteristics, such as difficult temperament, attachment problems, developmental abnormalities, and behavioral and emotional difficulties, may be contributors to risk, at least for physical abuse (Kolko, Kazdin, Thomas, & Day, 1993). However, as mentioned above, all of these characteristics can also be results of both exposure to and experience of family violence. Furthermore, child behavior has been found to be an insufficient explanation for child abuse (Ammerman, 1991; Pianta, Egeland, & Erickson, 1989).

Parental characteristics that have been associated with child physical abuse potential were outlined by Kolko et al. (1993): inconsistent, negative, or aggressive child-rearing practices; limited positive affect and social behavior; cognitive-attributional biases (such as the unrealistic expectations described above, as well as lack of acceptance or positive attributions); depression; and physical symptoms. Abusive families have been found to exhibit more coercive interactions, heightened conflict, and decreased cohesion and they seem to experience more stressful life events.

In the study carried out by Kolko et al. (1993) comparing mothers at high risk for abuse to low- and moderate-risk mothers, parental psychological dysfunction showed the strongest relationship to abuse potential. Parenting practices, as reported by subjects, did not differentiate between groups of mothers, nor did reports of family violence. High-risk mothers did, however, report more stressful life events and family problems. The children of high-risk mothers showed more antisocial behavior, depression, and self-injury. Other researchers (Becker-Lausen et al., 1992) have demonstrated a relationship between the experience of more stressful life events and increased depression in male and female college students and their reports of abusive childhood experiences.

A major flaw in most studies related to parenting, as Phares (1992) has pointed out, is the absence of data on fathers. When males are included in studies, it is often for the purpose of understanding victims or perpetrators, but not in relation to parenting. For example, a study of father-perpetrators of incest found that fathers with a childhood history of sexual abuse reported significantly more chaotic, dysfunctional families of origin than nonabused perpetrators (Hanson, Lipovsky, & Saunders, 1994). However, abused perpetrators were no different from nonabused perpetrators with regard to personality profiles and psychological symptoms, and both groups reported more dysfunction in their families of origin and more psychological symptoms, compared to normative data.

Likewise, Hunter (1991) assessed psychosocial maladjustment in adult males and females sexually molested as children. He found that the association between childhood sexual abuse and adult psychosocial dysfunction was as true for males as it was for females, with both sexes showing significantly more dysfunction than controls on a number of psychosocial variables.

A number of studies have shown increased psychopathology associated with increased levels of various types of maltreatment in childhood. Studies of both clinical and nonclinical populations have demonstrated that child abuse victims exhibit a variety of symptoms: posttraumatic stress disorder; cognitive distortions, such as a damaged self-image and low self-esteem; depression; anxiety; dissociation; and impaired self-reference, including boundary issues, a sense of personal emptiness, and "other directedness"—that is, hypervigilance and attentiveness to the needs of others, with accompanying lack of self-awareness (Becker-Lausen et al., 1992; Briere, 1992; Chu & Dill, 1990; Sanders & Giolas, 1991; Sanders, McRoberts, & Tollefson, 1989).

Becker-Lausen and Rickel (in press) reported that for college females, dissociation was significantly related to reports of becoming pregnant and reports of having an abortion during high school. For these young women, a history of childhood maltreatment alone was not associated with these events, although dissociation was found more generally to be a significant mediator between child abuse history and negative life outcomes. For college males, however, child abuse history was the only variable significantly related to reports of a girlfriend's becoming pregnant and reports of a girlfriend's having an abortion in high school.

For many years, the negative effects of childhood sexual abuse, indeed, even its very existence, were dismissed or diminished. In part because of this history, many researchers have tended to overemphasize the relationship between child sexual abuse history and mental health difficulties (Berliner, 1993). As childhood trauma, including all the various forms of child abuse and neglect, becomes an accepted focus of study related to the development of psychopathology, "abuse clinicians and researchers are more comfortable investigating the other possible contributors to negative adult outcomes" (Berliner, 1993, p. 429).

Community Violence

Violence in the larger community has been the focus of attention recently, as rates of violent crime have increased, primarily among youth. In fact, the United States has the shameful distinction of ranking Number 1 among industrialized nations for our homicide rate (APA Commission on Violence and Youth, 1993).

Homicide rates for children and youth have doubled since the early 1960s (Novello, 1992). For young black males and females, homicide is the leading cause of death (Centers for Disease Control, 1992). As noted above, much of the violence occurs within the family; far too many of these deaths are children killed by caretakers or women murdered by their male partner.

Whereas family violence occurs at all socioeconomic levels (although it is often exacerbated by stresses associated with poverty), street violence disproportionately affects the poorest of our children and youth, those trapped by poverty and segregation in decaying inner-city environments and afforded the least opportunities for education and upward mobility.

James Garbarino (1992) has studied children trapped in the "war zones" of our inner cities, and he found that such children live with a deep sense of hopelessness and despair. According to Garbarino, if you ask many of these children "What do you expect to be when you're 30?" they will answer, "Dead" (p. 39).

A number of reports have concluded that poverty is the single greatest risk factor for youth (APA Commission on Violence and Youth, 1993; NRC, 1993). The NRC noted that poverty has greatly increased in the past two decades, even during the periods of economic expansion in the 1980s. The result has been increasingly large gaps between the highest and lowest income groups, as well as a nearly one third decline in the real income of young families.

Teen Pregnancy: A Key Element

Teenage pregnancy in the United States is rampant, with 1 of 10 sexually active teens becoming pregnant each year. More than half of all pregnant teens keep and attempt to rear their babies.

U.S. teen pregnancy rates are more than twice those of Canada, Great Britain, and Norway; three times those of Denmark and Sweden; and seven times those of the Netherlands (Adler, 1993). Teen pregnancy affects all races, ethnic groups, and social classes. Although poverty and, more precisely, lack of opportunity, are significant factors in teen pregnancy, they do not fully explain it (Becker-Lausen & Rickel, in press).

For example, white U.S. teens become pregnant twice as often as their British counterparts, and six times more often than their Dutch peers (Alan Guttmacher Institute, 1986); yet U.S. teens are not more sexually active than their European counterparts.

Factors putting teens at risk for early pregnancy include low self-esteem, lack of educational opportunities, and diminished expectations for the future. A history of childhood maltreatment may also put teenagers at increased risk of becoming pregnant (Adler, 1993; Becker-Lausen & Rickel, in press; Butler, Rickel, Thomas, & Hendren, 1993).

Well-documented risks accrue to the offspring of teenaged mothers, including a high incidence of illness and mortality, decreased cognitive capabilities and academic success, and emotional difficulties (Rickel & Allen, 1987). Vulnerability to homicide may also be a risk for children and youth of teen mothers (McMahon & Johnson, 1993). In addition, early sexuality is related not only to permissive parenting, but also to excessive parental strictness and rigidity (Thomas, Rickel, Butler, & Montgomery, 1990).

Teen Mothers and the Detroit Parenting Project

Recognizing the significance of the issue of teen pregnancy, Rickel and her colleagues (Rickel, 1989) adapted the Detroit Parent Training Project for implementation with teenaged mothers. The researchers realized that by the time children are school aged, many parent-child interaction patterns are already well established and become resistant to change (Atlas & Rickel, 1988; Rickel, Williams, & Loigman, 1988). Thus, the project was designed to enhance parenting competencies and to further identify personality, situational, and attitudinal factors associated with early parenting (Butler et al., 1993).

Based on a peer advocacy model, college students were paired with young mothers for an academic year. Individual sessions were held several times weekly. Sessions were designed to enrich adolescent mothers' knowledge of child development and also to help them identify and more effectively manage stress.

A total of 420 participants were recruited from Detroit City and Wayne County public school alternative education sites, which have special programs for pregnant and parenting teens, as well as from the schools that feed into the two alternative facilities. Pre- and posttesting was conducted on maternal attitude and personality variables. The testing included the Rickel Modified CRPR, the original Minnesota Multiphasic Personality Inventory (MMPI), a social support network inventory, a life-change event questionnaire, and a detailed demographic questionnaire.

The first phase of the project, designed to determine base rates for adolescent maladjustment, indicated that pregnant and parenting teens reported significantly greater maladjustment than their nonpregnant, nonparenting counterparts in the public schools. After computer scoring of the MMPI, teens were placed into the following subgroups based on their two-point code types: normal, neurotic, characterological, socially alienated, and unclassified. Only 20% of the pregnant or parenting sample scored in the normal range on the MMPI, that is, with no clinical scale elevations greater than 65 T, the cutoff score recommended for adolescents.

In addition, significant differences were found between the MMPI personality subgroups relative to their self-reported parenting attitudes, as measured by the Rickel Modified CRPR. Teens in the neurotic subgroup reported significantly lower nurturance values than those with characterological profiles. For the dependent variable of restrictiveness, girls with profiles depicting social alienation differed significantly from those in the neurotic subgroup, with socially alienated teens espousing greater restrictiveness and/or authoritarian values than those in the neurotic subgroup. Interestingly, teens in the neurotic subgroup were low on both restrictive and nurturing parenting attitudes as measured by the Rickel Modified CRPR, which may indicate they do little parenting of their children. Future studies are needed to determine whether this finding is related to neglectful parenting.

Many school districts in the United States provide alternative education facilities for youthful mothers to attend while they are pregnant and for a time after giving birth. Such settings provide a rich opportunity for intervention targeted at enhancing parental competence. Because there appears to be a link between socially alienated personality types and self-reported restrictive parental attitudes, a simple screening using the Rickel Modified CRPR could identify those mothers who appear overly restrictive. A parenting intervention could be specifically developed with a goal of moderating parental restrictiveness while taking into account the special treatment needs of the socially alienated adolescent.

Implications for Research, Policy, and Practice

Elsewhere, we have proposed a link between a young girl's experience of an abusive or neglectful home environment and her vulnerability to becoming pregnant at an early age (Becker-Lausen & Rickel, in press). As suggested above, we also believe that teen pregnancy can too often be the beginning of a destructive path leading to poverty, family dysfunction, and even violence. Thus, preventing teen pregnancy should be one of society's priorities. Where we cannot prevent pregnancy from occurring at an early age, we must intervene to help young parents better nurture their children while we also help them to improve their own lives and delay additional pregnancies.

The Detroit Parent Project has demonstrated that parents can and do improve their parenting skills. Head Start also has a long-standing history of working with parents to improve the quality of their lives while helping them develop better parenting skills. The dramatic stories of the turnaround in the lives of some Head Start *parents* is what Edward Zigler (personal communication to E. Becker-Lausen, August, 1993) has termed "the untold story of Head Start," for few recognize this important aspect of the popular preschool intervention program.

Building Theoretical Models of Child Outcomes

In this chapter we have reviewed aspects of intergenerational influences on child outcomes and highlighted some of the findings from research thus far. We have attempted to describe some of the numerous factors that influence the child, including aspects of the parents and the environment.

From the research described, we propose the beginning of a theoretical model of these interactions, shown in Figures 10.1 and 10.2. The model has been divided into two figures in an attempt to make it easier to comprehend. Pivotal to this model are two constructs: restrictive parenting and nurturant parenting. We also postulate, as we have noted above, that teen pregnancy is a key outcome variable, which predisposes the next generation (i.e., if we then loop back to the beginning of Figure 10.1) to many of the negative outcomes described in the model.

Figure 10.1 provides the foundation for the beginning of the child's life: Environmental hazards act as moderators of the prenatal environment, both directly and indirectly, through their potential effects on genetic material (environmental hazards also continue to pose a potential threat to the developing child throughout his or

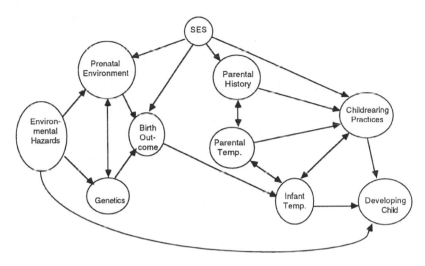

Figure 10.1. Intergenerational Transmission Model—Part I

her life). Genetic material interacts with the prenatal environment, acting as a moderator of birth outcome, both directly and indirectly. Socioeconomic status (SES) is a moderator of the prenatal environment (e.g., prenatal nutrition and health care) and also directly affects birth outcome (e.g., quality of perinatal care).

The resulting birth outcome (e.g., birth weight, birth abnormalities, neonatal health) moderates the infant's temperament. Infant temperament interacts with parental temperament as a mediator of the child's development. Parental temperament has been moderated by parental history, which to some degree has been shaped by SES. Parental history (e.g., how the parent was reared, abusive experiences in parent's childhood) moderates the parent's child-rearing practices, as does the parent's SES and the parent's temperament. Child-rearing practices in turn interact with the infant's temperament and, ultimately, moderate the child's development.

As we continue in Figure 10.2, we divide the child-rearing practices into the constructs of restrictive versus nurturant parenting, as has been described throughout the chapter. As we have described for Figure 10.1, these practices are moderated by the parent's SES (i.e., the potentially positive outcomes of nurturant parenting are affected by the child's exposure to conditions of poverty or, conversely, to the various advantages of higher status). Likewise, the family/home environment will moderate the effects of nurturant or restrictive parenting—that is, a boy who sees his nurturant mother being beaten by his father may be vulnerable to aggressive behavior, conduct disorder, or other negative outcomes, despite his mother's parenting skills, whereas a girl with restrictive parents whose home is otherwise relatively free of stressors may do well in school and be able to make the most of learning experiences in the world outside the home.

For simplicity, we have designed Figure 10.2 with the various negative or positive outcomes shown in clusters. Were we to attempt to add all the potential paths between SES, home environment, and child-rearing practices, and all the various outcomes, the diagram would be too confusing. Thus, Figure 10.2 depicts SES and home environment as interacting with one another and moderating the effects of child rearing, potentially leading to any of the various positive and negative outcomes listed in the clusters, with onset during childhood or adolescence.

The paths from restrictive and nurturant child rearing are shown to lead to negative or positive outcomes, respectively; here we are suggesting that these child-rearing styles mediate the effects of home environment and SES. Based on research so far, we believe that were restrictive or nurturant parenting to exist in a vacuum, they would lead in this manner to negative or positive child outcomes. But because they exist in a context of multiple influences on the child, we propose that the outcome for the child will result from the interaction between these child-rearing styles and the environment in which they are exercised.

What we are proposing, then, is that negative outcomes for the child and, ultimately for the adolescent and adult, are the end points of a dual pathway that begins before birth. Thornberry summarized his 5-year study of 4,000 youth in three U.S. cities by concluding that youth do not suddenly become violent, but that violence develops over time, usually from early childhood (Kantrowitz, 1993). Finding that just 15% of these teens committed 75% of the violent offenses, Thornberry discovered that the most violent teens tended to come from poor homes where there was interpersonal violence and abuse, and where parents were unemployed high school dropouts who began having children in their teens.

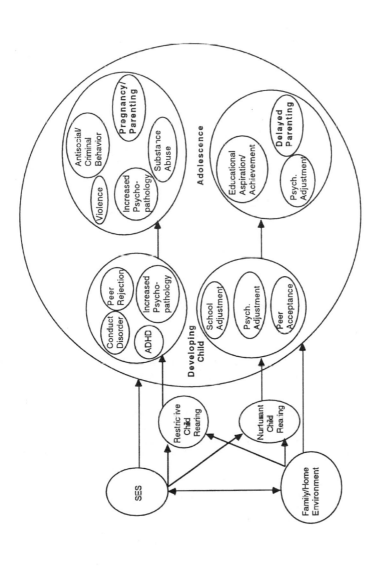

Figure 10.2. Intergenerational Transmission Model—Part II

NOTE: Family/Home Environment includes family violence, child abuse, parental conflict, parental substance abuse, and psychopathology.

We suggest that the process begins even before early childhood. A key policy implication is the need for multidisciplinary approaches to prevention, approaches that involve our major social systems—education, health care, mental health, child protection, and juvenile justice, to name a few. For not a single one of these variables is completely beyond society's control. Yet if we ignore, for example, health care access and nutrition needs for young mothers, our efforts to intervene with their preschoolers are likely to be inadequate.

Therefore, we call on researchers and policymakers of conscience in every relevant discipline to continue to demonstrate and add to the links in this critical chain, to evaluate prevention and intervention techniques, and to publicize findings as widely as possible, until all Americans understand that prevention can and will make a difference in this country's future.

References

Adler, N. (1993, April). *Adolescent pregnancy risk factors*. Presentation to staff, U.S. Congress, Washington, DC.

Alan Guttmacher Institute. (1986). *Teenage pregnancy in industrialized countries: A study*. New Haven, CT: Yale University Press.

Ammerman, R. T. (1991). The role of the child in physical abuse: A reappraisal. *Violence and Victims, 6*, 87-101.

Anthony, E. J., & Cohler, B. J. (1987). *The invulnerable child*. New York: Guilford.

APA Commission on Violence and Youth. (1993). *Violence and youth: Psychology's response*. Washington, DC: American Psychological Association.

Atkinson, R. L., Atkinson, R. C., Smith, E. E., & Bem, D. J. (1990). *Introduction to psychology* (10th ed.). New York: Harcourt Brace Jovanovich.

Atlas, J. G., & Rickel, A. U. (1988). Maternal coping styles and adjustment in children. *Journal of Primary Prevention, 8*, 169-185.

Azar, S. T., Robinson, D. R., Hekimian, E., & Twentyman, C. T. (1984). Unrealistic expectations and problem solving ability in maltreating and comparison mothers. *Journal of Consulting and Clinical Psychology, 52*, 687-691.

Azar, S. T., & Rohrbeck, C. A. (1986). Child abuse and unrealistic expectations: Further validation of the Parent Opinion Questionnaire. *Journal of Consulting and Clinical Psychology, 54*, 867-868.

Becker-Lausen, E., Barkan, S., & Newberger, E. M. (1994, May). *Physician ignorance of family violence: Implications for women's health*. Paper presented at the American Psychological Association Conference on Psychosocial and Behavioral Factors in Women's Health: Creating an Agenda for the Twenty-First Century, Washington, DC.

Becker-Lausen, E., & Rickel, A. U. (in press). Integration of teen pregnancy and child abuse research: Identifying mediator variables for pregnancy outcome. *Journal of Primary Prevention.*

Becker-Lausen, E., Sanders, B., & Chinsky, J. M. (1992, August). *A structural analysis of child abuse and negative life experiences.* Symposium presentation, 100th Annual Convention of the American Psychological Association, Washington, DC.

Berliner, L. (1993). Commentary: Sexual abuse effects or not? *Journal of Interpersonal Violence, 8,* 428-429.

Block, J. (1965). *The Child Rearing Practices Report.* Berkeley: University of California, Institute of Human Development.

Block, J. H., Block, J., & Gjerde, P. F. (1986). The personality of children prior to divorce: A prospective study. *Child Development, 57,* 827-890.

Briere, J. N. (1992). *Child abuse trauma: Theory and treatment of the lasting effects.* Newbury Park, CA: Sage.

Briere, J. N., & Runtz, M. (1993). Childhood sexual abuse: Long-term sequelae and implications for psychological assessment. *Journal of Interpersonal Violence, 8,* 312-330.

Browne, A. (1987). *When battered women kill.* New York: Macmillan Free Press.

Browne, A. (1991, July). Testimony before the Subcommittee on Children, Family, Drugs and Alcoholism of the Committee on Labor and Human Resources, U.S. Senate, 102nd Congress, hearing on *Behind closed doors: Family violence in the home* (pp. 13-18). Washington, DC: U.S. Senate Labor and Human Resources Committee.

Butler, C., Rickel, A. U., Thomas, E., & Hendren, M. (1993). An intervention program to build competencies in adolescent parents. *Journal of Primary Prevention, 13,* 183-198.

Center for the Study of Social Policy. (1993). *Kids count.* Washington, DC: Annie E. Casey Foundation.

Centers for Disease Control. (1992). *Morbidity and Mortality Weekly Report, 41*(34). Atlanta, GA: U.S. Department of Health and Human Services, Public Health Service, CDC.

Children's Defense Fund. (1992). *The state of America's children, 1992.* Washington, DC: Author.

Chu, J. A., & Dill, D. I. (1990). Dissociative symptoms in relation to childhood physical and sexual abuse. *American Journal of Psychiatry, 147,* 887-892.

Dekovic, M., Janssens, J., & Gerris, J. (1991). Factor structure and construct validity of the Block Child Rearing Practices Report (CRPR). *Psychological Assessment: A Journal of Consulting and Clinical Psychology, 3,* 182-187.

Demo, D. H., & Acock, A. C. (1988). The impact of divorce in children. *Journal of Marriage and the Family, 50,* 619-148.

Duvall, E. L. (1990). *The relation of marital satisfaction to parental functioning.* Unpublished doctoral dissertation, University of Georgia.

Farber, E. A., & Egeland, B. (1987). Invulnerability among abused and neglected children. In E. J. Anthony & B. J. Cohler (Eds.), *The invulnerable child* (pp. 253-288). New York: Guilford.

Felsman, J. K., & Vaillant, G. E. (1987). Resilient children as adults: A 40-year study. In E. J. Anthony & B. J. Cohler (Eds.), *The invulnerable child* (pp. 289-314). New York: Guilford.

338 THE FAMILY-SCHOOL CONNECTION

Field, T. M. (1990). *Infancy*. Cambridge, MA: Harvard University Press.

Garbarino, J. (1992, July). Testimony before the Subcommittee on Children, Family, Drugs and Alcoholism, Committee on Labor and Human Resources, U.S. Senate, 102nd Congress, hearing on *Children of war: Violence and America's youth* (pp. 37-45). Washington, DC: U.S. Senate Labor and Human Resources Committee.

Gelles, R. J. (1987). The family and its role in the abuse of children. *Psychiatric Annals, 17,* 229-232.

Gold, S. R., Milan, L. D., Mayall, A., & Johnson, A. E. (1994). A cross-validation study of the Trauma Symptom Checklist: The role of mediating variables. *Journal of Interpersonal Violence, 9,* 12-26.

Hanson, R. F., Lipovsky, J. A., & Saunders, B. E. (1994). Characteristics of fathers in incest families. *Journal of Interpersonal Violence, 9,* 155-169.

Hetherington, E. M., Cox, M., & Cox, R. (1986). Long-term effects of divorce and remarriage on the adjustment of children. In S. Chess & A. Thomas (Eds.), *Annual progress in child psychiatry and child development* (pp. 407-429). New York: Brunner/Mazel.

Hotaling, G., & Sugarman, D. (1986). An analysis of risk markers in husband to wife violence: The current state of knowledge. *Violence and Victims, 1*(2), 101-124.

Hunter, J. A. (1991). A comparison of the psychosocial maladjustment of adult males and females sexually molested as children. *Journal of Interpersonal Violence, 6,* 205-217.

Jones, D. C., Rickel, A. U., & Smith, R. L. (1980). Maternal child rearing practices and social problem solving strategies among preschoolers. *Developmental Psychology, 16,* 241-242.

Kantrowitz, B. (1993, August 2). Wild in the streets. *Newsweek,* pp. 40-46.

Kaufman, J., & Zigler, E. (1987). Do abused children become abusive parents? *American Journal of Orthopsychiatry, 57,* 186-192.

Kelder, L. R., McNamara, J. R., Carlson, B., & Lynn, S. J. (1991). Perceptions of physical punishment: The relation to childhood and adolescent experiences. *Journal of Interpersonal Violence, 6,* 432-445.

Kolko, D. J. (1992). Characteristics of child victims of physical violence: Research findings and clinical implications. *Journal of Interpersonal Violence, 7,* 244-276.

Kolko, D. J., Kazdin, A. E., Thomas, A. M., & Day, B. (1993). Heightened child physical abuse potential: Child, parent, and family dysfunction. *Journal of Interpersonal Violence, 8,* 169-192.

Lamb, M. E. (1986). The changing roles of fathers. In M. E. Lamb (Ed.), *The father's role: Applied perspectives* (pp. 3-27). New York: John Wiley.

McCurdy, K., & Daro, D. (1993). *Current trends in child abuse reporting and fatalities: The results of the 1992 annual fifty state survey.* Chicago: National Committee for Prevention of Child Abuse.

McMahon, C., & Johnson, S. (1993, July 9). Portrait of a city's tragedy. *Chicago Tribune,* pp. 1, 16.

Meredith, W. H., Abbott, D. A., & Adams, S. L. (1986). Family violence: Its relation to marital and parental satisfaction and family strengths. *Journal of Family Violence, 1,* 299-305.

National Research Council (NRC). (1993). *Losing generations: Adolescents in high-risk settings.* Washington, DC: National Academy Press.

Novello, A. (1992). From the Surgeon General, U.S. Public Health Service. *Journal of the American Medical Association, 267,* 3007.

Packer, A. J. (1992). *Differences in self-reported child rearing practices and family functioning between pre-recovering alcoholic fathers and recovering alcoholic fathers.* Unpublished doctoral dissertation, Boston College.

Payne, M. A., & Furnham, A. (1992). Parents' self-reports of child rearing practices in the Caribbean. *Journal of Black Psychology, 18,* 19-36.

Phares, V. (1992). Where's Poppa? The relative lack of attention to the role of fathers in child and adolescent psychopathology. *American Psychologist, 47,* 656-664.

Pianta, R., Egeland, B., & Erickson, M. F. (1989). The antecedents of maltreatment: Results of the Mother-Child Interaction Project. In D. Cicchetti & V. Carlson (Eds.), *Child maltreatment: Theory and research on the causes and consequences of child abuse and neglect* (pp. 203-253). New York: Cambridge University Press.

Plomin, R., DeFries, J. C., & McClearn, G. E. (1980). *Behavioral genetics: A primer.* San Francisco: W. H. Freeman.

Rickel, A. U. (1986). Prescriptions for a new generation: Early life interventions. *American Journal of Community Psychology, 14,* 1-15.

Rickel, A. U. (1989). *Teen pregnancy and parenting.* New York: Taylor & Francis.

Rickel, A. U., & Allen, L. (1987). *Preventing maladjustment from infancy through adolescence.* Newbury Park, CA: Sage.

Rickel, A. U., & Becker-Lausen, E. (1994). Treating the adolescent drug misuser. In T. P. Gullotta, G. R. Adams, & R. Montemayor (Eds.), *Substance misuse in adolescence* (pp. 175-200). Thousand Oaks, CA: Sage.

Rickel, A. U., & Biasatti, L. L. (1982). Modifications of the Block Child Rearing Practices Report. *Journal of Clinical Psychology, 38,* 129-134.

Rickel, A. U., Dudley, G., & Berman, S. (1980). An evaluation of parent training. *Evaluation Review, 4,* 389-403.

Rickel, A. U., Williams, D. L., & Loigman, G. A. (1988). Predictors of maternal child-rearing practices: Implications for intervention. *Journal of Community Psychology, 16,* 32-40.

Roberts, M. C., & Peterson, L. (Eds.). (1984). *Prevention of problems in childhood.* New York: John Wiley.

Sanders, B., & Becker-Lausen, E. (in press). The measurement of psychological maltreatment: Early data on the Child Abuse and Trauma scale. *Child Abuse & Neglect.*

Sanders, B., & Giolas, M. (1991). Dissociation and childhood trauma in psychologically disturbed adolescents. *American Journal of Psychiatry, 148,* 50-53.

Sanders, B., McRoberts, G., & Tollefson, C. (1989). Childhood stress and dissociation in a college population. *Dissociation, 2*(1), 17-23.

Santrock, J. W., & Sitterle, K. A. (1987). Parent-child relations in stepmother families. In K. Pasley & M. Ihinger-Tallman (Eds.), *Remarriage and stepparenting: Current research and theory* (pp. 273-299). New York: Guilford.

Silverman, I. W., & Dubow, E. F. (1991). Looking ahead to parenthood: Nonparents' expectations of themselves and their future children. *Merrill-Palmer Quarterly, 37,* 231-251.

Stark, E., & Flitcraft, A. (1988). Violence among intimates: An epidemiological review. In V. B. Van Hasselt, R. L. Morrison, A. S. Bellack, & M. Hersen (Eds.), *Handbook of family violence* (pp. 293-317). New York: Plenum.

Straus, M., Gelles, R., & Steinmetz, S. (1980). *Behind closed doors: Violence in the American family.* New York: Anchor.

Thomas, E., Rickel, A. U., Butler, C., & Montgomery, E. (1990). Adolescent pregnancy and parenting. *Journal of Primary Prevention, 10,* 195-206.

U.S. Bureau of the Census. (1992). *Current population survey.* Washington, DC: Government Printing Office.

Werner, E. (1988). Individual differences, universal needs: A thirty-year study of resilient high-risk infants. *Zero to Three, 8,* 1-5.

Widom, C. S. (1989a). Does violence beget violence? A critical examination of the literature. *Psychological Bulletin, 1,* 3-28.

Widom, C. S. (1989b). The cycle of violence. *Science, 244,* 160-166.

Wiehe, V. R. (1992). Abusive and nonabusive parents: How they were parented. *Journal of Social Services Research, 15,* 81-93.

The Family-School Connection: A Research Bibliography

COMPILED BY BRUCE A. RYAN

Abrams, J. C., & Kaslow, F. W. (1976). Learning disability and family dynamics: A mutual interaction. *Journal of Clinical Child Psychology, 5*(1), 35-40.

Adelman, H. S., & Taylor, L. (1991). Early school adjustment problems: Some perspectives and a project report. *American Journal of Orthopsychiatry, 61,* 468-474.

Allison, P. D., & Furstenberg, F. F. (1989). How marital dissolution affects children: Variations by age and sex. *Developmental Psychology, 25,* 540-549.

Amatea, E. S. (1988). Brief systemic intervention with school behavior problems: A case of temper tantrums. *Psychology in the Schools, 25,* 174-183.

Amatea, E. S. (1989). *Brief strategic intervention for school behavior problems.* San Francisco: Jossey-Bass.

Amatea, E. S., & Brown, B. (1993). The counselor and the family: An ecosystemic approach. In J. Wittmer (Ed.), *Managing your school counseling program: K-12 developmental strategies* (pp. 142-150). Minneapolis, MN: Educational Media.

Amatea, E. S., & Fabrick, F. (1984). Moving a family into therapy: Critical referral issues for the school counselor. *School Counselor, 31,* 285-294.

Amatea, E. S., & Sherrard, P. A. D. (1989). Reversing the schools's response: A new approach to resolving persistent school problems. *American Journal of Family Therapy, 17,* 15-26.

Amatea, E. S., & Sherrard, P. A. D. (1994). The ecosystemic view: A choice of lenses. *Journal of Mental Health Counseling, 16,* 6-21.

Amato, P. R. (1989). Family processes and the competence of adolescents and primary school children. *Journal of Youth and Adolescence, 18,* 39-53.

Amato, P. R. (1993). Children's adjustment to divorce: Theories, hypotheses, and empirical support. *Journal of Marriage and the Family, 55,* 23-38.

Amato, P. R., & Ochiltree, G. (1986). Family resources and the development of child competence. *Journal of Marriage and the Family, 48,* 47-56.

Amato, P. R., & Ochiltree, G. (1987). Child and adolescent competence in intact, one-parent, and step-families. *Journal of Divorce, 10,* 75-96.

Amerikaner, M. J., & Omizo, M. M. (1984). Family interaction and learning disabilities. *Journal of Learning Disabilities, 9,* 540-543.

Anderson, J. G., & Evans, F. B. (1976). Family socialization and educational achievement in two cultures: Mexican-Americans and Anglo-Americans. *Sociometry, 39,* 209-222.

Aponte, H. J. (1976). The family-school interview: An eco-structural approach. *Family Process, 15,* 303-311.

Armentrout, J. A. (1971). Parental child-rearing attitudes and preadolescents' problem behaviors. *Journal of Consulting and Clinical Psychology, 37,* 278-285.

Astone, N. M., & McLanahan, S. S. (1991). Family structure, parental practices and high school completion. *American Sociological Review, 56,* 309-320.

Bacon, W. F., & Ichikawa, V. (1988). Maternal expectations, classroom experiences, and achievement among kindergartners in the United States and Japan. *Human Development, 31,* 378-383.

Baker, D. P., & Stevenson, D. L. (1986). Mothers' strategies for children's school achievement: Managing the transition to high school. *Sociology of Education, 59,* 155-156.

Banner, C. N. (1979). Child-rearing attitudes of mothers of under-, average-, and over-achieving children. *British Journal of Educational Psychology, 49,* 150-155.

Barbarin, O. A. (1992). Family functioning and school adjustment—family systems perspectives. In F. J. Medway & T. P. Cafferty (Eds.), *School psychology: A social psychological perspective* (pp. 137-163). Hillsdale, NJ: Lawrence Erlbaum.

Barber, B. L. (1988). The influence of family demographics and parental teaching practices on Peruvian children's academic achievement. *Human Development, 31,* 370-377.

Barth, J. M., & Parke, R. D. (1993). Parent-child relationship influences on children's transition to school. *Merrill-Palmer Quarterly, 39,* 173-195.

Barton, K., Dielman, T. E., & Cattell, R. B. (1974). Child rearing practices and achievement in school. *Journal of Genetic Psychology, 124,* 155-165.

Baumrind, D. (1973). The development of instrumental competence through socialization. In A. D. Pick (Ed.), *Minnesota symposium on child psychology* (Vol. 7, pp. 3-46). Minneapolis: University of Minnesota Press.

Bayley, N., & Schaefer, E. S. (1964). Correlations of maternal and child behaviors with the development of mental abilities: Data from the Berkeley Growth Study. *Monographs of the Society for Research in Child Development, 29*(No. 6).

Becker, H. J., & Epstein, J. L. (1982). Parent involvement: A study of teacher practices. *Elementary School Journal, 83,* 85-102.

Beer, J. (1989). Relationship of divorce to self-concept, self-esteem, and grade point average of fifth and sixth grade school children. *Psychological Reports, 65,* 1379-1383.

Belsky, J. (1984). The determinants of parenting: A process model. *Child Development, 55,* 83-96.

Bernard, J. (1984). Divorced families and the schools: An interface of systems. In B. F. Okun (Ed.), *Family therapy with school related problems* (pp. 91-102). Rockville, MD: Aspen.

Bernstein, G. A., Svingen, P. H., & Garfinkel, B. D. (1990). School phobia: Patterns of family functioning. *Journal of the American Academy of Child and Adolescent Psychiatry, 29,* 24-30.

Biller, H. B. (1974). *Paternal deprivation: Family, school, sexuality, and society.* Lexington, MA: Lexington.

Bisnaire, L. M. C., Firestone, P., & Rynard, D. (1990). Factors associated with academic achievement in children following parental separation. *American Journal of Orthopsychiatry, 60,* 67-78.

Blechman, E. A., Kotanchik, N. L., & Taylor, C. J. (1981). Families and schools together: Early behavioral intervention with high risk children. *Behavior Therapy, 12,* 308-319.

Blechman, E. A., Taylor, C. J., & Schrader, S. M. (1981). Family problem solving versus home notes as early intervention with high-risk children. *Journal of Consulting and Clinical Psychology, 49,* 919-926.

Boike, M. F., Gesten, E. L., Cowen, E. L., Felner, R. D., & Francis, R. (1978). Relations between family background problems and school problems and competencies of young normal children. *Psychology in the Schools, 15,* 283-290.

Bornstein, M. T., Bornstein, P. H., & Walters, H. A. (1988). Children of divorce: Empirical evaluation of a group-treatment program. *Journal of Clinical Child Psychology, 17,* 248-254.

Braden, J. P., & Sherrard, P. A. D. (1987). Referring families to nonschool agencies: A family systems approach. *School Psychology Review, 16,* 513-518.

Bradley, R., & Caldwell, B. (1984). The relation of infants' home environments to achievement test performance in first grade: A follow-up study. *Child Development, 55,* 803-809.

Bradley, R., Caldwell, B., & Rock, S. (1988). Home environment and school performance: A ten-year follow-up and examination of three models of environment action. *Child Development, 59,* 852-867.

Bradley, R., Caldwell, B., Rock, S., Hamrick, H., & Harris, P. (1988). Home observation for measurement of the environment: Development of a home inventory for use with families having children 6 to 10 years old. *Contemporary Educational Psychology, 13,* 58-71.

Bronstein, P., Clauson, J., Stoll, M. F., & Adams, C. L. (1993). Parenting behavior and children's social, psychological, and academic adjustment in diverse family structures. *Family Relations, 42,* 268-276.

Brooks, E., Buri, J., Byrne, E., & Hudson, M. (1962). Socioeconomic factors, parental attitudes, and school attendance. *Social Work, 7,* 103-108.

Brown, D. (1983). Truants, families, and schools: A critique of the literature on truancy. *Educational Review, 35,* 225-235.

Brown, D. (1987). The attitudes of parents to education and the school attendance of their children. In K. Reid (Ed.), *Combatting school absenteeism* (pp. 32-44). London: Hodder & Stoughton.

Browne, B. A., & Francis, S. K. (1993). Participants in school-sponsored and independent sports: Perceptions of self and family. *Adolescence, 28,* 383-391.

Campbell, J. R., & Mandel, F. (1990). Connecting math achievement to parental influences. *Contemporary Educational Psychology, 15,* 64-74.

Carlson, C. (1993). The family-school link: Methodological issues of family processes related to children's competence. *School Psychology Quarterly, 8,* 264-276.

Carlson, C. I. (1987). Resolving school problems with structural family therapy. *School Psychology Review, 16,* 457-468.

Carlson, C. I., Hickman, J., & Horton, C. B. (1992). From blame to solutions: Solution-oriented family-school consultation. In S. Christenson & J. C. Conoley (Eds.), *Home-school collaboration: Enhancing children's academic and social competence* (pp. 193-213). Silver Spring, MD: National Association of School Psychologists.

Carlson, C. I., & Sincavage, J. M. (1987). Family-oriented school psychology practice: Results of a national survey of NASP members. *School Psychology Review, 16,* 519-526.

Chavkin, N. F. (Ed.). (1993). *Families and schools in a pluralistic society.* Albany: State University of New York Press.

Chen, C., & Uttal, D. H. (1988). Cultural values, parents' beliefs, and children's achievement in the United States and China. *Human Development, 31,* 351-358.

Cherian, V. I. (1989). Academic achievement of children of divorced parents. *Psychological Reports, 64,* 355-358.

Christensen, A., Phillips, S., Glasgow, R. E., & Johnson, S. M. (1983). Parental characteristics and interactional dysfunction in families with child behavior problems: A preliminary investigation. *Journal of Abnormal Child Psychology, 11,* 153-166.

Christenson, S., & Conoley, J. C. (Eds.). (1992). *Home-school collaboration: Enhancing children's academic and social competence.* Silver Spring, MD: National Association of School Psychologists.

Christenson, S. L., Rounds, T., & Gorney, D. (1992). Family factors and student achievement: An avenue to increase students' success. *School Psychology Quarterly, 7,* 178-206.

Clark, R. (1983). *Family life and social achievement: Why poor black children succeed in school.* Chicago: University of Chicago Press.

Clark, R. M. (1993). Homework-focused parenting practices that positively affect student achievement. In N. F. Chavkin (Ed.), *Families and schools in a pluralistic society.* Albany: State University of New York Press.

Cohn, D. A. (1990). Child-mother attachment of six-year-olds and social competence at school. *Child Development, 61,* 152-162.

Coleman, J. S. (1987). Families and schools. *Educational Researcher, 16,* 32-38.

Compher, J. (1982). Parent-school-child systems: Triadic assessment and intervention. *Social Casework: The Journal of Contemporary Social Work, 63,* 415-423.

Conger, R. D., Conger, K. J., Elder, G. H., Lorenz, F. O., Simons, R. L., & Whitbeck, L. B. (1992). A family process model of economic hardship and adjustment of early adolescent boys. *Child Development, 63,* 526-541.

Conklin, M. E., & Dailey, A. R. (1981). Does consistency of parental encouragement matter for secondary school students? *Sociology of Education, 54,* 254-262.

Conoley, J. C. (1987). Strategic family intervention: Three cases of school-aged children. *School Psychology Review, 16,* 469-486.

Conoley, J. C., & Gutkin, T. B. (1986). Educating school psychologists for the real world. *School Psychology Review, 15,* 457-465.

Coon, H., Fulker, D. W., DeFries, J. C., & Plomin, R. (1990). Home environment and cognitive ability of 7-year-old children in the Colorado adoption project: Genetic and environmental etiologies. *Developmental Psychology, 26,* 459-468.

Cooper, M. G. (1966). School refusal: An inquiry into the part played by school and home. *Educational Research, 8,* 223-229.

Cornell, D. G., & Grossberg, I. W. (1987). Family environment and personality adjustment in gifted program children. *Gifted Child Quarterly, 31,* 59-64.

Cowen, E. L., Lotyczewski, B. S., & Weissberg, R. P. (1984). Risk and resource indicators and their relationship to young children's school adjustment. *American Journal of Community Psychology, 12,* 353-367.

Crandall, V., Dewey, R., Katkovsky, W., & Preston, A. (1964). Parents' attitudes and behaviors and grade school children's academic achievement. *Journal of Genetic Psychology, 104,* 53-66.

Crouter, A. C., MacDermid, S. M., McHale, S. M., & Perry-Jenkins, M. (1991). Parental monitoring and perceptions of children's school performance and conduct in dual- and single-earner families. *Developmental Psychology, 26,* 649-657.

Crystal, D. S., & Stevenson, H. W. (1991). Mothers' perceptions of children's problems with mathematics: A cross-national comparison. *Journal of Educational Psychology, 83,* 372-376.

Datcher, L. (1982). Effects of community and family background on achievement. *Review of Economics and Statistics, 64,* 32-41.

Davids, A., & Hainsworth, P. K. (1967). Maternal attitudes about family life and childrearing as avowed by mothers and perceived by their underachieving and high-achieving sons. *Journal of Consulting Psychology, 31,* 29-37.

de Jong, P. F. (1993). The relationship between students' behaviour at home and attention and achievement in elementary school. *British Journal of Educational Psychology, 63,* 201-213.

DeBaryshe, B. D., Patterson, G. R., & Capaldi, D. M. (1993). A performance model for academic achievement in early adolescent boys. *Developmental Psychology, 29,* 795-804.

Delgado-Gaitan, C. (1991). Involving parents in the schools: A process of empowerment. *American Journal of Education, 100,* 20-46.

DiCocco, B. E. (1986). A guide to family/school interventions for the family therapist. *Contemporary Family Therapy, 8,* 50-61.

DiCocco, B. E., & Lott, E. B. (1982). Family/school strategies in dealing with the troubled child. *International Journal of Family Therapy, 4,* 98-106.

Dombalis, A. O., & Erchul, W. P. (1987). Multiple family group therapy: A review of its applicability to the practice of school psychology. *School Psychology Review, 16,* 487-497.

Dornbusch, S. M., Ritter, P. L., Leiderman, P. H., Roberts, D. F., & Fraleigh, M. J. (1987). The relation of parenting style to adolescent school performance. *Child Development, 58,* 1244-1257.

Dornbusch, S. M., & Wood, K. (1989). Family processes and educational achievement. In W. J. Weston (Ed.), *Education and the American family: A research synthesis* (pp. 66-95). New York: New York University Press.

DuBois, D. L., Eitel, S. K., & Felner, R. D. (1994). Effects of family environment and parent-child relationships on school adjustment during the transition to early adolescence. *Journal of Marriage and the Family, 56,* 405-414.

Dubow, E. F., & Tisak, J. (1989). The relation between stressful life events and adjustment in elementary school children: The role of social support and social problem-solving skills. *Child Development, 60,* 1412-1423.

Eccles, J. S., & Harold, R. D. (1993). Parent-school involvement during the early adolescent years. *Teachers College Record, 94,* 568-587.

Emery, R. E. (1982). Interparental conflict and the children of discord and divorce. *Psychological Bulletin, 92,* 310-330.

Emery, R. E., & O'Leary, K. D. (1982). Children's perceptions of marital discord and behavior problems of boys and girls. *Journal of Abnormal Child Psychology, 10,* 11-24.

Emery, R. E., & O'Leary, K. D. (1984). Marital discord and child behavior problems in a nonclinic sample. *Journal of Abnormal Child Psychology, 12,* 411-420.

Emery, R., Weintraub, S., & Neale, J. M. (1982). Effects of marital discord on the school behavior of children of schizophrenic, affectively disordered, and normal parents. *Journal of Abnormal Child Psychology, 10,* 215-228.

Entwisle, D. R., & Hayduk, L. A. (1978). *Too great expectations: The academic outlook of young children.* Baltimore: Johns Hopkins University Press.

Epstein, J. L. (1985). Home and school connections in schools of the future: Implications of research on parent involvement. *Peabody Journal of Education, 62,* 18-41.

Epstein, J. L. (1986). Parents' reactions to teacher practices of parent involvement. *Elementary School Journal, 86,* 277-294.

Epstein, J. L. (1987). Toward a theory of family-school connections: Teacher practices and parent involvement. In K. Hurrelmann, F. Kaufmann, & F. Losel (Eds.), *Social interventions: Potential and constraints* (pp. 121-136). New York: Aldine de Gruyter.

Epstein, J. L. (1990). School and family connections: Theory, research, and implications for integrating sociologies of education and family. *Marriage and Family Review, 12,* 99-126.

Epstein, J. L. (1990). School and family connections: Theory, research, and implications for integrating sociologies of education and the family. In D. G. Unger & M. B. Sussman (Eds.), *Families in community settings: Interdisciplinary perspectives* (pp. 99-126). Binghampton, NY: Haworth.

Estrada, P., Arsenio, W. F., Hess, R. D., & Holloway, S. D. (1987). Affective quality of the mother-child relationship: Longitudinal consequences for children's school-relevant cognitive functioning. *Developmental Psychology, 23,* 210-215.

Evans, I. M., & Okifuji, A. (1992). Home-school partnerships: A behavioral-community approach to childhood behavior disorders. *New Zealand Journal of Psychology,* 14-24.

Fagan, T. K. (1986). School psychology's dilemma: Reappraising solutions and directing attention to the future. *American Psychologist, 41,* 851-861.

Farrington, D. (1980). Truancy, delinquency, the home, and the school. In L. Hersov & I. Berg (Eds.), *Out of school: Modern perspectives in truancy and school refusal* (pp. 49-64). Chichester, UK: John Wiley.

Feagans, L. V., Merriwether, A. M., & Haldane, D. (1991). Goodness of fit in the home: Its relationship to school behavior and achievement in children with learning disabilities. *Journal of Learning Disabilities, 24,* 413-420.

Fehrmann, P. G., Keith, T. Z., & Reimers, T. M. (1987). Home influence on school learning: Direct and indirect effects of parental involvement on high school grades. *Journal of Educational Research, 80,* 330-337.

Feldman, S. S., Wentzel, K. R., Weinberger, D. A., & Munson, J. A. (1990). Marital satisfaction of parents of preadolescent boys and its relationship to family and child functioning. *Journal of Family Psychology, 4,* 213-234.

Feldman, S. S., & Wentzel, K. R. (1990). Relations among family interaction patterns, classroom self-restraint, and academic achievement in preadolescent boys. *Journal of Educational Psychology, 82,* 813-819.

Felner, R. D., Ginter, M. A., Boike, M. F., & Cowen, E. L. (1981). Parental death or divorce and the school adjustment of young children. *American Journal of Community Psychology, 9,* 181-191.

Felson, R. B. (1990). Comparison processes in parents' and children's appraisals of academic performance. *Social Psychology Quarterly, 53,* 264-273.

Fergusson, D. M., Dimond, M. E., & Horwood, L. J. (1986). Childhood family placement history and behaviour problems in 6-year-old children. *Journal of Child Psychiatry, 27,* 213-226.

Fincham, F. D., & Osborne, L. N. (1993). Marital conflict and children: Retrospect and prospect. *Clinical Psychology Review, 13,* 75-88.

Fine, M. J. (1992). A systems-ecological perspective on home-school intervention. In M. J. Fine & C. Carlson (Eds.), *The handbook of family-school intervention: A systems perspective* (pp. 1-17). Boston: Allyn & Bacon.

Fine, M. J., & Carlson, C. (Eds.). (1992). *The handbook of family-school intervention: A systems perspective.* Boston: Allyn & Bacon.

Fish, M. C., & Jain, S. (1985). A systems approach in working with learning disabled children: Implications for the school. *Journal of Learning Disabilities, 18,* 592-595.

Flanagan, C. A., & Eccles, J. S. (1993). Changes in parents' work status and adolescents' adjustment at school. *Child Development, 64,* 246-257.

Forehand, R., & Long, N. (1988). Outpatient treatment of the acting out child: Procedures, long term follow-up data, and clinical problems. *Advances in Behavior Research and Therapy, 10,* 129-177.

Forehand, R., Long, N., Brody, G. H., & Fauber, R. (1986). Home predictors of young adolescents' school behavior and academic performance. *Child Development, 57,* 1528-1533.

Forehand, R., Long, N., Faust, J., Brody, G. H., Burke, M., & Fauber, R. (1987). Physical and psychological health of young adolescents: The relationship to gender and marital conflict. *Journal of Pediatric Psychology, 12,* 191-201.

Forehand, R., McCombs, A., & Brody, G. H. (1987). The relationship between parental depressive mood states and child functioning. *Advances in Behaviour Research and Therapy, 9,* 1-20.

Forehand, R., McCombs, A., Long, N., Brody, G., & Fauber, R. (1988). Early adolescent adjustment to recent parental divorce: The role of interparental conflict and adolescent sex as mediating variables. *Journal of Consulting and Clinical Psychology, 56,* 624-627.

Forehand, R., & Nousiainen, S. (1993). Maternal and paternal parenting: Critical dimensions in adolescent functioning. *Journal of Family Psychology, 7,* 213-221.

Forehand, R., Thomas, A. M., Wierson, M., Brody, G., & Fauber, R. (1990). Role of maternal functioning and parenting skills in adolescent functioning following parental divorce. *Journal of Abnormal Psychology, 99,* 278-283.

Forehand, R., Wierson, M., Thomas, A. M., Armistead, L., Kempton, T., & Neighbors, B. (1991). The role of family stressors and parent relationships on adolescent functioning. *Journal of the American Academy of Child and Adolescent Psychiatry, 30,* 316-322.

Forehand, R., Wierson, M., Thomas, A. M., Fauber, R., Armistead, L., Kempton, T., & Long, N. (1991). A short-term longitudinal examination of young adolescent functioning following divorce: The role of family factors. *Journal of Abnormal Child Psychology, 19,* 97-111.

Freeman, M. A. (1970). *A comparative analysis of patterns of attitudes among mothers of children with learning disabilities and mothers of children who are achieving normally.* Unpublished doctoral dissertation, Northwestern University, Chicago.

Friedman, R. (Ed.). (1973). *Family roots of school learning and behavior disorders.* Springfield, IL: Charles C Thomas.

Ginsburg, G. S., & Bronstein, P. (1993). Family factors related to children's intrinsic/extrinsic motivational orientation and academic performance. *Child Development, 64,* 1461-1474.

Ginsburg, H. P., Bempechat, J., & Chung, Y. E. (1992). Parent influences on children's mathematics. In T. G. Sticht, B. A. McDonald, & M. J. Beeler (Eds.), *The intergenerational transfer of cognitive skills* (Vol. 2, pp. 91-121). Norwood, NJ: Ablex.

Goldenberg, C. N. (1989). Parents' effects on academic grouping for reading: Three case studies. *American Educational Research Journal, 26,* 329-352.

Goldstein-Hendley, S., Green, V., & Evans, J. R. (1986). Effects of teachers' marital status and child's family's marital status on teachers' ratings of a child. *Psychological Reports, 58,* 959-964.

Green, K., Fine, M. J., & Tollefson, N. (1988). Family systems characteristics and underachieving gifted adolescent males. *Gifted Child Quarterly, 32,* 267-272.

Green, R.-J. (1989). "Learning to learn" and the family system: New perspectives on underachievement and learning disorders. *Journal of Marital and Family Therapy, 15,* 187-203.

Green, R.-J. (1990). Family communication and children's learning disabilities: Evidence for Coles's theory of interactivity. *Journal of Learning Disabilities, 23,* 145-148.

Grolnick, W. S., & Ryan, R. M. (1989). Parent styles associated with children's self-regulation and competence in school. *Journal of Educational Psychology, 81,* 143-154.

Grolnick, W. S., & Slowiaczek, M. L. (1994). Parents' involvement in children's schooling: A multidimensional conceptualization and motivational model. *Child Development, 65,* 237-252.

Grych, J. H., & Fincham, F. D. (1990). Marital conflict and children's adjustment: A cognitive-contextual framework. *Psychological Bulletin, 108,* 267-290.

Guidubaldi, J., Cleminshaw, H. K., Perry, J. D., & Mcloughlin, C. S. (1983). The impact of parental divorce on children: Report of the nationwide NASP study. *School Psychology Review, 12,* 300-323.

Guidubaldi, J., Cleminshaw, H. K., Perry, J. D., Nastasi, B. K., & Lightel, J. (1986). The role of selected family environment factors in children's post-divorce adjustment. *Family Relations, 35,* 141-151.

Guidubaldi, J., & Perry, J. D. (1984). Divorce, socioeconomic status, and children's cognitive-social competence at school entry. *American Journal of Orthopsychiatry, 54,* 459-468.

Guttmann, J., & Broudo, M. (1989). The effect of children's family type on teachers' stereotypes. *Journal of Divorce, 12,* 315-328.

Hannon, P. (1987). A study of the effects of parental involvement in the teaching of reading on children's reading test performance. *British Journal of Educational Psychology, 57,* 56-72.

Hannon, P., & Welch, J. (1993). Bringing parents into initial teacher education in the context of a school partnership. *Educational Review, 45,* 279-291.

Hatano, G., Miyake, K., & Tajima, N. (1980). Mother behavior in an unstructured situation and child's acquisition of number conservation. *Child Development, 51,* 379-385.

Hauser, R. (1984). Some cross-population comparisons of family bias in the effects of schooling on occupational success. *Social Science Research, 13,* 159-187.

Hawkes, R. (1981). Paradox and a systems theory approach to a case of severe school phobia. *Australian Journal of Family Therapy, 2,* 56-62.

Heilbrun, A. B., & Harrell, S. N. (1967). Perceived maternal child-rearing patterns and the effects of social nonreaction upon achievement motivation. *Child Development, 38,* 267-281.

Heilbrun, A. B., & Waters, D. B. (1968). Underachievement as related to perceived maternal child rearing and academic conditions of reinforcement. *Child Development, 39,* 913-921.

Henderson, R. W. (1981). Home environment and intellectual performance. In R. W. Henderson (Ed.), *Parent-child interaction: Theory, research, and prospects* (pp. 3-32). New York: Academic Press.

Hess, R. D., & Camara, K. A. (1979). Post-divorce family relationships as mediating factors in the consequences of divorce for children. *Journal of Social Issues, 35,* 79-96.

Hess, R. D., Chih-Mei, C., & McDevitt, T. M. (1987). Cultural variations in family beliefs about children's performance in mathematics: Comparisons among People's Republic of China, Chinese-American and Caucasian-American families. *Journal of Educational Psychology, 79,* 179-188.

Hess, R. D., & Holloway, S. D. (1984). Family and school as educational institutions. In R. D. Parke (Ed.), *Review of child development research* (Vol. 7, pp. 179-222). Chicago: University of Chicago Press.

Hess, R. D., Holloway, S. D., Dickson, W. P., & Price, G. G. (1984). Maternal variables as predictors of children's school readiness and later achievement in vocabulary and mathematics in sixth grade. *Child Development, 55,* 1902-1912.

Hess, R. D., & McDevitt, T. M. (1984). Some cognitive consequences of maternal intervention techniques: A longitudinal study. *Child Development, 55,* 2017-2030.

Hetherington, E. M., Cox, M., & Cox, R. (1982). Effects of divorce on parents and children. In M. E. Lamb (Ed.), *Nontraditional families: Parenting and child development* (pp. 233-288). Hillsdale, NJ: Lawrence Erlbaum.

Hewison, J. (1988). The long term effectiveness of parental involvement in reading: A follow-up to the Haringey Reading Project. *British Journal of Educational Psychology, 58,* 184-190.

Hewison, J., & Tizard, J. (1980). Parental involvement and reading attainment. *British Journal of Educational Psychology, 50,* 209-215.

Heyns, B., & Catsambis, S. (1986). Mother's employment and children's achievement: A critique. *Sociology of Education, 59,* 140-151.

Hibbett, A., & Fogleman, K. (1990). Future lives of truants: Family formation and health related behaviour. *British Journal of Educational Psychology, 60,* 171-179.

Hilliard, T., & Roth, R. M. (1969). Maternal attitudes and the non-achievement syndrome. *Personnel and Guidance Journal, 47,* 424-428.

Hodges, W. F., London, J., & Colwell, J. B. (1990). Stress in parents and late elementary age children in divorced and intact families and child adjustment. *Journal of Divorce and Remarriage, 14,* 63-79.

Hoover-Dempsey, K. V., Bassler, O. C., & Brissie, J. S. (1987). Parent involvement: Contributions of teacher efficacy, school socioeconomic status, and other school characteristics. *American Educational Research Journal, 24,* 417-435.

Hoover-Dempsey, K. V., Bassler, O. C., & Brissie, J. S. (1992). Explorations in parent-school relations. *Journal of Educational Research, 85,* 287-294.

Huffington, C. M., & Sevitt, M. A. (1989). Family interaction in adolescent school phobia. *Journal of Family Therapy, 11,* 353-375.

Humphries, T. W., & Bauman, E. (1980). Maternal child rearing attitudes associated with learning disabilities. *Journal of Learning Disabilities, 13,* 54-57.

Isaacs, M. B., & Leon, G. H. (1988). Remarriage and its alternatives following divorce: Mother and child adjustment. *Journal of Marital and Family Therapy, 14,* 163-173.

Isaacs, M. B., Leon, G., & Donohue, A. M. (1987). Who are the "normal" children of divorce? On the need to specify population. *Journal of Divorce, 10,* 107-119.

Jacobs, J. E. (1991). Influence of gender stereotypes on parent and child mathematics attitudes. *Journal of Educational Psychology, 83,* 518-527.

Janes, C. L., Weeks, D. G., & Worland, J. (1983). School behavior in adolescent children of parents with mental disorder. *Journal of Nervous and Mental Disease, 171,* 234-240.

Jencks, C., Smith, M., Acland, H., Bane, M., Cohen, D., Gintis, H., Heyns, B., & Michelson, S. (1972). *Inequality: A reassessment of family and schooling in America.* New York: Basic Books.

Jowett, S., & Baginsky, M. (1991). Parents and education—issues, options and strategies. *Educational Research, 33,* 199-204.

Kandel, D. B., & Lesser, G. S. (1969). Parental and peer influences on educational plans of adolescents. *American Sociological Review, 34,* 313-223.

Karnes, F. A., & D'Ilio, V. R. (1988). Comparison of gifted children and their parents' perception of the home environment. *Gifted Child Quarterly, 32,* 277-279.

Katkovsky, W., Preston, A., & Crandall, V. J. (1964). Parents' achievement attitudes and their behaviors with their children in achievement situations. *Journal of Genetic Psychology, 104,* 105-121.

Kavanaugh, A., & Carroll, H. M. C. (1977). Pupil attendance in three comprehensive schools: A study of the pupils and their families. In H. M. C. Carroll (Ed.), *Absenteeism in South Wales* (pp. 40-49). Swansea, UK: University College of Swansea Faculty of Education.

Kaye, S. H. (1989). The impact of divorce on children's academic performance. *Journal of Divorce, 12,* 283-298.

Keirouz, K. S. (1990). Concerns of parents of gifted children: A research review. *Gifted Child Quarterly, 34,* 56-63.

Keith, T. Z. (1982). Time spent on homework and high school grades: A large-sample path analysis. *Journal of Educational Psychology, 74,* 248-253.

Keith, T. Z., Keith, P. B., Troutman, G. C., Bickely, P. G., Trivette, P. S., & Singh, K. (1993). Does parental involvement affect eighth grade student achievement? Structural analysis of national data. *School Psychology Review, 22,* 474-496.

Keith, T. Z., Reimers, T. M., Fehrmann, P. G., Pottebaum, S. M., & Aubey, L. W. (1986). Parental involvement, homework, and TV time: Direct and indirect effects on high school achievement. *Journal of Educational Psychology, 78,* 373-380.

Keith, V. M., & Finlay, B. (1988). The impact of parental divorce on children's educational attainment, marital timing, and likelihood of divorce. *Journal of Marriage and the Family, 50,* 797-809.

Kellaghan, T., Sloane, K., Alvarez, B., & Bloom, B. (1993). *The home environment and school learning.* San Francisco: Jossey-Bass.

Kinard, E. M., & Reinherz, H. (1986). Effects of marital disruption on children's school aptitude and achievement. *Journal of Marriage and the Family, 48,* 285-293.

Klein, R. S., Altman, S. D., Dreizen, K., Friedman, R., & Powers, L. (1981). Restructuring dysfunctional parental attitudes toward children's learning and behavior in school: Family-oriented psychoeducational therapy (Part 1). *Journal of Learning Disabilities, 14,* 15-19.

Klein, R. S., Altman, S. D., Dreizen, K., Friedman, R., & Powers, L. (1981). Restructuring dysfunctional parental attitudes toward children's learning and behavior in school: Family-oriented psychoeducational therapy (Part 2). *Journal of Learning Disabilities, 14,* 99-100.

Kurdek, L. A., & Sinclair, R. J. (1988). Adjustment of young adolescents in two-parent nuclear, stepfather, and mother-custody families. *Journal of Consulting and Clinical Psychology, 56,* 91-96.

Kurdek, L. A., & Sinclair, R. J. (1988). Relation of eighth graders' family structure, gender, and family environment with academic performance and school behavior. *Journal of Educational Psychology, 80,* 90-94.

Lamborn, S. D., Mounts, N. S., Steinberg, L., & Dornbusch, S. M. (1991). Patterns of competence and adjustment among adolescents from authoritative, authoritarian, indulgent, and neglectful families. *Child Development, 62,* 1049-1065.

Laosa, L. M. (1982). School, occupation, culture, and family: The impact of parental schooling on the parent child relationship *Journal of Educational Psychology, 74,* 791-827.

Lareau, A. (1987). Social class differences in family-school relationships: The importance of cultural capital. *Sociology of Education, 60,* 73-85.

Leach, D. J., & Siddall, S. W. (1990). Parental involvement in the teaching of reading: A comparison of hearing reading, paired reading, pause, prompt, praise, and direct instruction methods. *British Journal of Educational Psychology, 60,* 349-355.

Lee, V. E., & Croninger, R. G. (1994). The relative importance of home and school in the development of literacy skills for middle grade students. *American Journal of Education, 102,* 286-329.

Leibowitz, A. (1974). Home investments in children. *Journal of Political Economy, 82,* S111-S131.

Leibowitz, A. (1977). Parental inputs and children's achievement. *Journal of Human Resources, 12,* 242-251.

Lightfoot, S. L. (1978). *Worlds apart: Relationships between families and schools.* New York: Basic Books.

Little, L. F., & Thompson, R. (1983). Truancy: How parents and teachers contribute. *School Counselor, 30,* 285-291.

Loeber, R., & Dishion, T. J. (1984). Boys who fight at home and school: Family conditions influencing cross-setting consistency. *Journal of Consulting and Clinical Psychology, 52,* 759-768.

Long, N., & Forehand, R. (1987). The effects of parental divorce and parental conflict on children: An overview. *Developmental and Behavioral Pediatrics, 8,* 292-296.

Long, N., Forehand, R., Fauber, R., & Brody, G. H. (1987). Self-perceived and independently observed competence of young adolescents as a function of parental marital conflict and recent divorce. *Journal of Abnormal Child Psychology, 15,* 15-27.

Long, N., Slater, E., Forehand, R., & Fauber, R. (1988). Continued high or reduced interparental conflict following divorce: Relation to young adolescent adjustment. *Journal of Consulting and Clinical Psychology, 56,* 467-469.

Lorion, R. P., Cowen, E. L., Kraus, R. M., & Milling, L. S. (1977). Family background characteristics and school adjustment problems. *Journal of Community Psychology, 5,* 142-148.

Luster, T., & Dubow, E. (1990). Predictors of the quality of the home environment that adolescent mothers provide for their school-aged children. *Journal of Youth and Adolescence, 19,* 475-494.

Lusterman, D. D. (1985). An ecosystemic approach to family-school problems. *American Journal of Family Therapy, 13,* 22-30.

Lusterman, D. D. (1989). School-family interventions and the circumplex model. *Journal of Psychotherapy and the Family, 4,* 267-283.

Margalit, M., & Almougy, K. (1991). Classroom behavior and family climate in students with learning disabilities and hyperactive behavior. *Journal of Learning Disabilities, 24,* 406-412.

Margalit, M., & Heiman, T. (1986). Family climate and anxiety in families with learning disabled boys. *Journal of the American Academy of Child Psychiatry, 25,* 841-846.

Margalit, M., & Heiman, T. (1986). Learning-disabled boys' anxiety, parental anxiety, and family climate. *Journal of Clinical Child Psychology, 15,* 248-253.

Marjoribanks, K. (1979). *Families and their learning environments.* London: Routledge & Kegan Paul.

Marjoribanks, K. (1981). Family environments and children's academic achievement: Sex and social group differences. *Journal of Psychology, 109,* 155-164.

Marjoribanks, K. (1987). Ability and attitude correlates of academic achievement: Family-group differences. *Journal of Educational Psychology, 79,* 171-178.

Marsh, H. W. (1990). Two-parent, stepparent, and single-parent families: Changes in achievement, attitudes, and behaviors during the last two years of high school. *Journal of Educational Psychology, 82,* 327-340.

Masten, A. S., Garmezy, N., Tellegen, A., Pellegrine, D. S., Larkin, K., & Larsen, A. (1988). Competence and stress in school children: The moderating effects of individual and family qualities. *Journal of Child Psychology and Psychiatry, 29,* 745-764.

McCombs, A., & Forehand, R. (1989). Adolescent school performance following parental divorce: Are there family factors that can enhance success? *Adolescence, 24,* 871-880.

McConaughy, S. H., Achenbach, T. M., & Gent, C. L. (1988). Multiaxial empirically based assessment: Parent, teacher observational, cognitive, and personality correlates of child behavior profile types for 6- to 11-year-old boys. *Journal of Abnormal Child Psychology, 16,* 485-509.

McDevitt, T. M., Hess, R. D., Kashiwagi, K., Dickson, W. P., Miyake, N., & Azuma, H. (1987). Referential communication accuracy of mother-child pairs and children's later scholastic achievement: A follow-up study. *Merrill-Palmer Quarterly, 33,* 171-185.

McGillicuddy-De Lisi, A. V. (1988). Sex differences in parental teaching behaviors. *Merrill-Palmer Quarterly, 34,* 147-162.

McMann, N., & Oliver, R. (1988). Problems in families with gifted children: Implications for counselors. *Journal of Counseling and Development, 66,* 275-278.

Mednick, B. R., Baker, R. L., & Reznick, C., & Hocevar, D. (1990). Long-term effects of divorce on adolescent academic achievement. *Journal of Divorce, 13,* 69-88.

Miller, D. H., & Kelley, M. L. (1991). Interventions for improving homework performance: A critical review. *School Psychology Quarterly, 6,* 174-185.

Miller, D. R., & Westman, J. C. (1966). Family teamwork and psychotherapy. *Family Process, 5,* 49-54.

Milne, A. M., Ginsburg, A., Myers, D. E., & Rosenthal, A. S. (1986). Single parents, working mothers, and the educational achievement of school children. *Sociology of Education, 59,* 125-139.

Milner, E. (1951). A study of the relationship between reading readiness in grade one school children and patterns of parent-child interaction. *Child Development, 22,* 95-112.

Mink, I. T., Meyers, C. E., & Nihira, K. (1984). Taxonomy of family life styles: 2. Homes with slow-learning children. *American Journal of Mental Deficiency, 89,* 111-123.

Mink, I. T., & Nihira, K. (1986). Family life-styles and child behaviors: A study of direction of effects. *Developmental Psychology, 22,* 610-616.

Mink, I. T., Nihira, K., & Meyers, C. E. (1983). Taxonomy of family life styles: 1. Homes with TMR children. *American Journal of Mental Deficiency, 87,* 484-497.

Monsaas, J. A., & Englehard, G. (1990). Home environment and the competitiveness of highly accomplished individuals in four talent fields. *Developmental Psychology, 26,* 264-268.

Moon, C., & Wells, G. (1979). The influence of home on learning to read. *Journal of Research in Reading, 2,* 53-62.

Moorehouse, M. J. (1991). Linking maternal employment patterns to mother-child activities and children's school competence. *Developmental Psychology, 27,* 295-303.

Morrow, W. R., & Wilson, R. C. (1961). Family relations of bright high-achieving and under-achieving high school boys. *Child Development, 32,* 501-510.

Morvitz, E., & Motta, R. W. (1992). Predictors of self-esteem: The roles of parent-child perceptions, achievement, and class placement. *Journal of Learning Disabilities, 25,* 72-80.

Mufson, L., Cooper, J., & Hall, J. (1989). Factors associated with underachievement in seventh-grade children. *Journal of Educational Research, 83,* 5-10.

Mulholland, D. J., Watt, N. F., Philpott, A., & Sarlin, N. (1991). Academic performance in children of divorce: Psychological resilience and vulnerability. *Psychiatry, 54,* 268-280.

Muller, C. (1993). Parental involvement and academic achievement: An analysis of family resources available to the child. In B. Schneider & J. S. Coleman (Eds.), *Parents, their children, and schools* (pp. 13-39). Boulder, CO: Westview.

Murmane, R., Maynard, R., & Ohls, J. (1981). Home resources and children's achievement. *Review of Economics and Statistics, 63,* 369-377.

Natriello, G., & McDill, E. L. (1986). Performance standards, student effort on homework, and academic achievement. *Sociology of Education, 59,* 18-31.

Nelson, G. (1984). The relationship between dimensions of classroom and family environments and the self-concept, satisfaction, and achievement of grade 7 and 8 students. *Journal of Community Psychology, 12,* 276-287.

Nichols, W. C. (1984). Therapeutic needs of children in family system reorganization. *Journal of Divorce, 7,* 23-44.

Nicoll, W. G. (1984). School counselors as family counselors: A rationale and training model. *School Counselor, 31,* 279-284.

Nihira, K., Mink, I. T., & Meyers, C. E. (1981). Relationship between home environment and school adjustment of TMR children. *American Journal of Mental Deficiency, 86,* 8-15.

Nihira, K., Mink, I. T., & Meyers, C. E. (1985). Home environment and development of slow learning adolescents: Reciprocal relations. *Developmental Psychology, 1,* 784-794.

Nihira, K., Webster, R., Tomiyasu, Y., & Oshio, C. (1988). Child-environment relationships: A cross-cultural study of educable mentally retarded children and their families. *Journal of Autism and Developmental Disorders, 18,* 327-341.

O'Connor, S. C., & Spreen, O. (1988). The relationship between parents' socioeconomic status and education level, and adult occupational and educational achievement of children with learning disabilities. *Journal of Learning Disabilities, 21,* 148-153.

Paget, K. D. (1987). Systemic family assessment: Concepts and strategies for school psychologists. *School Psychology Review, 16,* 429-442.

Palmo, A. J., Lowry, L. A., Weldon, D. P., & Scioscia, T. M. (1984). Schools and family: Future perspectives for school counselors. *School Counselor, 31,* 272-278.

Pandy, K. (1984). Parent-child relationship and achievement: A review. *Child Psychiatry Quarterly, 17,* 139-148.

Parish, T. S. (1990). Examining teachers' perceptions of children's support systems. *Journal of Psychology, 124,* 113-118.

Parkinson, C. E., Wallis, S. M., Prince, J., & Harvey, D. (1982). Research note: Rating the home environment of school-age children: A comparison with General Cognitive Index and school achievement. *Journal of Child Psychology and Psychiatry, 23,* 329-333.

Parsons, J. E., Adler, T. F., & Kaczala, C. M. (1982). Socialization of achievement attitudes and beliefs: Parental influences. *Child Development, 53,* 310-321.

Patterson, C. J., Kupersmidt, J. B., & Vaden, N. A. (1990). Income level, gender, ethnicity, and household composition as predictors of children's school-based competence. *Child Development, 61,* 485-494.

Peck, B. B. (1971). Reading disorders: Have we overlooked something? *Journal of School Psychology, 9,* 182-190.

Pedro-Carroll, J. L., & Cowen, E. L. (1985). The children of divorce intervention program: An investigation of the efficacy of a school based prevention program. *Journal of Consulting and Clinical Psychology, 53,* 603-611.

Pedro-Carroll, J. L., Cowen, E. L., & Hightower, A. D. (1986). Preventive intervention with latency-aged children of divorce: A replication study. *American Journal of Community Psychology, 14,* 277-290.

Pellegrini, A., Brody, G., & Sigel, I. (1985). Parents' teaching strategies with their children: The effects of parental and child status variables. *Journal of Psycholinguistics Research, 14,* 509-521.

Perosa, L. M., & Perosa, S. L. (1982). Structural interaction patterns in families with a learning disabled child. *Family Therapy, 9,* 175-188.

Pettit, G. S., Dodge, K. A., & Bates, J. E. (1993). Family interaction patterns and children's conduct problems at home and school: A longitudinal perspective. *School Psychology Review, 22,* 403-420.

Pianta, R. C., Smith, N., & Reeve, R. E. (1991). Observing mother and child behavior in a problem-solving situation at school entry: Relations with classroom adjustment. *School Psychology Quarterly, 6,* 1-15.

Pinto, A., Folkers, E., & Sines, J. O. (1991). Dimensions of behavior and home environment in school-age children. *Journal of Cross-Cultural Psychology, 22,* 491-508.

Plas, J. M. (1986). *Systems psychology in the schools.* New York: Pergamon.

Portes, P. R., Dunham, R. M., & Williams, S. (1986). Assessing child-rearing style in ecological settings: Its relation to culture, social class, early age intervention and scholastic achievement. *Adolescence, 21,* 723-735.

Power, T. J., & Bartholomew, K. L. (1987). Family-school relationship patterns: An ecological assessment. *School Psychology Review, 16,* 498-512.

Pratt, M. W., Green, D., MacVicar, J., & Bountrogianni, M. (1992). The mathematical parent: Parental scaffolding, parenting style, and learning outcomes in long-division mathematics homework. *Journal of Applied Developmental Psychology, 13,* 17-33.

Pratt, M. W., Kerig, P., Cowan, P. A., & Cowan, C. P. (1988). Mothers and fathers teaching 3-year-olds: Authoritative parenting and adult scaffolding of young children's learning. *Developmental Psychology, 24,* 832-839.

Prom-Jackson, S. (1987). Home environment, talented minority youth, and school achievement. *Journal of Negro Education, 56,* 111-121.

Pryor-Brown, L., & Cowen, E. L. (1989). Stressful life events, support, and children's school adjustment. *Journal of Clinical Child Psychology, 18,* 214-220.

Radin, N. (1973). Observed paternal behaviors as antecedents of intellectual functioning in young boys. *Developmental Psychology, 8,* 369-376.

Ramsey, E., Walker, H. M., Shinn, M., O'Neill, R. E., & Stieber, S. (1989). Parent management practices and school adjustment. *School Psychology Review, 18,* 513-525.

Rasku-Puttonen, H., Lyytinen, P., Poikkeus, A. M., Laakso, M. L., & Ahonen, T. (1994). Communication deviances and clarity among the mothers of normally achieving and learning-disabled boys. *Family Process, 33,* 71-81.

Reid, W. J., & Crisafulli, A. (1990). Marital discord and child behavior problems: A meta-analysis. *Journal of Abnormal Child Psychology, 18,* 105-117.

Renken, B., Egeland, B., Marvinney, D., Mangelsdorf, S., & Srouf, L. A. (1989). Early childhood antecedents of aggression and passive-withdrawal in early elementary school. *Journal of Personality, 57,* 257-281.

Rogers-Wiese, M. R., & Kramer, J. J. (1988). Parent training research: An analysis of the empirical literature 1975-1985. *Psychology in the Schools, 25,* 325-330.

Roseby, V., & Deutsch, R. (1985). Children of separation and divorce: Effects of a social role-taking group intervention on fourth and fifth graders. *Journal of Clinical Child Psychology, 14,* 55-60.

Rothbaum, F. (1988). Maternal acceptance and child functioning. *Merrill-Palmer Quarterly, 34,* 163-184.

Rowe, K. J. (1991). The influence of reading activity at home on students' attitudes towards reading, classroom attentiveness and reading achievement: An application of structural equation modelling. *British Journal of Educational Psychology, 61,* 19-35.

Rubin, D. (1968). Mother and father schemata of achievers and underachievers in primary school arithmetic. *Psychological Reports, 23,* 1215-1221.

Rumberger, R. W. (1987). High school dropouts: A review of issues and evidence. *Review of Educational Research, 57,* 101-121.

Rumberger, R. W., Ghatak, R., Poulus, G., Ritter, P. L., & Dornbusch, S. M. (1990). Family influences on dropout behavior in one California high school. *Sociology of Education, 63,* 283-299.

Rutter, M. (1994). Family discord and conduct disorder: Cause, consequence, or correlate? *Journal of Family Psychology, 8,* 170-186.

Ryan, B. A. (1994). *The family-school connection: A research bibliography.* Unpublished manuscript, Department of Family Studies, University of Guelph, Guelph, Ontario.

Ryan, B. A., & Barham, R. M. (1984). Family systems, counselling, and school problems. *Canadian Counsellor, 18,* 72-78.

Ryan, B. A., Barham, R. M., & Fine, M. (1985). The functional role of school problems in a child's family. *Interchange, 16,* 1-13.

Ryan, B. A., & Sawatzky, D. D. (1989). Children's school problems and family system processes. *International Journal for the Advancement of Counselling, 12,* 215-222.

Santrock, J. W., & Tracy, R. L. (1978). Effects of children's family structure on the development of stereotypes by teachers. *Journal of Educational Psychology, 70,* 754-757.

Sawatzky, D. D., Eckert, C., & Ryan, B. A. (1993). The use of family systems approaches by school counsellors. *Canadian Journal of Counselling, 27,* 113-122.

Schiff, M., Duyme, M., Dumaret, A., Stewart, J., Tomkiewicz, S., & Feingold, J. (1978). Intellectual status of working-class children adopted early into upper-class families. *Science, 200,* 1503-1504.

Schneider, B., & Coleman, J. S. (Eds.). (1993). *Parents, their children, and schools.* Boulder, CO: Westview.

Scott, W. A., & Scott, R. (1989). Family correlates of high-school student adjustment: A cross-cultural study. *Australian Journal of Psychology, 41,* 269-284.

Scott-Jones, D. (1984). Family influences on cognitive development and school achievement. *Review of Research in Education, 11,* 259-304.

Searight, H. R., Searight, P. R., & Scott, E. (1987). Family environments of children with school behavior problems. *Psychological Reports, 60,* 1263-1266.

Seginer, R. (1983). Parents' educational expectations and children's academic achievements: A literature review. *Merrill-Palmer Quarterly, 29,* 1-23.

Seginer, R. (1986). Mothers' behavior and sons' performance: An initial test of an academic achievement path model. *Merrill-Palmer Quarterly, 32,* 153-166.

Seginer, R., Cohen, Y. B., & Zukerman, S. (1988). Mothers' characteristics and first-grade boys' performance: Testing an academic achievement path model. *Journal of Genetic Psychology, 149,* 349-361.

Sheridan, S. M., Kratochwill, T. R., & Elliott, S. N. (1990). Behavioral consultation with parents and teachers: delivering treatment for socially withdrawn children at home and school. *School Psychology Review, 19,* 33-52.

Shinn, M. (1978). Father absence and children's cognitive development. *Psychological Bulletin, 85,* 295-324.

Shybunko, D. E. (1989). Effects of post-divorce relationships on child adjustment. *Journal of Divorce, 12,* 299-313.

Simons, R. L., Conger, R. D., Whitbeck, L. B., & Conger, K. J. (1991). Parenting factors, social skills, and value commitments as precursors to school failure, involvement with deviant peers and delinquent behavior. *Journal of Youth and Adolescence, 20,* 645-664.

Slaughter, D. T. (1987). The home environment and academic achievement of black American children and youth. *Journal of Negro Education, 56,* 3-20.

Smith, A. H. (1978). Encountering the family system in school-related behavior problems. *Psychology in the Schools, 15,* 379-386.

Smith, M. B. (1968). School and home: Focus on achievement. In A. H. Passow (Ed.), *Developing programs for the educationally disadvantaged* (pp. 87-107). New York: Teachers College Press.

Smith, T. E. (1990). Parental separation and the academic self-concepts of adolescents: An effort to solve the puzzle of separation effects. *Journal of Marriage and the Family, 52,* 107-118.

Solomon, D., Houlihan, K. A., Busse, T. V., & Parelius, R. J. (1971). Parent behavior and child academic achievement, achievement striving and related personality characteristics. *Genetic Psychology Monographs, 83,* 173-273.

Spacone, C., & Hansen, J. C. (1984). Therapy with a family with a learning-disabled child. In B. F. Okun (Ed.), *Family therapy with school related problems* (pp. 46-58). Rockville, MD: Aspen.

St. John, N. (1972). Mothers and children: Congruence and optimism of school-related attitudes. *Journal of Marriage and the Family, 34,* 422-430.

Steinberg, L., Elmen, J. D., & Mounts, N. S. (1989). Authoritative parenting, psychosocial maturity, and academic success among adolescents. *Child Development, 60,* 1424-1436.

Steinberg, L., Lamborn, S. D., Dornbusch, S. M., & Darling, N. (1992). Impact of parenting practices on adolescent achievement: Authoritative parenting, school involvement, and encouragement to succeed. *Child Development, 63,* 1266-1281.

Steinberg, L., Mounts, N. S., Lamborn, S. D., & Dornbusch, S. M. (1991). Authoritative parenting and adolescent adjustment across varied ecological niches. *Journal of Research on Adolescence, 1,* 19-36.

Sterling, S., Cowen, E. L., Weissberg, R. P., Lotyczweski, B. S., & Boike, M. (1985). Recent stressful life events and young children's school adjustment. *American Journal of Community Psychology, 13,* 87-98.

Stevenson, D. L., & Baker, D. P. (1987). The family-school relation and the child's school performance. *Child Development, 58,* 1348-1357.

Stevenson, H. W., Chen, C., & Uttal, D. H. (1990). Beliefs and achievement: A study of black, white, and Hispanic children. *Child Development, 61,* 508-523.

Stevenson, H. W., & Lee, S. (1990). Contexts of achievement. *Monographs of the Society for Research in Child Development, 55*(1-2, Serial No. 221).

Stevenson, H. W., Lee, S. Y., Chen, C., Lummis, M., Stigler, J., Fan, L., & Ge, F. (1990). Mathematics achievement of children in China and the United States. *Child Development, 61,* 1053-1066.

Stevenson, J., Simpson, J., & Bailey, V. (1988). Research note: Recurrent headaches and stomachaches in preschool children. *Journal of Child Psychology and Psychiatry, 29,* 897-900.

Stolberg, A. L., & Bush, J. (1985). A path analysis of factors predicting children's divorce adjustment. *Journal of Clinical Child Psychology, 14,* 49-54.

Stolberg, A. L., Camplair, C., Currier, K., & Wells, M. J. (1987). Individual, familial and environmental determinants of children's post-divorce adjustment and maladjustment. *Journal of Divorce, 11,* 51-70.

Stolberg, A. L., & Garrison, K. M. (1985). Evaluating a primary prevention program for children of divorce. *American Journal of Community Psychology, 13,* 111-124.

Stone, G., & Peeks, B. (1986). The use of strategic family therapy in the school setting: A case study. *Journal of Counseling and Development, 65,* 200-203.

Stratton, C. W. (1993). Strategies for helping early school-aged children with oppositional defiant and conduct disorders: The importance of home-school partnerships. *School Psychology Review, 22,* 437-457.

Swanson, R., & Henderson, R. W. (1976). Achieving home-school continuity in the socialization of an academic motive. *Journal of Experimental Education, 44,* 38-44.

Taylor, D. (1986). The child as go-between: Consulting with parents and teachers. *Journal of Family Therapy, 8,* 79-89.

Teachman, J. D. (1987). Family background, educational resources, and educational attainment. *American Sociological Review, 52,* 548-557.

Thomas, A. M., & Forehand, R. (1991). The relationship between paternal depressive mood and early adolescent functioning. *Journal of Family Psychology, 4,* 260-271.

Thompson, M. S., Alexander, K. L., & Entwisle, D. R. (1988). Household composition, parental expectations, and school achievement. *Social Forces, 67,* 424-451.

Thompson, M. S., Entwisle, D. R., Alexander, K. L., & Sundius, M. J. (1992). The influence of family composition on children's conformity to the student role. *American Educational Research Journal, 29,* 405-424.

Thompson, R. J., Lampron, L. B., Johnson, D. F., & Eckstein, T. L. (1990). Behavior problems in children with the presenting problem of poor school performance. *Journal of Pediatric Psychology, 15,* 3-20.

Tittler, B. I., & Cook, V. J. (1981). Relationship among family, school, and clinic: Toward a systems approach. *Journal of Clinical Child Psychology,* 184-187.

Tizard, J., Schofield, W. N., & Hewison, J. (1982). Collaboration between teachers and parents in assisting children's reading. *British Journal of Educational Psychology, 52,* 1-15.

Tocci, C. M., & Engelhard, G. (1991). Achievement, parental support, and gender differences in attitudes toward mathematics. *Journal of Educational Research, 84,* 280-286.

Toro, P. A., Weissberg, R. P., Guare, J., & Liebenstein, N. L. (1990). A comparison of children with and without learning disabilities on social problem-solving skill, school behavior, and family background. *Journal of Learning Disabilities, 23,* 115-120.

Trute, B., & Hauch, C. (1988). Building on family strength: A study of families with positive adjustment to the birth of a developmentally disabled child. *Journal of Marital and Family Therapy, 14,* 185-193.

Tschann, J. M., Johnston, J. R., Kline, M., & Wallerstein, J. S. (1989). Family process and children's functioning during divorce. *Journal of Marriage and the Family, 51,* 431-444.

Useem, E. L. (1992). Middle schools and math groups: Parents' involvement in children's placement. *Sociology of Education, 65,* 263-279.

Useem, E. L. (1991). Student selection into course selection sequences in mathematics: The impact of parent involvement and school policies. *Journal of Research on Adolescence, 1,* 231-250.

van Doorninck, W. J., Caldwell, B. M., Wright, C., & Frankenberg, W. K. (1981). The relationship between twelve-month home stimulation and school achievement. *Child Development, 52,* 1080-1083.

Verdiani, F. A. (1971). A comparison of selected child rearing activities used with achieving and nonachieving school children (Doctoral dissertation, Columbia University, 1970). *Dissertation Abstracts International, 31,* 4894A.

Vevier, E., & Tharinger, D. J. (1986). Child sexual abuse: A review and intervention framework for the school psychologist. *Journal of School Psychology, 24,* 293-311.

Victor, J. B., Halverson, C. F., & Wampler, K. S. (1988). Family-school context: Parent and teacher agreement on child temperament. *Journal of Consulting and Clinical Psychology, 56,* 573-577.

Visser, D. (1987). The relationship of parental attitudes and expectations to children's mathematics achievement behavior. *Journal of Early Adolescence, 7,* 1-12.

Vogel, E. F., & Bell, N. W. (1968). The emotionally disturbed child as the family scapegoat. In N. W. Bell & E. F. Vogel (Eds.), *A modern introduction to the family* (pp. 412-427). New York: Free Press.

Wagner, D. A., & Spratt, J. E. (1988). Intergenerational literacy: Effects of parental literacy and attitudes on children's reading achievement in Morocco. *Human Development, 31,* 359-369.

Wallerstein, J. S. (1991). The long-term effects of divorce on children: A review. *Journal of the American Academy of Child and Adolescent Psychiatry, 30,* 349-360.

Walsh, P. E., & Stolberg, A. L. (1989). Parental and environmental determinants of children's behavioral, affective and cognitive adjustment to divorce. *Journal of Divorce, 12,* 265-282.

Watson, T., Brown, M., & Swick, K. J. (1983). The relationship of parents' support to children's school achievement. *Child Welfare, 62,* 175-180.

Webster-Stratton, C. (1989). The relationship of marital support, conflict, and divorce to parent perceptions, behaviors, and childhood conduct problems. *Journal of Marriage and the Family, 51,* 417-430.

Webster-Stratton, C. (1990). Long-term follow-up of families with young conduct problem children: From preschool to grade school. *Journal of Clinical Child Psychology, 19,* 144-149.

Weiss, H. M., & Edwards, M. E. (1992). The family-school collaboration project: Systemic interventions for school improvement. In S. Christenson & J. C. Conoley (Eds.), *Home-school collaboration: Enhancing children's academic and social competence* (pp. 215-243). Silver Spring, MD: National Association of School Psychologists.

Wentzel, K. L., Feldman, S. S., & Weinberger, D. A. (1991). Parent child rearing and academic achievement in boys: The mediational role of socio-emotional adjustment. *Journal of Early Adolescence, 11,* 321-339.

Westerman, M. A. (1987). "Triangulation," marital discord and child behaviour problems. *Journal of Social and Personal Relationships, 4,* 87-106.

Westerman, M. A., & Schonholtz, J. (1993). Marital adjustment, joint parental support in a triadic problem-solving task, and child behavior problems. *Journal of Clinical Child Psychology, 22,* 97-106.

Weston, W. J. (Ed.). (1989). *Education and the American family: A research synthesis.* New York: New York University Press.

Wetchler, J. L. (1986). Family therapy of school-focused problems: A macrosystemic perspective. *Contemporary Family Therapy, 8,* 224-240.

Whitehead, L. (1979). Sex differences in children's responses to family stress: A re-evaluation. *Journal of Child Psychology and Psychiatry, 20,* 247-254.

Widlak, P. A., & Perrucci, C. C. (1988). Family configuration, family interaction, and intellectual attainment. *Journal of Marriage and the Family, 50,* 33-44.

Wierson, M., Forehand, R., & McCombs, A. (1988). The relationship of early adolescent functioning to parent-reported and adolescent-perceived interparental conflict. *Journal of Abnormal Child Psychology, 16,* 707-718.

Williams, J. M., & Weeks, G. R. (1984). Use of paradoxical techniques in a school setting. *American Journal of Family Therapy, 12,* 47-57.

Wolfendale, S. (1983). *Parental participation in children's development and education.* London: Gordon & Breach Science Publishers.

Wood, J., Chapin, K., & Hannah, M. E. (1988). Family environment and its relationship to underachievement. *Adolescence, 23,* 282-290.

Wood, J. I., & Lewis, G. J. (1990). The coparental relationship of divorced spouses: Its effect on children's school adjustment. *Journal of Remarriage and Divorce, 14,* 81-95.

Wyman, P. A., Cowen, E. L., Hightower, A. D., & Pedro-Carroll, J. L. (1985). Perceived competence, self-esteem, and anxiety in latency-aged children of divorce. *Journal of Clinical Child Psychology, 14,* 20-26.

Ziegler, S. (1987). *The effects of parent involvement on children's achievement: The significance of home/school links.* Toronto: Toronto Board of Education.

Zimiles, H., & Lee, V. E. (1991). Adolescent family structure and educational progress. *Developmental Psychology, 27,* 314-320.

Zuccone, C. F., & Amerikaner, M. (1986). Counseling gifted underachievers: A family systems approach. *Journal of Counseling and Development, 64,* 590-592.

Index

About the Editors

Gerald R. Adams is Professor in the Department of Family Studies at the University of Guelph. He is a Fellow of the American Psychological Association and has been awarded the James D. Moral Research Award from the American Home Economics Association. Currently he has editorial assignments with the *Journal of Adolescence, Journal of Primary Prevention, Journal of Early Adolescence,* and *Social Psychology Quarterly.*

Thomas P. Gullotta is CEO of the Child and Family Agency in Connecticut. He currently is the editor of the *Journal of Primary Prevention.* He is a book editor for the **Advances in Adolescent Development** series and is the senior book series editor for **Issues in Children's and Families' Lives.** In addition, he serves on the editorial boards of the *Journal of Early Adolescence* and *Adolescence* and is an adjunct faculty member in the psychology and education departments of Eastern Connecticut State University. His published works focus on primary prevention and youth.

Robert L. Hampton received his AB degree from Princeton University, his MA and his PhD from the University of Michigan. He is Professor of Sociology and Undergraduate Dean of the University of Maryland, College Park; Research Associate in the Family Development Program, Children's Hospital Center, Boston; and Research Associate in Medicine (General Pediatrics), Harvard Medical School, Boston. He has published extensively in the field of family violence, including two earlier books: *Violence in the Black Family: Correlates and Consequences* and *Black Family Violence: Current Research and Theory.* His research interests include interspousal

364

violence, family abuse, community violence, stress and social support, and institutional responses to violence.

Bruce A. Ryan is Associate Professor in the Department of Family Studies at the University of Guelph. He earned a doctorate in Educational Psychology from the University of Alberta and has served in numerous positions of responsibility at the University of Guelph and in child and family service associations and agencies in Ontario. His current research interests and most recent publications are focused on the relationship between family processes and school outcomes for children.

Roger P. Weissberg is Professor of Psychology at the University of Illinois at Chicago. He as published more than 60 research articles and chapters focusing on issues related to preventive interventions with children and adolescents. He has also cowritten nine curricula on school-based programs to promote social competence and prevent high-risk, antisocial problem behaviors. Formerly, he was director of Yale University's NIMH-funded Prevention Research Training Program for Predoctoral and Postdoctoral Trainees (1989-1993). He is a recipient of the William T. Grant Foundation's 5-year Faculty Scholars Award in Children's Mental Health, the Connecticut Psychological Association's 1992 Award for Distinguished Psychological Contribution in the Public Interest, and the National Mental Health Association's 1992 Lela Rowland Prevention Award.

About the Contributors

Ellen S. Amatea, PhD, is Professor in the Department of Counselor Education at the University of Florida where she teaches in the marriage and family therapy, school counseling, and mental health counseling programs. She was editor of the *Florida Family Therapy News* from 1985 to 1987 and authored the book *Brief Strategic Intervention for School Behavior Problems,* as well as numerous book chapters and articles focusing on the application of family systems and ecosystemic concepts and intervention methods in the school setting. In addition, she has conducted workshops and consultations with school systems and mental health agencies on family school intervention methods.

Lisa Armistead is Assistant Professor of Psychology and a member of the Institute for Behavioral Research at the University of Georgia. Her research has had two foci: the identification of variables that buffer children and adolescents from divorced and interparental conflict effects, and the role of family factors in forecasting social competence among young adults. She currently serves as Co-Principal Investigator of the Centers for Disease Control grant on the influence of chronic physical illness on parenting and child functioning.

Evvie Becker-Lausen, PhD, is Assistant Professor of Clinical Psychology at the University of Connecticut. She was a 1992-1993 Congressional Science Fellow sponsored by the American Psychological Association, working for the U.S. Senate Labor Subcommittee on children, chaired by Senator Christopher J. Dodd. She was a 1993-1994 Fellow at Boston Children's Hospital and Harvard Medical School and a 1991-1992 Psychology Fellow at Harbor-UCLA Medical Center. She is the recipient of a National Research

Service Award, a member of the APA Committee on Legal Issues, and a member of the board of directors for Connecticut's Children's Law Center. Prior to receiving her doctorate (University of Connecticut, 1991), she was Public Information Officer for the National Aeronautics and Space Administration and received a NASA Special Achievement Award in 1985.

Karen Price Carver is Assistant Professor of Human Development at Washington State University. Her research interests include family demography, adolescence, and human health. She is currently involved in a long-term project assessing the impact of families on the educational outcomes of siblings as part of the Family and Child Well-Being Network funded by the National Institute of Child Health and Human Development.

Jane Corville-Smith received her BA and MA degrees from Laurentian University (Ontario, Canada) and is presently a doctoral candidate in the Department of Family Studies at the University of Guelph. She is particularly interested in issues pertinent to adolescence. Earlier employment included working with troubled teens placed under the care of the courts. Her research interests have included examining potential predictors and correlates of adolescents' educational and occupational aspirations, students' attitudes toward bilingualism, and, more recently, the reasons or motives governing student's decisions not to attend school regularly.

Randal D. Day is Associate Professor in the Department of Human Development at Washington State University. His research interests focus on fathering and family health with a particular interest in issues of fertility. He specializes in secondary data analysis of national longitudinal data sets. In addition, he has authored two books and several articles about teaching family science.

Joyce L. Epstein is Co-Director of the national Center on Families, Communities, Schools, and Children's Learning and Principal Research Scientist and Professor of Sociology at the Johns Hopkins University, where she received her doctorate. She has published extensively on the effects of school, classroom, family, and peer environments on student learning and development, with numerous theory, research, and practical publications on school, family, and community partnerships. Her most recent publication is *School and Family Partnerships: Preparing Educators and Improving Schools*. She is Chair-Elect of the Sociology of Education Section of the American Sociological Association and serves on the editorial boards of several journals. She is the recipient of the Academy for Educational Development's 1991 Alvin C. Eurich Education Award for her work on family-school partnerships.

Rex Forehand is Research Professor of Psychology and Director of the Institute for Behavioral Research at the University of Georgia. He has been on faculty at the University of Georgia for the past 24 years. During that time, his research efforts have focused on the role of family stressors on parenting and on the functioning of children within the family. In particular, his research efforts have targeted the effects of interparental conflict and divorce on young adolescents. Many of his efforts have examined the cross-situational influences of family stressors on the functioning of adolescents in the schools. He is a licensed clinical psychologist, a diplomat of clinical psychology, a member of eight editorial boards of journals in family and child psychology, and currently the Principal Investigator on a Centers for Disease Control grant to examine the influence of chronic physical illness on parenting and child functioning.

Robert-Jay Green, PhD, is Professor and Coordinator of Family-Child Psychology at the California School of Professional Psychology, Berkeley/Alameda. In 1980, he cofounded and for 11 years codirected Redwood Center Psychology Associates, Inc.—one of the San Francisco Bay Area's leading training institutes for family therapy. He is the author of more than 40 publications on family processes, clinical training, and the practice of family therapy, including a family relations questionnaire (*California Inventory for Family Assessment,* developed with Paul D. Werner) and two books (*Family Therapy: Major Contributions,* edited with James L. Framo, 1981, and *Voices of Women Family Therapists,* written with Sukie Magraw and Sarah Stearns, in press). He is on the board of directors of the American Family Therapy Academy, a Fellow of the American Association for Marriage and Family Therapy and the American Psychological Association, and serves on the editorial boards of *Family Process, Journal of Marital and Family Therapy,* and *Cultural Diversity and Mental Health.*

Patricia A. King, MEd, has over 20 years experience in early childhood programs including state-funded and private nursery schools and child care centers and Project Head Start. Her experience includes teaching, directing nursery schools and child care centers, coordinating a network of child care centers, consulting both privately and publicly funded centers, developing curricula, and organizing staff development activities. She researched and developed the preschool, kindergarten, and infant-toddler curricula implemented by the Children's Discovery Centers of America. Currently Director of Early Childhood Services at Child and Family Agency of Southeastern Connecticut, Inc., she is also the administrator of the New London Family Resource Center, which includes the Smith-Bent Children's Center. The Smith-Bent Children's Center, as a site for a federally funded demonstration project, is developing and piloting a preschool violence prevention curriculum with a parent education component.

Karla Klein is currently a graduate student in the clinical psychology program at the University of Georgia. Her research has focused on the use of longitudinal data in predicting functioning of late adolescence from early family factors. She was recently elected to the APA Student Science Directorate.

Seyong Lee completed his PhD at the Johns Hopkins University in 1994. His dissertation, "Family-School Connections and Students' Education: Continuity and Change of Family Involvement from the Middle Grades to High School," uses the NELS:88 base-year and follow-up surveys of students to study how family background, family structure, race, gender, and school sector affect family involvement in high school students' education and the effects on student attitudes, attendance, behavior, academic commitment, report card grades, and student achievement. The study shows that many types of involvement are important for high school students. A sociologist, he is a research fellow at the Population and Development Center at the Seoul National University in Korea.

Robert W. Plant, PhD, is a licensed clinical psychologist and Director of Clinical Services at Child and Family Agency of Southeastern Connecticut. Since completing his academic and clinical training at the University of Rochester and Yale University Medical School, he has worked as a provider and administrator of mental health services for adults and children. He has written articles on a variety of mental health topics and has published in both professional journals and popular magazines. In his current position as clinical director, he provides and supervises services to children and families and has worked with school systems and community organizations to establish preventive programs and improve access to mental health services.

Annette U. Rickel was an American Psychological Association Senior Congressional Fellow in Washington, D.C., where she worked in the Senate and the House of Representatives. In addition, she served on the President's Task Force for National Health Care Reform. She is on leave from Wayne State University where she is Professor of Psychology and Director of the Community Psychology Program. She received her doctoral degree from the University of Michigan and is a Fellow and Past President of the APA Society for Community Research and Action. She has published 3 books and 50 articles and chapters.

Diane Scott-Jones is Associate Professor in the Department of Psychology at Temple University. Her interests are in social development, family processes, and the development of African Americans and other ethnic minorities. Her current research, which is part of the federally funded Center on Families, Communities, Schools, and Children's Learning, includes two major projects: a study of families' roles in their children's education and schooling and a study of the educational and developmental outcomes of adolescent childbearers and their children. Her work has been published in many sources, including the *American Journal of Education, Journal of Adolescent Research, Journal of Early Adolescence, Phi Delta Kappan,* and *Review of Research in Education.*

Peter A. D. Sherrard, EdD, is Associate Professor of Counselor Education at the University of Florida where he teaches in the marriage and family therapy and mental health counseling programs. He is licensed as a marriage and family therapist and mental health counselor in Florida. He holds the diplomate in counseling psychology from the American Board of Professional Psychology and the diplomate in marriage and family therapy from the American Board of Family Psychology. His scholarly interests focus on the use of social construction theory in marriage and family therapy training and intervention practice. He was associate editor for practice of the *Journal of Mental Health Counseling* (1987-1993), president of the North Central Florida Association for Marriage and Family Therapy (1991), and corecipient of the 1992 AMHCA Research Award.

Jay D. Teachman is Professor and Chair of the Department of Human Development at Washington State University. He is one of seven principal investigators in the Family and Child Well-Being Research Network funded by the National Institute of Child Health and Human Development. His current research interests revolve around the use of sibling data to better understand the impact of families on children.